Peter Jukes is a British writer and journalist. Through his TV appearances and regular columns on the Daily Beast website and in *Newsweek* he has become one of the UK's most authoritative commentators on the News International phone-hacking scandal and the Leveson Inquiry. He has written on the links between culture and politics for the *Independent*, *New Statesman* and *Prospect* magazine and is a high-profile contributor to US political blogs. Jukes is also a dramatist for theatre radio and television, whose credits include *Matador*, *In Deep*, *Bad Faith*, *Waking the Dead, The Inspector Lynley Mysteries* and *Sea of Souls*. His account of living in the modern city, *A Shout in the Street* (Faber & Faber, 1990), was called 'a dream of a book' by John Berger. He lives in London.

The Fall of the
House of Murdoch

The Fall of the House of Murdoch

FOURTEEN DAYS THAT ENDED A MEDIA DYNASTY

Peter Jukes

Illustrations by Eric Lewis

unbound

This edition first published in 2012

Unbound
32–38 Scrutton Street, London, EC2A 4RQ
www.unbound.co.uk

Typeset by Lorna Morris
Cover design by Dan Mogford

A CIP record for this book is available from the British Library

ISBN 978-1-908717-42-9

Printed in England by Clays Ltd, Bungay, Suffolk

CONTENTS

LIST OF FIGURES

dla mojego kochanego małego anioła

FOREWORD

Sometimes it helps to be an outsider. For the last twenty-five years as a professional writer I've never dared to think of myself as a journalist, even though
reading Ernest Hemingway it seemed to me the best job in the world when I
was teenager – a way of both interpreting the world and changing it. Instead
I've devoted most my time to drama, cultural commentary about new technology, cities and entertainment and viewed many of my closest friends, who are
journalists, with a mixture of envy and suspicion. In return, they have a right to
be sceptical about a practitioner of fiction engaging in an issue so fraught with
problematic facts: all I can say is that dealing with myths, rhetoric, deceptions
and self-deceptions has turned out to be very useful when exploring the scandal
around News International and its unhealthy dominance of British public life.

So my qualifications for writing this book are not from inside the news industry, but as a close observer of it. I also lack another key qualification: I've
never been a fully paid-up 'Murdoch basher' and was probably better known as
a 'BBC basher' first. From a *New Statesmen* piece in 1994 about 'The Death of
the TV Author' to a *Prospect* magazine article in 2009 'Why Britain can't do The
Wire', I've explored the relative decline of pluralism and quality television, the
last article emphasising the monopoly stranglehold the BBC was developing in
drama. For my pains I was called into a three-hour long meeting with the BBC's
head of drama, Ben Stephenson, during which I inadvertently compared him to
John Major. It's probably a coincidence, but I haven't had a commission from TV
Drama since. Since I've obviously developed a penchant for career suicide taking
on another potential employer in the form of News Corp, the biggest publisher
and richest broadcaster in the UK, was the natural next choice.

There are legions of others, however, who have taken far more risks than I have in
order to bring the details of this story to the light of day: the Hacked Off campaign,
the hundreds of victims who fought long and initially unpromising court battles, the
Dowler Family, the McCanns, the family of the murdered private investigator Daniel Morgan, the police blogger Richard Horton and – of course – the trio of Mark
Lewis, Nick Davies and Tom Watson: lawyer, investigative journalist and Member of
Parliament. This book is partly a tribute to them and the many other journalists who
dared to question their own profession. Before he died in 2010, my friend and mentor

Tony Judt said – in conversation with Tim Snyder – that investigative journalists are the closest thing we have these days to public intellectuals in the mode of Orwell or Camus. Though this book concentrates on so many of the failures of journalism in the UK, it's actually filled with respect for its highest ideals.

As for my jumping on a bandwagon, I ought to explain the bandwagon jumped on me. The main reason I ended up writing *The Fall of the House of Murdoch* was the online encouragement of hundreds of other bloggers I've encountered while writing a series of 'diaries' on the US blog Daily Kos about the phone-hacking scandal when it broke in July 2011. Many of these people are credited in the acknowledgements and one of them – Eric Lewis – has provided illustrations for the ebook. Despite the trolls and sock puppets and echo-chambers the experience of blogging has been like an electrifying jolt to my non-fiction writing and the live interaction restored my mojo for politics, journalism and debate. So I owe it all to my first audience online and their encouragement. Since those diaries were originally crowd-sourced, it's only appropriate that it should have been commissioned and supported by the unique crowd-funded publishing model Unbound. So let's hear it for the wisdom, wit and occasional buffoonery of crowds. Without them, the outline of this book would still be languishing on some publisher's slush pile.

One professional qualification I do have, after all, which has helped me to write the developing story: a sense of drama. When people try to imagine the whole saga, the hundred-year history of the Murdoch dynasty, the international dimensions and colourful cast and then connect this backstory to those incredible fourteen days in July that closed the *News of the World*, they often reach for mythic or dramatic metaphors. One of the most popular Twitter search phrases during the scandal in the summer of 2011 was the hashtag #Murdoch4Shakespeare, used to share hundreds of lines from the works of our greatest dramatist appropriate to the saga. The Murdoch Movie has already been scripted in magazine and newspapers articles and humorous YouTube videos (Anthony Hopkins to play Rupert, Hugh Grant to play… err… Hugh Grant). But looking at the interweaving narratives and historical scope of the Murdoch family and its media empire, it's far too vast for one movie. Perhaps a trilogy like *The Godfather*? But even that isn't complex or labyrinthine enough. No, the only format that could encompass the parallel storylines and different precincts – Fleet Street, New York, Parliament, Catford – is that of a long-running TV series, like *The Wire*, *The Sopranos* or *Mad Men*.

Oddly enough, I happen to know something about the format of long-running dramas…

One thing that makes US TV drama stand out from our sadly declined British domestic output is that it mixes genres and has psychologically complex central characters. As I explored in my *Prospect* essay, we Brits are all too simplistic about our distinctions between crime shows and comedies, satire and tragedy. These days we expect our leads to be lovable heroes or downright damnable serial-killing villains. But the great US TV dramas always keep us guessing morally: is Tony Soprano really a complete monster? Is Don Draper just a shallow womanising ad man? I feel the same way about the character of Rupert Murdoch – for all the ill I think he's wrought there are dimensions to his fractured complex character which are admirable, show him capable of change and may yet surprise us. I have no personal animosity against the man. That doesn't change the thesis of this book – which is a social and cultural and economic indictment of much of the last thirty years – but I hope to play the ball not the man and separate the sin from the sinner.

The other great innovation of US TV drama is that it is constantly shifting in tone, playing with time sequences, keeping us on our feet, not knowing whether we're in a flash forward or a dream sequence, and disrupting simple linear narrative. The structure of this book aims to reflect that; for while it is hung around the fourteen days after the breaking of the Milly Dowler story on 4 July 2011, it flashes back over a whole century of the Murdoch legacy, and also flashes forward to the revelations of the Leveson Inquiry over the following year. I hope it's not too confusing for that; this tangled yarn needed a firm narrative frame, but themes and characters should be more important than chronology.

Though it has turned into a deeply serious book, *The Fall of the House of Murdoch* tries to avoid being sombre, plodding or dull. There's a lot of detail here, but much more has been kept out of the way to keep the pace unencumbered: an exhaustive account of a major event like this shouldn't also be exhausting. Though I'm passionately convinced that our media is undergoing a profound historic conflict, that doesn't mean there isn't a chance for a bit of levity and facetiousness. The hacking scandal and all that has followed has many comic moments – from Horsegate to LOLgate to Rupert's Twitter outbursts – and the illustrations of Eric Lewis in the ebook edition provide a vital service in reminding us that only rational people can laugh and only ideologues take themselves seriously all the time.

On that humorous score, when the publishers Unbound decided this book would become one of their new projects in November 2011, they sent out emails to major news and TV organisations announcing *The Fall of the House of Murdoch*. They almost immediate received an email back from the *Sun*'s news editor asking: 'Is this some kind of joke?'

I'll leave that decision to my readers.

MAIN CHARACTERS

PRESS

Rupert Murdoch (b.1931)   CEO and Chair of News Corp

James Murdoch (b.1972)   Former Chair of BSkyB and News International

Rebekah Brooks (b.1968)   Editor of the *News of the World* 2000–2003

Editor of the *Sun* 2003–2009

CEO News International 2009–2011

Andy Coulson (b.1968)   Editor of the *News of the World* 2003–2007

Conservative Party Communications Chief 2007–2010

Chief Government Press Officer 2010–2011

Les Hinton (b.1944)   CEO News International 1995–2007

Dow Jones Publisher 2007–2011

Tom Crone   News International Legal Affairs Manager 1985–2011

Kelvin MacKenzie (b.1946)   Editor of the *Sun* 1981–1994

Frédéric Michel   Head of News Corp Public Affairs Europe 2009–

Neville Thurlbeck   *News of the World* Journalist 1990–2011

Paul McMullan   *News of the World* Journalist 1998–2002

Nick Davies (b.1953)   *Guardian* Journalist

Glenn Mulcaire (b.1970)   Private Investigator

Jonathan Rees   Private Investigator

Elisabeth Murdoch (b.1968)   Media Proprietor

Matthew Freud (b.1963)   Public Relations

POLITICS

David Cameron (b.1966)   Conservative Prime Minister 2010–

Margaret Thatcher (b.1925)   Conservative Prime Minister 1979–1990

George Osborne (b.1971)   Conservative Chancellor of the Exchequer 2010–

Tony Blair (b.1953)   Labour Prime Minister 1997–2007

Gordon Brown (b.1951)   Labour Chancellor of the Exchequer 1997–2007

Labour Prime Minister 2007–2010

Alastair Campbell (b.1957)	Labour Prime Minister's Press Secretary and Spokesman Director of Communication and Strategy 1997–2003
Vince Cable (b.1943)	Lib Dem Business Minister 2010–
Jeremy Hunt (b.1966)	Conservative Secretary of State for Culture, Media and Sport 2010–
Nick Clegg (b.1967)	Lib Dem Deputy Prime Minister 2010–
Ed Miliband (b.1969)	Labour Opposition Leader 2010–
John Major (b.1943)	Conservative Prime Minister 1990–1997
Tom Watson (b.1967)	Current Culture, Media and Sport Select Committee Member
Chris Bryant (b.1962)	Former Culture, Media and Sport Select Committee Member
Rudy Giuliani (b.1944)	Former Mayor of New York City
Newt Gingrich (b.1943)	Former Speaker of the House

LAW, POLICE AND VICTIMS

Lord Justice Brian Leveson (b.1949)	Chair of the Leveson Inquiry
Robert Jay QC (b.1960)	Counsel to the Leveson Inquiry
John Yates (b.1959)	Former Assistant Commissioner Metropolitan Police
Andy Hayman (b.1959)	Former Assistant Commissioner for the Metropolitan Police
Sir Paul Stephenson (b.1953)	Former Commissioner for the Metropolitan Police
Ray Adams	Former Police Commander and NDS Head of Security
Richard Horton (b.1964)	Police Constable and former blogger
Milly Dowler (b.1988)	Murdered circa 21 March 2002
Daniel Morgan (b.1949)	Murdered 10 March 1987

4 July 2011
Bad Press

To say that Rupert Murdoch ruined my life, and probably ruined yours, is only partly hyperbole.

In a career spanning more than half a century, Murdoch has carved out an almost mythic place for himself as the modern media mogul, a species distinct from the purely print-based press barons of the past. From the early days in Australia, when he added TV stations to the newspaper legacy of his father, his was a cross-platform project that spanned different formats and quickly developed international ambitions. The acquisition of the *News of the World* in 1969 was followed four years later by Murdoch's relocation to New York and purchase of magazine and newspaper franchises in the US. By the eighties News Corp was a global conglomerate characteristic of the late twentieth century: able to navigate national taxes and regulations by shifting operations and earnings across international boundaries.

Along the way, Murdoch's media strategies have broken many borders. His trademark papers, from the downmarket *New York Post* and the *Sun* to upmarket titles like the *Australian*, *The Times* and the *Wall Street Journal*, prove that he can address the nuanced interests of the governing elites as well as appeal to the popular concerns of their constituents. Almost invariably, he has changed the terms of the game in the markets he has entered, appearing to circumvent national laws on competition, monopoly and cross-ownership regulations. In the process, Murdoch has defeated or superseded rival dynasties: the Halifaxes, the Packers, the Carrs, the Bancrofts – even the Windsors. By 1996 he was named by *Time Magazine* as the fourth most powerful person in the US. In the next decade he also made the leap into new media, having brushed off rivals such as Ted Turner and Michael Eisner, he was rubbing shoulders with Bill Gates and Steve Jobs.

In his iconoclastic biography of Picasso, *The Success and Failure of Picasso*, the art critic and novelist John Berger describes the Andalusian artist as a 'vertical invader', an outsider from the poor south whose energy so shook the Parisian art world that he rose rapidly to a position of great wealth, eminence and isolation. One can see a similar drive towards confrontation and disruption in Murdoch, although – from a background of relative wealth and prestige in Australia – the invasion is more lateral than vertical. One of Murdoch's few constant refrains over the years has been his hatred of the 'establishment', and a desire to challenge 'snobs' and 'elites'. Like a wired-up, globalised Citizen Kane, he's a horizontal invader who courts and then challenges every hierarchy he meets (except his own) with a radical restlessness.

By 2010, as chairman and chief executive of News Corp, Murdoch presided over the third biggest media conglomerate in global terms, but with two distinct advantages over his rivals: an unprecedented concentration of power in the English-speaking world and a unique level of personal control over his company, which he ran almost as a 'one man show'. By then Murdoch owned nearly 70 per cent of the Australian Press and many TV stations, over 40 per cent of the UK's press circulation and a controlling interest in its biggest pay-TV broadcaster, BSkyB. In both these countries his domination of the media – and by extension politics and political coverage – was dubbed a 'Murdocracy'. Three generations of politicians have regarded Murdoch as a 'Kingmaker'. Britain's former deputy prime minister, John Prescott, claimed the mogul had more sway over the Prime Minister than he did. The Watergate investigator, Carl Bernstein, says of Murdoch in the US: 'it's hard to think of any other individual who has had a greater impact on American political and media culture in the past half century.' Murdoch's waspish official biographer Michael Wolff makes an even more sweeping claim, contending that Murdoch's TV station Fox News has 'helped transform American culture into a two-nation state. The Tea Party is its child.'

In 2011 the legacy was almost complete, with one remaining challenge: how to retain the Murdoch brand in a publicly-listed company and solve the thorny issue of the family's role in the corporation. The problem of who among his children would inherit control had been creating frictions for over a decade, with his eldest son Lachlan bounced from the News Corp board by internal rivalries and his eldest daughter setting up her own company *Shine* (though it was subsequently bought back into the News Corp fold for $663 million). But a strategy had finally been worked out. Murdoch's second son James, having initially shown no taste for corporate life, had proved himself as head of News International in the UK and sat on the board as head of News Corp's European and Asian interests. To seal his role as heir apparent, James devised a strategic plan code-named 'Rubicon' to take over the remaining 61 per cent of BSkyB and establish a broadcast digital monopoly to match the one his father had created in publishing thirty years before.

Then, during a few weeks in July 2011, two weeks before the British government was prepared to allow the £8 billion takeover to go ahead, a long-rumbling story of illegal privacy intrusion erupted into public consciousness with the Milly Dowler phone-hacking scandal. Revelations followed of further hacking victims, police pay-offs and email intrusion, and three new official investigations were established to investigate allegations of phone hacking, police corruption and computer hacking (operations Weeting, Elveden and Tuleta). In an attempt to stem the contagion, the *News of the World* was closed after 168 years. The biggest-selling English-language newspaper in the world, which had thrived on a diet of scandal about other institutions and dynasties, suddenly became the scandal itself.

Closure didn't contain the problem: more arrests followed, including Prime Minster David Cameron's former communications chief, Andy Coulson, and the CEO of News International, Rebekah Brooks. Allegations spread to other News International titles and expanded to include surveillance and intimidation of politicians and lawyers, regular bribes to corrupt officials and a corporate cover-up. After an emergency parliamentary debate, New Corp's bid for BSkyB was withdrawn. James's succession strategy was in tatters and he and his father were forced, by the command of the serjeant-at-arms, to appear in Parliament before MPs.

The man who 'owned the news' suffered, in his own ungrammatical words, 'the most humble day of my life'.

However, the damage didn't stop there: in the months ahead over fifty people were arrested, sixteen of them senior editors from News International. Rebekah Brooks, the CEO, was charged with three counts of perverting the course of justice and Andy Coulson with perjury. Meanwhile, the Leveson Inquiry into the culture, practices and ethics of the press, set up by David Cameron in the firestorm of the summer, would run three modules for the next nine months: three acts exploring the relationships between the press, the police and senior politicians – with powers to compel witnesses who had to testify under oath. What a drama ensued. With a starry cast of players, including Rupert and James Murdoch, David Cameron, Tony Blair, Rebekah Brooks, Sienna Miller, Hugh Grant, it became the best show in town with a compelling storyline. What began as a scandal about illegal intrusions into privacy became a wider scandal of backdoor access and the hidden political clout of a rich media organisation, too big to fail, too big to jail. By the summer of 2012, the Leveson Inquiry, which started as an investigation into privacy intrusion in the press, had turned into a forensic examination of the state of the nation, putting three public institutions and our whole ruling political and media class on trial.

This book seeks to explain how this all happened by following the twists and turns of those two weeks in July 2011. It also flashes back nearly a hundred years, to the origins of the Murdoch dynasty and historical antecedents to the crisis that was to come. The story flashes forward too, through the first year of the Leveson Inquiry, which developed its own momentum and drama as the Murdoch dynasty fell from grace, and began to fall from power, while its death throes shook the foundations of the British state.

THEATRE OF COMPLICITY

Looking back on those tumultuous fourteen days in July, from the initial revelation of the hacking of teenage murder victim Milly Dowler's phone to the Murdochs questioning by British MPs, it's hard not to feel shock at the industrial scale of the hacking, blagging, surveillance and intimidation and disgust at the collusion of senior politicians and subornment of public officials. There is also the forensic thrill of the chase as multiple investigations, both legal and journalistic, pieced together a pattern of alleged corporate malpractice and cover-up which began to look, in the words of former prime minister Gordon Brown, like a 'criminal media nexus'.

By the time Rupert and James Murdoch were summoned to appear before the Department of Culture, Media and Sport's (DCMS) select committee (after an initial refusal), this feeling became, for many, both vindication and a sense of justice finally being done. At last, Rupert Murdoch, one of the most powerful unelected political forces of the last thirty years was compelled to face the people's elected representatives in Parliament. British commentators compared it to the fall of Mubarak or the Death of God and even in the US – where Department of Justice investigations were still pending – liberal opinion was enjoying something akin to a Schadenfreude-fest.

However, buried under the various emotions which escaped from the Pandora's Box of 'Hackgate', there is one last unexpected feeling that emerges – a feeling of guilt.

Why guilt? I personally hadn't hacked anyone's phone. True, I worked briefly in a News International subsidiary in the nineties, but as a freelancer and in a multimedia project that never happened. I have many friends and colleagues in journalism, some who work for News International, but they weren't at the tabloid end; they didn't routinely invade privacy or engage in the politics of personal destruction. But I still feel somehow complicit.

This sense of complicity comes from being a passive bystander. I remember complaints by actors I worked with that they had their wedding rings erased in photoshopped pictures when out on the town, or their partners set up in compromising romantic stings. I'd seen countless politicians and celebrities tarnished or destroyed by public exposure of illegally accessed material. But what could anyone do about it? The only means of redress were the same press and media who targeted them in the first place.

There were plenty of warnings about the hubris at the centre of News International, but they only become clear in hindsight. In his 2009 MacTaggart lecture James Murdoch outlined the plan for Sky to replace the BBC as the nation's major broadcaster. This was all part of the strategy revealed later as the Rubicon process, but back then, only an insider would have realised the deal being done.

Then I had a brief glimpse inside that magic circle. At a conference in July 2010 about the future of news in the digital age, a senior News International journalist and a Tory special adviser suggested that there was too much news 'for free' and public service provision needed to be reduced (British–American Project, 2010). Though there were several BBC executives present, they made little protest; but the prospect of a News Corp dominated 'market in news' appalled me. This was only days after the corporation had launched its bid for the remaining 61 per cent of BSkyB. When I spoke out about this, I was chastised for being alarmist. A Conservative special advisor told me: 'we just want to cut the BBC down to size a bit'.

Three months later in its Comprehensive Spending Review the coalition government cut the BBC's budget by 16 per cent by freezing the licence fee and forcing the corporation to take on the cost of the World Service – previously paid for by a Foreign Office grant. This was done in the back rooms of Whitehall and without any form of consultation with the people who are supposed to own the BBC: the public who pay the licence fee.

Finally, a month or so before the Hackgate scandal erupted, I was invited to a dinner with a junior minister at the DCMS when the issue of the BSkyB takeover came up. I tried to argue for the merits of a mixed economy in broadcasting and the dangers of News Corp having a cross-platform monopoly, but though the minister nodded at the principle it was evident the decision was a juggernaut somewhere high above his pay grade. If senior politicians, journalists and BBC executives treated News Corp with reverence, what could a lowly freelance writer do?

In retrospect, all the information was there – and must have been seen and understood by many professionals in the media business – and yet few protests were raised and the story never gained much public exposure. Claire Enders, of Enders Analysis, warned that the net effect of this takeover would be to make a combined BSkyB and News International 'a force de frappe which none of their competitors could match', with the *Financial Times* describing it as a 'Berlusconi moment'. (Ender's disagreed: 'The level of concentration [of News Corp media] already seen in the UK is substantially greater than would be allowed in Italian law. We are already way past any Berlusconi moment in Britain.') But the biggest merger in British media history barely made it out of the specialist papers, or remained buried deep in the business section. The key role of the press – to provide accountability – was compromised because it couldn't cover itself.

This is where the guilt comes from – or perhaps it is better described as a form of shame – the kind of shame when one is confronted with an unpleasant spectacle but can do nothing about it. Time and again I've seen this mixture of helplessness and inevitability in the faces of competitors, employees, policy wonks and even radical opponents when it comes to the activities of Murdoch and News Corp. In theological terms, we were guilty of succumbing to the mortal sin of despair.

We were wrong. That's one of the key lessons of this story. By falling for the Murdoch myth of invincibility, we gave it power. As soon as the *News of the World* was perceived as toxic, it was closed, and the Murdoch name tainted by association. Days before the scandal broke, News International parties and soirees were events any politician or public figure would be loath to ignore; almost overnight, senior executives like Rebekah Brooks and James Murdoch became a deadly third rail, which few politicians wanted to touch.

We were wrong, *en masse*, and it was only the persistence of a few brave individuals who, despite years of threats and obstruction, managed to bring an all-powerful corporation to account: a lawyer from Manchester who refused to be intimidated by corporate legal power; two parliamentarians who risked reputation and preferment by pursuing an organisation that still had the power to make or break their political careers; and a newspaper, the *Guardian*, and its lead investigator on the issue, Nick Davies.

In a saga which does much to discredit the practices of the British press, Davies – partly supported by the *New York Times* – proved that the era of investigative journalism isn't dead. The *Guardian* was not alone in trying to resist the BSkyB takeover, for both the *Daily Mail* and the *Daily Telegraph* joined the BBC and Channel 4 in a coalition against it. But the *Telegraph*'s campaign spectacularly backfired when, in a sting interview with the business minister Vince Cable who was overseeing the BSkyB bid, two young undercover female journalists got him to boast he was 'at war' with Murdoch. Though this section of the interview was excised from the *Telegraph* scoop, it was soon leaked to Will Lewis at News International who passed the news on to Robert Peston at the BBC. In just a few fateful hours before Christmas 2010, the Prime Minster recused Cable and passed on responsibility for the bid to Jeremy Hunt, who had conceded in an interview published on his website that he was a 'cheerleader' for Murdoch.

By early July 2011, the biggest media takeover in British history was only days away from approval. Had the hacking story broken much later, the quasi-judicial process would have taken its course and been much harder to undo through judicial review. Whatever the furore, in practical terms News Corp's dominance of the UK media would have been unassailable. Murdoch would have been even more powerful than Berlusconi in Italy, given the firewalls of accounting practices in Australia and the protection afforded by his US citizenship. No British subject – though very much subject to the Murdochs' ideals and influence – would have ever been able to hold them to account. A potentially invincible hegemony was only confronted and confounded at the eleventh minute of the eleventh hour through a tiny number of people who refused to bow to the inevitable.

A LIFELINE LOST

When I say that Murdoch ruined my life and probably did yours, this is not just a tongue-in-cheek tribute to his commercial success, but also a wink towards the way his tabloid model has changed our discourse. Instead of the bland brain-numbing government-controlled Newspeak envisaged by George Orwell in the 1940s, we have a livelier, brash commercial equivalent: the mockery and mayhem of the Murdoch-led tabloids, which could perhaps be described as '*Sun*speak'.

Like a red top headline, my hyperbole is personalised, provocative, turning a complex issue into a drama, lurking with animus, betrayal, passion and anger. If Murdoch loves the physicality of print and tabloid ink flows in his veins, then this is how his rebarbative DNA has been dispersed into our culture. It's not all for the bad – few things ever are – and compared with the mandarin tones of US or British publishing before his arrival, Murdoch's graphic language had much to commend it. But framing a protest in the language of your opposition is tantamount to offering a false flag of tribute. So let me try a less tabloid-inspired explanation of what Murdoch's influence over my culture has really meant to me.

Though my early childhood was fairly comfortable and middle class, my teens were pretty desperate. My father, discharged from the army as a manic depressive, was bankrupted twice in the early seventies, leaving my mother and the four remaining children she had at home penniless and about to be evicted from a repossessed house. To be declared homeless – bad enough in itself – also meant that my nine-year-old foster brother would have to be returned to a children's home despite living with us for five years. Fortunately, my mother had just trained as a social worker and she managed to get a job on a vast psychiatric hospital in the Buckinghamshire countryside. With that job came cheap subsidised accommodation.

For years I lived in a pebble-dashed semi on a grim wind-blown sixties estate over the road from the even grimmer Victorian mental institution. My mother, now separated from my father, was working all hours. Our diet seemed to consist of frozen hamburgers and peas, and for various reasons I didn't understand, I began to act up. By the time I was fourteen I was regularly smoking and drinking. I came twenty-fourth in my class of thirty, and having received five detentions in one term, I was threatened with suspension. My closest friend at the time, and the only schoolmate who lived within walking distance, was also troubled (he ended up in prison). My mother would complain about my deteriorating accent, and those of the girls who would ring for me, and we inevitably rowed. But apart from my mother's stoicism, there were a few other rays of quality and hope: the odd book she left around, the out-of-tune upright piano, the family heirloom silverware I'd polish for Christmas and the weekly sound of *The Sunday Times* plopping onto the doormat.

It's hard to explain to anyone younger than me just what a breath of intelligence and insight *The Sunday Times* was under the inspired editorship of Harold Evans. I still have vivid memories of its photomontages in the sixties, from the colour pictures of the first moon landing to the black-and-white shots of a naked John Lennon and Yoko Ono. In those tough teenage years I read little, but would use the weekly newspaper – especially the Review Section – as visual source material for pencil drawing, the one activity beyond television, school and going out that filled my time. The black-and-white photos were particularly easy to sketch; I remember copying an ancient woman painting and smiling (I have no idea who she was), a man fishing in a river (his name turned out to be Jonathan Raban) and a rotund bald Frenchman, with an amazing moustache and huge bags under his eyes. His name was Gustave Flaubert.

At some point, the accompanying text of the newspaper must have percolated my brain, for I have some recollection of mastheads billing an important (but to me, dull) series called the Crossman Diaries (published in the face of government opposition). More engaging were the well-illustrated Insight articles about the Israelis recovering their hostages in a raid on Entebbe, terrorist attacks and army shootings in Northern Ireland. At the back of the Review Section there was also a funny, intelligent take on the week's television, written by someone called Dennis Potter. I began to wander from my weekly diet of soaps and pop programmes to follow-up these tips to dramas and documentaries.

The Sunday Times was a cultural lifeline for me as a teenager. Something of the inquiring, open spirit of that newspaper must have got through my thick shaggy seventies haircut. Within a couple of years, books by Ernest Hemingway had joined science fiction on my bookshelf and I dreamt of being a journalist or an explorer – or maybe both – when I grew up. A few years later I won a scholarship to study literature at Cambridge University, with a particular interest in politics and current affairs. Before I graduated, I actually appeared in *The Sunday Times* Review Section, when James Fenton, the theatre critic, generously reviewed one of my student plays.

What happened to *The Sunday Times* when it was acquired by Murdoch in 1981 is the subject of another chapter, but the short version is that I doubt many teenagers were inspired by the bloated whale of a paper it became, with multiple shrink-wrapped supplements, as if column inches alone accorded insight (though it clearly added more advertising revenue). The reputation for meticulous fact-checking was blown apart by the fiasco of the fake Hitler diaries it published. The famed Insight team, which had exposed the spy ring around Kim Philby and the truth of Bloody Sunday in Northern Ireland, was diminished by episodes such as the libelling of a witness to the killing of three IRA members in Gibraltar by the SAS and the McCarthy-esque smearing of the Labour leader Michael Foot as a KGB agent. Instead of exposés of the corporate negligence around the Thalidomide drug, the paper printed a later discredited argument that HIV was not the cause of AIDS in Africa. Editorial independence was slowly eroded until, under Andrew Neil's editorship, it became a relatively uncritical cheerleader for the Thatcherite revolution.

I still believe it's rare for a cultural legacy to be all good or all bad and not all the formative influences of Murdoch's audience can have been as negative as mine. For my kids at least they have Murdoch partially to thank for the parodic multi-layered wit of *The Simpsons* appearing on his Fox Network, which include two episodes in which Murdoch turns up to play himself, accompanied by the Darth Vader theme from *Star Wars*. No doubt there are many football fans who praise Murdoch for Sky's acquisition of football rights and the creation of the Premier League – though there are many supporters of lower league football who claim this has ruined the game, and I doubt it would compensate many Liverpool supporters after the *Sun*'s coverage of the Hillsborough football stadium disaster under the editorship of Kelvin MacKenzie (see Chapter 5).

A moral cost–benefit analysis of Murdoch's influence on the English-speaking world is a vast task, given his reach and the hundreds of papers and TV channels he owns. However, when it comes to the self-declared core function of News Corp – the provision of information about the modern world – the verdict is pretty clear: it failed.

BEYOND WATERGATE

Sensationalised Fleet Street reporting wasn't invented by the *Sun* or the *News of the World*: the so-called gutter or yellow press has been successfully tormenting celebrities, politicians and opponents in public life for over a hundred years. Part of the argument of this book is that it's not just individual moral failure that led to the scandal of phone hacking and bribing state officials, but a collective ethos. As a market leader in Fleet Street, News International could be said to exercise a modal monopoly in an increasingly cut-throat business, in which scoops and scandals gathered huge economic rewards, developing the practices that other media owners were forced to copy to survive.

Because of this wider institutional malaise, ever since the Milly Dowler revelations in July 2011, the scandal of News International has been compared to Watergate. Carl Bernstein has made the comparison himself (and proffered the title 'Murdochgate') while John Dean, lead counsel to Richard Nixon, has said the potential ramifications are actually 'bigger than Watergate'. There are some useful parallels with the scandal around Nixon's government in the early seventies, especially in the way the attempt to suppress the initial crime only served to expand it. At the Leveson Inquiry, Murdoch admitted there was such a 'cover-up' at News International and in judging the civil actions lodged by phone-hacking victims Lord Justice Vos would claim that the destruction of computers and deletion of emails raised 'compelling questions about whether [NGN – a subsidiary of NI] concealed, told lies, actively tried to get off scot free'. But the Watergate analogy soon runs out of usefulness.

In the case of Watergate the ruthless power of the state was exposed by fearless journalists. The hacking scandal, the revelations of police corruption and back-door lobbying of government, present an almost completely inverted image, with the state appearing either cowed or complicit with the ruthless powers of journalism. Indeed, Murdoch's press often uses the language of Watergate to justify its actions, claiming they are defending ordinary people against the establishment. This is the core paradox we are left to resolve: in the name of holding power to account, parts of News International became an unaccountable power. While it still complains of 'witch-hunts' and 'Stasi-like' state intimidation, we are presented with a picture of a news gathering organisation that has allegedly bribed, intimidated and eavesdropped on police, army officials, civil servants, senior politicians, the wife of a prime minister and the heirs to the throne, appearing almost as a private sector version of East Germany's infamous secret police.

If there's one certain legacy of Murdoch's decades-long dominance of the British press, it is the deterioration of the image of investigative journalist from truth-teller to sleazy extortionist. You can see this sad transmogrification in the depiction of British journalists by Hollywood film-makers. To add to the stock-in-trade English stereotypes of effete villains, dashing spies, zany comedians and mop-haired pop stars, a new archetype was born: the ruthless, venal, privacy-invading tabloid journalist, epitomised by the British ex-pat hack Peter Fallow in Tom Wolfe's *The Bonfire of the Vanities*. As Murdoch became the leading force in the British press, the cultural reputation of British journalism sank to a new low.

Murdoch's reaction to this kind of cultural and moral criticism has been to shrug it off as old-fashioned snobbery, arguing that as his circulation figures prove, he is only giving the people what they want, and if you object to that, you're an elitist. Murdoch's favourite retort to critics of his tabloids – whether in TV interviews or testy replies on Twitter – is 'Don't buy them then!' He was even more explicit about this equation of populism with democracy when he appeared at the Leveson Inquiry in April 2012: 'I'm held to account by the British people,' Murdoch told Counsel for the Inquiry Robert Jay QC. 'They can stop buying the paper. I stand for election every day.' If people vote every morning by buying his papers, then his press has a public mandate to do whatever they want to do.

There are questionable assumptions here. Are *Sun* readers buying politics, horoscopes, football results or outsized breasts? If I buy more copies of *The Sunday Times* do I have more votes? But Murdoch is brilliant at expressing the assumptions of laissez-faire politics in a punchy popular way: you can't buck the market and the market is always right.

As I intend to show, any examination of the regulations, barriers to entry and concentrated ownership of the media would suggest that this market is far from open and free. And although news is certainly a market, it's not only a market; news is also a public good, vital for the functioning of a democracy, so much so that the requirement to report impartial information about elections and manifestoes is written into British electoral law.

Forty years after Rupert Murdoch first entered the UK market by buying the *News of the World*, James Murdoch reiterated his father's libertarian fallacy in his landmark MacTaggart lecture. He may have tried to dress it up with new media radicalism and MBA smartness, but the message was just the same: 'The only reliable, durable, and perpetual guarantor of independence is profit.' The title of James's speech *The Absence of Trust* – a barely concealed attack on the BBC Trust – has thickened with irony since 2009, especially as it was made only a year after he had authorised a million-dollar pay-out to a phone-hacking victim complete with stringent confidentiality clauses: a news organisation vigorously trying to conceal news about itself. But the paradox is entirely consistent with James's message: if news is to be entirely market driven, then money can buy the news.

Days after the Hackgate scandal erupted, according to a feature in the Daily Beast, an anonymous former senior News Corp employee stated:

> *This scandal and all its implications could not have happened anywhere else. Only in Murdoch's orbit. The hacking at* News of the World *was done on an industrial scale. More than anyone, Murdoch invented and established this culture in the newsroom, where you do whatever it takes to get the story, take no prisoners, destroy the competition, and the end will justify the means ... Now Murdoch is a victim of the culture that he created. It is a logical conclusion, and it is his people at the top who encouraged lawbreaking and hacking phones and condoned it.*

(Bernstein, 2011)

There is no doubt there is a lucrative and important 'market in news', but if news is *only* a market, the phone-hacking scandal shows us the consequences. The logical extension of chequebook journalism is that it can buy private details of unlisted phone numbers, social security numbers, computer passwords and voicemail pin codes. It can buy detectives who blag their way into bank accounts and medical records. It can suborn police officers for tip-offs on celebrities and crime stories. It can payoff informants for kiss-and-tell stories. It can hire the best lawyers and threaten litigants. It can authorise massive hush fees with non-disclosure orders. More insidiously, it can buy more media space to trash and harass political opponents. It can pay its favoured defenders big fees for ghost-written columns. It can become a kind of protection racket until a newspaper owner becomes a political legislator in his own right, a twenty-fourth member of the cabinet. It can enter the back door of Number 10 the day after a contentious national election. It can, through insider lobbying and back channels to government, seal the expansion of its commercial interests and media power until opposition to it is drowned out. In the name of the free market, it can monopolise it. In the name of free speech, it can chill it.

The moral of the story is: a dominance of the market in news ends up perverting the news.

CAPTIVE MINDS

The hacking scandal erupted in a year of many crises including the collapse of regimes in Tunisia, Egypt and Libya; a global financial meltdown which had turned from a liquidity crisis three years earlier into a wider sovereign debt crisis in the eurozone. Commentators have made comparisons between Murdoch's slow-motion demise and the toppling of tyrants in the Arab Spring, but the connection with the economic crisis is more pertinent.

Murdoch has always enjoyed a close relationship with bankers and shown a fondness for leveraged buyouts since his earliest Australian acquisitions. A personal friend of the junk bond trader Michael Milken, Murdoch has both deployed the aggressive techniques of deregulated globalised finance and stoutly defended its principles editorially.

The rise and fall of the House of Murdoch in the English-speaking media world is therefore inseparable, both in business form and ideological content, from the successes and failures of the Anglo-Saxon model of capitalism.

For two hundred years the liberal market economy has been underpinned by the concept of a free press and that pluralism, accountability, transparency and access to accurate information are vital to an open society as well as to a functioning market. The foreign friends I talk to, especially in former communist countries where democracy and the market economy is still seen as precious and precarious, pose a simple question about the phone-hacking scandal and its aftermath: 'How did you let one man get so much power?'

It isn't as if we weren't warned in advance about Murdoch's predilections for monopolistic commercial power combined with political clout. Over the decades there have been thousands of articles, hundreds of books (see a fraction in the Bibliography) and a raft of TV documentaries spelling out the dangers that lay in wait if Murdoch's media power was allowed to grow unfettered. They have been stunningly ineffective.

Back in the sixties, when Murdoch was aiming to take over the *News of the World*, part of the resistance to his bid was old-school snobbery about a colonial outsider and, in a bit of deft jujitsu, Murdoch played the cultural cringe against the 'old boys' network'. A BBC film shows him animatedly regaling the TV audience how he'd been called a 'moth-eaten kangaroo' by his rival, Robert Maxwell. This allowed Murdoch to portray himself, in stark defiance of the facts (he was the son of a millionaire and educated at Oxford), as the man-in-the-street, the ordinary bloke willing to take on the snooty establishment. *Private Eye*'s 'Dirty Digger' barb has survived much longer as a sobriquet but also falls into this class warfare trap. As Murdoch proceeded to take over the Times Group, establish Sky Television offshore and take over BSB, the chorus of disapproval got louder but made no difference. In 1994, in an otherwise powerful last television interview with Melvyn Bragg, the famous TV dramatist and polemicist, Dennis Potter, explained how he'd named the pancreatic cancer that would soon kill him 'Rupert'. Potter then went on to say, 'There is no one person more responsible for the pollution of what was already a fairly polluted press, and the pollution of the British press is an important part of the pollution of British political life.' Though seventeen years later some may see a prescient warning in Potter's words, pathologising the Murdoch phenomenon has done little to combat its rise.

And neither has the attempt to neutralise it. Around the same time, having suffered a third successive election defeat, and with Murdoch's popular daily tabloid claiming 'It's the Sun Wot Won it' for the Tories in 1992, the Labour Party came to the same conclusion, and the architects of New Labour – Tony Blair, Gordon Brown and Peter Mandelson – made a strategic decision that a policy of dialogue and containment might be wiser with News Corp. As Blair explained, 'It is better to ride the tiger's back than let it rip your throat out.' A year after becoming leader of the Labour Party, Blair attended a conference on Hayman Island, off the Australian coast, hosted by News Corp. In terms of election endorsements, the rapprochement was pretty successful (the 1997 election campaign saw the tabloid declaring: 'The *Sun* Backs Blair'), but New Labour's courtship of Murdoch required them to trim their media legislation and other policies until – some would argue – they were dancing to his music.

As we will see in Chapter 9 the whole story of New Labour and its relationship with News Corp is slightly more interactive than this. Murdoch had been a Labour supporter at Oxford; he'd agitated for the election of the Australian Labor leader Gough Whitlam in the seventies (before conniving in his dismissal a few years later) and had good working relationships with the Australian Labor leaders Bob Hawke and Paul Keating. This has led many journalists and analysts to conclude that Murdoch's ideology is actually fairly unimportant to News Corp: he pursues his business interests aggressively and will court politicians of whatever persuasion as long as they don't threaten his commercial activities with regulation.

If the left's critique of Murdoch has failed, either by being personally charmed and neutralised by him, or launching into ad hominem attacks, the right has – if anything – been even more supine. Of course Murdoch supported the radical Thatcherite agenda for ten years, led by one of Thatcher's key confidantes, Woodrow Wyatt. But in the mid-nineties Murdoch abandoned them for another three elections and Wyatt confided to his diary 'Rupert has behaved like a swine and a pig'. The Murdoch press might have maintained an editorial antipathy to the European Union – thus satisfying the core post-Thatcher test of ideological soundness for the core Euro-sceptics – yet, on virtually every other level of social conservatism or economic liberalism, Murdoch's commercial activities should have drawn ire from the right as much as the left.

For a one-nation Tory or a right-wing nationalist, Murdoch – an American citizen who indulged in a long albeit unproductive dance with the Chinese Communist Party – had little to offer. To the true followers of Friedrich Hayek or Adam Smith, the contradiction is even more egregious: did they not notice this avatar of free market philosophy was rapidly establishing monopolies across the world through cosying up to politicians? Did they not get the cognitive dissonance between a so-called meritocrat and man of the people wanting to turn his company into a family dynasty?

The failure to counter Murdoch's media concentration is, with some notable exceptions, a failure of the whole UK political establishment. Like the Dreyfus case in France at the turn of the last century, the phone-hacking scandal revealed deep fissures not only in politics but the whole of civil society (see Chapter 10). Our political culture failed because we didn't seem to have the language to describe what was happening.

Part of the problem is that our tools for analysing the role of media ownership and freedom of expression are firmly rooted in eighteenth-century notions of government censorship and a free press: they take little account of the globalised media conglomerates of the twenty-first century. The two-year Leveson Inquiry into the culture, practices and ethics of the press has been framed under these assumptions, with a remit which mainly looks at the competing balances between no regulation, self-regulation and state regulation of free speech. However, the issue of free speech – a legal guarantee to protect civil society from interference or censorship by the state – is very different to the concept of a free press in a highly competitive and commercialised world where the media are the key sector in the information economy.

Nearly all our concepts of censorship and freedom of expression are variants on those principles first outlined by John Milton in *Aeropagitica*, developed by J.S. Mill in his essay *On Liberty*, and enshrined in the first amendment of the US constitution. This Enlightenment emphasis on freedom of thought and empirical enquiry holds that no one person is in full possession of the truth, and that discovery of it requires competition of ideas, a sceptical citizenry exposed to argument and counter-argument, rather than having issues centrally decided by State or Church. Of course, this understanding has been vital to the growth of modern democratic societies and the alternative – centralised control of the press – is a key characteristic of totalitarian and authoritarian regimes, whose first move in a period of social repression is usually to smash printing presses or park their tanks outside TV stations.

In his novel *Nineteen Eighty-Four*, George Orwell extrapolated the idea that controlling the news agenda was the way to control society and in his brilliant appended essay on Newspeak outlined the way that the apparent disclosure of truth could be turned into its obverse. The dangers of state control of the press have understandably become the obsession of most discussions of free speech for the second half of the twentieth century, especially when the Iron Curtain was still in place. However, Orwell himself, when discussing the realities of Britain in the 1940s, acknowledged that centralised ideological control over our discourse was not the only issue. As he writes in his classic essay *The Prevention of Literature* (1946):

> In our age, the idea of intellectual liberty is under attack from two directions. On the one side are its theoretical enemies, the apologists of totalitarianism, and on the other its immediate, practical enemies, monopoly and bureaucracy. Any writer or journalist who wants to retain his integrity finds himself thwarted by the general drift of society rather than by active persecution. The sort of things that are working against him are the concentration of the press in the hands of a few rich men, the grip of monopoly on radio and the films, the unwillingness of the public to spend money on books, making it necessary for nearly every writer to earn part of his living by hackwork…

And in case it should be overlooked, Orwell repeats the premise at the end of the essay:

> To keep the matter in perspective, let me repeat what I said at the beginning of this essay: that in England the immediate enemies of truthfulness, and hence of freedom of thought, are the press lords, the film magnates, and the bureaucrats…

We'll never know what Orwell would have made of Rupert Murdoch, a press lord and film magnate, with the bureaucracy of News Corp virtually under his sole control. But over sixty years later, with the collapse of communism and the near hegemony of market economics, new private bureaucracies have arisen; corporations which, in an age of transglobal capital and borderless exchange, could be argued to have become as powerful as many nation states. I would argue that throughout the phone-hacking and police bribes scandal we've seen vivid evidence of *corporate censorship*.

Lowell Bergman experienced this when he tried to air his *60 Minutes* CBS documentary about the tobacco industry whistle-blower Jeffrey Wigand in 1995. While the secrets of the CIA or FBI had been exposed by journalists under the public interest defence, corporate law had no such get-out clause. As Bergman said in a PBS interview:

So there's no question that it was fair game to use confidential information from the government. But the new rule was: Don't use confidential information if it comes from the inner-workings of a Fortune 500 company, where the source has signed a confidentiality agreement.

The threat of civil litigation from the tobacco companies over the confidentiality agreement could have bankrupted CBS so they suppressed the first broadcast.

Hard censorship is only the most egregious example of the chilling of free speech. As Orwell points out, the suppression of dissenting voices doesn't have to be negative, it can be achieved through the soft censorship of promoting of the favourable point of view, the acquiescent op-ed, the politically correct line. Though it's not bribery, the blandishment of large fees on favoured politicians or public figures for their opinion pieces both co-opts them and the readership. *Suppressio veri, suggestio falsi.* All it takes to promote falsehood is to prevent the truth.

This is not just a parochial concern for media experts, regulators and journalists; misinformation can have much more serious and devastating casualties than just the truth. In *Flat Earth News*, written years before he broke the Hackgate scandal, the *Guardian* journalist Nick Davies explored how the decline of independent investigative journalism played a large part in allowing the falsehoods about Iraqi's weapons of mass destruction to become prevalent before the 2003 invasion. Botched intelligence about WMDs, combined with the disinformation about Saddam Hussein's regime and Iraqi reactions to a US invasion, led directly to the debacle that followed: an insurrection that cost around 100,000 Iraqi lives and that of more than 4,000 American service personnel.

It would be wrong to blame News Corp for the partiality of the press and media, but here we have a first-hand 'plurality' test. As a war of choice, the Iraq invasion was one of the most controversial foreign policy decisions of my lifetime. It generated such international dissent that key NATO allies were at odds in the UN Security Council. It brought Blair's government to the brink in a vote of the House of Commons and generated one of the biggest mass protests in Britain's history. How well did News Corp's extensive newspaper holding reflect that diversity of international public opinion about the Iraq War?

There's a simple statistical answer to this. Despite international disagreement in the Security Council, major dissent from allies and the largest ever protest demonstration in the UK, of Murdoch's 175 newspapers scattered across the globe, ALL came out in favour of the Iraq invasion in spring 2003 (Page, 2011).

Such a level of conformity is almost Orwellian. It proves that private bureaucracies are as capable of stifling dissent as the state bureaucracies. It proves that global competition between corporations doesn't necessarily lead to diversity, but rather a monoculture hidden under the market mechanics of pluralism.

Before he died tragically young of Lou Gehrig's disease, the British-born historian Tony Judt wrote an article in praise of the Polish poet Czeslaw Milosz's seminal account of the hold of Stalinism on young intellectuals in *The Captive Mind*. Having used the book as a teaching aide since the seventies, Judt noticed how thirty years later, students seemed to have no comprehension of how any thinking person could be seduced by such a totalitarian delusion. He goes on to explain how this is a sign of malaise rather than liberation:

> ...the true mental captivity of our time lies elsewhere. Our contemporary faith in 'the market' rigorously tracks its radical nineteenth-century doppelgänger—the unquestioning belief in necessity, progress, and History ... But 'the market'—like 'dialectical materialism'—is just an abstraction: at once ultra-rational (its argument trumps all) and the acme of unreason (it is not open to question). It has its true believers—mediocre thinkers by contrast with the founding fathers, but influential withal; its fellow travellers—who may privately doubt the claims of the dogma but see no alternative to preaching it; and its victims, many of whom in the US especially have dutifully swallowed their pill and proudly proclaim the virtues of a doctrine whose benefits they will never see. Above all, the thrall in which an ideology holds a people is best measured by their collective inability to imagine alternatives.

Our complicity with Murdoch's media project – our inability to think of any alternative – has ominous parallels with this. The News Corp story raises similar questions about the apparent 'freedom' of free markets and how that connects with the similarly slippery kind of 'freedom' displayed by the current model of the free press. Born during the expansion of mass electronic media and now trying to survive the online assault of new media, News Corp's crisis is also inseparable from the other 'problem of free': how the public good of truthful and accurate news can be promoted in an era where there is a digital abundance of information combined with a crisis in reliability and authority.

In the Information Age, the provision of news moves from being a precondition of the functioning of society to one of its most profitable activities. Just as the shadow banking system, originally devised to provide liquidity to financial markets, actually became bigger than the banking system itself, the medium of news has become the message in a way that Marshall McLuhan could not have foreseen. The US and the UK are now primarily knowledge economies, devoted to the processing and packaging of information. We accept Bloomberg, Reuters and the FT provide important signalling mechanisms to help financial markets function, but news is more than just the raw material of data mining facts and figures. Whole sectors of our economy are now in secondary data industries, devoted to turning information into workable and predictive knowledge. As for the tertiary industries, you could class many activities, from politics to sport to entertainment, as exactly that, manufacturing meaning from information about the world and creating motivating narratives for its inhabitants.

With vast interests from marketing to Hollywood films to sports to new educational software, News Corp clearly sits at various points on this supply chain of information. For Britons, the company has so many monopoly positions in newspapers, publishing, sports and film rights, it could be called the Standard Oil of the Information Age. But, though publishing has sunk to less than 20 per cent of its revenues, the company still brands itself as a news company, providing information about the world. And it's on that level it should be judged.

One of the key revelations of the phone-hacking scandal is a massive malfunction in the company's core activity. The pages ahead will describe a culture in which crucial bits of information were withheld from the public for commercial or political leverage. In effect, Murdoch turned news into a currency that could be traded, sometimes with the public, sometimes with other players under the counter. This in itself is not news; newspaper proprietors have been parlaying gossip and scandal for centuries. But the scale and aggression of this modus operandi are unique to Murdoch's empire.

In this sense, Murdoch was merely following the trends in many other companies in the world of modern finance. One can look at News Corp's various gambles over the years – from the cross promoting of Sky in the *Sun* to the promotion of favoured politicians – as a trading in news *futures*, i.e. betting on outcomes rather than current events. And just as this kind of derivative trading is liable to consume the original activity (as it has in the shadow banking system and various commodity and energy markets) I would argue that News Corp has gone from being a news organisation to a highly speculative and often *anti*-news organisation and has thus failed its primary purpose. It's hard to imagine any other industry surviving such a scandal: a construction company building skyscrapers that collapse or an airline company making planes that regularly fall out of the sky. In the past, such corporate malpractice has been eventually brought down by media exposure. If the media itself is faulty, the safety valve has gone.

Half a century in the making, the fourteen days that closed the *News of the*

World exposed not only the flaws of one man or one multinational corporation or indeed one society or nation, but an international culture which, by connecting free expression with the free market, had somehow ended up violating key freedoms in the process. And that's why – beyond the scandal and the personalities, beyond the party politics, boardroom battles and dynastic squabbles – the story of the fall of the House of Murdoch holds many lessons for us yet.

I

5 July 2011

Not the Morning News

Though it could claim to be one of the most important front page stories the *Guardian* newspaper had ever published, there are four important ways in which its front page exclusive about the hacking of murder victim Milly Dowler's phone by *News of the World* was not really news.

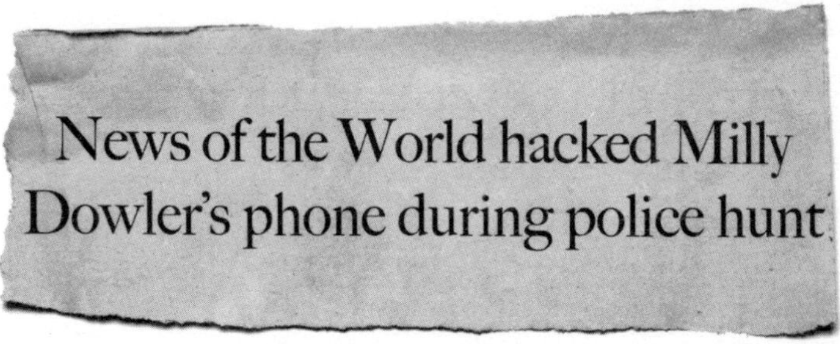
News of the World hacked Milly Dowler's phone during police hunt

Figure 1.1 Guardian, *5 July 2011*

First, in a pedantic technical sense by the time the presses rolled late Monday night and early Tuesday, the *Guardian*'s story wasn't new. As the article history on the *Guardian* website makes clear the story had broken online at 16:29 Monday afternoon. Within minutes news of the hacking of Milly Dowler's phone was tweeted by thousands and appeared as breaking news on TV channels and radio stations. Within hours it was the subject of comment and analysis, supplemented by more revelations from other newspapers, websites and broadsheets throughout the world. Whatever 'news' means – a concept as elusive as 'modernity' or time itself – by the criteria of novelty, currency or immediacy the print publication of the front page on Tuesday morning was already 'old news'.

Second, in terms of 'newsworthiness' there might seem to have been a rare consensus among the broadsheets about their headlines on Tuesday 5 July.

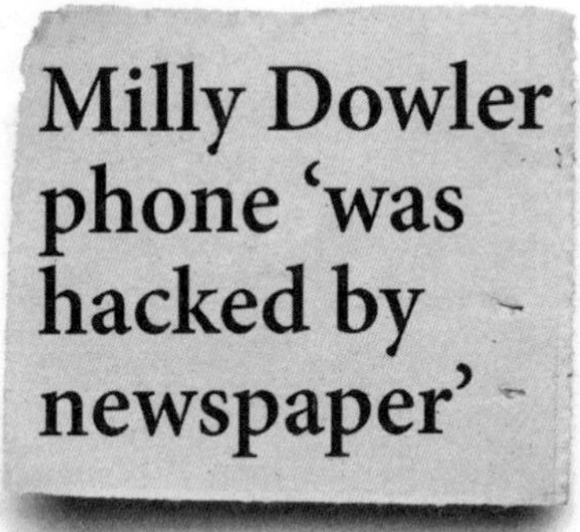
Milly Dowler phone 'was hacked by newspaper'

Figure 1.2 Daily Telegraph, *5 July 2011*

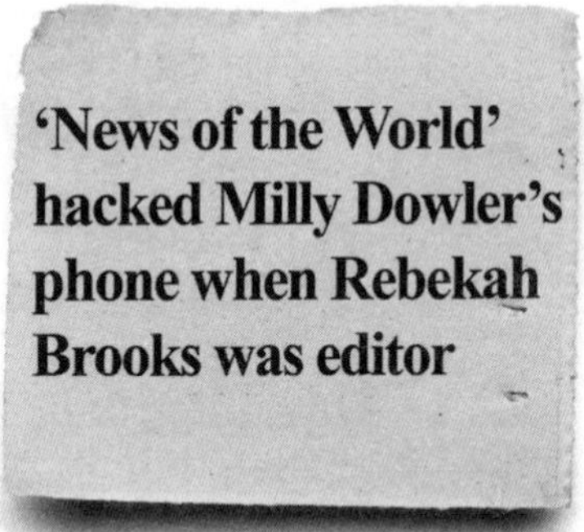
'News of the World' hacked Milly Dowler's phone when Rebekah Brooks was editor

Figure 1.3 Independent, *5 July 2011*

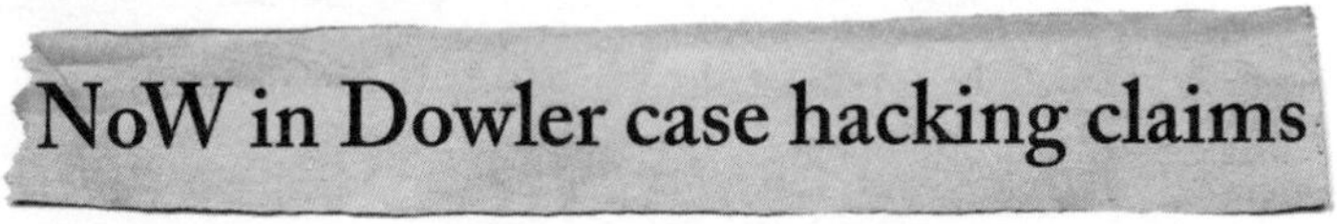
NoW in Dowler case hacking claims

Figure 1.4 Financial Times, *5 July 2011*

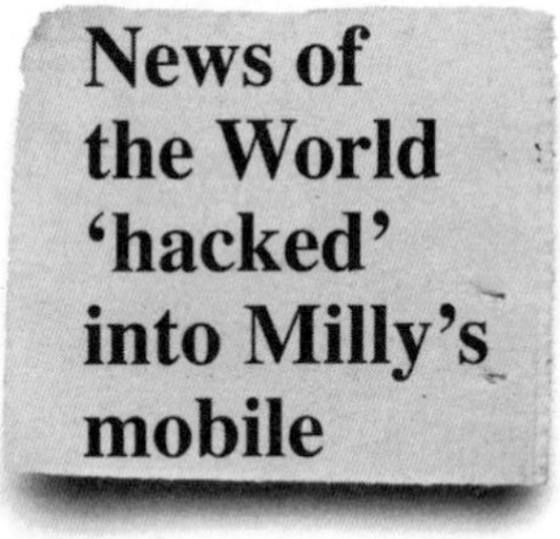
News of the World 'hacked' into Milly's mobile

Figure 1.5 The Times, *5 July 2011*

In one way or another, all the broadsheets covered the Milly Dowler story on their front pages. But they are only a fraction of the market: the *Sun*, *Daily Mail*, *Daily*

Mirror, *Daily Star* and *Daily Express* have a circulation of around 7.5 million, compared with 2 million or so who buy the *Daily Telegraph*, *The Times*, *Financial Times*, *Guardian* and *Independent*. For the bulk of Britain's newspaper readers the Milly Dowler story was distinctly not news.

If the market is the final measure of newsworthiness, then a picture of Prince William embracing his wife after a canoeing trip was nearly four times more important than the first dramatic act of the hacking scandal, since it dominated the front pages of the mass circulation papers, while Milly Dowler was nowhere to be seen.

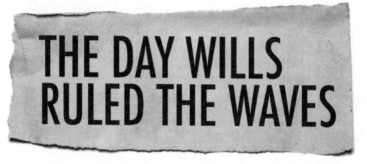

Figure 1.6 Daily Mail, *5 July 2011*

Figure 1.7 Daily Mirror, *5 July 2011*

Figure 1.8 Daily Star, *5 July 2011*   Figure 1.9 Daily Express, *5 July 2011*

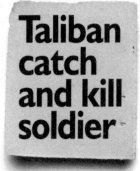

Figure 1.10 Sun, *5 July 2011*   *Figure 1.11* Metro, *5 July 2011*

Third, and most significant, the extensive hacking of the mobile phones of royalty, celebrities, politicians and people in the public eye was already a very old story. If you wanted to know the reality of phone hacking, or indeed what happened to Milly Dowler's phone when she disappeared in 2002, all you had to do was read between the lines.

MILLY

Accessing mobile voicemail messages without permission has been illegal in the UK since the Computer Misuse Act 1990, which carries a two-year prison sentence as a maximum penalty and has no 'public interest' defence. However, throughout the early nineties when mobile phones became ubiquitous, several newspaper scoops were derived from some kind of interception and recording of analogue phone signals. The two most famous are a six-minute bedtime 'Tampon' conversation between Prince Charles and Camilla Parker Bowles on a mobile phone (recorded December 18 1989 and published by the *Sunday Mirror* and the *Sunday People* in 1993) and the Squidgygate tape of a private conversation between Princess Diana and a close friend (published by the *Sun* in 1992).

In 2000 the Regulation of Investigatory Powers Act (RIPA) made intercepting a message while 'in the course of transmission' illegal. Around this time mobile telephony shifted from analogue to digital and intercepting encrypted signals required expensive technology, generally only available to the security services. However, a back door was left open: voicemails could be accessed remotely through a pin number. Much like the default admin passwords left on computers in the eighties, these pins were often left unchanged from their defaults. One of the first to discover this loophole was Steve Nott who alerted various newspapers to the security breach. As he claimed under oath to the Leveson Inquiry, the newspapers decided to use the security breach for 'their own purposes' rather than publish the story. Even phone users who changed their pin codes were still vulnerable to simple password attacks, with data such as dates of birth culled from other sources. If that failed, a bit of social engineering could solve the problem; dedicated investigators could ring the mobile phone service provider, either pretending to be the customer or an employee, and get the pin code set to default.

On the evening of 21 March 2002 after their 13-year-old daughter Milly failed to return from school, Bob and Sally Dowler rang the police. Within twenty-four hours a nationwide search for Milly was launched, and soon videos and photos of the missing teenager were broadcast on prime-time television. The *News of the World* which, under the editorship of Rebekah Brooks and her deputy editor Andy Coulson, had built a reputation for covering child murders, began a furious campaign.

Figure 1.12 News of the World's *Milly Dowler story, 14 April 2002*

Three weeks after Milly's disappearance, in the first edition of the *News of the World* on Sunday 14 April, a major story by-lined by Robert Kellaway had some interesting details.

To any casual reader the details of the messages, not only their content, timing and more importantly the tone of the callers, indicate that these have been listened to by the journalist. It's not even concealed. There's no suggestion of a police source. The *News of the World*, arrogating command of the investigation and trying to sell up a scoop, seems to know more about Milly than the police.

We now know that Milly was already dead, murdered by Levi Bellfield and dumped in Hampshire woodland where her body would not be found for two years.

On Wednesday, March 27 – six days after Milly vanished – a Midlands employment agency appears to have phoned the number of the mobile owned by the bubbly teenager, whose real name is Amanda.

At 10.13am a woman claiming to be an employee left a message saying: "Hello Mandy. We're ringing because we have some interviews starting. Can you call me back? Thank you. Bye bye."

Voice

The caller says the interviews are for work at a company which makes computer equipment. She leaves a phone number.

Next day at 7.48am a female voice says: "Leave a message now." A man then says: "Mortlake in Putney by Tangies." He signs off: "Piggo baby."

On April 2 at 9.50am a mystery voice leaves another brief cryptic message.

There has been no sign of Milly since she vanished walking to her home in Walton-on-Thames, Surrey, on March 21 at 4pm.

Figure 1.13 News of the World *article by Robert Kellaway, 14 April 2002*

We also know now that senior editors of the *News of the World* were at that time '110 per cent' convinced they knew where Milly was on the basis of hacking her voicemail. One of these was a message from a 'recruitment caller' offering a job and (according to the *Wall Street Journal*) the Sunday paper had sent out eight reporters and photographers to stake out an ink-cartridge factory in Epson for three days. When Milly failed to turn up, and investigations proved that Milly wasn't even on the factory's books, the *News of the World* – stumped for any story – came up with a new scandal: that some hoax caller had rung the factory impersonating a recruitment agency.

Later editions of the *News of the World* changed the original story, removing some of the more incriminating detail, adding some minimal fact checking. The recruitment company wasn't a hoax caller, they'd just come up with the wrong number for a client seeking work. But still the tabloid persisted in churning the non-story into a lurid smear: someone mentally disturbed had now called the recruitment agent impersonating Milly.

> *The hunt for missing Milly Dowler took a shocking twist last night when it emerged a deranged woman has been posing as the missing youngster.*
>
> *Police believe the sick hoaxer called into a recruitment agency pretending to be Milly.*
>
> *Staff at the Midlands bureau failed to recognise the name as that of the missing girl and took the woman on their books.*
>
> *It is thought the hoaxer even gave the agency Milly's real mobile phone number. Police believe she may have got it by gaining the trust of people who knew the schoolgirl.*
>
> *The agency used the number to contact Milly, real name Amanda, when a job vacancy arose and left a message on her voicemail AFTER the 13-year-old vanished at 4pm on March 21.*
>
> *It was on March 27, six days after Milly went missing in Walton-on-Thames, Surrey that the employment agency appears to have phoned her mobile.*

News is a rough draft of history and a breaking story is like a series of jotted notes, but this scribbled nonsense covers old errors with new: the paper had missed the simple explanation of a wrong number call. A police investigation of this would have quickly discounted the red herring. But the *News of the World* wanted its sensational exclusive and didn't want to divulge its illegal source, so clumsily tried to cover its tracks. It would continue to pepper its pages with useless speculation for the next two weeks. When their persistent interference with a missing person investigation failed, and they were eventually ignored by Surrey Police, the newspaper sought retribution by suggesting in print the investigating officers were incompetent.

In the past, tabloid newspapers have been accused of acting like judge and jury during criminal trials, but here we have them acting like the leading investigators during a major murder inquiry (the concatenation of errors, followed by bluster and threats toward the police are forensically documented by Tim Ireland on his Bloggerheads site). Most disturbingly, the paper used its access to illegal information to encourage Milly's parents that she was still alive and even pressure them into delivering an exclusive interview.

For those who have eyes to see, it's clear that even ten years ago the Sunday tabloid considered itself better than the police and above the law, which of course they were in more ways than one. It also must have been blindingly obvious to any journalist, police officer or senior News International management at the time that Milly's voicemail had been hacked by *News of the World*.

WILFUL BLINDNESS

Throughout the early noughties, there was plenty of other evidence of phone hacking lying around in plain sight. The *Daily Telegraph* did a database search of the British Newspaper Library in Colindale and came up with dozens of articles with direct mentions of phone messages from public figures such as Sven-Göran Eriksson, Ulrika Jonsson, Jude Law, Chris Bryant, Chris Tarrant, Ronaldo, Prince Harry and his girlfriend Chelsy Davy, including precise dates and locations. As Tim Ireland points out, the hacking of young murder victims' phones seems to go back to 2001 when the text messages of 15-year-old Danielle Jones formed the basis for another *News of the World* story.

Days after News International journalists were disturbing the police's attempts to trace Milly Dowler, at a newspaper awards ceremony sponsored by the mobile telephony giant Vodafone, the then business editor of the *Sun*, Dominic Mohan, thanked the mobile phone company's 'lack of security' for providing exclusives for his rival, the *Daily Mirror*. It may have been a jest, but it certainly wasn't a joke.

A few months later, in November 2002, detectives from the newly created Information Commissioner's Office (ICO) found a cache of records implicating various newspapers in illegal access to police and government records from a private investigator in south England. Raiding a second private investigator, Steve Whittamore, the officers of Operation Motorman found extensive evidence of requests from major British newspapers for information. There were hundreds of journalists making hundreds of request for illegal searches of private medical records, social security details, pin numbers and bank accounts. When the senior investigating officer asked his boss why his office weren't charging the newspapers in question with criminal offences, he was told by his boss they were 'too big to take on'.

In January 2003, Andy Coulson replaced Rebekah Brooks (then Wade) as editor of *News of the World* while she took over its daily sister paper, the *Sun*, as its first female editor. Both of them appeared, along with Murdoch and Les Hinton, then chief executive of News International, before the House of Commons DCMS select committee in March 2003, which was preparing a report on media intrusion and privacy. Questioned by Chris Bryant, Member of Parliament for Rhondda, Brooks admitted 'We have paid the police for information in the past', but was saved from further incriminating herself by an interjection from her former deputy, Andy Coulson: 'We have always operated within the code and within the law.'

Here, on camera, in the committee room of the House of Commons, was prima facie evidence of another crime – the subornment of police officers for payment. Yet Rebekah Brooks stayed in her job as editor of the *Sun* for the next three years and even hosted and started sponsoring the Police Bravery Awards in 2005, a notorious booze-up for police officers and journalists.

The year 2006 should have been the breaking point. In May the Information Commissioner finally published a report based on the discoveries of Operation Motorman (*What price privacy now?*), which explained the vast lucrative market in illicit information through deception and corruption and how the documentation seized from Whittamore had named 305 journalists in thousands of offenses under Section 55 of the Data Protection Act.

If this this wasn't enough, the arrest and trial of Clive Goodman and Glenn Mulcaire should have opened the floodgates of outrage. Royal aides had long been suspicious that Royal Household phones were compromised, but without hard evidence had to accept the security breach with resignation. But when in 2005 *News of the World*'s royal editor Clive Goodman published several trivial scoops in his Blackadder column (including one about Prince William's sore knee), using information that could only have been culled from hacked calls, the police were called in by Clarence House, the Royal Household for the Prince of Wales and his two sons. An investigation called Operation Caryatid was mounted that autumn and detectives soon traced Goodman making the calls and the activity of a private investigator working for the *News of the World*, Glenn Mulcaire.

The private investigator and the royal editor were arrested in August 2006. Goodman admitted to making 487 phone calls to intercept private messages of three royal aides and pleaded guilty to conspiracy to intercept communications. He received a sentence of four months the following January. Mulcaire pleaded guilty to conspiracy and eight offences under RIPA. He was sentenced to six months imprisonment. Before sentencing, the public prosecutor David Perry QC laid out some of the extent of the hacking. He told the court that Mulcaire had an annual contract worth £104,988 with the *News of the World* for 'research and information services' with an additional £12,300 made in cash payments (this had lasted five years). Mulcaire's notebooks also contained many details – pin number and phone network security passwords – of the supermodel Elle Macpherson. The court heard how Mulcaire had also intercepted the voicemail of the publicist Max Clifford, MP Simon Hughes, football agent Skylet Andrew and the Professional Footballers' Association's chief executive Gordon Taylor. On the day of Goodman's sentencing Andy Coulson resigned as editor of the *News of the World*, but not without an angry sideswipe at the judge and railed at the Home Secretary for the injustice of the criminal courts (Burden, 2008, pp. 140–1).

Here, finally, the truth could have been exposed. This was a story hard to miss for any investigative journalist who dared, or cared, to investigate their own trade. Mulcaire's large annual income would be an unlikely reward for just half a dozen targets. Moreover, anyone could see that, though he was charged with hacking the Royal Princes, Mulcaire came from a background in football; since it was announced in open court that a sports agent and senior footballing executive were among his targets, and with a supermodel, a member of parliament and a publicist on the list, it wouldn't take a genius or insider to figure out that the *News of the World*'s private investigator wasn't just working for Goodman's Blackadder column. Other journalists must have also been clients for his material.

Nonetheless, the explanation of Les Hinton, a key member of the Press Complaints Commission (PCC) and Murdoch's longest serving lieutenant, was accepted without rebuttal. As the then CEO of News International, he told the Commons culture select committee that Goodman was 'the only person involved in phone hacking at *News of the World*'. His boss, Murdoch, went even further: 'If you're talking about illegal tapping by a private investigator, that is not part of our culture anywhere in the world, least of all in Britain.'

In May 2007 the PCC, the official overseer of journalistic ethics and behaviour on Fleet Street, came up with their own view and agreed wholeheartedly with new editor of the *News of the World*, Colin Myler, that Mulcaire and Goodman were a 'rogue exception': 'There is no evidence to challenge Mr Myler's assertion ... that no-one else at the *News of the World* knew that Messrs Goodman and Mulcaire were tapping phone messages for stories.'

'No-one else' ... 'the only person' ... 'the rogue exception'? Any tabloid Fleet Street journalist could have told you that phone hacking was rife at that time. Any parliamentarian reviewing the evidence of the ICO and the *What price privacy now?* report could have seen illegal access to private data was a booming secondary industry. And any policeman, glancing at the 11,000 entries in Mulcaire's meticulous records, would have known that Hinton and the PCC were either duped or duplicitous.

To put it into context, phone hacking was not just some marginal specialist interest at this point. Data protection, the importance of securing private information against theft and misuse, was a major theme of the times. The virtual burglaries and robberies of 'identity theft' were in the papers every other day and banks were beginning to aggressively sell insurance against the loss of personal information and compromise of financial identities. In those days most people knew someone who had their credit or debit card cloned and used to buy goods illegally – either abroad or in the UK. (It was around this time that my car tax disc was stolen and I was sent speeding tickets for another car with the same number plate.) Yet when it came to this crucial form of identity theft by the most power media organisation in the country – the virtual breaking in and stealing of personal information from private phone messages – something which could only been motivated by the financial gain of increased newspaper circulation, the most meagre and mendacious assurances of senior management seemed to be swallowed whole.

Something was rotten in the state of the nation. Three of the key pillars of society – the press, the police and Parliament – failed us when it came to the early outings of the hacking story. The security implications alone don't bear thinking about. The family of the head of state, members of Parliament, senior cabinet ministers and senior police officers were also on Mulcaire's list. Bear in mind this was at the height of the 'War on Terror' when many other individual rights were being overridden by the exigencies of 'national security'. With the police mute, journalists reticent and our lawmakers not willing to make an issue of it, only the fourth pillar – the legal establishment – chipped away at this facade. In court, the prosecuting counsel had named a dozen or so other victims from Glenn Mulcaire's notebooks. It was the civil cases launched with this information that slowly began to force News International and the police to disclose more.

The founder of the Hacked Off campaign, former journalist Brian Cathcart, has suggested some kind of monument or honour should be made for the civil litigants who started on this long, expensive and dangerous road which finally breached News Corp's corporate defences. Having personally known victims of phone hacking and tabloid stings, I can understand why most victims tend to lie low: contesting the claims of the tabloids, no matter how outrageous, can just make you more of a target. This has been a tradition even with those who win costly libel cases (such as Elton John or Hugh Grant): the tabloids persist in vendettas against successful litigants, partly out of vengeance, but also out of simple legal 'don't fuck with us' financial calculation. Cathcart (2012) explained how anyone who decided to pursue in the courts was in for a rough time:

> *...every politician knew that the Sun and the News of the World could wreck their reputations, and that these papers had more access to the prime minister (and his two predecessors) than any backbencher and most ministers. Suing probably looked like political suicide to most MPs.*
>
> *Across television, cinema and sport, from Hollywood to India, News Corporation owns or controls far more than any other company, so if you were an actress, a sportsman, a football agent or a PR person you risked much more than your time and money by suing – you risked your livelihood.*
>
> *As for ordinary people whose phones had been hacked, you might think they had nothing to lose by suing, but think again: this is a company that employed private investigators on an industrial scale. Would you be happy to have every aspect of your private life secretly investigated, and if the*

> *slightest blemish was found – perhaps involving a vulnerable relative – to*
> *have that exposed in the press?*

Because many of the original phone-hacking victims were celebrities or politicians, the sympathy for their plight among the public may have been limited, but even a celebrity is relatively powerless before the wheels of the fame and infamy-making machine of News International's tabloids. Before long, even the lawyers who represented these victims would become targets of smear and surveillance themselves; the family of the lawyer Mark Lewis, and a fellow lawyer Charlotte Harris, were followed by Derek Webb, a former policeman turned private investigator hired by News International in 2010. Parliamentarians who campaigned on their behalf, such as MP Tom Watson, would also be targeted and News International were even alleged to have planned to follow the whole DCMS select committee investigating them, to dig up dirt (Watson and Hickman, 2012).

Shame is a powerful force and the existential threats of public disgrace are hard to overestimate. There are several documented cases where individuals have killed themselves shortly after a Murdoch tabloid exposé. In 1964 Murdoch's Sydney tabloid the *Daily Mirror* leaked a schoolgirl's sex diary which falsely accused a fellow pupil – Digby Bamford – of promiscuity; 13-year-old Bamford was expelled from school and committed suicide by hanging himself on a clothes line. In 1971 the *News of the World* accused some of the young dancers in the audience of BBC One's music show *Top of the Pops* of 'promiscuity' too and claimed Samantha MacAlpine, aged 15, had a leather-bound book which would expose the scandal. MacAlpine committed suicide the day after the story was published. Other suicides were more slow motion. In the Leveson Inquiry, former *News of the World* reporter Paul McMullan admitted how he befriended Jennifer Elliott, daughter of actor Denholm Elliott, took photos of her topless and wrote several articles about her decline (tipped off by police sources for £500 payments). McMullan conceded the coverage contributed to Jennifer's suicide in 2003.

ROGUE REPORTER

It was through the victims' evidence that Nick Davies began to assemble his story of systematic lawbreaking at News International he explained in his evidence at the Leveson Inquiry. Davies first became interested in intrusions into privacy when researching his 2008 book *Flat Earth News*, which, although it mainly explores the commercial imperatives that have driven newspapers into the business of turning out celebrity and PR 'churnalism' rather than journalism, has a whole chapter devoted to the 'black arts' of surveillance, the science of 'bin-ology' or going through people's rubbish for personal data (what the Americans call 'dumpster diving') and phone hacking. The book was well received, but made no big impact on the public sphere. However, in terms of sources and reputation, it put Davies in prime position to explore the hacking story as it unfolded.

The first lead turned out to have been almost accidental. As related in Tom Watson and Martin Hickman's book, *Dial M for Murdoch*, Davies was tipped off during a dinner party conversation with a senior police officer; when he asked whether the number of phone-hacking victims suggested by Mulcaire's notebooks was in its hundreds, the police officer replied 'no, thousands'. In 2008, after a testy BBC Radio 4 exchange with the *News of the World* managing editor, Stuart Kuttner, Davies was contacted by a whistle-blower appalled at the cover-up.

In 2009, a year after the publication of *Flat Earth News*, News Group Newspapers (the subsidiary of News International that runs the *News of the World* and the *Sun*) paid more than £1 million to settle the legal cases of a further phone-hacking victim, the head of the Professional Footballers' Association, Gordon Taylor. The size of this pay-out – at least twenty times the amount for any previous compensation for intrusion into privacy – was an indication that something very big was at stake.

In his first big *Guardian* exposé of 8 July 2009, Davies finally demolished the whole 'rogue reporter defence' of the Mulcaire/Goodman trial. Advanced legal disclosure had revealed potentially thousands more phone-hacking victims in Mulcaire's papers and many more journalists using the private investigator's material. Davies said the unsayable – in print – and remonstrated with senior News Corp executives for misleading a parliamentary select committee, the Metropolitan Police for failing to notify many victims, the Crown Prosecution Service for omitting to pursue all the possible charges and the PCC for swerving the duty of a proper investigation. This article and its allegation made the top of the BBC's bulletins and one of Murdoch's former favoured editors, Andrew Neil, called it the 'most important media story in years'. For all the vaunted power of the BBC, what was the wider reaction to this allegation of lawbreaking by a major media corporation and a potential cover-up in 2009?

Crickets…

Days later, *Observer* editor Peter Wilby noticed the stunning silence of Fleet Street. Even worse, the PCC, tasked with controlling the worst excesses of the press, actually condemned the *Guardian*'s investigation as overdramatic and providing no new evidence. Assistant commissioner John Yates, head of specialist operations, claimed that there were only a dozen phone-hacking victims and that 'no additional evidence has come to light' and 'no further investigation is needed'. Murdoch was psychologically interesting: 'If that had happened I would know about it.'

Undeterred, Davies kept up the campaign through 2010, leaking details of other victims sampled from Mulcaire's files – John Prescott, George Michael, Jade Goody, Kate Middleton, Princess Michael of Kent – and in April going full throttle for the blocked Met investigation:

> *Something very worrying has been going on at Scotland Yard. We now know that in dealing with the phone-hacking affair at the News of the World, they cut short their original inquiry; suppressed evidence; misled the public and the press; concealed information and broke the law.*

(DAVIES, 2010)

Again, the response of the rest of Fleet Street was a stunning silence. An academic survey of the year 2009 and 2010 shows that whereas the *Guardian* had written 237 articles on the subject, the *Independent* had written 83, the *Daily Telegraph* 46 and *The Times* 43. Tabloid coverage was even scanter, with the Associated Press group only covering the hacking revelations in 38 articles, the *Sun* with 17, and the *Daily Mirror* and the *Sunday Mirror* 11 between them. Numbers alone don't do the Fleet Street self-censorship in this instance any justice. As Bennett and Townend (2012) suggest, 'often journalists covered phone hacking in a minimal manner, reporting angles that undermined any basis for further investigation or attacking those who believed it deserved attention as a news story.'

Carl Bernstein and John Dean might compare the hacking scandal to Watergate, but the painstaking journalistic investigation of Richard Nixon's White House seems to move at lightning speed compared to the hacking scandal affair. It took two years from when Woodward and Bernstein first latched onto the circumstances of the Watergate break-ins in 1972 to Nixon's resignation and another year for the masterminds of the Committee for the Re-Election of the President to be indicted and jailed.

In comparison, Davies and the *Guardian* had a harder uphill task. For a start they were taking on the world's third largest media conglomerate, which already had 43 per cent of the newspaper readership in the UK and was developing plans to be the sole owner of the country's monopoly satellite broadcaster, BSkyB. News International had vast coffers to fight debilitating legal battles. It also had – as already demonstrated by the bland assurances of the regulator – the most influential voice on the PCC. Davies also faced a wall of indifference and silence from the official representatives of the Metropolitan Police.

After the 2010 general election when David Cameron had entered 10 Downing Street as head of the coalition government and installed Andy Coulson as the chief press spokesman for the whole government, the right-wing commentator Peter Oborne wrote in outrage:

> ...*the Tory leader is embracing a history of pay-offs, venality and wire-taps ... We only know this thanks to the investigative work carried out by* Guardian *reporter Nick Davies. Davies's work, however, has gained no traction at all in the rest of Fleet Street, which operates under a system of omerta so strict that it would secure a nod of approbation from the heads of the big New York crime families.*

> (OBORNE, 2010)

The code of silence in Fleet Street would continue for a while yet.

DISCLOSURE

In October 2010 another figure from right of centre stepped forward to emphasise the role of the press to speak truth to power, fearlessly, from whatever quarter:

> ...*a free society requires an independent press: turbulent ... enquiring ... bustling ... and free ... That's why our journalism is hard-driving and questioning of authority. And so are our journalists ... Now, it would certainly serve the interests of the powerful if professional journalists were muted – or replaced as navigators in our society by bloggers and bloviators. Bloggers can have a social role – but that role is very different to that of the professional seeking to uncover facts, however uncomfortable.*

This is a great image of the benign effects of what Blair once called the 'feral press'. Like maggots that eat dead flesh, the superficially unpleasant process of media disclosure can have a therapeutic effect, cleaning the necrotic wounds in the body politic which, left untreated, could infect the whole.

And who was this brave journalist who put his head above the parapet to take on unaccountable bloggers and to argue for journalistic investigation and disclosure no matter how painful? One K.R. Murdoch. (Keith is actually Rupert's first name.)

It's worth re-reading the informatively titled speech 'Free markets and free minds: the security of opportunity' that Murdoch delivered at the inaugural Margaret Thatcher lecture in October 2010. Like James Murdoch's MacTaggart lecture the year before, the text now abounds in ironies. A lot of the assertions are uncontroversial – a formal recitation of the values of free speech, transparency and accountability. I suspect Rupert Murdoch himself believes in everything he said. But whatever the espoused ideology of its chairman and chief executive, the actual practice of News Corp's subsidiary spoke a very different truth.

The half century trajectory of Murdoch's global media invasion is the subject of this whole book, but the specifics of 2010 are worth noting here. At this point, Murdoch had been described by Labour's deputy press spokesman Lance Price as being like the twenty-fourth member of the cabinet: 'No big decision could ever be made inside No 10 without taking account of the likely reaction of three men – Gordon Brown, John Prescott and Rupert Murdoch.' This political influence extended to his family and favoured lieutenants, a network of relationships that were personal as well as political; Brown's wife Sarah famously hosted a 'sleep-over' party for Rebekah Brooks and Elisabeth Murdoch at Chequers a couple of years earlier. Meanwhile, the previous Labour Prime Minister, Tony Blair, had just become godfather to one of Murdoch's daughters with Wendi Deng. Likewise, as he later made clear in his testimony to the parliamentary select committee, Murdoch himself was also good friends with Brown and supported his bid to succeed Blair. The media mogul's two daughters played with the children of the outgoing prime minister, and his wife Wendi Deng was close to Sarah Brown.

However touching these family rendezvous, other dynastic considerations were afoot. As part of his manoeuvring to become heir apparent, James Murdoch was planning a 'Wapping Two' to combine BSkyB and News International to launch a dominant digital platform, but this required a takeover of the remaining shares and the approval of the government. Labour would have a difficult time, especially given the Brown–Blair civil war, nodding through the deal. But there was an alternative waiting in the wings, someone who was not only a near neighbour and friend of one of Murdoch's protégés, Rebekah Brooks, but a Conservative who was intent on de-toxifying the 'nasty Tory' image of the past and who had the potential to be positive post-partisan figure and true heir to Blair: David Cameron. The MP for Witney was already, by all accounts, a member of the 'Chipping Norton set' along with Brooks, Elisabeth Murdoch and her husband Matthew Freud (see Chapter 9).

Though Labour certainly lost the ensuing election in May 2010, the Tories didn't win it sufficiently enough to form a government on their own. But News Corp's spread bet still paid dividends. After two weeks of wrangling (which apparently included several warnings about his advisor's past) Andy Coulson was installed as the Prime Minister's Director of Communications when the coalition government was formed. Within a week of taking office, Cameron invited Murdoch for a private meeting; though to his chagrin this entailed entering Number 10 by the back door. We'll never know what was discussed at those private social meetings, but as John Biffen (the Tory minister who waved through Murdoch's purchase of Times Newspapers) once said: 'Whenever you find a senior politician and a powerful media owner in private conclave, you can be certain that the aims of a healthy, plural democracy are not being well-served.'

The lobbying was not of course just one sided. By the time the Rubicon process came to a head, and the BSkyB bid was revealed, a media coalition, including the BBC, had formed to oppose the overwhelming cross-platform news advantage the takeover would have posed in the UK. The *Guardian*'s campaign to reveal the secrets of phone hacking at Wapping can't be separated from this threat of media hegemony. So urgent was the campaign to stop Murdoch before the BSkyB decision that the *Guardian* sought crucial intervention from across the Atlantic. The paper's editor, Alan Rusbridger, picked up the phone and called his counterpart, Bill Keller, editor of the *New York Times*.

In June 2010 three *New York Times* journalists arrived in the UK to pursue the phone-hacking story (according to *Vanity Fair* there was already a newspaper war brewing between Murdoch – now owner of the *Wall Street Journal* – and the rival Sulzberger dynasty who owned the *New York Times*). The *New York Times*'s reputation for double sourcing, fact checking and diligence were legendary, and the ability to throw three reporters at one foreign story for three months was a rare advantage few Fleet Street papers still had.

The 6,000-word *New York Times* article published on 1 September 2010 took the hacking story to a whole new level. Not only did it finally bust the 'rogue reporter' defence with various unnamed sources, but two former *News of the World* journalists – Sean Hoare and Paul McMullan – went on record claiming that phone hacking was rife under the editorship of Andy Coulson. Surely this would have blown the scandal wide open, force other papers to report it and finally gain the attention of public opinion? But rather like the 'expensive delicate ship' that missed the death of Icarus in W.H. Auden's poem *Musée des Beaux Arts*, public opinion had other things on its mind and sailed calmly by.

The list of known hacking victims was growing and now included some of the most senior lawmakers and law enforcers: former deputy prime minister John Prescott and a former deputy assistant commissioner, Brian Paddick. Mark Lewis, a lawyer acting for one of the original phone-hacking victims, told the DCMS select committee that one of the original investigating officers claimed the number of hacking victims in Mulcaire's notebooks could be as high as 6,000. At a Society of Editors dinner the head of the PCC, Baroness Peta Buscombe, went to the aid of News International and claimed she had evidence from the Met that the police officer had been misquoted. A year later Buscombe was successfully sued for libel by Lewis (and the Met too in 2010) but at the time the PCC was actively discouraging reports of more extensive phone hacking, bringing out yet another report that year denying the wider claims.

Nevertheless, the slow drip drip of private litigation couldn't be so easily contained. In December 2010 Sienna Miller's lawyers announced they now had evidence that her phone was hacked. More importantly, a constant stream of requests, early day motions in Parliament, written and verbal questions from a small number of MPs, most notably Tom Watson and Chris Bryant, was beginning to prise away at the police decision not to prosecute further in 2006. As public employees, the Metropolitan Police and Crown Prosecution Service were both open to, and subject to, Freedom of Information Act requests. These revealed extensive meetings between senior Met officers with News International executives during the phase when Mulcaire's files were being discussed.

At this point, News Corp was on the brink of achieving a key strategic goal of Rubicon – taking over the whole of BSkyB. The bid had managed to pass the supine EU monopoly test and dodge the Competition Commission, but still faced the hurdle of satisfying Ofcom's 'plurality test' which had been inserted into the 2003 Communications Bill to guarantee a diversity of news sources. Without a clear majority the Conservatives couldn't easily replace Ofcom (as Cameron and James Murdoch had previously mooted in separate speeches), so the only way out was to avoid referral entirely. The problem resolved itself, however, when in December 2010 two *Daily Telegraph* journalists posing as constituents covertly recorded the business minister, Vince Cable, explaining how he had referred the bid to Ofcom: 'I have declared war on Mr Murdoch and I think we're going to win'.

Cable's revealed bias would have opened any decision to a judicial review and he had to be replaced. When Cameron awarded oversight of the bid to the culture secretary Jeremy Hunt – an admirer of News Corp and in close contact with both James Murdoch and his senior lobbyist Frédéric Michel – the Rubicon process looked back on track. But it had to get a move on. In January 2011, when the Sienna Miller legal case revealed that hacking at the *News of the World* was not restricted to a single 'rogue reporter' something shifted behind the scenes at Scotland Yard. Director of Public Prosecutions, Keir Starmer, kept on asking the Metropolitan Police to look at their files and the police finally launched a new investigation and re-examined the copious details in Mulcaire's notebooks, assigning 45 officers commanded by the friendly but formidable Deputy Assistant Commissioner Sue Akers to the job. This became the now historic police inquiry, Operation Weeting.

In retrospect, the critical factor here was not the press reporting of phone hacking, nor the parliamentary questions, but the Sienna Miller case and the legal demand placed on News International to preserve key documents. Days before Operation Weeting was announced, key emails were deleted from the inboxes of new *News of the World* editor Colin Myler and his boss James Murdoch. A senior *News of the World* assistant news editor was sacked and – seeing the writing on the wall in terms of containing the story – Andy Coulson resigned as head of communications for the Prime Minister, claiming that the events of the past were making him a distraction: 'I stand by what I've said about those events but when the spokesman needs a spokesman, it's time to move on' (Telegraph, 2011a). In retrospect, a decision had been made to sacrifice Coulson to protect the BSkyB bid. And it seemed to work…

As for the rest of the press, or public opinion, the ship sailed calmly on.

Over the next few months more hacking victims were identified: comedian Steve Coogan, sports presenter Andy Gray and Labour MP Chris Bryant. Then, in March 2011, with the collapse of a murder trial against private investigator Jonathan Rees, the lifting of reporting restrictions allowed the press to discuss the connection between his firm Southern Investigations and News International. Rees had been regularly employed by *News of the World* when Coulson was editor – notwithstanding a criminal conviction for planting cocaine on a woman during a child custody battle and being investigated no less than five times over the murder of his former business partner Daniel Morgan (see Chapter 10). In the same month a BBC One *Panorama* programme alleged that a former News International senior executive editor, Alex Marunchak, had paid Rees for exclusive material based on confidential police sources and that Marunchak had also received information hacked via a Trojan from the computer of a British army intelligence officer (see Chapter 11).

The next month, in April 2011, no less than three *News of the World* employees were arrested on suspicion of phone hacking by officers from Operation Weeting: the chief reporter, news editor and a reporter. But apart from the *Guardian* the story barely broke through the front pages of the broadsheets. And as for the tabloid journalists who must have seen something extraordinary – many of their colleagues falling out of the sky – they had something better to do and sailed obliviously on.

May 2011 wasn't interested either – despite John Prescott and others achieving a judicial review of the hacking files. June 2011 was indifferent, despite the arrest of two more former *News of the World* journalists.

Though Nick Davies had, by now, written over a hundred stories on the phone-hacking scandal, by the beginning of July 2011 this was still a rumbling non-story, a parochial concern of a few diehard news insiders or – take your pick – some smear campaign by the left-leaning *Guardian* and liberal BBC.

Looking back, it's hard to believe in Britain's mythical reputation as the envy of the world for its 'free press' over this time. As described by Murdoch in his Thatcher lecture, the press was a feral but necessary cleansing force, ferociously devoted to exposing scandal and corruption at whatever cost, confronting sclerotic hierarchies, challenging those in power.

If there's any further refutation of the contention of Murdoch and his son, that the free market automatically leads to a free press, or that reliance on profit is the guarantor of independence, then it is these nine long years of silence, subterfuge and cover-up from the first *News of the World* articles on Milly Dowler in 2002, clearly based on her voicemail messages. Despite reams of other evidence available for any conscientious journalist – or even a lay reader of material in the public domain – the story of extensive illegal activity in the newsrooms of Wapping, a litany of intrusion, electronic burglary, deception and blagging, was just not news.

Corporate conspiracy is only one of the explanations for the media silence on this issue. Though rumours of a 'non-aggression pact' have been denied by senior Fleet Street editors, the ownership is narrow enough to form an unconscious cartel of self-interest when it comes to exposing nefarious journalistic practices. There was also a widespread feeling in news rooms that this was a 'meeja' story, of little interest to the wider public (Bennett and Townend, 2012, p. 150). And, in a perverse twist, the longevity of the Hackgate story, stretching back over nearly a decade, counted against it. The PCC drew on this spurious definition in its 2009 report when it opined the *Guardian*'s revelations 'did not quite live up to the dramatic billing they were initially given' and was 'old information … already in the public domain'.

The much vaunted role of the fourth estate to 'speak truth to power' had been inverted – it tacitly spoke of the truth of power. The main story about the 'market in news' over that decade was that it failed to deliver the most significant news about itself.

FALSE HOPE

While the hacking of Milly Dowler's phone wasn't news in so many ways and had been ignored and then repressed for nearly a decade, there's one fourth and final twist to this story which acts as a salutary reminder about the problematic relationship between a breaking story and accuracy. The old popular Russian saying about the communist party newspapers in the Soviet Union, *Isvestia* (news) and *Pravda* (truth) is still relevant: *v Pravde net izvestiy, v Izvestiyakh net pravdy* – in the truth there is no news, and in the news there is no truth. News and truth are far from synonyms and to break a story is often to betray it.

In terms of that famous *Guardian* front page from 5 July, the sub-heading 'EXCLUSIVE: Paper deleted missing schoolgirl's voicemails, giving family false hope' was not entirely accurate. The suggestion was that *News of the World* journalists had discovered the voicemail box was full and deleted messages to leave space for new ones to be left. As Bob and Sally Dowler explained at the Leveson Inquiry, the activity of their daughter's voicemail gave then 'false hope' their daughter was still alive. Though this was the understanding of police investigators at the time, their subsequent discoveries six months later clouded the deletion theory with doubt. The stored messages could have very well been removed automatically by the mobile phone service provider.

The police's new assessment led to a massive storm of bluster and counter accusation. The managing editor of the *Sun* accused the *Guardian* of 'sexing up' the whole story. Murdoch was reportedly so furious about the perceived misrepresentation that he brought forward his plans to re-launch a *News of the World* replacement – the *Sun on Sunday*. In a foretaste of what would happen two months later when ten *Sun* journalists were arrested for allegedly paying bribes to the police, loud cries of 'witch-hunt' came from News International's Wapping headquarters.

In a BBC Two *Newsnight* interview at the time, Davies faced former *News of the World* features editor Jules Stenson, who accused him of 'shoddy journalism'. But Davies' grilling by the presenter Jeremy Paxman was much more informative because it directly addressed the issue of truth.

PAXMAN: *This central allegation, the most scandalous perhaps of the lot, that a murdered girl's voicemails were deleted by the* News of the World *which you claimed to be a fact wasn't a fact was it?*

DAVIES: *No you're getting it all wrong here. The story that we published in July was squarely based on all of the evidence available and was correct in saying that her voicemail had been deleted and it remains the case that NI are not denying that* News of the World *journalists may have been responsible for those deletions.*

PAXMAN: *You say in the copy that the messages were deleted by journalists in the first few days after Milly's disappearance. You don't know that.*

DAVIES: *You're getting the problem slightly wrong, you've misunderstood it. The problem is whether or not they were responsible for deleting the particular messages which caused the friends and family to have false hope. That is now in doubt.*

PAXMAN: *Do you know for a fact what you state as fact in this article?*

DAVIES: *Everybody who was involved in this story accepted that it was true.*

PAXMAN: *You're not answering.*

DAVIES: *You've asked the wrong questions.*

PAXMAN: *Oh, I am so sorry.*

DAVIES: *You've misunderstood the problem.*

PAXMAN: *This is the key question. Was it true?*

DAVIES: *Everybody involved in that story believed it was true. The day after I published that story I sat down for two hours with Glenn Mulcaire, the private investigator at the centre of this thing, and subsequently he issued an apology and he didn't disagree with a single word…*

PAXMAN: *But you state it as a fact, you don't say it was a police belief.*

DAVIES: *Everybody involved in that story accepted that that story was true and continued to accept until four months later evidence that was not available, to everybody's surprise, showed that one element of that story was now in doubt…*

PAXMAN: *You don't report it as a belief you report it as fact.*

DAVIES: *And everyone accepted that it was true, the police accepted it in London and Surrey, the private investigator, News International — nobody disputed a word of that story … Nobody dissented from it. In retrospect it was in doubt.*

It's important to remember that the deletion of Milly Dowler's messages themselves was not the headline of the article by Nick Davies and the *Guardian*'s crime correspondent, Amelia Hill – it was only a subheading. As we have learned from the historical record, the *News of the World* was running many stories on the basis of listening to Milly's messages and severely wasting police time. But leaving aside whether this 'significant error' in the *Guardian* article actually changed the dynamics of the Milly Dowler story and the hacking revelations that ensued, it is valuable as a reminder that journalism is always approximate.

Paxman tried to make an absolute distinction between 'belief' and 'fact', but 'facts' represent provisional accepted truth rather than some unchanging absolute. Especially now, in a twenty-four hour news cycle, the press's place as the so-called 'first draft' of history is more fluid and changeable, more like a set of notes or chapter headings in a Wikipedia stub, destined to be edited, reverted, resourced and rewritten hundreds of times. One of the benefits of online publication is not only that articles can be seamlessly amended and republished but older versions are also stored and can be compared with later revisions. The effect is like a virtual palimpsest of changing interpretations and details. The final article may lose its authority because it is never truly 'finished', but perversely that very uncertainty brings us closer to the 'truth'.

Certainly, the *Guardian* was quick to alert their readership to the changing explanations for the deletion of the voicemails on Milly's phone in Spring 2012. As soon as the police issued a revised statement a full correction was available on the *Guardian* site under the original story, with an explanation of the 'significant' error by Davies himself and follow-up piece by David Leigh. A *Guardian* timeline of the investigation of Surrey Police and their interactions with the *News of the World* was published in January 2012 on the website. After months of further investigation, Operation Weeting published its own timeline. In a written statement to the Leveson Inquiry in May 2012, Detective Chief Inspector John Macdonald concluded that, because of missing technical data so many years after the event, 'reaching a definitive conclusion' as to whether Milly Dowler's voicemail messages were deleted deliberately or automatically 'is not, and may never be possible'.

Who or what caused the deletion of Milly's voicemails and the 'false hope' moment is almost proof of Heisenberg's Uncertainty Principle – that the closer an event is inspected the more nebulous it becomes.

Before we sanctify the *Guardian* or elevate it to a *Pravda*-like status, it's worth reiterating that the relationship between breaking news and truth can be inversely proportional, for getting a story out very often overrules getting a story completely right. My personal experience of every newspaper story I have been either directly or peripherally involved with is that they always get substantial facts wrong. Part of this is just the nature of writing about reality: witnesses misremember, misinformation spreads, clichés stick, manual errors of transcription happen, and that's before a story is changed through the subbing and editing process. This kind of error is endemic to the broadsheets as much as the tabloids; the main difference is that the more reputable papers at least nod towards the kind of dry double-sourced accuracy exemplified by the *New York Times*.

I had my own brief unpleasant experience of this when I appeared on the front page of the *Guardian* in August 2004. Under commission to write a drama series about political lobbying for Initial Productions and BBC Drama in 2003, I had met dozens of lobbyists, parliamentarians and journalists to research the issue. Amazingly, the then famed (and soon to be notorious) Ian Greer of Ian Greer Associates invited me to shadow his team at the Tory Party conference. Already I was getting hints of the 'cash-for-questions' scandal that would erupt the following year, not least from the *Guardian* parliamentary correspondent David Hencke (as he relates in his evidence to the parliamentary select committee). I could see the potential corruptions of the system – and was mortified by the fact that Greer was lobbying for the Bosnian Serbs just while they were raining down sniper fire, tank and mortar shells on the besieged city of Sarajevo. These insights formed the narrative backbone of the planned series *Conflict of Interest*, which centred on the story of Jeremy Church (a stand-in for Greer) and a senior minister called Tavistock (a fictional version of the soon-to-be disgraced Neil Hamilton). I wrote the first episode and delivered it in spring 1994.

After initial enthusiasm from the BBC's head of drama series, Michael Wearing, I received a letter from his assistant with bad news: they couldn't proceed with the show in the 'current political climate'. Now there are a million reasons for saying 'no' to a drama commission and a million often unrelated ways of letting a writer down. Deflated, but used to the vagaries of the freelance writer's life, I thought no more of it and moved onto other projects.

In August 1994 I heard the surprising news that Michael Wearing was resigning from the BBC. Wearing had been a hero of mine since I first met him as a judge at a National Student Drama Festival a decade earlier, where he spoke about making the iconic *Boys from the Blackstuff* – the classic Alan Bleasdale series about Liverpool under Thatcherism – which was one of the main reasons I wanted to write TV drama in the first place. I called Hencke both to complain about Wearing's leaving the BBC and to update him about the progress of *Conflict of Interest*. I explained that I'd been told, in writing, that the show would be hard to place 'in the current political climate' but refused to pass on the letter lest it cause the assistant some problems. Hencke asked if he could at least quote me about Wearing's importance and history; carried away by my own vanity, I went ahead.

The next day was one of the more hectic days of my life. I was off early in the morning to do a drama recce in Wales, but was stopped short when a copy of the *Guardian* came through the front door. My heart thudded, partly in excitement, partly in fear. I had guessed this would be a small piece in the media pages. Instead, it was front page news! Hencke, still digging away at Greer and the lobbying story, had turned a correlation into causation and seemed to be implying that Wearing had resigned because political pressure had cancelled my project.

By the time I returned from my trip to Wales, there were dozens of messages flashing on my answerphone (I had no mobile in those days). They started with congratulations from my agent for getting the front page and a request from the *Guardian* supplement for a full-fledged article. But as the messages went on, they became more disconcerting. A producer I knew said Wearing hadn't fully resigned and was in negotiations for more money. By the end of the messages my agent was telling me NOT to speak to any press. She had been leant on by senior BBC management who reminded her I was still bound by the confidentiality clauses of my development deal. By the end of that night I was hearing rumours from senior lobbyists that I would 'never work at the BBC again'.

Whatever my personal career angst – much of it self-inflicted – Hencke had more than a legitimate public interest reason in pursuing Greer and Hamilton and the lobbying question scandal, even if it meant railroading an unknown dramatist in the meantime. Even back then I completely understood this and by 1995, with the cash-for-questions scandal broken nationwide, with resignations and the arrests of senior Tory ministers, the sacrifice seemed worth making. The whole affair became a touchstone for how complacent, out of touch and corrupt the Conservative Party was after sixteen years in power.

That was the big story and while there were many factual inaccuracies in the investigative process – and no doubt other personal collateral damage – the public interest of the bigger picture, a tale of politicians on the take and influence bought and sold, justified the means. There may be no absolute truth in news, but that doesn't mean accuracy and veracity isn't an aspiration. You may not arrive at a complete account of events, but you'll get things completely wrong if you don't try to.

Contrast the cash-for-questions investigation with the kind of coverage provided by the *News of the World* during Milly Dowler's disappearance, or many tabloid papers through the eighties and nineties, and you'll see the debasement of the investigative process into one of front page splashes, personal invective or emotive manipulation. As Kelvin MacKenzie said at the Leveson Inquiry: 'There's no absolute truth' – which explains a lot about the *Sun* under his editorship. However, in his testimony to the Royal Courts of Justice, MacKenzie was merely echoing the words of his former boss, Rupert Murdoch, who said after the fiasco of the hoax Hitler diaries: 'After all, we are in the entertainment business.'

Twenty years later, the tabloids appeared to have eschewed absolute objectivity, even as an aspiration, and fallen into an absolute relativism. How a family's grief over their missing daughter could become the stuff of 'entertainment' is the subject of the next chapter, but forgetting the near obscene outcome, depraved motives, or illegal means of the *News of The World*'s hacking, the inescapable fact is that journalists will always intrude and that the reality for any individual involved in a big story will nearly always be a form of misrepresentation and intrusion – at least on a personal emotional level.

There has always been, and always will be, an element of callousness in journalistic investigation. To paraphrase one the first great British press barons, Lord Northcliffe, news is public information which usually someone wants to keep private. Depending on the story, this may involve deceiving witnesses or targets, or indeed threatening them with non-accuracy if they don't disclose. Such were the tactics of Woodward and Bernstein, and any legitimate journalist covering a big important story will tell you this. Most journalists protect their sources for reasons of trust, loyalty and continued information, but ultimately you're just a piece in a jigsaw – a 'source' – and if you're more than that, then the journalism is compromised. The individual has to be subordinate to politics in this instance. In the words of Peter Mandelson, 'You can be friendly with journalists, but journalists are never your friends.' If a story is in the public interest then the private relationship is always secondary.

The clear difference between the *News of the World* and the investigative discoveries of the *Washington Post* in the seventies, the *Guardian* in the nineties, or indeed the *Daily Telegraph* when it revealed the scandal of MPs' expenses, is precisely this justification of a wider public interest: the bigger political picture is the exposure of unseen corruption and – eventually – an assurance of more accuracy and transparency in public life.

Just looking at the three different versions of the *News of the World*'s coverage of Milly Dowler on 14 April 2002, you can see very little public interest in terms of informing the public, or indeed helping the police. Instead there are several degrees of obfuscation and obstruction. Not only did *News of the World* journalists (ineptly) try to conceal the hacking of Milly's phone, they consistently lied to witnesses about their identities. Having got the initial story of a runaway wrong, they first blamed the recruitment agency and then whoever called the recruitment agency as a 'sick hoax'. This is not ground-breaking journalism. This is clumsy and bullying covering of tracks.

The same habits of intrusion, deception and bullying counter accusation would characterise the attitude of many News International journalists for the next decade. Right up to the Leveson Inquiry in 2012, *News of the World*'s former senior reporter Neville Thurlbeck suggested – until refuted by a Surrey Constabulary investigation – that the Surrey police had given his paper access to the Dowler messages.

Two senior officers in charge of the original missing person probe at the time – one of whom is now the deputy chief constable of Surrey Police – were placed under investigation by the Independent Police Complaints Commission (IPCC) in June 2012 for allegedly failing to explore the *News of the World*'s blatant phone hacking.

In this instance of phone hacking the contrast with Watergate journalism couldn't be clearer. During Watergate the Nixon administration blocked Woodward and Bernstein wherever they went. Faced with a wall of silence from those in power, the two American journalists had to occasionally dissemble and divert to secure a bigger story in the public interest. But behind the walls of fortress

Wapping, the *News of the World* journalists pulled rank and power, dissembling and diverting in order to conceal the bigger story *from* the public interest.

TROLLING AND TRUTH

In his last book, published in 2002, the moral philosopher Bernard Williams made an important distinction between truth and truthfulness, pointing out that those postmodernist thinkers who dismiss the concept of objective reality because it is distorted by power, class bias and ideology, can end up serving those very distortions.

Though more an ideologue than a postmodernist philosopher, editor Kelvin MacKenzie seems to prove Williams' point when he casually dismissed the idea of 'absolute truth'. Without a pursuit of the idea of truth, no matter how unobtainable, there's no aspiration towards accuracy, no ability to accept you've got it wrong and to try again. Truthfulness is the basis of empirical open-minded enquiry; the capacity to assert a premise, test it and to come up with something better if it fails. Without some kind of standard of truthfulness, loose comments are as good as hard facts, reportage is no better than an op-ed; without some standard of truthfulness opinion itself declines into sophistry, sophistry into captious rhetoric and ultimately into the personal insults which are the default mode of shock-jocks and tabloid *Sun*speak.

Ultimately, the internet term trolling, coined first on Usenet forums, is the best term for this kind of provocative discourse, which seeks to inflame rather than illuminate. Trolling is not a form of communication but of communication interference. It's a way of winning an argument by either ignoring it, changing the subject, wasting time or trying to discredit your opponent with ad personam smears or making an interlocutor lose their temper. All these rhetorical tricks, though replete with logical fallacies, were brilliantly outlined by Arthur Schopenhauer in *The Art of Controversy* in the early nineteenth century. British tabloids and American shock-jocks deployed the same tactics on a mass audience.

This kind of political 'trolling' is deeply embedded in much of print and broadcast journalism as was revealed by the *Sun*'s senior editorial team, when several of their colleagues were arrested by police in 2012 under suspicion of bribing police officers. Two female tabloid journalists challenged the Murdoch biographer Michael Wolff and the campaigning MP Tom Watson on Twitter. After a to-and-fro of allegation and counter-allegation, the tabloid journalists finished their argument with an unanswerable rebuttal. Both called their interlocutors 'fat'.

As for the revelation of the hacking of Milly Dowler's voicemail, apologists for News International were still trying to discredit Davies and Hill's story in February 2012, even though it had just be nominated as 'Scoop of the Year' in the Press Guild Awards. James Delingpole from *The Times* conveniently forgot about the public revulsion when he claimed that the *News of the World* was a victim of 'a vindictive campaign by the *Guardian* and the BBC' (The Big Questions, 2012). Just before that the columnist Toby Young, freshly recruited to write a column for Murdoch's newly launched *Sun on Sunday*, tweeted to the comedian Graham Linehan: 'That murdered girl thing? Check the *Guardian* story. Turned out to be balls. Get off your high horse.' Young went on to tweet: 'The story that the News of the World hacked Milly Dowler's phone turned out to be wrong' – from a position of no absolute truth to absolute error in two tweets.

In Chapter 5 I look more closely at *Sun*speak, a modern commercial equivalent of Orwell's Newspeak, but in my view some of its precepts can be laid bare. The 'get off your high horse' attack is the default position. Everyone's bad. Those who think they're better are snobs, elitists, hypocrites. Meanwhile, don't get ideas above your station. If you claim the moral high ground, we'll drag you down in the gutter with us. Nick Davies and Amelia Hill's entire *Guardian* scoop can therefore be called 'shoddy journalism' because of one possible corrigible error. A story that doesn't get everything right is no different from a story that gets everything wrong. It's pure moral relativism and, as Toby Young goes on to demonstrate, this kind of postmodern anti-journalism ends up in the promotion of an absolute lie.

Over the years, working hand-in-hand with the canard that 'if the people buy a newspaper it can't be wrong', this tabloid cynicism about accuracy has infected our political culture. *Sun*speak has transformed the legitimate and healthy scepticism of our journalists into something unhealthy, closed and immune to rebuttal and proof. If everyone is bad, and nothing changes under the sun, why try to change anything? Why engage in politics or hope or any kind of inquiry? The lying bastards are always lying to us: that's all you know and all you need to know. But selectively holding institutions and politicians hostage is not the same as holding them to account.

Yet there's good news here. For all the loud remonstrations about the *Guardian*'s purported 'error' about the Dowlers' 'false hope', and Murdoch's claim that the misreporting of this forced him to close the *News of the World* when otherwise he would not have, the bad press could not be undone.

Public opinion – more like an oil tanker than an expensive delicate ship in this instance – had sailed and nothing would turn it round.

2

6 July 2011
The Death of Privacy

The Tuesday 5 July 2011 Milly Dowler story will always be seen as the catalyst in the Hackgate scandal, the moment when a story of corrupt newspaper practices broke to a wider audience. Had the 'false hope' subheading not been added to the *Guardian's* front page, the outcome would have been the same. As the 6 July headlines show, even the tabloids couldn't ignore the story.

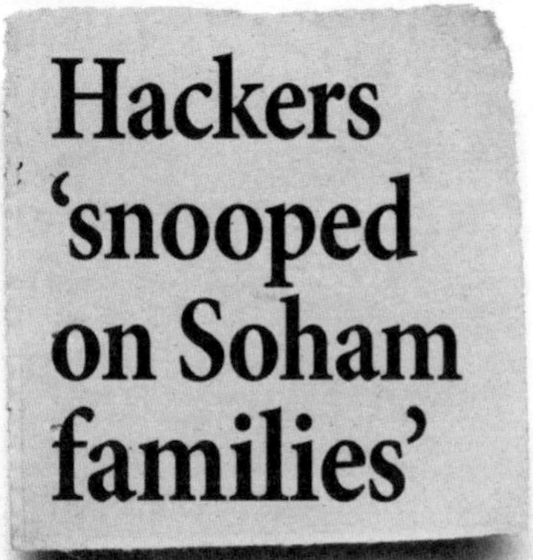
Hackers 'snooped on Soham families'

Figure 2.1 Daily Telegraph, *6 July 2011*

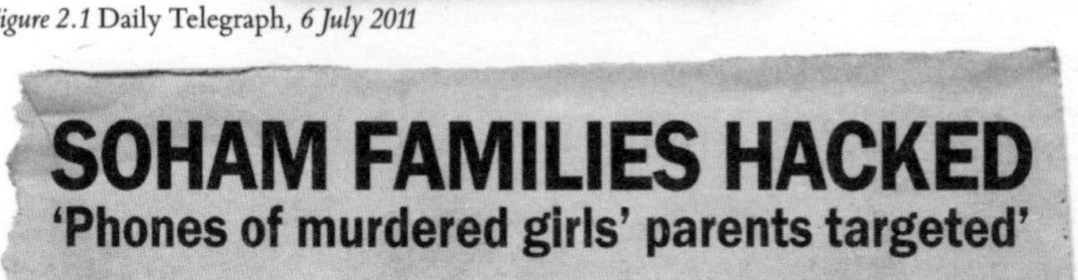
SOHAM FAMILIES HACKED
'Phones of murdered girls' parents targeted'

Figure 2.2 Daily Mirror, *6 July 2011*

NEW OUTRAGE AS SOHAM PARENTS ARE DRAGGED INTO THE HACKING SCANDAL

Figure 2.3 Daily Express, *6 July 2011*

Holly, Jessica, Maddie, Sarah, Milly... were they all targets of hackers?

Figure 2.4 Metro, *6 July 2011*

News of the World hackers 'targeted the parents of Holly and Jessica'

Holly & Jessica linked to hacking scandal

Figure 2.5 Daily Mail, *6 July 2011*   *Figure 2.6* Daily Star, *6 July 2011*

By Wednesday new phone-hacking victims as emotive as Milly Dowler were revealed. The photo of two ten-year-old girls in red Manchester United football tops – a striking image repeated on most tabloid front pages – was of Jessica Chapman and Holly Wells, who were murdered by their school caretaker in 2002 in Soham, Cambridgeshire. Their families were alleged to be potential phone-hacking victims on Mulcaire's list. Also mentioned are two other recent British child crime cases: eight-year-old Sarah Payne, murdered in 2000, and Madeleine McCann, who was abducted from a holiday apartment in Portugal just before her fourth birthday in 2007. The suggestion that their relatives' phones had been hacked and their messages listened to by *News of the World* journalists would have served as a tipping point even without the Dowler revelations. If anything, these were even more high-profile stories.

For the previous decade these extremely rare cases of child murder or abduction have dominated tabloid coverage. It's easy to see why: all the victims were telegenic, vulnerable, very young and white. A mix of innocence, sex and murder provides a perfect trifecta for the modern tabloid because it sells a simplified version of moral absolutes while permitting vicarious rubbernecking. But that's not where the discomfort lies.

There is public interest in the press making a splash about missing children because the publicity can help the police track them down. But over the years the tabloids have carried on pursuing these stories long after many of the victims are buried and the perpetrators apprehended and imprisoned. Lacking hue and cry, most of the subsequent coverage then concentrates on those peripheral to the crime, particularly the bereaved families who become – through infamy rather than fame – celebrity victims. This tabloid obsession with child murder, especially as it begun to lead the coverage of mainstream broadcasters like BBC and Sky News, felt uncomfortable at the time, an intrusion into private grief which overstepped a moral boundary. We now know that it overstepped several legal boundaries as well.

Figure 2.7 News of the World, *Sarah's Law campaign*

All the tabloids, but the *News of the World* in particular, found ways to keep the photos of the victims on their front pages. For many years any headline including the words Soham, Sarah Payne or Madeleine McCann usually resulted in increased circulation. Rebekah Brooks personally led a campaign to name and shame sex offenders which she called 'Sarah's Law' (much like Megan's Law in the US) after Sarah Payne. At various launches and press events, the editor of the *News of the World* stood side by side with the dead girl's mother, Sara Payne. Brooks became her friend and provided her with a mobile phone. It was later revealed that her phone number was also on Glenn Mulcaire's list.

The tabloid fascination with child murder has killed privacy by invading the privacy of death. But what did the *Sun*, Britain's biggest selling tabloid have to say about these shock-horror revelations about its sister paper to the *News of the World*? The *Sun* led with a headline about some spurious IVF lottery to win a baby and a photo of Victoria Beckham heavily pregnant in a red dress, with the leaden pun 'Victoria Becktum'.

Again, News International was mute when it came to news about itself.

CEREAL KILLERS

For over a century stories of murder and perversity have been a staple of the yellow press, something to ponder over breakfast, or to pass the time while commuting to work. One can just reel off names – Jack the Ripper, Dr Crippen, John Christie, the Lindbergh baby, Jeffrey Dahmer, the Yorkshire Ripper, Fred and Rosemary West, O.J. Simpson – to see that murder not only sells papers, it's a cultural event. Sex and death are of course compelling biological processes, but they're also deeply subjective experiences. We keep on gazing at them from the outside to grasp their meaning, only to find ourselves more baffled and alienated than before. More repellent than pornography, the depiction of death and mortality is oddly more acceptable. Violence on TV never causes the same outrage as nudity or sexuality and the privacy of mortality is constantly violated by the popular press, whether it's a photo of TV presenter Russell Harty dying of hepatitis, a demented Frank Sinatra being wheeled around his garden, Elvis Presley in his casket or the bath Whitney Houston died in.

Child murder is a particularly powerful sub-category of this fatal genre, for there our prurience over sex and death can be disguised with clear-cut moral righteousness and cultural commentary. The Moors Murderers Ian Brady and Myra Hindley provided the media with a long-running drama series that lasted from the early sixties until 2002 when Hindley died. The murder of two-year-old James Bulger in Bootle, Merseyside in 1993 by two other children prompted another such wave of emotional catharsis and self-reflection. (Later it emerged that James's mother, Denise Fergus, was also a victim of phone hacking.) Protagonists in these bloody scenarios take on an almost legendary quality; they openly act as didactic or symbolic figures that allow us to discuss the state of the nation, the problems of family life, drugs, sexuality or social breakdown.

In such cases, then, the Murdochian tabloid defence that they're 'only giving the people what they want' has some justification. But the irony is that just as the coverage is become more graphic and obsessive, child murder has actually becoming vanishingly scarce, with a child's chance of being killed by a stranger around a million to one. Indeed, the UK has seen a large fall in interpersonal violence over the last 150 years, with the exception of a modest blip in the sixties, which declined again in the mid-nineties. Paradoxically, we're presented with more media representations of violence just as it is declining in our personal lives (Pinker, 2011).

Perhaps the shortage of victims explains the change in tabloid coverage of crime since the time of the press barons Rothermere and Beaverbrook in the UK, Hearst and Pulitzer in the US. Macabre details still abound, but the narrative now focuses more on the psychological rather than bodily trauma. The voyeurism has less to do with physical damage than with the subjective apprehension of the mental states of victims and aggressors. Like amateur forensic psychiatrists we hone in on the inner life of violence, the prior psychological compulsions that will drive this potential killer to meet that potential target. Some of this could be construed as precautionary; humans spend most of their time thinking about other humans and our ability to conjure a 'theory of mind' about psychopaths and predict their actions could have a great evolutionary advantage – especially if you happen to meet a serial killer. But the ludicrousness of the proposition only shows how out of kilter these obsessions have become with the realities of everyday life. The morbid obsession with serial killing and sex crime actually diverts our understanding of the strangeness of others rather than enhancing it.

This trend towards forensic psychology in press crime coverage has been inspired by other kinds of writing: crime fiction such as Thomas Harris's *The Silence of the Lambs* or even great non-fiction writing such as Truman Capote's *In Cold Blood*. But Murdoch played an important part by turning it into a newspaper norm.

Around the time Murdoch took over the *New York Post*, David Berkowitz ('Son of Sam') went on his fourth shooting spree, injuring two girls walking in the streets of New York. As more shootings and killings took place in the first half of 1977, the unfolding story developed into the 'Summer of Sam'. Murdoch's publication won the newspaper circulation war through hysteriaand fear of crime. According to his managing editor at the time, who had thought this was an aberration 'Rupert wrote headlines. Rupert shaped stories. Rupert dictated the leads in stories. Rupert was everywhere for two or three weeks' ('Who's Afraid of Rupert Murdoch?', 1981). But this was no aberration. It was the beginning of a worrying new trend.

The publicity around Berkowitz did not just mirror events – in another form of journalistic form of the Heisenberg principle – it influenced the serial killer's behaviour. Like Jack the Ripper before him, and Peter Sutcliffe afterward, Berkowitz ended up sending letters to the press. For the first time the newspaper coverage of murder helped to create a new social phenomenon – the 'killer as celebrity'. In the UK, thirty years on, the next phase of innovation took place – the 'celebrity victim'.

Why this degree of privacy intrusion happened so extensively in Britain first is down to many factors, the most obvious being the intense competitiveness of its newspaper market. Thanks to its early industrialisation and rapid railroad construction, England had a large but geographically compact readership in which a newspaper printed overnight could be delivered to most doors by the morning. Though the number of titles has declined, the national newspaper market still is uniquely crowded and cut-throat. News International's growing domination of this market is partly down to Murdoch's effective form of political lobbying, but one can't deny him his adept instinct for populistic appeal. From Page Three topless girls to angry resentment about immigrants and intellectuals, Murdoch has pitched his ear to the lowest common denominator in British life. And the key innovation of the turn of the twenty-first century was an increasing emphasis on the celebrity columns of the *Sun* and the *News of the World*. It's there where the new cult of the 'celebrity victim' was born and where the pursuit of stories about them pushed the moral boundaries of journalism to the edge of obscenity.

BIZARRE

It's no accident that the pre-eminent editors of the Hackgate era, Piers Morgan, Andy Coulson and Dominic Mohan came through the *Sun*'s column devoted to show business celebrities: Bizarre. As readership began to flag at the beginning of the new millennium, time-consuming investigative journalism was cut down and a cheap, popular intensive replacement was needed. Celebrity journalism filled the gap.

Celebrity columns like Bizarre are easy to write because – for the most part – material is provided by publicists who need to launch a new book, film, recording or career and their clients are soft targets for self-disclosure. Sometimes the shine of celebrity begins to reflect back on the columnist, interviewer or editor who, as in the case of Morgan, arrogate some of the celebrity to themselves. Many show business writers flout their personal friendships with their supposed sources, glowing in the borrowed light (Mohan signed off his last Bizarre column with the boast 'Getting hammered with ROD, partying with MADONNA, tea at ELTON'S house – it's been the greatest five years of my life.')

Apart from the puff and fluff of positive PR, show business gossip is also heavily dependent on the negative story, the inevitable bad news which celebrities want to suppress. Given the realities of stardom, the availability of partners and the temptations of excess, there's a constant stream of informants coming forward with kiss-and-tell stories of drug abuse, sexual indiscretion and domestic strife. Add to that a lucrative cash hand-out (hundreds of thousands of pounds for a particularly salacious story) and this kind of journalism is as challenging as catching flies with honey. Here's a handy 'cut and keep' guide for *News of the World* readers from 24 October 2004, to use their mobile phone cameras to earn a 'wedge of wonga':

> *We pay big money for sizzling shots of showbiz love-cheats doing what they shouldn't ought to. A-listers looking the worse for wear or Premiership idols on the lash the night before a crucial game.*
>
> *Recently we've brought you fantastic pictures of Robbie Williams' latest girlfriend … We've also had pictures of Charlotte Church and — on the razzle.*
>
> *Just have your camera phone handy when you're out on the town and watch for the big names. Then simply point and shoot and get in touch with us.*

You could call this a form of citizen journalism – or a recruitment drive for secret informers. This kind of untrammelled, unregulated 'market in news' leads to an invitation to everyone in the country to shop their fellow citizens for cash.

Though the daily British tabloids and US weekly 'tabs' are the market leaders on the sleaze end of celebrity, it's hardly a uniquely Anglo-Saxon phenomenon. Go to any country in Europe – Poland for example – and the magazine racks are identical: an array of gossip, fashion, sex, cooking and lifestyle tips from the rich and famous, whose airbrushed faces look interchangeable with any other set of celebrities, even though you don't know who they are. The iconographics of modern fame are almost universal. The paparazzi (the name is a bit of giveaway) became a byword for celebrity-chasing photographers in the

Rome of Federico Fellini's *La Dolce Vita* in the early sixties. *Paris Match* still excels with the long lens and 'pap' shot and of course it was in the French capital that Princess Diana was pursued to her death by an international pack of press photographers on motorcycles.

The death of Diana typifies the tension within celebrity journalism. Though it looks like a symbiosis between the famous and the media, the relationship is often more parasitic – and the parasitism goes both ways. Princess Diana would use the press to selectively leak stories when it suited her and then avoid them when it did not; this competing co-dependency creates an uneasy equilibrium.

Both sides of the PR equation need each other but fight to control the agenda. Even in the most benign interviews around the launch of a book or film, perfume or fashion range, this tension is audible. The interviewer complains the star is late, brusque or uncommunicative or that the celebrity is too open and disingenuous, or lying. The star in question is uneasy; they know they could be set-up at any moment, but also are contractually obliged to get publicity for their new venture or re-launch. The interviewee begins to open up – but then looks embarrassed, self-justifying and retracts any authentic claims. Such interviews, especially in the upmarket papers, usually end on the same dying fall discord: the journalist trying to come to some conclusion about the genuineness of their subject; the subject trying to second-guess public reception and to avoid judgement before slipping away.

In the popular press, this oscillation between forced intrusion and self-disclosure becomes much more extreme and even violent. It leads to young women being chased down the street by half a dozen burley men – a pursuit which would be a crime, except if the young woman is the film actress Sienna Miller and the men in pursuit photographers. It leads to the disturbing spectacle of a young woman having her emotional breakdown caused by the media, filmed by the media (for example, Britney Spears). The chthonic forces unleashed by this contradiction can ultimately result in the tragedy of Princess Diana who – like her Greek namesake's admirer, Actaeon – was pursued and torn apart by her own hounds. There is a mythic undercurrent to so much of our celebrity worship that it begins to enter a religious dimension.

CELEBRITY CULTURE

For millennia our storytelling has revolved around magical and legendary figures. Christianity created a system of iconography, transforming local pagan deities into official saints, constructing complex allegories connecting contemporary events to biblical stories. Yet even in early Christian art the temptations of 'shock-horror' are evident and depictions of divinity verged on the kind of voyeurism we see in the modern press. The image of the Crucifixion, for example, starting from the heroic upright Christus-figure of the Byzantine and Roman-esque eras, was transformed in the late Middle Ages to the suffering pietà, the son of Mary, covered with wounds, slumped on the Cross. As the monastic idea of 'imitating' Christ became the dominant approach, the physical suffering of his body became more and more the object of attention. By the late Gothic period, especially in Northern Germany, statues and paintings of the Passion went from affective sympathy to something much more intrusive and obscene, nearly pornographic, with green rotting flesh, copious blood and gaping wounds.

When the power of the Church declined, non-religious political figures provided an alternative iconography, and here the precedents for the Princess Diana myth were laid. Monarchs were deliberately offered up as venerable symbols: Elizabeth I memorialised as the Virgin Queen or Gloriana, borrowing lustre from the banned Marian cult of the Virgin Mary, a clever game of populist statecraft around her marriageability and sexual availability which prefigures Diana. (Oddly enough, monarchy is one of the few instances in which the sex life of a public figure is of real political interest, because 'who bonks who' has direct effect on the succession, as dynastic election takes place *in utero*.) Even supposedly egalitarian republics aren't immune from this kind of hero-worship. It was Stalin who denounced the cult of personality of Lenin, at the same time he was turning leader-worship into a Soviet state religion.

Over the last hundred years, stars – film stars, TV stars, pop stars, sports stars – have occupied the niches vacated by the gods. The dream factories of Hollywood were the first to industrialise fame and spawned a secondary industry of newspaper, magazine, radio and, eventually, TV celebrity coverage. As Hollywood went into decline in the sixties, the star system found new sectors to colonise. Television comedians and soap stars took some of the shine, but the pop industry was the big benefactor, creating a stream of poster children from Elvis through the Beatles to Madonna and Michael Jackson. Sports too became a space for exploitation, but the most striking thing about the late twentieth century is the amalgamation of all these various branches of culture into one huge myth-making PR sphere. As the mass media converged, different facets of stardom co-operated to advantage, with sports stars appearing in films and pop stars marketing fashion – endless forms of celebrity endorsements combined with ghost-written autobiographies, tie-ins with book deals, TV shows and newspaper serialisations. Sometimes these brand liaisons are so total they appear personal and romantic; Victoria and David Beckham being a prime example of a cultural convergence of sport, fashion and pop.

Often called 'show business for ugly people' politics couldn't escape the appetite for celebrity. The campaign of Senator Kennedy to become President of the United States deployed all the marketing and advertising skills of Madison Avenue, and during his presidency his family life with Jacqueline and their children was regularly used to create an emotional identification with the public. Even more helpfully, President Reagan was a well-known Hollywood actor before he entered politics; subsequent presidential hopefuls are now obliged to borrow some of the reflected light of stardom by playing saxophone on a chat show or shooting basketball rims as part of their political campaign.

For all the glamour of the star system, we shouldn't forget that there's a hard-nosed business principle working behind the scenes. As an indication of the permeation of publicity into information, Britain now has more PR people (47,800) than journalists (45,000) and Nick Davies' intensive statistical study of the content of broadsheet papers concludes that the majority of press stories are now recycled material from the publicity machine:

> *60% of these quality-print stories consisted wholly or mainly of wire copy and/or PR material, and a further 20% contained clear elements of wire copy and/or PR to which more or less other material had been added ... The highest quota proved to be in* The Times, *where 69% of news stories were wholly or mainly wire copy and/or PR ... And these are conservative figures. They left out the tabloids...*

(DAVIES, 2008)

By 2012, the number of PR press handlers was reported to have doubled to nearly 100,000 while jobs in journalism were in decline.

Scholarly essays are written about the semiotics of Greta Garbo, the meaning of Marilyn Monroe and the feminism of Audrey Hepburn, but these often overlook the impersonal ways identities have been mass manufactured, marketed, accessed and accessorised. In Hollywood the real people behind the icons – whether it be Judy Garland or Rock Hudson – had little in common with their media representations. Recognising the impersonality of their images, many famous figures became reclusive, going off the grid, to avoid further exposure. Others were driven to addiction or indeed psychosis by the strangely isolating wilderness of mirrors that media attention entails (now apparently a personality disorder diagnosed as Acquired Situational Narcissism).

Nevertheless, the downsides of fame had their upsides for the industry. A parallel shadow celebrity system grew up alongside the official one, dedicated to iconoclasm rather than iconography. It started small with Hollywood scandal magazines like *Confidential* (the model for the fictionalised *Hush-Hush* magazine in James Ellroy's *L.A. Confidential*) but then burgeoned out into publishing (Kitty Kelley being an expert in this form) and now has become the crucial dynamic in of press coverage of film, TV, sports and politics.

The *Sun*'s Bizarre column, the alma mater for Morgan, Coulson and Mohan, is the direct descendant of these trends. The celebrity gossip of the column can range, in a couple of days on the same target, from the fatuous, through the congratulatory, to the libellous. It's often said that the press and media build up celebrities only to knock them down, but the symbiosis/parasitism divide is dynamic and dialectical. A good rehab scandal can re-launch the career of a fading actor and a pop star swearing on TV is about as damaging as throwing a television set out of their hotel window. For one of the most famous *Sun* headlines, 'Freddie Starr Ate My Hamster', the PR specialist Max Clifford stated that, though the story was untrue and Freddie Starr wanted his manager to stop it running, Clifford approved it becoming the front page of Britain's best-selling daily because no matter how bizarre or mendacious the headline, it would be good for his client's career.

No publicity, the cliché goes, is bad publicity. Indeed, one of the reasons that Andy Coulson was hired as David Cameron's chief communications adviser was because he had managed to turn some potentially damaging revelations about the Shadow Chancellor George Osborne into the spun gold of PR (more of this in Chapter 4). However, the PR machine has one severe limitation. For most of the last century the public figures it relied on were well-known for some other exiguous reason, a visible skill such as being the first to cross the Atlantic solo, playing baseball or golf superlatively, leading the country, or landing on the moon. The commercial problem is obvious: celebrity coverage is onerously dependent on an outside achievement. The brilliant innovation of the last decade or so has been the creation of a new class of celebrities who have no talent whatsoever and are famous for just being famous.

Many of the self-made celebrities of our era – Paris Hilton, Kim Kardashian, Katie Price (aka Jordan), Jade Goody – made their names by violating their own privacy. A couple of recent innovations aided them. One was the rise of the internet and digital production, which democratises the means of production, distribution and exchange, and has given rise to that impressive cultural achievement of amateur porn. Both Hilton and Kardashian rose to their celebrity status through the popularity of apparently illicit personal sex videos which created a feeling of spontaneity and intimacy which hundreds of wannabes have tried to copy since.

The other – slightly different – factor in the rise of the new celebrity culture was the decline of public service broadcasting in the UK. Britain, once home to the pioneering public service documentaries, became the leading exporters of reality TV shows across the world. This was mainly due to the country's TV documentary sector searching for lucrative new horizons when domestic output withered. Many of the elements of the social observation genre were bowdlerised in reality TV shows like *Big Brother*, *Survivor*, *Wife Swap*: kitchen-sink realism, shaky 'fly on the wall' camera, ad hoc confessionals in the middle of events. But reality TV is anything but spontaneous, documentary or realist. Like the mock-udrama comedy *The Office*, reality TV is a scripted pastiche of the documentary tradition of fly-on-the-wall and *cinéma trouvé* – only undeclared. Regardless of their complete ersatz quality, these reality TV shows became the seed bed for the new celebrity boom of the early twenty-first century.

Fame for fame's sake is the ultimate goal of shows like *The X-Factor* and *Britain's Got Talent*. Though skill or aptitude is supposed to be the benchmark, it is so hedged and manufactured that the products are either standardised to the point of anonymity or actually substandard. The main reason for watching these shows is all to do with the vagaries of publicity and fame, to see how wannabes deal with failure and success and to bet on who everyone else thinks will win. To use old economic terms, the intrinsic *use-value* of any person appearing on these shows (or in the endless magazines and papers that provide supporting cover) is virtually zero. It's their *exchange-value*, like cards of baseball or football players, that counts.

Justin Bieber is hot, because, well he's hot. He's on the front page. He's trending on Twitter. In this way celebrity culture is just another news derivative market – a purely speculative activity, a bet on who will fall and who will rise. And like other forms of gambling, the house always wins. Simon Cowell – whose crucial break into America came thanks to an important introduction to Murdoch – takes his fees and commissions regardless of whether his stars crash and burn. Indeed, as with the elevation and then breakdown then recuperation of the Scottish amateur singer Susan Boyle, there's often as much to be made on the short bet as the long.

FETISHES

It was Karl Marx who, in his first chapter of *Das Kapital*, explored the distinction between and intrinsic use-value of an artefact and its relative exchange-value on the market. In this regard, the rock, film or sports stars of the twentieth century usually had some kind of residual use-value, some talent or skill to attract attention. Compared to them, the celebrities of the early twenty-first century are almost wholly useless. They are celebrated for being celebrities. Their trajectory is entirely geared around their speculative value, the velocity of their fame and its half-life among newspapers and other media. Watching them is like watching the bond markets on a bad day: a fascinating lesson in group hysteria which can turn from ramping success to nose dive.

Many of the practices which led to the hacking scandal derive from insider dealing in this vast clearing house of fame and infamy. Again, the Murdochian response to this trend is easy to anticipate: so what if most of our newspapers are now given over to the celebration of celebrity? The tabloids are just following market demand and giving people what they want. Though there's an element of truth in this, it's also deeply disingenuous for the CEO and chairman of one of the world's largest media companies.

Michael Wolff encapsulates Murdoch's trajectory in a sentence:

> *From 1954 until 1968, he was building a midsize Australian newspaper company; from 1968 until 1980, he was turning himself into an international publishing entrepreneur ... by this time (2003) he had turned News Corp it a vast 'integrated multiplatform content-creation and distribution conglomerate'.*

(WOLFF, 2008, P. 305)

In the light of these vertical supply chains of fame and meaning, it's easy to see why the *Sun*'s Bizarre column becomes the editorial model. News Corp's interests stretch from news to marketing to sports, cinema and book publishing. Murdoch owns a vast catalogue of film titles thanks to his acquisition of Twentieth Century Fox and the same film celebrities appear on his TV programmes and in his gossip columns. Despite Murdoch's schoolboy aversion to sports, he won exclusive rights to the British Premier League in 1991 and snatched the National Football League from CBS in 1993; footballers regularly appear on front page sex exclusives. The upstream and downstream exploitation of rights create many economies of scale; for example, a celebrity chef who can appear on his own TV channel or gossip column, with a book deal and newspaper serialisation, all in the same week.

Such pre-eminence in the fame market leaves it open to extensive commercial exploitation and some abuse. 'Giving the audience what they want' in Murdoch's terms is therefore barely distinguishable from 'getting them to give me what I want'. Though her phone was hacked, the supermodel Elle MacPherson never brought a civil case against *News of the World* – though within a few months she had a dedicated series in another News International title. The then 13-year-old child prodigy singer Charlotte Church was first offered £100,000 to perform Pie Jesu at Murdoch's wedding to Wendi Deng, but Church was told by Matthew

Freud that she would get a 'good press' if she waived the fee. (Even though she did, the *News of the World* would still write over thirty stories based on hacking the voicemail boxes of Church and her direct family.) A cross-platform modal monopoly like News Corp doesn't just respond to the market, it changes market conditions. Like the Heisenberg principle in quantum physics, in which observing a phenomenon affects it, the mass media don't just broadcast to society, they alter what they communicate and who they communicate to.

Once again, News Corp is not alone in this cross-platform exploitation of the fame game, but it did pioneer its creation and today stands as an exemplar of – or perhaps a warning about – the social and economic trends of the last thirty or so years.

One of the key qualities of post-industrial societies is that they become devoted to creating demand, eliciting new desires and dissatisfactions as a solution to the problem of over-production. With higher median wages, rising living standards and relative affluence, the consumer society is defined by a demand not only for consumer items and gadgets, but more immaterial goods: designer or luxury brands, tourism, culture, the arts. More often than not these 'lifestyle choices' are associated with the brand of a famous personality.

You see this in every big marketing campaign; it is hitched and personified in an individual, from the face of L'Oreal to Chanel. Sometimes the connection is legitimate and causal – such as Apple's co-founder and CEO Steve Jobs being the 'face' of the iPhone and iPad – but more often than not it's pure illusion. But the role of celebrities is central. They embody a simple way of navigating through a bewildering number of consumer choices. More vitally, they connect directly to our imaginative inner lives, providing efficient, glamorous, care-free or romantic figures we could aspire to. We copy how they dress, what they eat, where they live, how they party, how they work, who they date and try to see ourselves in the mirror looking like them.

In the heavily mediated modern world the terms of trade have changed drastically since Marx described the 'fetishism' of commodities in the mid-nineteenth century. In a prescient passage, Marx struggled with the 'mystical' quality of consumer goods which took on a bizarre secondary life that he could only explain by analogy to the 'mist-enveloped regions of the religious world':

> *A commodity is therefore a mysterious thing, simply because in it the social character of men's labour appears to them as an objective character stamped upon the product of that labour … There is a definite social relation between men, that assumes, in their eyes, the fantastic form of a relation between things.*

(TUCKER, 1978)

A century and a half later the cult of celebrity reveals another phase of fetishism. From having transformed our social relations into a relationship between things, the media market has turned things on their head again and transformed a relationship between products into an association of personalities. Thus our personal connections, first reified into material possessions, are re-animated in a Frankenstein world of bit parts and loosely assembled personality traits. The world of celebrity is as fantastical and strange as anything remarked in Marx's description – for a dip into the surreal just glance at *OK!*, *Hello!* or *Nuts* magazine. But there's a common principle in all the bewildering epiphenomena; personality has been turned into a fetish: character commodified.

To achieve this magical transformation of commodities into people, people need to be turned into commodities, and this is the direct connection with the industrial hacking of celebrities. As many have remarked, most trenchantly Richard Sennett in his book *The Fall of Public Man*, the main thrust of consumer society has been to privatise public collective space. You can see this process physicalised in the geography of our cities and the exodus to the gated communities and enclaves. But the real colonisation of late twentieth-century life was of our inwardness. It saw the rise of what Sennett calls the 'tyranny of intimacy' in which private relationships became the main focus of our social authenticity and value. Since the personal is now deemed political, we demand of our public figures more intimate disclosures. By one of those paradoxes of the market, as public space is privatised, privacy is publicised.

It's this new Klondike of inner personal space that sets the context for the *News of the World* newsroom during the noughties and their routine intrusions into personal privacy. New media are not exempt from the problem either. Indeed, they rely on a new version of it. Google's commercial model is essentially premised on the personal revelations you make when making an internet search, which is then turned into targeted direct advertising. Facebook – which recently launched a \$100 billion initial public offer on the US stock market – is another adaption of this: a do-it-yourself celebrity mechanism. With our relationship status, educational and work qualifications, pap photos, favourite bands, lifestyle choices all promoted online with constant updates, we've all became adept managers of personal PR. At the same time we reveal, often openly but sometimes without realising, where we travel, our friends, our favourite bands and TV shows. Some apps actually download our entire address books. This forms the invaluable aggregate database for advertisers and credit rating agencies which Facebook hopes will justify the massive investment. Online, despite numerous apologies from Facebook CEO Mark Zuckerberg, we regularly violate our own privacy and give it away for free to a company which then sells it to the highest bidder.

As former *New York Times* editor Bill Keller was told by a tech friend, the only difference between the billionaire media mogul Zuckerberg and the billionaire media mogul Murdoch was this: 'When Rupert invades your privacy it's against the law. When Mark does, it's the future.'

We are soon reaching a point where the celebrity equation will be turned on its head. While we seek information about the stars, it's actually the information revealed about us which is (in aggregate) much more valuable. These days retailers are always trying to predict our next move, using the extraordinary amount of information they amass and process with the most sophisticated analytical software and neuroscientific research to understand our identifications. As the *New York Times* explained in a story about how just one US retailer, Target, creates a guest ID for everyone who enters one of its stores:

> *Also linked to your Guest ID is demographic information like your age, whether you are married and have kids, which part of town you live in, how long it takes you to drive to the store, your estimated salary, whether you've moved recently, what credit cards you carry in your wallet and what Web sites you visit. Target can buy data about your ethnicity, job history, the magazines you read, if you've ever declared bankruptcy or got divorced, the year you bought (or lost) your house, where you went to college, what kinds of topics you talk about online, whether you prefer certain brands of coffee, paper towels, cereal or applesauce, your political leanings, reading habits, charitable giving and the number of cars you own.*

Our routine violation of our privacy online is one of the main subjects of Chapter 10, but our complicity in this should not be overlooked; the emotional urge to exfoliate and disclose intimate secrets is by no means confined to the tabloid press.

WICKERMEN

Many thinkers and writers in the twentieth century had dystopian visions of the death of privacy and the demise of personal secrecy. The best-known of course is *Nineteen Eighty-Four*, Orwell's vision of state controlled news and propaganda is informed by his experience during the wartime BBC. His vision of state intrusion into private life through the audio-visual suasion of 'Big Brother' and the concept of 'thoughtcrime' has been one of the most lasting indictments of the power of totalitarian regimes to politicise personal space and obliterate the individual. Despite Orwell's democratic socialist origins, and the specific warning about Stalinism in his work, *Nineteen Eighty-Four* has become a default reference for the libertarian right for any kind of media regulation or collective provision. Rupert Murdoch cited it in an early MacTaggart lecture in 1989 and again in 1993 at a major speech in London's Mansion House praising the liberating qualities of his own BSkyB. In 2009, in his MacTaggart lecture, James Murdoch had accused the BBC of being an Orwellian organisation, stifling plurality through its free, popular, online news service. The Murdochs' copy of *Nineteen Eighty-Four* must be very dog-eared indeed.

However, there's another futurist vision of the role of mass media which in recent years has been seen by many as more prophetic. Aldous Huxley's *Brave New World* describes a world where individuality has also been eroded – not by state propaganda, but by a mass media of conformist consumerism. Here, the individual is not coerced into accepting the state's ideology with the psychological torture of Room 101. In *Brave New World* thoughtcrime is replaced by thoughtlessness; individuality is corroded by consumption and pleasure. As inhabitants of this particular dystopia we live in a velvet prison created by an immersive virtual reality of the 'feelies' and an all-encompassing media world where we spend our time 'amusing ourselves to death' (Postman, 1985). Of course, both books weren't actually attempts to predict the future, but an imaginative extrapolation of trends – the Americanisation of the thirties or the Sovietisation of the forties. But if there were a contest between the two for the most successful prediction of the future, Huxley's would surely win: these days, if you mention the worlds 'Big Brother' it's more likely to conjure a reality TV format first devised in Holland.

The reality TV show *Big Brother* seems to confirm that an immersive entertainment sphere, though designed to appease rather than oppress us, would still be invasive and debilitating. Unlike the Orwellian world where our privacy is violated through extracted confessions and betrayals, here we offer it up willingly for the metrics of attention. Through Twitter and Facebook and comment sections on major news sites or blogs, we are free to express ourselves, though at what level of honesty, or awareness of the loss of our intellectual property, is an open question. For all the theories that online social networking would lead to a flourishing of dissent, free thought, social action and dialogue, one only has to note (as its editor Paul Dacre boasted to the Leveson Inquiry in February 2012) that the *Daily Mail*'s website, almost exclusively devoted to celebrity revelations, had overtaken the *New York Times* to become the most popular news site in the entire world with 100 million visitors a month, to see that we are just as likely to forsake hard news for the virtual shadow world of PR.

On the other hand, the phone-hacking scandal shows that perhaps Orwell's dark imprecations are still relevant. Like their owner, many of Murdoch's lead writers and columnists use the *Nineteen Eighty-Four* argument that state surveillance is the one and only threat to our individual liberty (a warning they quickly forget when it comes to law and order or the threat of terrorism). Personal secrecy is everywhere and always threatened by the state.

This knee-jerk libertarianism was on display when ten of the *Sun's* senior staff were arrested in February 2012. The daily tabloid's veteran political chief and close confidante of Murdoch, Trevor Kavanagh, explicitly compared the three Hackgate police operations – Weeting, Elveden and Tuleta – to a 'witch-hunt' and warned that this 'huge operation driven by politicians threatens the very foundations of a free Press'. He cited a Reporters without Borders press freedom index that showed Britain had slipped to twenty-eighth place in 2011 without, however, actually studying the report; Britain's ranking didn't slip because of police prosecutions of phone hacking or police bribery, but because the phone-hacking scandal had shown the press to be violating the rights to privacy and, above all, because our 'surreal' libel laws chills free press. Kavanagh – as one of the veterans of the tabloid dailies – inverts the image of a witch-hunt, confusing the persecution of the powerless with the prosecution of the powerful.

Another News International stalwart writing in the *Daily Mail*, Richard Littlejohn, was even more explicit. In a piece called 'Scotland Yard Stasi and this sinister assault on a free Press' he repeats Kavanagh's misinterpretation of the free press data and then goes on to describe the police arrests as 'gestapo tactics' and a 'deranged witch-hunt'. Triple downing on his hyperbole, using Fascism, communism and the inquisition as his benchmarks, Littlejohn goes on to claim: 'The Establishment has declared war on the Press and by extension our very democracy.' This is what I call the 'Wickerman Defence': assemble several straw-men arguments, add lashings of volatile victimhood, insert into a pile of martyrdom and ignite.

The Orwellian expostulations of Kavanagh and Littlejohn were rapidly repeated by other journalists, from Piers Morgan to the crime correspondent at *The Times*, Sean O'Neill, who complained about the chilling effect of the police inquiries on press contact with police and tweeted endlessly about the cost of the police investigations Weeting, Elveden and Tuleta, which after a year had quadrupled its staff to 185 and was anticipated to run at least another three years at an estimated cost of £40 million. (When I tried to argue a counter-case with O'Neill on Twitter he – like Toby Young – blocked me; another free speech triumph.)

Here, the moral relativism of tabloid politics comes back to bite its perpetrators. The same journalists who were quick to complain the police didn't investigate or prosecute other crimes vigorously enough, were complaining about dawn raids and public expense when it came to their own. The inability of so much of the media to cover themselves objectively would continue a long time after the Milly Dowler scandal. Lord Justice Leveson opened his inquiry with the question 'who watches the watchmen?' when it comes to the press, but that suggests the need for oversight and the recursive problem of 'who watches the watchmen who watch the watchmen?' What many journalists have demonstrated during the hacking scandal is a lack of self-reflection and wilful blindness over themselves.

The litany of press intrusion revealed by the Leveson Inquiry shows that it went well beyond the hacking of a dead teenager's phone or indeed pursuing a princess to her death. In a form of surveillance most secret police states would not have dared to contemplate, the *News of the World* hacked the phones of senior ministers such as former deputy prime minister John Prescott and Peter Hain, once responsible for security in Northern Ireland. Senior political aides, police officers, union leaders and military officials were also targets. In a civil case launched in January 2012, Cherie Blair also sought compensation from News International for being a victim of *News of the World* phone hacking, leading to the assumption that her husband – the Prime Minister of the country – could have had his private conversations routinely overheard. All of this, though known to the police, was ignored by them. The surveillance state was weak compared to privatised corporate surveillance.

Beyond the celebrities and the politicians, some of the most upsetting cases of phone hacking involved ordinary people who just happened to be associated with a celebrity. As a close member of my family experienced personally, mere association with someone who is associated with someone famous, could make you a target of phone hacking. The reason for this is that targets don't leave messages on their own phones, so hacking their circle of friends will provide much more information. Even more invidious were the cases of those who found themselves in the media spotlight through some personal tragedy because a relative had been killed, or made the news in some other involuntary way through a relationship with a celebrity, and had their privacy violated by the accident of association.

Regardless of the circumstances, these were people who had phones bugged, their whereabouts 'pinged' through triangulation of the phone signals, personal medical and financial records inspected, their private lives put under surveillance and – in some cases – their homes broken into. Others found their private diaries, letters and emails published without permission; their confidences betrayed and their personal affairs, romantic or professional, exposed in the worst light. Personal trust between lovers, spouses, parents and children were irretrievably damaged when victims, unable to work out the source of these intimate disclosures, inevitably blamed those closest to them. Careers were ruined. Reputations were dragged through the mud. People became paranoid and isolated, unable to believe their former partners, closest friends or immediate siblings. The consequence of massive media intrusion, the feeling of all eyes being upon you, created a feeling of complete isolation which, in several cases, let to attempted suicide.

Littlejohn was right about his metaphor of communist surveillance apparatus, but wrong about the target. If the prevalence of hacking is reminiscent of anything, it recalls the power of intrusion of the Stasi in East Germany or the Polish internal security forces under martial law. People might not have been tortured or murdered in the crude way of Stalin's NKVD in the thirties – the model for Orwell's 'Thought Police' – but the oppression was still there and the apparent immunity of those responsible for it. For the victims it must have been a dystopian nightmare.

Take the case of Charlotte Church who, having sung at Rupert and Wendi's wedding, and while only in her teens, became the object of dozens of sensationalist press stories, sometimes about her sex or social life, or that of her parents'. Church's mother Maria, after being cruelly characterised as a 'Welsh dragon' attempted suicide just before an affair of her husband's was due to be published by the *News of the World* in 2005. News International's attitude to this was revealing; as Church explained to the *Guardian*, the *News of the World* wanted 'Part Two' of the story, complete with pictures of her mother's injured arms. They told Maria: 'If you give us a story, an exclusive about your self-harming, your attempted suicide, your relationship with Charlotte, then we won't print that story and that story will never see the light of day.'

The hounding of her mother was the main reason Charlotte Church was the last of the first tranche of cases to settle in the High Court before an open trial in February 2012. And the intimidation wasn't all extra-legal. A key factor that made Church settle was because her mother's mental state would have become an important element of the case, opening her to cross questioning:

> You just have to look at the court room, look at News International and their 25 lawyers and then look at the individuals with maybe their three lawyers and one barrister and a couple of juniors. You are fighting a massive corporation with endless resources, a phenomenal amount of power and it is just made really difficult ... They were just going to drag my parents through the mud again and I couldn't let that happen.

(O'CARROLL, 2012A)

If there's any doubt about the human cost of such a rampant violation of privacy, just read the witness statements of Kate and Gerry McCann who testified at the Leveson Inquiry in late 2011. Within a year of their three-year-old daughter's disappearance, the couple became the targets of an all-out campaign in the press (especially by the *Daily Express*) who decided that they were responsible for killing their daughter. Under oath Kate McCann described how photographers would jump out of bushes and hit her car to get a frightened reaction: 'journalists said we stored her body in a freezer'. And when *News of the World* published the personal diaries in which Kate wrote to her missing daughter, without her permission and after she had protested, she told the court she felt 'totally violated'.

That ordinary people should become harassed and demonised because of their association with a celebrity, or because of the death or suicide of a close family member, is surely a moral horror worthy of Orwell.

Murdoch's defence in cases like this has been that he is not responsible for what some of his journalists do. Not only does this position fail to meet the rules of governance and principles of corporate accountability, it's also demonstrably untrue, as his oversight of the Australian newspapers whose stories had led to teenage suicides through the sixties and seventies and his active participation in the *New York Post* reporting of the Son of Sam attacks in 1977 shows, Murdoch forged a culture of privacy violation which – when his papers came under the economic pressures of the nineties and noughties – became even more shocking and reprehensible.

In the name of freedom of the press, Murdoch and his defenders on Fleet Street and admirers elsewhere have breached our freedom. They cried 'wolf' so often about state oppression they end up howling themselves. Like lycanthropes, they forgot to look in the mirror.

At the Leveson Inquiry, Paul McMullan, a previous editor at the *News of the World*, and admirable if only for his openness, said: 'Privacy is for paedos.' This lawless sense of entitlement to other people's secrets, in flagrant violation of the law, while not confined to News International, was incomparably prevalent there for, as *Private Eye* editor Ian Hislop explained to Lord Justice Leveson, 'it could get away with whatever it liked because it was embedded in our political culture'. The historic dynamics which enabled one media company to become so entrenched in the British establishment is the subject of the next two chapters.

3

7 July 2011
Grow or Die

Thursday 7 July 2011 saw yet more allegations of hacking, most emotively into the phones of war widows – the partners of service personnel killed in action overseas. This would prompt the British Legion to declare in disgust in an official statement: 'We can't with any conscience campaign alongside the *News of the World* on behalf of armed forces families while it stands accused of preying on these same families in the lowest depths of their misery.'

Meanwhile, the rest of the day's headlines concentrated on the internal fallout from Hackgate – 'Murdoch Empire in Crisis' – or explored the political repercussions of the scandal, particularly as it affected the BSkyB takeover and Number 10's association with Andy Coulson. By now even the *Sun* finally put a (tiny) mention of the story on the front page – Hacking: PM vow – though overshadowed by teenage sexuality and footballers' antics with strippers and models.

Figure 3.1 Sun, *7 July 2011*

To a large extent, the clamour in the morning headlines was being rapidly out-paced and the real dramatic action was unfolding online. Thanks to grass-roots campaigning sites like Avaaz, 38 Degrees and Political Scrapbook, hundreds of thousands were emailing major *News of the World* advertisers, petitioning them through simple internet hyperlinks to boycott the Sunday tabloid. The Twit-ter accounts of the Co-operative, Virgin Media and easyJet were bombarded by tweets. By Wednesday Ford had cancelled its contract, joined by Vauxhall, Mit-subishi, the Co-op, Lloyds TSB, Virgin Holidays and npower. Early on Thursday *News of the World* announced it was pulling all its advertising that week. Realising how toxic the brand had become, James Murdoch made a dramatic announce-ment that afternoon.

FIREFIGHTING

One of the most effective strategies of Murdoch's has been to be ahead of events, especially in a crisis, or negotiating the purchase or sale of an asset or rights deal. He has been adept at reading other people, guessing what they think his next move might be – and then doing completely the opposite. This effrontery is of-ten overrated and has got Murdoch into almost as much trouble as it has landed him the advantage, but at this moment an aggressive move was desperately need-ed. News Corp had been on the back foot for nearly a week, responding to a welter of bad press with unfocused sporadic firefighting.

Today things would change. In what was seen as a calculated move to rescue the £8 billion BSkyB bid on which his succession project depended, James Mur-doch announced the closure of the *News of the World*:

> *The good things the News of the World does, however, have been sullied by behaviour that was wrong. Indeed, if recent allegations are true, it was inhuman and has no place in our company. ... The News of the World is in the business of holding others to account. But it failed when it came to itself.*
>
> (TELEGRAPH, 2011B)

Even if hedged in the McKinsey-esque platitudes, the closing of a 168-year-old newspaper was a high-impact move, designed to instil shock and awe among the wavering journalists of Fleet Street and cauterise a poisoned brand before it in-fected other parts of the corporation. It would not succeed. Even at the time, the strategy of sacking of 200 staff at the *News of the World* but leaving all the senior executives in place would create something of a backlash. There was also justified suspicion that the closed paper would soon be replaced by a *Sun on Sunday* since the domain name had been surreptitiously registered days before (it would take another eight months for the launch).

We now know that, behind the scenes, there was a struggle between corporate reputational management and the more visceral politics of personal loyalty and family protection – an inevitable struggle in such a top down organisation stamped with one man's authority.

According to most reports at the time, Murdoch himself was against closing the paper, but his children (who had never really cared for the tabloid legacy of his empire) persuaded him. As the civil cases had revealed, News International had been engaged in a cover-up, destroying journalists' computers, deleting incriminating emails en masse for the previous three years despite a legal obligation to preserve all evidence of phone hacking. Secrecy is fine for corporations – just not for anyone else.

The email deletion, outlined by News International management in 2009, intensified a year before the Hackgate scandal, after a legal claim by Sienna Miller on 6 September 2010 demanding all relevant legal documents. HCL, the firm contracted to oversee News International's live emails, were told to delete emails nine times from May to July 2010. Again, the Watergate analogy returns to haunt this corporate coverage, only in this case it's not voice tapes with 'expletives deleted' but an email audit trail, unwittingly preserved on outsourced back-up servers.

What was really going on in News Corp at the time can be partially reconstructed thanks to inside sources, some excellent investigative journalism and witness statements lodged in the Leveson Inquiry, particularly Rupert Murdoch's evidence, revealed on the day his son took the stand at the Royal Courts of Justice in late April 2012.

In the overall narrative of this book, and the deep background to the story, the hacking scandal at the *News of the World* – and the corporate dangers it posed – can only really be understood in the context of the Rubicon process, News Corp's £8 billion takeover of BskyB, which was to be the largest media acquisition in British history and simultaneously James Murdoch's bid for succession. This had been planned for at least three years – probably longer – with careful behind the scenes lobbying mainly focused on gaining Conservative Party support, neutralising the opposition of most other media outlets in the country and trying to deflect the growing suspicions of the Labour Party.

The removal of business secretary Vince Cable from oversight of the bid just before Christmas 2010 was a boost for News Corp, especially since his replacement – the culture secretary Jeremy Hunt – was a self-declared 'cheerleader' for Murdoch. However, the media regulator Ofcom (though trimmed by the

coalition during its austerity budget in September 2010) was still insistent on ex-
amining the issues of plurality such that a potential monopoly in broadcasting
and print could involve. As was shown by the entry into evidence at the Leveson
Inquiry of the almost daily communications between James Murdoch's senior
UK lobbyist Frédéric Michel and Adam Smith, Hunt's special advisor, News
Corp came up with 'undertakings in lieu' – in other words, proposals to keep
Sky News separate and independent in order to avoid the Ofcom investigation.
This carefully choreographed move Michel claimed would be 'game over for the
opposition'. An email of 23 January explains how Hunt (or at least his senior ad-
visor) needed to 'build some political cover' but promised 'we would get there in
the end and he shared our objectives'. On the evidence of the emails, News Corp
had both input and advance notice into the quasi-judicial process.

The panic really started hitting the organisation with the formation of Operation Weeting in January 2011. Subsequently, on 5 April 2011, senior *News of
the World* reporter and editor Neville Thurlbeck was arrested, on the grounds that
he was the recipient of the transcribed hacked voicemail revealed through earlier
legal disclosure of parts of Mulcaire's notes – the email that would later become
universally known as the 'for Neville' document. On 12 April another editor,
James Weatherup, was arrested; but this time News International deployed lawyers to remove documents before the police arrived. A similar threat of obstruction was alleged to have happened when the royal reporter Clive Goodman was
arrested for the original hacking case in 2006, with burly photographers physically intimidating officers from Operation Caryatid who wanted to remove paperwork. The police backed down then. This time deputy assistant commissioner
Sue Akers threatened to arrest the obstructing lawyer.

(In the meantime, the lobbyist Frédéric Michel was telling his boss, James
Murdoch, that he had briefed Jeremy Hunt on the 'NoW issues' and that the
hacking allegations would 'not play any part in his decision'.)

A few days later, Rebekah Brooks and James Murdoch hosted a transatlantic
conference call with Rupert Murdoch's long-term legal counsel, Lon Jacobs, and
head of News Corp's education division, Joel Klein, a lawyer and former chancellor of the New York City school system. Jacobs wanted the internal investigation
moved to New York away from the conflicts of interests that seemed to be impeding
the News International subsidiary running things from the London end. But this
move had the danger of taking control of the scandal away from James and making him vulnerable to his rivals for succession in New York.

Things soon came to a head at a top level face-to-face crisis meeting (reconstructed by *Businessweek*) in Murdoch's Mayfair town house in May. The key
players from News Corp arrived early: Murdoch hosted the event and was joined

by Rebekah Brooks, James Murdoch, Chase Carey (News Corp's chief operating officer), Joel Klein and his outside legal adviser and friend Brendan Sullivan Jr, who had risen to fame defending the Iran–Contra defendant, Lieutenant Colonel Oliver North. Over cocktails they discussed the growing scandal and how the internal investigation should be run.

By the time Jacobs and his colleagues Will Lewis and Simon Greenberg arrived for dinner, the decision was fait accompli: the internal inquiry would be run by Brooks in London. The New York option was thrown out. Brooks was still running the investigation (which was in effect an investigation into herself) when she was arrested in July 2011.

His advice ignored, Jacobs resigned from News Corp soon afterwards, ending 15 years as a key member of Murdoch's inner Praetorian Guard. But Murdoch's decision to let Brooks run the hacking investigation, as James continued to pursue his personal Rubicon of the BSkyB bid, would backfire disastrously within weeks. But this is the benefit of hindsight: the biggest media merger in UK history – which would leave broadcasting dominated by the Murdochs just as much as Fleet Street – was within sight.

On 27 June 2011, a mere week away before the Milly Dowler revelations, Brooks (on her own evidence to the Leveson Inquiry) was sent an email from Frédéric Michel reassuring her that the culture minister Jeremy Hunt would green light the BSkyB bid as he believed 'phone hacking has nothing to do with the media plurality issues'. Michel was asking Brooks for information on 'phone-hacking/practices' for Hunt so that he could 'advise him privately in the coming weeks and guide his and No 10's positioning'. Hunt planned to approve the bid by the summer after a brief public consultation. It was pencilled in for 18 July.

Leaving the national politics aside for a moment, these briefly glimpsed meetings provide a scene-setting for News Corp internal politics – a complex combination of personal loyalty, family connection, political lobbying and boardroom manoeuvring – against a rapidly shifting background of public taste, which Murdoch had for years managed to second-guess or manipulate, but which would soon be completely out of his control. Here too, the struggle between corporate interests and personal imperatives plays out. For years the New York HQ had been trying to distance itself from the UK newspaper division which provided only 3 per cent of the company's profits. Murdoch's own instincts were torn between his affection for his British tabloid staples – the *Sun* and *News of the World* – which had provided the cash flow that enabled his expansion across the Atlantic. Added to this was internal tension as an external clash in his personal loyalty towards others, especially to James who was chair of News International at the time, and next in line to take over from his father when he retired.

While one might condemn the obsession with personality, the dynamics of News Corp is inseparable from one man's control and a family name. Ironically, given this media family have thrived on exposing the private lives of others, the Murdochs are highly secretive. Nonetheless it's virtually impossible to talk about the history of News Corp without plunging into the personal history of Murdoch himself. To comprehend the levels of influence and access Murdoch has attained in three Anglophone countries – Australia, Great Britain and the United States – we need to go back to his family background and personal motivations.

LORD SOUTHCLIFFE

If there's one catchphrase that is repeated again and again by Murdoch, his family and many of his employees, it is that they are taking on the 'The Establishment'. The definitive article is the trick – because with his global reach there are many establishments that Murdoch has confronted, joined, repudiated and even created.

Born in Melbourne in March 1931, son of Sir Keith Murdoch, Australia's biggest newspaper proprietor, Murdoch had little need to be a vertical invader. He was already near the top of Australian society, his father having been friendly with one Australian prime minister after another, a visitor to Harry Truman's White House and with strong connections to the cream of British society. Perhaps Murdoch had just enough horizontal contacts with other elites, dynasties and hierarchies to want to challenge them.

That's the paradox of the lateral invaders, the insider/outsiders: they're driven by the dual motors of entitlement and privilege, resentment and exclusion. Though privileged by today's standards, Murdoch was born just outside the biggest establishment ever known: the British Empire. His trajectory over the next 80 years only makes sense if you see it against this exclusive global hierarchy. In 1931 – though challenged for economic dominance by the US and military dominance by Germany – Britain was still, just, the world's biggest empire and Australia, though politically independent under dominion status, was still culturally dominated by a country far away, captured by the manners and *moeurs* of a nineteenth-century imperium.

Keith Murdoch was born in Melbourne to parents who were both children of Presbyterian ministers; his father had broken from the Church of Scotland for its pro-English bias. To this extent a non-conformist anti-establishment strand was genuinely part of the background of the Murdoch history. While the Murdoch family's friends included the then Australian Prime Minister Alfred Deakin, Keith himself would go on to befriend several subsequent prime ministers. However, his parents weren't rich. On matriculating from Camberwell Grammar School

Keith worked at *The Age* newspaper for four years on a miserable wage before he was able to save enough money to attend the London School of Economics. In London, he wasn't happy. Many letters of introduction to important newspaper editors failed to win him any work and treatment of an acute childhood stammer was only moderately successful. While horribly lonely, he gained an appreciation of how the fittest survived that he declared in a letter home would make him a power once he returned home.

Britain during its Edwardian heyday was a cascading hierarchy of snobbery, and it is inevitable Keith would have encountered various elites who would have looked down on him as a colonial parvenu. Keith returned to Australia without finishing his degree. By 1914 he was an assiduous political correspondent for the Sydney *Sun* in Melbourne and World War I afforded him his biggest break. Rather than enlist, he used his writing to further his career. With a grasp of the logistics of the newspaper business, Keith secured the backing of the new Australian prime minister, Andrew Fisher, and the defence minister to check the mail arrangements for the large contingent of Australian and New Zealand, now fighting in the Mediterranean. Though he was supposed to only be inspecting the administrative headquarters in Cairo, thousands of ANZAC troops were now engaged in a bitter and bloody battle against the Turkish in the Dardanelles. Keith used his connections to get in contact with General Sir Ian Hamilton, commander of the Mediterranean expeditionary force, to head over to Gallipoli. He was granted permission, providing he would subject any of his reports to military censorship.

Though he only spent four days in Gallipoli, Keith came across a story too big to censor. The eight-month campaign devised by the naval secretary, Winston Churchill, to open up a second front and dominate the entrance to the Black Sea and occupy Constantinople had gone awry from its inception in April 1915: a lightning strike turned into a quagmire and by August, when Keith arrived, thousands of troops were stuck on the Peninsula suffering heavy casualties under Turkish guns. A botched naval bombardment was followed by an amphibious assault and an unsuccessful assault on well-prepared Turkish defences which left 43,000 British, 15,000 French, 8,700 Australian, 2,700 New Zealand and 1,370 Indian casualties.

The fiasco of the Gallipoli campaign is the origin of ANZAC day in Australia and New Zealand, dedicated to the dead of that and all subsequent conflicts, a day equal to or perhaps greater in significance than Remembrance Day. Gallipoli has become a sacred motif of national wartime sacrifice, as well as of incompetent leadership and the creaking class hierarchies of the British Empire in its sunset days. It has been mythologised in text, song and celluloid – most notably in the

Mel Gibson film, *Gallipoli*, which Rupert Murdoch helped finance. As a proportion of their population, New Zealand had the highest number of casualties per
capita, but Australia wasn't far behind. Gallipoli therefore became, like the Som-
me or Verdun, a metaphor for the wastefulness of ordinary soldiers caught up in
an industrial-scale war, with the added piquancy that these 'lions led by donkeys'
were Australians and New Zealanders sent to their deaths by effete 'poms' from
the English military brass.

By the time Keith arrived in the Dardanelles, the casualties were mounting.
Spending little time at the front, Keith met the *Daily Telegraph* correspondent,
Ellis Ashmead-Bartlett, on the isle of Imbros. Though bound by tight military
censorship Ashmead-Bartlett had written a letter to the British Prime Minister,
Herbert Asquith, exposing some of the failures of command in the campaign.
Keith agreed to smuggle out the letter, but as he proceeded on to London he
was betrayed by military police in France by another journalist and Ashmead-
Bartlett's whistle-blowing account was confiscated.

By the time he arrived in London, Keith had written his own 8,000-word
version of the exposé, with a particular emphasis on the valour of the Australians
and the deficiencies of the British officers and staff, which he sent to the Australian prime minister. Acting more as a 'news broker' than an actual reporter, he
contacted Lord Northcliffe, editor and proprietor of *The Times*, who then introduced him to members of the British cabinet.

Lord Northcliffe (Alfred Harmsworth) was, along with Lord Beaverbrook
and his younger brother Viscount Rothermere, one of the pre-eminent press
barons of the era of commercial papers. At different times Northcliffe owned
The Times, the *Daily Mail* and the *Daily Mirror*, the *Observer*, *The Sunday Times*
and the *Sunday Dispatch*, effectively dominating the British press as it had never
been before. His eye-grabbing headlines, 'DO DOGS COMMIT MURDER?'
and 'WHY JEWS DON'T RIDE BICYCLES', were commercially successful and
from this he assumed some kind of democratic assent: 'A newspaper is to be made
to pay. Let it deal with what interests the mass of people. Let it give the public
what it wants' (Fyfe, 1930). Northcliffe's editorship of the *Mail* in the run up to
World War I was so virulently anti-German that, when hostilities broke out, a
German warship was sent to shell his house on the south coast, killing his gar-
dener. During the war itself, his *Times* was so successful in attacking the government of Prime Minister Asquith that Northcliffe brought it down and he was
instrumental in getting David Lloyd George to replace him.

It was in the world of press power and political machination that Keith's letter
could be used as a political bombshell. With the help of Northcliffe's paper, the
revelations it contained were deployed in a successful press and parliamentary

campaign to get the soldiers out of the Dardanelles, General Hamilton sacked and the general's departure would in turn lead to Winston Churchill leaving the cabinet. The troops were stealthily evacuated with almost no further casualties and back home Keith was anointed the 'Hero of Gallipoli'.

Seventy-five years later *The Times* – once owned by Northcliffe and now by Rupert Murdoch – ran an account of Keith's Gallipoli exploits, with the legend 'The Journalist Who Stopped the War'. The fact that Keith was, at the same time, advancing his career and influence, hardly discredits the outcome. The motivations of whistle-blowers and dedicated investigative journalists are irrelevant. They can be seeking fame, revenge or remuneration, but what matters is the information they get out into the public sphere so that we can make a democratic evaluation. As we have seen, Murdoch praises these feral qualities of the press and he's right to do so: the competition to get a scoop is the mechanism of media disclosure, that however venal the motive or partisan the agenda, a sufficient variety of sources of information should cancel out any bias.

However, the 'competition of ideas' concept of free speech, explicated by J.S. Mill's *On Liberty*, implies an open market, with few barriers to entry and fair rules; the market in news today, which retains a lot of monopoly features, rarely attains those ideals. Information is as often or not traded below the counter, bargained for something else, cash or influence and often withheld. There are many barriers from original eye-witness accounts to final publication. In terms of the Gallipoli scandal, Keith Murdoch was not a 'journalist' who stopped the war; he was, however, certainly a brilliant arbitrageur, who ended up brokering a deal between a reporter and a powerful press baron. This must have been a vivid lesson for his son: news is not just information, but a currency with huge political leverage.

It was Northcliffe who first grasped this system at the dawn of the democratic age of mass media; as he said in his famous aphorism, 'News is something somebody else doesn't want you to know.' He became Keith Murdoch's lifelong friend and mentor and in a way the patron of the whole Murdoch project. Keith learned from him that a successful press baron can make or break governments by mediating information between politicians and the newly enfranchised electorate. While in London, Keith became an intermediary for the Australian prime minister in London, acting as his publicist, speech-writer and organising dinner parties with senior British politicians like Lloyd George. Towards the end of World War I, he visited the Australian contingent on the Western Front and wrote vivid dispatches as an unofficial war correspondent. But the objectivity was vitiated by political spin and Keith got involved with unseemly behind the scenes machinations by using both his media access and friendship with the

Australian prime minister to change the command of the Australian Corps during a vital offensive. On this occasion Keith overplayed his hand and fell out with the Australian prime minister (Serle, 1986).

However, politicians come and go; newspaper proprietors can outstay them. Keith was the only Australian journalist to witness the signing of the Treaty of Versailles and returned to Australia as chief editor of the *Melbourne Herald*. Under Northcliffe's tutelage, Keith managed to simultaneously improve its content and circulation through a mixture of political controversy, arts journalism and celebrity contributions. After a bitter circulation war with the Sydney *Sun* he acquired the tabloid picture-style paper and turned it into the biggest-selling newspaper in Australia. Like Rupert, Keith was an early adopter of new media and saw the benefits of cross-media ownership, getting heavily involved in the burgeoning sector of radio stations and supply chain deals, merging cable services in the Australian Associated Press. In deference to his role model, Northcliffe, Keith was now dubbed 'Lord Southcliffe' by his employees.

Had Keith's career ended here then the journalistic legacy of the 'Hero of Gallipoli' taking on the Establishment for the common man and then returning to create a popular accessible press, would be hard to reproach. But establishments are plural and one can expose the deficiencies of another while efficiently serving another and in Keith Murdoch's case, the double aspect of information trading was irresistible. According the Bruce Page, the former *Sunday Times* Insight editor, who has written the most comprehensive account of Murdoch's Australian newspaper roots, 'To [Keith] Murdoch, stories were currency, and were most valuable when unpublished: by the 1930s he was an experienced practitioner of intrigue' (Page, 2011, p. 44).

By the 1930s Keith was not only friend to several previous prime ministers, but though a complicated set of mergers and acquisitions, also now chairman of Australia's biggest news organisation, the Herald and Weekly Times Group (HWT). His media clout made him a kingmaker and he wasn't afraid to wield his political power. When Joseph Lyons split from the incumbent Labor Party, Keith Murdoch's press stepped in and dominated news-stands with their support for Lyons's more conservative break-away party. Lyons's victory in the 1931 election was largely attributed to the role played by the Herald Group and Keith Murdoch was duly knighted.

Press barons don't have to suffer the vagaries of the election cycle – an advantage they have over politicians, but also a temptation towards autocracy. Before long Keith's increasingly imperious attitude to the democratic process was revealed when Lyons's Cabinet put forward an ownership restriction in the new broadcast industry. They proposed that no one proprietor should own more than five radio stations; Keith already owned seven. Furious at the Prime Minister, Keith railed 'I put him there and I'll put him out', and fired off an angry letter to Lyons accusing his cabinet of personal hostility. The Australian leader's obsequious five-page reply is a vivid demonstration of where the real power lay: 'No word hostile to you has ever been uttered in Cabinet. On the contrary, all ministers realise only too well what the Government and Party owe to the papers of your group' (Munster, 1985). The ownership rules were quietly dropped.

As Orwell noted around this time, the threats to a free press don't just come from bureaucrats and commissar, but also from over-mighty press barons who think themselves above the electoral process. Eighty years later, Keith's son would also complain in an unguarded tweet, 'To hell with politicians! When are we going to find some to tell the truth in any country? Don't hold your breath' (Murdoch, 2012b). The phone-hacking scandal would reveal that much of Britain's political class had become subservient to Murdoch's abusive charm.

For all his success in building up a media group which could hold the government to account and/or to ransom, there were two flaws in Keith Murdoch's strategy which came back to haunt him in later life. One was an authoritarian streak. During the Second World War, with his close government contacts and media dominance, Keith was appointed as Director-General of Information by Lyons's successor, Robert Menzies, and soon sought authority to correct 'misstatements' in the press and force all news outlets to publish government stories. The furore was universal among politicians and the press (except his own Herald Group) and Keith was forced to resign his government post.

The other weakness was the dispersed ownership of the HWT group. Though he built up the company to pre-eminence through a complex set of mergers and partnerships, Keith never assembled enough personal equity to control it and remained an employee rather than a true proprietor. Having created a series of complex interlocking shareholdings as a defence from hostile takeover, his piecemeal ownership was potentially vulnerable to attack from inside; and this is what happened. Before his death, during a prolonged battle with cancer, Keith tried various moves to sort out his affairs, at one point using company funds to hive off a separate company, News Ltd, much to the disgust of rivals on the HWT board. With much of his personal estate tied up in death duties and properties, Keith tried to keep the newspaper investment locked away in the trust of Cruden Investments, with his wife Dame Elisabeth Murdoch (still alive as I write, having reached her 103rd birthday) and Keith's successor as chair of the Herald Group, Harry Giddy, acting as executors.

It wasn't a well-thought-out plan. Keith Murdoch was so mistrusted by his own board that – on news of his death – his former deputy immediately brought in builders with jackhammers to open the dead man's office safe. Rupert, called back from his last year at Oxford, but still missing the funeral, nearly lost his bequest when Giddy insisted that Elisabeth sell all the newspaper assets to pay off debts. She acquiesced to the sale of Keith's upmarket Queensland newspapers (which Giddy pocketed and then sold for a profit) but managed to hang on to the downmarket, scrappy title the Adelaide *News*.

It's not hard to speculate what the effect of this plundering of his father's bequest had on Rupert. A close family friend called the sale of Cruden assets a 'theft' and a 'terrible business': 'And if I felt like that and I wasn't Sir Keith's son, how do you think Rupert felt?' (Chenoweth, 2001, p. 26). Over half a century later, Rupert's mother's anguish can still be heard in an interview with Michael Wolff:

> It was very hard to know what to do, because he wanted to keep certain properties and we knew that it was not possible. And that was hard, as I said, it was a very hard time because I insisted that we were not going into enormous debt and I'm sure that was the right thing. But I think he will always regret it very much that I didn't allow him to hang on to [the] Queensland interest because, you know, we just couldn't go owing a lot of money at that stage. Rupert was too young.

(WOLFF, 2008, P. 69)

As well as the outer compulsion, there were also combative inner family dynamics. Keith, who often disparaged his son Rupert, set tough terms for the inheritance in the codicils to his will:

> I desire that my said son Keith Rupert Murdoch should have the great opportunity of leading a useful, altruistic and full life in newspaper and broadcasting activities and ultimately occupying a position of high responsibilities on that field with the support of my trustees if they consider him worth of that support.

(CHENOWETH, 2001, P. 28)

Not only did Rupert's inheritance come at the cost of shock and grief, with so many conditions attached, the legacy must have been as much burden as gift. At first Rupert refused to take over the remaining paper and a meeting with his mother about what was expected of him left him 'shaken to his foundations'. Bequests, like mortgages, are literally 'dead hands' – the expectations of the past weigh like a nightmare on the brains of the living.

KEITH'S LEGACY

Though it has already lasted nearly twice as long, there are plenty of echoes, writ large and over several continents, of the father's career in that of his son. Rupert's taste for political intrigue and back-room dealings for one; a habit of befriending and then betraying politicians, colleagues and rivals is another. There's also an undeniable drive to technological innovation combined with a canny grasp of demotic appeal – Keith created Australia's first tabloid in the *Herald Sun*, and was ahead of his time in spotting the importance of broadcast media. But he was also – like his son Rupert would be – drawn to anti-competitive meddling. Keith opposed the formation of the public service Australian Broadcasting Corporation because the government refused to let the Herald Group be the sole supplier of information. Rupert's decades-long attacks on the BBC smack of the same rivalrous jealousy. And if James Murdoch hadn't combined his bid for BSkyB with a simultaneous plan to decimate the BBC, perhaps history would have been different and he might still be chair of the British satellite channel.

It seems to be family tradition – an entrepreneurial impulse to compete combined with an autocratic need to control. The urge to compete can lead to new rivals, new arguments, new territories; an openness to adventure and opportunity, the enterprise of the innovator and buccaneer. But the urge to transform the world can quickly sour into an anxious and occasionally manic need to control it, make it conform and disable any forces that threaten that. Bereft of a competitor to challenge him, the mogul becomes paranoid and unable to read the public mood anymore. Like Orson Welles's *Citizen Kane*, the idealistic innovator declines into a tyrannical manager, to a lonely recluse isolated in his Xanadu. Winning the game and outbidding everyone else at the table actually means losing it.

For all the similarities between *père et fils*, perhaps the differences between Keith and Rupert are more significant and symptomatic. For some reason, despite the long annals of patriarchy, we tend to assume driven sons are trying to vindicate their fathers. Picasso's father was a failed painter; William James's a failed essayist; Yeats's a failed playwright; Dickens's was declared bankrupt. But anxiety of paternal influence works both ways. Ambitious people are driven by a dual desire to justify their parents and transcend them; as Ivan Karamazov said 'Who doesn't desire his father's death?'

George W. Bush exemplifies some of these ambiguities. Many people have assumed the invasion of Iraq was some kind of revenge for Saddam Hussein's attempted assassination of his father, George Bush Snr, who had routed Hussein from Kuwait a decade before. However, a brief inspection of George W.'s key staff show it was the tight cadre who most disagreed with his father on Iraq who became most powerful during the son's administration. If anything, the policies of Donald Rumsfeld and Dick Cheney were *revenge* for George Bush Snr's refusal to go all the way to Baghdad in 1991 rather than vindication of it. The need to overcome and incorporate the paternal influence creates a dynamo of contradictions. When asked about how often he consulted with his father during his presidency, George W. Bush could only resolve the tension by resorting to a divine get-out clause: 'I speak to a Higher Father.'

Without looking for a Murdoch equivalent to the Charles Foster Kane's 'Rosebud' moment, an ambivalence toward the paternal will is striking: Keith's strictures beyond the grave would both be repudiated and overcome. While Rupert praised his father's journalism and business acumen, he also came to bury it. Though trained nominally as a journalist, Rupert never spent anything like the same time actually writing stories as his father, nor did he assume the same degree of full-scale editorial responsibility; though he has always meddled with the papers he has owned, it has been by proxy, as proprietor rather than editor. This could be construed as a transparent lack of transparency or the canny desire to avoid his father's fate as the salaried employee.

Likewise, though clearly fascinated by politics, Rupert has never taken any public office as his father did during World War II (nor to his credit has he accepted any honours or titles). This could be prudent, given the disastrous consequence of Keith Murdoch's appointment as director-general, or a form of cowardice, an abdication of his duties and public life. Compared to his father, Rupert has never built any lasting partnerships with equals or mentors. His longest standing colleagues have always been inferiors – like Les Hinton, who was finally ousted from News Corp in 2011 during the two weeks that the phone-hacking scandal raged. But once again this could be a protective wise move given how Keith's comrades tried to pillage his legacy.

Above all, the most glaring difference between father and son is this: while Keith made foreign jaunts, he stayed in Australia and remained a patriot to his particular hierarchy. Rupert's loyalties have, to the contrary, always been split. Though he proclaimed to the Australian courts that he was a deep patriot in order to keep his TV licences, Rupert became an American citizen within a couple of years of that pronouncement in order to gain US TV licences. Though his corporate HQ is in New York, most of Rupert's most valuable interests are in Los Angeles and yet he hated living on the West Coast. As the unfolding hacking story proved, some of his deep professional loyalties remained in his London headquarters in Wapping. If there's any principle to come out of his multi-layered patriotism, it is a mixture of the calculated bet and something more poignant: the lack of trust of someone who is a permanent global trotter, touring his many properties, but never quite at home. His father's past is a history lesson here; no matter if you're a friend of the prime minister or have built up the most powerful media empire in the land, they can still take that away from you. They can screw you up. The thrust of the lateral invader owes something to the wariness of the outcast or refugee.

WORKFLOWS

Though Keith Murdoch was by all accounts often cutting and scathing, he was a hands-off father – Rupert's mother was the disciplinarian (Chenoweth, 2001, p. 11). After her husband's death, Lady (now Dame) Elizabeth constantly reminded her son to 'live up to his father's approval' and 'justify his faith'. While Keith was still alive it was Elisabeth who insisted Rupert should be sent to boarding school at Geelong, though that was not a family tradition. Murdoch resented the disciplinarian atmosphere there and was terrible at sports, though he did end up editing two journals. Then, much like the nepotistic favours among media folk today, Rupert got a brief internship on his father's paper (driven there by chauffeur) before he followed the family tradition of crossing half the world to finish his education.

Rupert's three years reading politics, philosophy and economics at Worcester College, Oxford, suggest a stirring of rebellion against his own privilege. He placed a bust of Lenin on his mantelpiece, which he and his college friends would toast as their 'Great Leader' and tormented his father with the notion that he was developing 'alarming left-wing views'. Though he was one of the wealthier undergraduates with a car and the best rooms in college, Rupert joined the Cole Group, Oxford's most famous socialist society. However, his brief career as Labour supporter was tarnished when he was suspended by the Labour Club for using illicit methods while campaigning to be secretary.

One thing seems not to have changed since those days – Rupert's complete lack of reverence for the British monarchy. Despite it clashing with the state funeral of George VI, he went ahead and threw a cocktail party, only to be thrown into a lake because of his disrespect. Interviewed years later, fellow undergraduates varied between remembering Murdoch's 'kindliness' and his political bombast. The reserve, the borderline mixture of shyness and a twinkly sense of mischief are about the only common threads in their accounts. During the summer Rupert worked for three months at the *Birmingham Gazette*, which the editor had organised as a favour to Murdoch's father and which Rupert repaid when he left by suggesting he should be sacked.

Keith's death in 1952 interrupted Rupert's studies and initially he was not keen on taking over the downmarket Adelaide *News*. He scraped his degree at

Oxford – understandable given the distance he had to travel and the shock of his father's death. Before Rupert returned to his homeland, the 22-year-old graduate went to work for a few months for the other famous British news tycoon of the day, Lord Beaverbrook, in his greatest commercial creation, the (sadly these days much derided and declined) *Daily Express*.

At this point in the early fifties, British newspapers were enjoying a post-war bonanza in advertising and sales and – prior to the rise of TV news – vast circulations. Fleet Street was not just a metonymy in those days, but actually a narrow conclave of streets turned into a busy industrial quarter, dominated by noisy rotary presses, truckloads of printing ink and reams of paper coming in, truckloads of newspapers going out. This booming sector had already created its tycoons, many of whom were ennobled. But it was also home to some of the most powerful organised labour in the form of the print unions. The tight, daily assembly line of newspaper production was a macho environment for both workers by hand and workers by brain. Journalists assembled in the smoky news rooms until the paper was put to bed and then assembled at the smoky pubs long before they would go to bed too. Lunchtimes were long and boozy. Everyone knew each other. Gossip was traded, sources bought drinks. This was a mixture of blue- and white-collar bravado in the heyday of mechanical mass reproduction.

This is also the zenith of the independent commercial newspaper. The production of most newspapers has rarely been met by its cover price and the actual content required some other kind of subsidy. In the nineteenth century this subsidy was largely provided by interested parties trying to change public opinion for charitable, political or commercial gain – a form of extended pamphleteering. With the exception of *The Times*, no newspaper could call itself independent. Newspapers just weren't profitable in themselves, they were a means to an end. But in America before the Second World War, and in Britain afterwards, the growth of a consumer society meant the creation of a whole new stream of lucrative revenue – advertising.

Thanks to this new-found commercial independence, the newspaper proprietors of the first half of the twentieth century became some of the most powerful figures in both media and politics, yet never wholly owned by their domain. Many of these figures had the same insider/outsider tensions as the Murdochs, with a similarly imperious attitude towards politicians. Lords Northcliffe and Beaverbrook were actually briefly cabinet members and thought they could control the government. Beaverbrook, from a Canadian background, openly despised the government of Stanley Baldwin during the thirties and with the help of Northcliffe's brother, Lord Rothermere, did everything he could to bring Baldwin down. When their newspaper campaigns failed to achieve that objective, they went into direct political confrontation creating a United Empire Party, which challenged the government in by-elections with a formidable 'Buy British' campaign.

For a brief moment we can talk about the power of the 'British press barons', plural. Like the unruly aristocrats under Tudor monarchs, Northcliffe, Rother-mere and Beaverbrook were an independent power who could use their populist power-base to directly challenge the political parties of the day. Many thought that Baldwin didn't stand a chance against the combined unelected might of Beaverbrook and Rothermere (*A Point of View: Power of the Press*, 2012). But in a stunning turnaround – perhaps the last time until the Leveson Inquiry that overweening media power in Britain would be challenged – Baldwin made a cru-cial speech which demolished the campaign of 'Buy British' the press barons had used as an excuse to attack him. Baldwin pointed out that, for all their nationalist demagoguery, most of the money made by the two proprietors came from US advertising revenues making US products household names in the UK. With a rider added by Baldwin's cousin, Rudyard Kipling, Baldwin saw off the press barons days before the election, using a phrase that remains a resonant indictment of the commercial independent press to this day: 'power without responsibility – the prerogative of the harlot throughout the ages'.

It's in this macho, inky, stinky politicised environment that Murdoch had his first experience of the powerhouse of the modern press and it must have opened his eyes. The brief sojourn at the *Herald* could not have prepared him for his job on the *Daily Express* earning ten pounds a week as a sub-editor – though he did stay at the Savoy. By being on the right side of the thirties debate and conscript-ing socialists, liberals and conservatives in the campaign against Hitler, the *Daily Express*, unlike most other Fleet Street titles, entered the fifties with no collabora-tion or gainsaying to explain.

From Michael Foot to James Cameron the *Express* boasted some of the era's finest journalists and opinion formers. It was also a powerhouse of design inno-vation. Beaverbrook's daily embodied all the best of a mid-market newspaper, one which could convey quality news in a popular way and popular news in a quality way, which Rupert would seek to emulate for the rest of his newspaper career.

Not since the invention of hot metal (also called line casting or linotype) fifty years before, which allowed changes in typeface size, had such a revolution in the appearance of newspapers taken place. The paper's editor, Arthur Christiansen, did away with staid columns and reimagined the front page as a free modernistic space where the montage of image and text could do for the popular press what free verse and Russian constructivism had done for poetry and photomontage. This is when newspapers became cinematic rather than linear; the eye panning across the page in long takes of serious subjects – zooming in for the provocative or saucy close-up. To make this floating visual/textual ensemble fizz required not just sharp picture editors or great foreign correspondents, but diligent editors and sub-editors, who could trim, twist and rewrite copy to make the semantic impact attuned to the design.

Many biographers have said that printers ink runs in Rupert Murdoch's veins and conclude that it was in Fleet Street the toxin first infused into him. It's certainly true that Murdoch first learned the value of gossip as political and social currency there. Twenty-five years later, when he became proprietor of the *New York Post*, Murdoch modelled his notorious 'Page Six' gossip section on the *Express*'s pseudonymous 'William Hickey' column that ran for over fifty years beginning in 1933. 'The Page' as it is known in New York parlayed the lowest kind of celebrity dirt into commercial and political gold and was the model for the British daily tabloid *Sun*'s Bizarre column – which eventually led to the *ne plus ultra* of privacy intrusion with the hacking of a dead schoolgirl's phone.

However, some of the influence was positive. The indelible visual legacy of Christiansen's creation is clear in Murdoch's own publications as is the emphasis on the role of the subs. Every editor who has worked for Murdoch talks about his keen eye for copy, image, headline size and column width and his hands-on approach, scoring dummy copies with red lines, readjusting the layout, subbing the text. This is evident in a BBC documentary from the early eighties when he is shown snatching copy from his editors in Australia ('Who's Afraid of Rupert Murdoch?', 1981). Murdoch's biographer Michael Wolff – who spent over sixty hours with the mogul during the late noughties – observed the same hands-on, sleeves rolled up, interventionism; despite now owning hundreds of papers, Murdoch's main focus is still his newspapers and he's constantly on the phone to his dozens of editors around the world and annotates the incoming daily copies:

> *He gets his newspapers wherever he is in the world, gets out his red pen—just like his father before him—and puts a cross through stories that shouldn't have run, circles a photo and draws an arrow to show where it should have been placed, notes a headline that should have been two lines rather than one, and so on.*

(WOLFF, 2008)

All this, despite Rupert's various denials – most recently at the DCMS select committee in Parliament – that he intervenes as a proprietor.

Murdoch's brief stint in Fleet Street wasn't just about understanding format and copy, it was also an apprenticeship in a large complicated industrial process.

The upstream and downstream logistics of daily newspapers are both diffuse and extremely time-critical: how can you get breaking news from the wires first? Is there a cheaper supply of newsprint paper? How do you get your paper to the newsagent quicker? How to make sure he puts it on the front shelf? Some of the understanding of workflows is technical and managerial; a change in print technology can mean that electricians rather than unionised typesetters can now run your machines. Some of it is more commercially strategic: can I buy this news service? Or that marketing and distribution channel? Or cross invest in sports? Ultimately, there is the political and social test: will a well-phrased headline and graphic image animate public opinion and cause debates in the House of Commons? Are the legislators listening to me?

A vast industrial process, dedicated to a physical object with enormous cultural and political significance, to be distributed to and consumed by millions every day, the publication of a twentieth-century national newspaper really has few parallels in any other part of the media business. In this light, it's completely understandable that, many years later in 1993, ensconced in Hollywood, having successfully bought a studio and launched a whole US TV network, Rupert would still muse: 'The movie business is interesting and challenging, but it can't compare to owning and running a newspaper' (Klein, 1993, p. 12). Already the nostalgia for the glory days of Fleet Street was upon him and the sentimentality towards the tough bravado of his London days would cost Murdoch dear in a couple of decades.

LEVERAGE

Whatever he learned from his early apprenticeship in the UK, Rupert took back to Australia, and for the next sixteen years he would stay there, doggedly expanding his narrow perch at the Adelaide *News* across the entire continent. Though Australia only has a population of 15 million people, its vast distances and logistical hurdles, with newspapers and broadcasters based in unique, discrete city markets under regional governments thousands of miles away from each other, would be the perfect preparation for a man who would build a global corporation based in Sydney, London, New York, Los Angeles and Hong Kong. News Corp Nation is also here seen in embryo (see Chapter 8).

Building his Australian Empire (and apparently the Murdoch family do call it an 'empire') would prepare Rupert for the battle ahead. An important element of this struggle was atavistic – a tribal battle with other dynasties reminiscent of the Medicis or Borgias. In Australia the key rivals were the Packers and the Fairfaxes:

the former descending into physical brawls in the sixties, the latter Murdoch was still lambasting in his tweets in 2012. In the UK, the families were less boisterous and either desperate to get out of newspapers, like Lord Thomson who owned *The Times* and *The Sunday Times*, or weak and easily deceived, like Sir William Carr who owned *News of the World*.

Murdoch would remain obsessed with the family element right up until the phone-hacking scandal. It is a peculiarity of the newspaper market in the US that it was until recently still dominated by family-owned businesses – the Sulzbergers at the *New York Times*, the Grahams at the *Washington Post* and the Bancrofts at the *Wall Street Journal* – a factor Murdoch has exploited to great benefit in the case of the latter, which he took over in 2007. Though a product of a newspaper dynasty himself, Murdoch mercilessly spots the inefficient, effete and easy to dominate elements among the legatees. He knows how to manipulate their fears and resentments, their sibling rivalries and sentimentalities, and then drive a wedge through these weaknesses to quickly gain control and sell off the family silver. Though appearing as a sentimental patriarch himself, Murdoch acts like a rebel against tradition, seeing rich pickings in assumed loyalties.

Most of Murdoch's company has been formed through takeovers, often financed with large loans or intra-company share issues and followed by asset stripping and consolidation. The margins in newspapers are tough – a war of attrition over pricing and circulation. In the Australian context at least, victory is absolute. Most cities today can only sustain one daily paper. If that paper is yours you've cornered the market and have a great cash cow, but apart from more horizontal integration with wire services or distribution, the only way up is out. Accumulating enough reserves of cash to make that leap can take years, maybe generations.

Murdoch solved this zero-sum financial problem by defying his mother's imprecations and accumulating more debt in the form of bank loans and complex share holdings. In this he was an early adopter of what would be, by the eighties, the transformation of late twentieth-century corporate capitalism – mergers and acquisitions based on massive leverage. As early as thirty years before Murdoch spotted a new opportunity and made a key strategic move: he left the National Bank of Australia, where he was a small customer, for the boutique Commonwealth Bank in Sydney, where he was one of the biggest. With a major loan from the Commonwealth Murdoch used debt to make his first move out of Adelaide, where he purchased magazines in Melbourne and *The Sunday Times* in Perth. He managed to break the zero-sum game of the captured market by speculating on his future earnings.

Important changes are afoot here. In this new context, convincing customers about your product is actually secondary to winning approval for your credit line. Like the perverse logic of the paradox of thrift (which means the more you try to save the less you actually save) the paradox of debt makes borrowing self-reinforcing, with favourable deals for buying in bulk: the more you owe your bank, the more you own it. But that debt requires servicing, so there has to be a constant stream of new revenues, and given the tightness of the markets, increased profits are unlikely. The best source of income is selling a recent acquisition at a profit, often to another sub-division of your company. You then use the cash generated to either pay off the loan or to service another bigger, better loan to buy another media outlet. More than creating companies, you're involved in buying and selling them. Sometimes (as we'll see with the Fox Network in Chapter 8) magical accounting rules allow you to treat debt as an asset and therefore borrow more on the basis of what you've already borrowed. But like a pyramid scheme you need an ever-increasing cycle of activity to keep afloat. The deal flow and constant merry-go-round of money is everything.

This 'grow or die' business model would be the operating principle for News Corp over the next sixty years. It's this leverage buy-out strategy which makes Murdoch the perfect exemplar of the neo-liberal Thatcher/Reagan era a quarter of a century before it became dominant, when Murdoch would deploy the junk bond broker Michael Milken to finance the founding of the Fox Network. The model would almost lead to disaster in the early nineties when News Corp could not service its debt.

Murdoch, still a close friend of the former federal felon Milken, is unrepentant about this model. Indeed, Murdoch's chief ideologue, Irwin Stelzer, was for the four years before its collapse lauding companies like Enron as the poster children for innovative new business in Murdoch's papers, *The Sunday Times* and *Weekly Standard*, vaunting Enron's off balance sheet deals and creative accounting procedures even after the energy giant's fraudulent self-dealing and make-believe audits were exposed. Stelzer, who had actually been on Enron's advisory board, carried on praising their business model even after the corrupt energy company collapsed.

As one of Murdoch's favoured economists, it would be logical to deduce that Stelzer's belief in modern innovations of high finance capitalism are shared by Rupert. And three important consequences flow.

First, it would appear that the quality of a newly acquired newspaper or media organisation itself is not necessarily the priority. The main investment is in the purchase and that debt has to be serviced and dividends paid on the new share. Any future investment in plant or personnel must deliver significant cost savings or increased market share. If that doesn't happen, asset-stripping, resale or closure can often be just as profitable. Indeed, that's what would happen during Murdoch's first phase of acquisition; within a few years he would close the Melbourne *Herald* and merge it with the Sydney tabloid *Sun*.

Second, for all the buccaneering free market approach, the key deals actually involve a small number of parties. To sort out a loan, share purchase or issue to acquire a new company (especially if it is a family-owned company like the *Wall Street Journal*) requires a narrow set of transactions with family members, bankers and lawyers. Insider knowledge counts, personal trust and commitment are as important as future revenue projections. For all his shyness and outsiderdom, Murdoch is clearly a past master at this kind of deal making. On a one-to-one level he's constantly charmed editors, rival owners and proprietors, bankers, bond holders and large shareholders. Even through the first phase of the phone-hacking crisis, that personal trust is what kept the largest shareholders relatively quiet.

Finally, the biggest commercial threat is actually government regulation. As Keith Murdoch discovered, the key players are politicians who, through monopoly, citizenship or cross-ownership rules, can stifle this grow or die model. Again, this is more like a court than a market; a relationship with a handful of defined players who can be privately approached. Ownership of an outlet such as a national TV station or newspaper is both an end and means; while legislators can block a merger or takeover, a powerful media outlet can also stall or vitiate their political careers. It's a trade-off – and by necessity a secret one, because if the public knew a politician was being targeted or favoured as a quid pro quo, then the good or bad publicity would lose is effectiveness. News manipulation only works unseen – the leverage operated below public consciousness: the word in your ear, the confidential chat, the apparently unmotivated printed innuendo. In this way the origins of the Murdoch mystique owe less to the arts of public communication and more to the powers of private confidence.

Underlying this trade in confidences is also an assumption of trust. From Murdoch's early days in Oxford and then Adelaide, the accounts of his trustworthiness and loyalty vary from person to person, but one thing doesn't change: the quietness and reserve. This personal non-disclosure leaves ample space for others to project what they want into his decision-making processes. Indeed, both detractors and admirers of Murdoch spend inordinate amounts of time speculating over his next move. He encourages a personal investment into his secrecy, which admirers can mistake for intimacy. If Murdoch's career has been based on any one factor, it has been this ability to instil a sense of fealty in his bankers, his shareholders, his business partners and his employees – and then to betray it when the time is right.

For all Murdoch's apparent sentimentality and long-term commitment to his core newspapers like the *New York Post*, the *Sun* and *News of the World*, the main thrust of most of his acquisitions is to buy cheap, cut costs, sell quickly for a profit or close to reduce competition. Though numerically, newspapers still form a remarkable number of News Corp's holdings – around 200 – global publishing is becoming a declining fraction of News Corp's $50 billion capitalisation. Nomura analysts estimated that newspapers will go from contributing 11 per cent of operating profit in 2011 to 4.2 per cent in 2014. By 2011, the print division of News International delivered only 1 per cent of the corporate profits of News Corp while a marketing division, News America, accounted for 12 per cent. For these reasons alone, and without the cost of hundreds of millions for defending the Sunday tabloid in private litigation, it had been rumoured for months before July 2011 that News International was thinking of saving costs by replacing *News of the World* with a more cost-effective Sunday version of the *Sun*.

If News International journalists had studied Murdoch's business history a little more closely, they would not have been shocked by the sudden closure of its lead title, despite its 2.7 million readers, on the afternoon of 7 July 2012.

4

8 July 2011
Playing the Man

Abrupt and shocking though it was, the closure of the *News of the World* failed to contain the growing crisis. The next day it significantly escalated as the former editor and prime minister's communications supremo, Andy Coulson, was arrested by appointment and his house searched.

Not only did Coulson's arrest take the scandal right into the heart of government – he had been, up until six months previously, the government's chief press officer – but the criminal allegations had by now also deepened as well as widened. Coulson was interviewed at length by detectives from Operation Weeting on suspicion of 'conspiring to intercept communications' and by officers from Operation Elveden in regard to 'corruption allegations contrary to Section 1 of the Prevention of Corruption Act 1906'. The phone-hacking charges were serious enough, but allegations that a handful of police officers were illegally paid £100,000 by the newspaper would, in very short order, constitute a threat to News Corp's operations in the US.

As arrests in 2012 at the *Sun* would remind journalists and editors, there is no statutory 'public interest' defence for bribing a state official to obtain a story in the UK. (There is also no such defence for computer hacking – something which even *The Times*'s long-serving in-house lawyer seemed unaware of until the paper was challenged for doing it during the Leveson Inquiry.) Bribery was, however, far more potentially grievous for News Corp, as the parent company of these papers was a US corporation. Allegations of bribery of police officers opened it up to prosecution under the United States' Foreign Corrupt Practices Act of 1977, which prohibits payments to foreign officials by US companies and individual US-born or naturalised citizens. Both are subject to large fines, while the individuals – whether the company's agents or its executives and including those who merely connived or turned a blind eye to the bribery – can be imprisoned for as long as five years. Rupert, James and Lachlan Murdoch, all of whom have sat on the News Corp board, are naturalised US citizens.

By this point in the scandal, on 8 July, over a billion dollars had been wiped off the value of News Corp (NWSA) shares.

TWO YEARS OF TROUBLE

If the long smouldering Hackgate scandal was in danger of creating a conflagration at the US parent company, flames were also lapping around the feet of Britain's senior politicians.

A close friend of Rebekah Brooks, Andy Coulson had worked alongside her since the late nineties, first through the *Sun*'s Bizarre show business column and then as her deputy at the *News of the World*, succeeding her as editor in 2003 – at the height of the alleged phone hacking by the paper. He stayed on as editor until January 2007 when he resigned after the sentencing of Goodman and Mulcaire. Just six months later, Coulson was hired by David Cameron to head up communications for the Conservative Party, then in opposition and trailing in the polls. The Conservative leader and his right-hand man, the shadow chancellor George Osborne, with their Oxbridge and public school backgrounds, were easily portrayed as upper-class and out of touch. Coulson, brought up in a public housing council estate and educated at a state-run comprehensive school, was seen by them as a tabloid expert who could guide the party's news operations with a tough populist touch. Since Coulson and Osborne, to a certain extent, modelled their collaboration on the dynamic dualism of Blair and Brown in their early days, Coulson was as capable of doing for the Tories what the former *Daily Mirror* political editor Alastair Campbell had done for New Labour.

According to both their statements to the Leveson Inquiry, it was Osborne who approached Coulson to take the job as the Conservative's communications chief, though the BBC correspondent Guto Harri had also been in the running. It was an odd alliance: the editor of a salacious Sunday tabloid and the son of a wealthy family who had married into the Tory establishment (Osborne's father-in-law is the Tory grandee Lord Howell, who was part of the Thatcher government that allowed Murdoch's purchase of Times Newspapers Group Newspapers to go ahead). But the would-be chancellor and Coulson had encountered each other before and in what at first blush look like inauspicious circumstances.

Two years earlier, in autumn 2005, while Osborne was running Cameron's leadership campaign, the left-leaning *Sunday Mirror* was on the brink of running an exclusive about a youthful drug-taking Osborne in the weekend before the leadership election. The source was Natalie Rowe, who ran an escort agency and was known as a dominatrix, and who was then going out with one of Osborne's college friends. She had produced a photo from the early nineties, which showed the chan-

TOP TORY, COKE AND THE HOOKER

Shadow Chancellor caught in shock picture

Figure 4.1 News of the World, *October 2005*

cellor to-be sitting on her lap behind a table, on which appear to be lines of cocaine. Rowe claimed – and still claims – that Osborne had used these class-A drugs. In the week before the Conservative Party Conference publication of this scoop could have caused major problems for Cameron and his campaign manager.

Somehow the *News of the World* got advance wind of their rival's exclusive and ran, what is called in Fleet Street, a 'spoiler'. The paper Coulson edited ran a front page headline 'Top Tory, Coke and the Hooker'. Inside was a double-page spread with the same photo, but with the addition of comments of Osborne, going on record denying the allegations and talking sadly about how drugs had ravaged the lives of his friends. (Oddly enough the article appeared on the same page as a column by William Hague, the former Tory Party leader who, according to the Register of Members' Interests, was being paid £200,000 a year by Coulson to write a column for the *News of the World*.) Though it has since been revealed that both Rowe and senior *Mirror* editors were also victims of phone hacking at the time, there's no evidence yet that the intrusion played a role in the spoiler. The tactic of contacting the subject of a scandal and saying 'Tell us your story and we'll make it more favourable' is an inveterate tabloid staple.

Though Coulson claimed during the Leveson Inquiry that his headline hardly did Osborne any favours, the prominent phone-hacking victims' lawyer Mark Lewis has pointed out that the *News of the World* published a much more favourable account of events than the *Sunday Mirror* and if anything managed to portray Osborne as less posh and aloof, producing a positive effect. In an accompanying editorial the paper maintained its support for Cameron. The threat to his campaign was averted and David Cameron won the party ballot that December. In any event, Coulson's ability to dominate Fleet Street with spoilers and exclusives clearly impressed Osborne, who approached the former *News of the World* editor despite the hacking allegations. When Coulson was hired by Conservative HQ, his annual income was reported to be £475,000, though his salary from the Conservative Party was only £270,000. The discrepancy is explained by a severance package from News International which was paid in instalments.

For all these reasons, on the day of Coulson's arrest, Cameron was on the defensive, having to justify his appointment of Coulson in 2007 and taking him along with him into Number 10 in May 2010:

> *I thought it was right to give that individual a second chance ... I have spoken to him. I have seen him, not recently and not frequently. But when you work with someone for four years, as I did, and you work closely, you do build a friendship, and I became friends with him ... he became a friend and is a friend.*

(HM Government, 2011)

This 'second chance' defence looks weak in retrospect. When the coalition government was formed in 2010, Cameron was warned on several occasions about Coulson's connections to criminality, and not just phone hacking. According to Francis Elliott and James Hanning (2012), concern was even expressed by the royal family – victims of Coulson's royal reporter's phone hacking – who had thought the Coulson communications role would only last while the Conservatives were in opposition. There were other warnings from senior figures on both the left and right, including former Liberal Democrat leader Paddy Ashdown and Conservative columnist Peter Oborne. Even more significantly, the *Guardian*'s editor, Alan Rusbridger, was particularly emphatic about Coulson's close collaboration with a private investigator, Jonathan Rees, who had been investigated for murdering his former business partner, Daniel Morgan, and corrupting police officers and conspiring to fit up an innocent person with cocaine (more of this in Chapter 10). The story was moving on from hacking to corruption to darker stories of drugs and murder...

The government's position was becoming intolerable. In Parliament, despite the many connections the previous administration had with News International, the new Labour Leader Ed Miliband was drawing attention to the Cabinet's current connections, especially Cameron's with Coulson, and numerous known social and business meetings with Rebekah Brooks and James Murdoch. Internally, the Tory's coalition partners, the Liberal Democrats – which of all the mainstream British political parties had neither occasion nor the inclination to court News International – were firm that something had to be done. Cameron announced to Parliament on 8 July that there would be a public inquiry into the phone-hacking scandal, though the terms of reference had yet to be determined. Under the same withering domestic pressure, the culture secretary Jeremy Hunt bowed to the inevitable and did what Vince Cable tried to do six months before – refer News Corp's BSkyB bid to Ofcom, the broadcasting regulator, to reassess whether the corporation's directors were 'fit and proper' to own the country's largest pay-TV broadcaster outright.

Shares in BSkyB closed down that day 7.64 per cent at 750p, their lowest in nearly five months.

Meanwhile, with its newsroom locked down and turned into a police incident room, Rebekah Brooks was addressing the staff of the *News of the World*. The staff of the Sunday tabloid she used to edit were facing redundancy and the 'town hall' meeting was less deferential than usual. As can be heard in a secret recording of the meeting, Brooks began to talk about what a 'difficult day' it was for her, when TV editor Tom Latchem interrupted and accused her of 'arrogance': why was she keeping her job while 200 staff members were losing theirs? If she'd resigned earlier it might have saved hundreds of jobs.

Brooks's reply was a masterful mixture of empathy, aggression and self-serving illogic. She made vague promises about a new title opening soon and that there would be job offers elsewhere in the organisation. She then went into a pitiable plea about the usual '*Guardian*, BBC witch-hunts' and how she wasn't a cabinet minister and had worked at the paper since she was nineteen years old. There was a flash of anger over the suggestion that her resignation earlier might have saved the paper; she hadn't resigned because she felt it her duty to steer News International through this troubled time and 'make a difference'. All in all, she claimed that she was the victim as much as anyone else, blaming the police for not investigating hacking properly the first time round and denouncing 'advertisers so willing to believe anything negative about the *News of the World*'; she came up with a line which Murdoch would repeat before a parliamentary sub-committee a few days later: 'people we trusted let us down'. Senior management had power but no responsibility. They were victims too.

Having reiterated that she would not resign, Brooks made an observation that would prove more accurate: 'worse revelations are yet to come and you will understand in a year why we closed *News of the World*'. In a prophetic tweet, a former *News of the World* journalist, Sophy Ridge, remarked that there could be 'two years plus of trouble'.

It's hard to think of an equivalent calamity which could close the biggest selling English-language newspaper and simultaneously threaten the fate of a national government and one of the world's biggest media conglomerates. How did the fate of one get so entangled with the other? How did Britain's ruling elite ally itself so closely with a company controlled and dominated by a foreign national, whose tax base was in Australia and whose corporate head-quarters were in New York?

For more of an answer to this we have to go back to News Ltd's expansion into News International and Murdoch's first great leap forward from Australia to the UK.

UNDERDOG

When he looked back on the Australian part of his career at a session of the Aus-tralian Broadcasting Tribunal in 1979, Murdoch seemed to remember it as a case of Jack the Giant Killer. He talked about the Fairfaxes and Packers – old rival newspaper-owning dynasties as though they had always had the upper hand: 'They are the monolithic companies in my country. My life has spent fighting, starting with a very small newspaper, standing up to their attempts to push me out of business at the age of twenty-three in Adelaide…' (Page, 2011).

There's no doubt Murdoch struggled, having been deprived of the full legacy of his father's Herald Group. During his decade or so apprenticeship as proprietor of the Adelaide *News* Murdoch was firmly guided by the senior editor installed by his father – Rohan Rivett. For nearly a decade, the paper cut a steady course and even caught a moment of international kudos.

The rape and murder of nine-year-old Mary Olive Hattam in Ceduna in Sep-tember 1958 drew the attention of both national and world news organisations. After a peremptory search for the killer, an illiterate Aboriginal, Rupert Max Stuart, was arrested and charged with the murder. Stuart was sentenced to hang in Adelaide the next year but – sniffing out a legitimate story – Rivett sent his top crime reporter to double-check the police's version of events. The paper soon turned up evidence that Stuart had a firm alibi from his employer for the time of the killing. The Adelaide *News* went big on the potential miscarriage of justice and basically accused the state's legal system of 'institutionalised racism' towards a non-white defendant. It's to Murdoch's credit as well as Rivett's that they pursued this campaign so strenuously that a judicial review was opened to re-examine the case. When the *News* questioned the staffing of the commission the paper was charged with seven counts of libel and one of 'seditious libel'. In this instance at least, Mur-doch's talk of 'taking on the establishment' was not mere rhetoric.

However, Murdoch's stomach for fighting the status quo and racial justice didn't last long. He quietly settled the defamation case in 1960. A few weeks later he sacked his long-standing editor Rivett because of his 'left-wing bias' (Shawcross, 1992). The changed political context was a controversial speech about race made by the Australian Premier Sir Robert Menzies in which he claimed the pre-eminence of White Australia was 'unaltered and unalterable'. The *News* editor had responded by excoriating the prime minister's theories as 'racial prejudice' and warning it was in danger of 'building up a reservoir of ill-will' with Australia's northern neighbours. Rivett was given his notice a few days later.

After this dismissal, Murdoch's two papers changed their anti-establishment, anti-racist attitude 180 degrees. A joint editorial was run simultaneously in the Sydney *Mirror* and the Adelaide *Times*: 'to permit an admixture of European and Asian races to develop in Asia would probably result in tensions which would defeat all attempts to retain the friendships of our Northern neighbours'.

Over the years, as they moved bases across three continents, the Murdoch family seem to have since developed a cosmopolitan attitude to matters of ethnic background. But once again, you can't transliterate the personal into the political in a simplistic fashion. Social acceptance of multiracial relationships has changed in the fifty years since this editorial was published. Certainly, Murdoch's cultural attitudes, generally conservative in nature, are not set in stone, but it's unlikely that he could have changed his beliefs about race in a matter of a few weeks. It seems more likely that a deeper family tradition is reaffirming itself: ideology is expedient; other interests predominate. Around the time Rivett was sacked, News Ltd was looking to expand into lucrative TV and radio licences, which required government approval. Taking on Sir Robert Menzies, though socially honourable in retrospect, was probably commercial suicide at the time.

For the next six or seven years, Murdoch would compete with the other Australian dynasties – the Packers and Fairfaxes – occasionally offering himself up as an opposition to their monopolies, but just as often doing deals and carving up the proceeds. Intellectually, Murdoch had already recognised – like his father – the need for cross-platform ownership and the increasing role of entertainment over news. But his progress was slow and there was no step change. He had not matched his father's influence or domination of the Australian media, let alone broken into the global scene. What Murdoch needed, like Keith before him, was a powerful political player and protector who he could advance and who could repay the favour. Eventually Murdoch found one in the deputy prime minister, John 'Black Jack' McEwen.

TOP TABLE

News Ltd had supported McEwen and his Country Party from the early sixties. In 1964, realising he lacked political traction, Murdoch launched Australia's
first national newspaper based in the country's political capital, Canberra. It was
an upmarket publication, designed for politicians and opinion formers and was
initially edited by the highly regarded Maxwell Newton (but who left, under
a cloud, a year later). The *Australian* has struggled, financially, for most of its
lifetime and could never be justified in purely commercial terms. But in political
terms, as an effective vehicle for lobbying, elevating his preferred candidates and
trashing competitors, the *Australian* soon became very cost-effective. In 1967 it
paid out a huge political dividend.

Harold Holt, who had been elected Liberal leader and Prime Minister,
drowned in a swimming accident in December 1967. McEwen was now acting
Prime Minister while a new leader was elected to the majority Liberal Party.
There were two viable candidates who could stand for internal election: John
Gorton and Billy McMahon. Gorton was deemed light-weight and easy to ma-
nipulate. McMahon was a force in his own right and least likely to acquiesce to
McEwen's plans. He had to be stopped.

Using information gained by the Australian Secret Service, McEwen decided
to damage McMahon by tarnishing one of his closest supporters (none other than
Murdoch's former editor at the *Australian*, Maxwell Newton) with spurious allegations that he was a 'foreign agent' because he worked for JETRO (the Japan Ex-
port Trade Organisation). Newton was placed under surveillance by the Australian
Secret Service on McEwen's orders. A dodgy dossier of innuendo and 'sexed-up'
claims of espionage was cooked up and promptly handed over to Murdoch.

Protecting your sources is one thing, but the young newspaper proprietor was
sitting on a huge story: the acting leader of the country was using the apparatus of
state to sabotage one of his opponents in his own cabinet (echoes of the Westland
affair in the UK many years later). Rather than disclose the true picture, Murdoch
selectively leaked the highly damaging implications of espionage. The *Australian* ran the headline: 'WHY MCEWEN VETOES MCMAHON: FOREIGN
AGENT IS THE MAN BETWEEN THE LEADERS'. McMahon was discredited
by the smear, lost the race and McEwen got the prime minister he wanted.

The JETRO scandal also prefigures some of the covert goings on that would be
unearthed during the phone-hacking scandal: a newspaper seeking to deliver electoral victory for a specific politician, the collusive role of illegal information gathering
and the police. This mix of political intrigue, confidence trading and the character assassination of the hatchet job would be a key factor during Thatcher's difficult periods

in government too. Rather than follow his much trumpeted principle of exposing the secrets of the establishment, Murdoch chose to collude with the security services in black ops. Twenty years later, Murdoch's *Sunday Times* allegations would lead with equally spurious allegations, coming from secret security sources, that the former Labour leader, Michael Foot, was a KGB agent. Foot won an apology and substantial damages, but the smear that he took KGB gold as Agent Boot still sticks to this day. A classic ad personam tactic – playing the man rather than the ball – the politics of personal destruction has become a fundamental operating principle of many of Murdoch's press and media outlets (not to mention many of his journalists).

So much for being anti-establishment; the establishment just happens to cover whoever your enemies are at any given time. In 1974 Murdoch was again a key player in political intrigue when he connived in the 'dismissal' of Gough Whitlam – a Labour prime minister he had previously supported – so that the more conservative Malcolm Fraser could take his place. Murdoch's papers were so extreme in their anti-Whitlam selection and massaging of news stories that he faced a revolt and walkout from his own staff at the *Australian*. Demonstrators took to the streets to support the striking journalists.

In pursuit of his commercial-political goal, Murdoch even jettisoned his inveterate republican chippiness towards the British monarchy. Despite sitting on an amazing scoop – that Australian politicians were conspiring with the Crown appointed Attorney General to organise a bloodless coup – Murdoch chose to suppress what he knew. So much for his dislike of colonialism; its archaic undemocratic powers are fine if they serve your own ends. So much for speaking truth to power; it's only useful if it serves your commercial interests. Otherwise, if the whistle is likely to be blown on your friends and not your enemies, silence, suppression and censorship is the order of the day. The anti-news aspect of News Corp was created in News Ltd in the sixties and seventies.

This eagerness to collaborate with politicians, often irrespective of their ideological colours, has led some of the best analysts of Murdoch to conclude that he is ultimately apolitical. Richard Stott, in a review of the first edition of Bruce Page's 2003 Murdoch biography, commented that Murdoch:

> ...is shown to be manipulative, devious, bullying, ruthless and unscrupulous. But that just makes him a newspaper proprietor. What makes him special is that he isn't interested in the usual playthings of newspaper owners such as Beaverbrook, Northcliffe and William Randolph Hearst, namely political power for mischievous personal ends. For him it is the currency to secure a bigger and better deal or to consolidate current ones.

(STOTT, 2003)

In his otherwise prophetic book *Flat Earth News*, Nick Davies adopts this either/ or formula: 'He uses his media outlets as tools to secure political favours, and he uses those political favours to advance his business … his politics are never as big as his wallet'.

But why the either/or of ideological interests versus commercial interests? Why not both?

Despite his plaint to the Parliamentary Select Committee last summer – 'I wish politicians would stay away from me!' – the evidence suggests that Murdoch surrounds himself with them: secret meetings with Thatcher; Blair flying out to Hayman Island; Cameron to the Aegean; coming in the back door of Number 10; a succession of ministers for lunch, dinner and tea. There's no possible social reason for such encounters, other than that he actually likes talking 'issues', and not just back issues of the *Sun on Sunday*.

Throughout his two-day hearing at the Leveson Inquiry, Murdoch's most insistent statements, underscored by emphatic hand banging, were that his politics were not determined by his business interests. The one time he caused a real kerfuffle among his lawyers was when he diverged from their script to decry Paul Dacre, in charge of the *Daily Mail*, for reportedly putting commercial considerations foremost: 'The most unethical thing I've read for a long time.'

On this primacy of politics over money making, Murdoch would find support from a surprising quarter. David McKnight's recently published book *Rupert Murdoch: An Investigation of Political Power*, written before the hacking scandal broke, agrees that 'Murdoch is at least as devoted to propagating his ideas and political beliefs as he is to making money.' As a student of politics, philosophy and economics, and a youthful admirer of Lenin, Murdoch seems to have learned that it's never an either/or if you can have it both ways. Whatever your liberal or conservative attitudes to sexuality, race, reproductive rights or the character of political leaders, it's the actual practice and economic interests that determine behaviour. In the jargon of Marxism – base determines superstructure; hard realities are more important than soft opinions.

If you study Murdoch's relations with Thatcher, Reagan, Blair and Brown, you do see the same ability to personally charm politicians, without actually being influenced by their beliefs. It's in the *form* of Murdoch's activities, in his business practices and dealings with government, that you can see his real politics, not in the mere *content* of its editorials. The fact that politicians can advance his business interests is completely synchronous with Murdoch's concentration on the virtues of 'free' markets and a minima of state involvement. A core tenet of neoliberal thinking is that the pursuit of profit is a political virtue, because it combines freedom with efficiency. This belief is transformed in Murdoch's rhetoric in a moral argument which has dominated English-speaking political economy, from Fleet Street to Wall Street, for at least two generations.

Despite all appearances, Murdoch has been as much an ideologue as a quiet, dedicated financial empire builder. There are few successful media owners who have been quite so vocal about their beliefs. Five months after the hacking scandal, Murdoch even joined Twitter to put across his case; the irony of perhaps the single most powerful man in global media, turning to Twitter in order to put his point of view across. Every year Murdoch siphons off hundreds of millions of dollars to subsidise loss-making titles such as *The Times*, the *Australian*, the *New York Post* and the *Wall Street Journal* – much to the reported dismay of his News Corp board. And for what? These papers act as mouthpieces for his views or to gain him respect and credibility from the political classes.

Only ever met PMs when asked, believe it or not. And NEVER asked for anything. That is, I never asked for anything!

Figure 4.2 Tweet from @rupertmurdoch, 4 February 2012

Which brings us to the wealth fallacy: that the bottom line is all Murdoch cares about. Though the smartest commentators suggest his manoeuvres have been purely motivated by financial gain, beyond a certain level or riches, when you have more than five houses and cars, what do extra millions or billions buy you? The answer is power and significance: power to influence events, significance of recognition of your thought and worth. This desire to be heard, and if not loved, feared and respected, is a much better explanation of a man who, in his eighties, felt impelled to join a social networking site. But Murdoch's hour-long interrogation during the Leveson Inquiry put paid to the myth that money is everything – indeed, it suggested that he is a politician manqué.

As for the riches, all the evidence shows that, until he met Wendi Deng in his seventies, Murdoch has never had a lavishly luxurious lifestyle compared to his billionaire peers. He was always much more interested in the currency of reputation, stories about politicians and rivals, and lambasting public figures for misbehaviour, than the baubles of the super-rich. Beyond day-to-day gossip and intrigue, the overall arc of his activity over the decades seems to be to secure his influence and place in history. His current preoccupations, beyond trying to fire-fight various scandals, seem to be all tied up with children and education.

So the immaterial part of Murdoch's legacy obsesses him as much as the material. Wealth translates – with the right apparatus – into power. Power translates into influence on formative minds. Creating meaning leads to narrative significance. Significance means your legacy has been real and everything else not in vain.

Back in 1969, 'Black Jack' McEwen quickly rewarded Murdoch for his key role in defeating his enemy. The favour was converted to hard cash when currency regulations were preventing Murdoch from buying an ailing British newspaper. McEwen called Gorton – the prime minister Murdoch had helped install – and, blandishing him with a bottle of Scotch, got his signature to lift the currency restriction. The deal went ahead. It was a crucial moment for Murdoch's first great foreign bridgehead, the purchase of the *News of the World*.

CULTURE WARS

Murdoch's bid for the *News of the World*, using all the expertise gained in Australia, allowed him to rediscover the energy of outsider status while re-launching himself on the global stage. As we've already seen, by casting himself as a 'moth-eaten kangaroo' in the fight to win the paper, Murdoch could play the despised colonial country boy, once more tilting his lances at the bastions of privilege. This was a neat trick, especially since he was up against a real outsider in Czech-born Robert Maxwell (though the latter's affected upper-class accent might have fooled some). It also conveniently hid the fact that Murdoch had been invited to make a bid by the owner, Sir William Carr, who rightly believed that Maxwell was semi-criminal, but wrongly believed Murdoch would abide by his promise to keep the family voice on the board. And of course all this was greased by cash liberated from Australian currency restrictions thanks to the McEwen deal (Chippindale and Horrie, 1990, pp. 3–6).

At the shareholders' Extraordinary General Meeting (EGM) for the *News of the World* in January 1969, Murdoch looked quiet, shy and lacking in confidence and bluster compared to Maxwell, but in reality the reticence was a sign of confidence. Maxwell's Pergamon Press had offered *News of the World* shareholders a £27 million share swap for control, but Murdoch knew he had already won because, as well as News Ltd's newly released cash, he had city insiders Hambros Bank behind him, and had persuaded Carr family loyalists that he would look after them. Murdoch's Sydney *Daily Mirror* had also dished some timely (if richly deserved) dirt on Maxwell. So the deal was already sealed. The tense drama of shareholders democracy at the EGM was a sham. Murdoch had already deployed his insider charm and a triumvirate of bankers, dynasts and bad press.

The paper he took over – the paper he would have to close in shame some forty-two years later – was already famed for its 'shock-horror' stories of illicit sex and extraordinary violence, which had an unfailing appeal to six million British readers. Like most newspapers during the television boom, it had shed a quarter of its readership over the previous decade, but its slogan 'All Human Life is Here' still represented an ideal combination: privileged ownership with a commercial instinct for demotic gossip and sleaze.

Murdoch did little to change these fundamentals. Indeed, they were embedded in the class structure of twentieth-century Britain. I discovered the same working principles when I went to work for commercial television in the nineties. Though purporting to be anti-elitist and demotic, nearly all the executives were privately schooled and Oxbridge educated as many News International staff still are. With a few exceptions, the people who made the decisions about what a popular audience should watch would never be seen in a room with one of the mass consumers they catered to. They didn't much care for the content they produced either. Though they would use the popularity of their products to berate friends and rivals who made less money, the bosses of commercial television and the popular press would often let on how they despised the audience who lined their pockets.

There had been great innovators in the democratisation of news and culture in the glory days of the *Daily Express*, the *Daily Mirror* and the new kinds of TV journalism and drama of Granada Television in the sixties and seventies. But many of the people I've worked with since that heyday, whether at HIT entertainment after the death of the Muppets creator Jim Henson, or under Nick Elliott when the regional system of ITV commissioning was being centralised, merely rode on the back of previous innovations. Caught between a licence to print money by raiding the public's worst taste and a genuine belief (as Murdoch seemed to have in his student days) in a media which could combine both quality and popularity, many of these people I met were angry. The battle between low commercial instincts and high public service ideals has been one of the most active fronts in Britain's culture wars over the last three decades. Often the combat zone could be found within a single brain, in which the cynicism conceals a disappointed social romanticism, which makes the cynicism all the more bitter and defensive.

As much of the salacious, mendacious and stupid behaviour depicted in the 'News of the Screws' confirmed, the attempt to appeal to the man and woman in the street contained a barely disguised disappointment – almost a kind of disgust – about what the ordinary Briton was really like. To a certain extent, the Tory masters of the media did fulfil a public service – for themselves – by keeping the masses ignorant and distracted with bread, breasts and circuses, so that the more important affairs of state and entitled money-making could go on unhindered. For all his anti-establishment shtick, Murdoch's first venture into British publishing only kicked that paradox of class further down Fleet Street and into the gutter. He didn't attempt to change the dynamics of British snobbery and its powerful inverse, he just accentuated it. Like his father, he could flatter to deceive old family money and he quickly reneged on his promise to the Carr family. But his next attempt to be part of a rising 'Room at the Top' meritocratic generation backfired badly.

One of Murdoch's earliest *News of the World*'s exclusives was the publication of the memoirs of Christine Keeler, the call girl at the heart of the Profumo scandal earlier in the sixties. But this was no scoop and the recycling of old scandalous news, an apparent tilting at fallen icons, undermined the initial welcome impression that Murdoch would be a breath of fresh air in the stuffy world of press ownership, something on a par with his compatriots Clive James or Germaine Greer. Murdoch managed to alienate both the old noblesse oblige Tory generation with his treatment of Carr and Profumo and the new up and coming sixties icons with his mercenary downmarket appeal. The latter led David Frost to humiliate Murdoch on a London Weekend Television (LWT) interview and *Private Eye* to coin the 'Dirty Digger' sobriquet, which has stuck ever since.

Whether out of revenge or mere insurance, Murdoch made a move to take over LWT, the broadcasting station which held the capital's monopoly weekend licence, but in 1970 was financially shaky. The cross-ownership rules entailed that, though he might have had a holding, Murdoch could not interfere in the actual programming of the channel. Murdoch promised the regulator, the Independent Television Association, that he would abide by the rules, but as soon as he had his placemen on the board, he started attending programming meetings. Challenged about his undertakings to the regulator and rules on cross-ownership Murdoch merely demurred according to Page (2011), 'Yes, but that's before I came.'

There are harbingers of the phone-hacking scandal in the subsequent outcry. In Parliament MPs upbraided Murdoch's downmarket tendencies and raised questions about whether he was a 'fit and proper person' by the stipulations of the television licence. Bernard Levin complained about the toothless regulator. David Frost used his clout and LWT stock holdings to block him. A past master of using public platforms to attack commercial rivals, Murdoch smarted at being outgunned and outwitted and complained of 'character assassination'. He would soon turn this episode into another round of 'Rupert versus the Establishment', claiming he was victimised for resurrecting the Profumo scandal and challenging those in power. As Murdoch told Alexander Cockburn in an interview for the *Village Voice* in 1976:

> *I just wasn't prepared to join the system ... Maybe I just have an inferiority complex about being an Australian. My wife accuses me of this sometime ... It's very difficult not at some point to be sucked into the establishment. The last thing I wanted was to be a bloody press lord. I think when people start taking knighthoods and peerages it really is telling the wold you've sold out.*

Notice the sixties language of middle-class rebellion, the fear of being 'sucked into the establishment' and 'selling out'. The irony is so heavy it points to some qualitative change in Murdoch's conservatism. There's no longer any regard to the old conservative Burkean traditions of stability and continuity. Murdoch adopts a more American language of New Class populism: a right-wing radicalism which would be a growing part of the counter-revolution in the US, where he then lived, and which borrowed much of the insurrectionary language of the left. Like many neo-cons in the US and many Thatcherites in the UK, this movement could claim many former left-wing thinkers among its founders: Paul Johnson and Woodrow Wyatt in the UK, or Richard Perle, Norman Podhoretz and Paul Wolfowitz in the US. Most of these neo-liberal neoconservatives began their early adult lives on the left and were described, in Irving Kristol's words, as 'liberals mugged by reality'. They were also normally influenced by doctrinaire theoretical Marxism – a bit like Murdoch in his college rooms with his bust of Lenin. The big difference is that, where the left describes the 'creative destruction' of capitalism in which 'all that's solid melts into air' in sorrow, they evoke it with relish.

The irony of a millionaire legatee media mogul talking in the language of radical rebellion hasn't escaped attention. It was captured in the vivid imagery of former Australian prime minister Paul Keating when he described the anti-establishment right-wingers like Murdoch 'cloaking their well-nourished frames in the rags of the powerless'. But it's important that Murdoch's rhetoric is portrayed as a *cultural* war rather an economic one. By any measure of redistribution of wealth, the last forty years of neo-liberal dominance in the US and UK has seen average wage levels flatline or decrease in real terms, with rising inequality as a result. The cultural levelling Murdoch seemed to celebrate has, in economic terms, led to quite the opposite.

Another self-serving myth from Murdoch's early years in the UK, which has been used to mitigate his growing monopoly control of the market, is that he revolutionised and reinvigorated the tabloid market in the late sixties and early seventies. On the technical side, from the News International move to Wapping, through Murdoch's big surge into satellite and pay-TV, to his disastrous forays into the internet, the innovation disappears on closer inspection. In simple circulation terms, as Bruce Page points out, Murdoch did not stop the slide of the *News of the World* readership. In the first decade of his ownership the Sunday tabloid lost a quarter of its readership and had declined by 1979 to under five million (Page, 2011, p. 109). If Murdoch's innovation is going to hang on anything it's not on the expanded circulation of his Sunday tabloid. The real innovation lay elsewhere.

Much more central to the British version of the Murdoch myth is the acquisition of the ailing daily *Sun* later in 1969. The tabloid had been haemorrhaging millions a year and News Ltd bought it for a mere £800,000. The *Sun* had been a working-class stalwart, originating from the once best-selling *Daily Herald*, which was heavily tied to the Union movement. At first Murdoch did little to change its politics and basically followed the lead of his veteran editor, Larry Lamb. Bruce Page contends that the design and tone was basically purloined from Lamb's former paper, the *Daily Mirror* (the real Mecca for young journalists like Roy Greenslade who saw the *Sun* merely as a stepping stone to the *Mirror*, which he would later edit). A visual comparison makes Page's point.

While the *Sun* looks like a pale imitation of Christiansen's *Daily Express* from the fifties the *Mirror* looks decades ahead, with a new 'red top' colour and vibrancy that marks it out as part of the era of Andy Warhol and pop art. Under the leadership of Hugh Cudlipp, the *Daily Mirror* had also been the best-selling daily and market leader for nearly twenty years. Though Cudlipp never actually edited the paper he was, according to Greenslade, 'the inspiration behind the whole concept, the design, the campaigns, the promotional stunts and the gimmicks that involved reader participation. He also wrote many of its iconic headlines' (Greenslade, 2009).

A year later, in 1970, the *Sun* had transformed itself through a full redesign: but into what? It's so obvious. The white sans serif text on red masthead and the full caps headline on the right-hand column. The use of underlining, sub-boxes and constant scaling of the text size leads you to turn the front page over.

The update confirms Page's point: Murdoch's new *Sun* was really pirated from its main competitor. Alongside the slavish plagiarism of the front page, the other major innovation would be the topless 'Page Three Girl' introduced the same year. Inserting soft porn erotica in a daily tabloid might have done much to attract attention (a *Private Eye* front page caption 'Thanks for the Mammaries') and publicity – the old tactic of the *succès de scandale* – but it hardly supports a claim to revolutionary change. Once again, the shiny surface thing can distract us from more important changes underneath.

Murdoch's real innovation at this time was in form rather than content: amortising cost savings by using the massive *News of the World* presses in Bouverie Street to print millions of copies every day, instead of just once a week for the Sunday tabloid. Murdoch also adeptly deployed television advertising – a cross-promotional innovation he'd learned in Australia – to great effect to market his 'soaraway *Sun*' to the square-eyed TV-centred readership of the seventies. Advertising heavily targeted the TV soaps such as *Coronation Street* which (unlike the US) dominated the prime-time as well as daytime schedules.

In this instance the strict standards of balance and diversity that dominated broadcast regulation in the UK actually created an opportunity for Murdoch. As Chippindale and Horrie explain in *Stick it Up Your Punter!*, 'The *Sun*'s role had been to provide material such as soft porn, wall-to-wall football coverage and wild political bias, which were absent from British television before its '80s deregulation (1990, p. 485). Though the design was stolen from the *Mirror*, Murdoch and Lamb made a cross-platform leap that made the *Sun* the first popular newspaper for the 'television age'.

It was a phenomenal success. In ten years the *Sun*'s readership quadrupled and overtook the *Daily Mirror* to reach four million by the time of Thatcher's election in 1979. There's no doubt about the immense cultural and political impact of the *Sun* on Britain and the lessons Murdoch learned there would be replicated, with varying success, across the world. As we will see '*Sun*speak' was a powerful form of discourse that would have an important impact on the politics of the 1980s. But the *Sun* did not re-invent the tabloid market or arrest its decline. Indeed, the readership didn't expand. Those extra four million readers came at the expense of the *Daily Mirror* and the *Daily Express*, both now declining from their glory days.

Gaining a market share like this was still a huge achievement and Murdoch's business acumen in outwitting his competitors deserves credit in itself. But the idea that he recreated and saved the popular British tabloid is bunk: he cornered it. But the victors of history get to rewrite it, especially those who buy ink by the barrel, so the Murdoch myth about his meritocratic tabloid origins still dominates the mainstream.

ENEMIES WITHIN

For all the soaraway success of the *Sun* through the late seventies and eighties a strange anomaly remains. Though he would dominate the British press throughout this era, Murdoch had actually left the country by 1973 and his control over Fleet Street was from a distance – either by telephone or during whirlwind impromptu visits as he toured his growing commercial interests now flung far across the world, from Sydney to New York.

There have been various explanations of the move to the US. The furore over the attempt to regurgitate the Profumo scandal via the Keeler diaries allegedly led to Murdoch and his second wife Anna feeling ostracised from society. However, Anna always claimed that the murder of Muriel McKay, wife of a News Corp executive, kidnapped under the mistaken belief she was Anna Murdoch, made her feel uncomfortable living full-time in London.

To add to the sense of physical insecurity, we should remember that post-colonial feeling of national insecurity was also a key factor in outward migration from Britain in the seventies. Some left for the bastions of white privilege in places like South Africa. Others looked to the US to restore the feeling of supremacy now that Britain was no longer the world superpower. Among the various groups who felt British decline most acutely, Murdoch's social network in London is particularly prominent. Most of the key members of the right-wing 'Mayfair set' he socialised with from his London town house – Sir Jimmy Goldsmith, Jim Slater, Tiny Rowland, David Stirling (the man who founded the SAS), John Aspinall and Lord Lucan – would leave in the late seventies, often under the shadows of financial scandal, and in Lord Lucan's case, much worse: on the run for murdering his nanny.

Yet, in another sense, Murdoch wasn't really relocating, no matter where his domestic base would be. As his then-wife Anna said eight years later 'We moved base. We never really left England' ('Who's Afraid of Rupert Murdoch?', 1981). With 'bases' in dozens of different time-zones since the sixties, Murdoch has never really lived anywhere. He would maintain a hectic jet-set lifestyle for the next forty years, with its attendant grumpy jet-lag: in sheer terms of air miles he's probably accumulated a couple of trips to the moon; the now defunct supersonic jet, Concorde, was really made for him. Through those decades, Murdoch has really only been a citizen of News Corp nation, a transnational corporate state (see Chapter 8). His restlessness and social mobility has been transformed into geographical dislocation: the vagrancy of the super-rich.

Though the first half of Murdoch's career can be seen as an attempt to escape the legacy of colonialism, there are some interesting parallels between the virtual empire he has created and the British 'empire' he was born into. Murdoch accentuated the class warfare of the society he had chosen to leave: White Van Man against Loony Lefty; Spongers versus Council Home Buyers; Upmarket versus Downmarket; Populars versus Unpopulars. In the case of the Wapping dispute, or the flying pickets of the miners' strike, these culture wars expressed and sometimes aggravated real pitched battles taking place on Britain's streets. But coming from a media mogul with an international imperium, this tactic of sowing of dissent looks very familiar.

By the late seventies an absentee landlord, enamoured by Nixon, Murdoch controlled his British dominions with the familiar strategy of divide and rule. For decades Murdoch would play British political leaders off against each other – Heath, Thorpe, Foot, Thatcher, Heseltine, Kinnock, Major, Blair, Brown, Cameron. During the first six months of the Leveson Inquiry, when it emerged that the coalition government was not going to play by the old rules, Murdoch started encouraging Alex Salmond, the leader of the Scottish Independence Party.

> Alex Salmond clearly most brilliant politician in U.K. Gave Cameron back of his hand this week. Loved by Scots.

> Let Scotland go and compete. Everyone would win.

Figure 4.3 Tweets from @rupertmurdoch, 19 February 2012

The man who did so much to define modern jingoism, whose papers had so berated the interference of the European Union in British sovereignty was ready – at the drop of a hack – to encourage the break-up of Great Britain.

5

9 July 2011
Fortress Wapping

Over this weekend in July, as journalists put to bed the last edition of *News of the World*, News International's headquarters came under siege in a way they had not done since the eighties. This time the ugly red brick compound at Wapping, with its double perimeter fence, razor wire and prison-like appearance, wasn't surrounded by thousands of trade unionists and police: News International's headquarters were besieged by journalists and camera crews from around the world covering the widening scandal. Once again Fortress Wapping became the locus for an economic and cultural storm that would have historic significance in the life of the British nation. A dividing line, first drawn there twenty-five years ago, was coming full circle.

AGGRESSIVE VICTIMHOOD

This was the weekend that Rupert Murdoch flew in to manage the phone-hacking crisis. The landing of his private Boeing 737 at Luton airport was covered by 24-hour news stations as if he were a head of state, a released hostage or a national football team returning home after heady foreign victories or heavy defeat. Murdoch's crisis management mainly consisted of supporting his son, being snapped in the back of his limo in shorts and most memorably – when asked what his priority was – gesturing to his protégé Rebekah Brooks and saying 'That one'.

Murdoch's loyalty to the CEO of News International was touching, until you took the time to consider that hundreds of other employees were losing their jobs, partly in an effort to save hers. However, the 81-year-old's paternal protectiveness towards Brooks illustrates how Murdoch was at the same time both old-fashioned and unorthodox. Though many of his downmarket newspapers displayed a boorish attitude to women, often verging on misogyny (and as a rare female tabloid editor

Brooks had attracted more derogatory comments than most), Murdoch's encour-agement of her through her twenty-year career at News International shows that when it comes to sexism – as with matters of race – Murdoch's tolerances are often more liberal than those he projects on his audiences.

Despite her prestige, wealth and marriage to the TV actor Ross Kemp, de-spite even her legendary off-handedness to employees, Brooks exuded an air of pale vulnerability throughout her dizzy ascent up the hierarchy of Fleet Street. Murdoch called her 'larrikin', an Antipodean phrase to describe someone who is both otherworldly and great fun. Her charms led to close personal friendships with three successive British prime ministers, not to mention an array of celebri-ties, senior police officers and lawmakers. And this is one of the occasions when I can confirm the biographical fallacy, because Brooks is one of the few major players in the Murdoch extended family saga I have actually met.

It was a brief but completely revealing encounter at the Hay-on-Wye book festival in 2006, when she was still Rebekah Wade, and a year after she was held for a night in a police cell for allegedly assaulting her husband, Ross Kemp. I ar-rived at a late-night party only to bump into Rebekah on the dance floor. She first chatted with a friend of mine with such a touchy-feely friendliness that I thought they were old friends (they'd never met). And then for some inexplicable reason I found myself dancing and chatting with her.

It was quite remarkable. I've worked in the British media for over twenty years and it's extremely cliquish. At most social events the powerful ones are aloof, guarding their drinks and opinions carefully, making sure they're seen with the right people and that their emotional unavailability leaves admirers begging for more. But here was one of the most powerful people in the British media scene, talking away to a complete stranger in a way that made me feel like the important one. Brooks complained that everyone at the festival hated her (it was sponsored in those days by the *Guardian*) and then we sat, drinking and talking in a corner, only disturbed by a rather ferocious dark haired assistant who clearly didn't like me and the fact that Brooks apparently did. The about-to-be installed Chief Executive of News International was friendly, funny, tactile and quite endearingly indiscreet, telling me about her brief night in the cells after the police were called to a 'domestic dispute' with her then husband. As she told me that Murdoch was waiting for her outside the cells that morning in a car, her eyes misted over; she was almost in tears.

That this same woman managed to charm three successive British prime min-isters with clashing personalities and interests – Blair, Brown and Cameron – makes complete sense. Charismatic politicians like Bill Clinton have the ability to make you feel like the most important person in the world when you meet them, but Brooks's talent was more subtle. She made you feel important, interesting and aroused an urge to protect, a bit like a red top version of Marilyn Monroe.

One can speculate about all kinds of preconditions for this reversed charisma: a borderline personality which turns empathy into a form of victimhood; the narcissism that charms other people for useful ends. But the Machiavellian motivations don't quite work in this instance, because – as an obscure writer – I had exactly zero-use value. If Samuel Johnson's dictum is true and the measure of a person's morality is how they treat someone who can do them absolutely no good, then Rebekah Wade (as she was then) on that occasion, and towards me, was a pretty kind moral person.

We're back to the tyranny of intimacy – the tabloid myth – that personal morality indicates political worth, that a person's private life is necessarily an indicator of their role in public life. There are too many instances of great politicians with dubious personal morals – from Lloyd George to Bill Clinton – to make this a facile leap. This is also why the typical left-wing personal attacks on Murdoch and his lieutenants have not only been ineffective, but also buy into *Sun*speak tabloid assumptions. It's worth restating for the record here that I have no personal animosity to Rupert Murdoch or his children. I know people who are either friends with, or have closely collaborated with, James, Rebekah and Elisabeth. I've heard many stories of Rupert's personal kindness and charm and loyalty to employees hit by tragedy or illness. As this one encounter shows, good people by Samuel Johnson's standard can – through social pressure and institutional power – end up oblivious to the bubble they live in and do radically bad things to defend it.

It was early in the morning by the time we stopped talking: the party was winding down and the music stopped. I think we exchanged phone numbers at some point, but to be honest, my memory is occluded by alcohol. One thing I do remember though, vividly, not long before we went our different ways. Brooks's assistant had spotted a photographer snapping us on a digital camera from the corner of the room by the door. By this point in the evening, mainly due to drink and Brooks's tactile tendencies (but also due to the protective streak she elicited) I guess I might have had my arm around her. Brooks got up and told me that if he saw those photos 'Ross would kill you' and went over to talk to the bearded young photographer. I couldn't hear what they said, but she seemed to be charming him too. Within a couple of minutes she returned with the entire flash drive of his camera, probably all the shots he'd taken that day.

I shook my head and asked: 'How did you do that? What did you say to him? Did you say that if you don't give me that you'll never work again?' Brooks shrugged. I continued: 'Or did you say to him if you give me that, you'll never have to worry about work again?'

She laughed, but never answered. But that's the moment I realised that Murdoch's reflected power was like a distortion field. This kind of power changes everything around you, sometimes visibly, sometimes not, until your view of the world is skewed by the lensing effect of adoration, antipathy and influence. Like celebrities, media power brokers can sometimes dominate the room and become the cynosure of all eyes. But unlike the stars, the media moguls control the mechanisms of fame and can adopt a cloak of invisibility when they want. They can turn it on and off like a light switch. Rare indeed in these days, they have the exceptional ability to enjoy both power and privacy. This stealth celebrity is something I'd never quite seen before, just as I'd never met a powerful person who had replaced the sociopath's manipulating charm with a borderline personality's ability to turn themselves into powerful victims you feel you want to protect.

However, the personal here does become political. If you look back over Brooks's rise to become Queen of Fleet Street, it has mainly been predicated on a form of victimhood. Her great campaigns over children – whether through hacking the phone of Milly Dowler, 'Sarah's Law' and naming and shaming paedophiles on the front pages of the *News of the World* or the forced revelation that Gordon Brown's four-month-old son suffered from cystic fibrosis – all aggressively pursued stories of celebrity victims, turning victims into celebrities, just as they had on occasion turned celebrities into victims.

Maybe that is why I never called back.

STOCKHOLM SYNDROME

The weekend the *News of the World* closed would be accompanied by much mythologising about its past and a legitimate soul searching about the future of the British press – understandable considering Murdoch owned a third of it. Many journalists I know, disgusted at the phone-hacking revelations, and understanding that parts of the press needed a thorough cleaning up, were still worried by the precipitous closure of the world's best-selling English-language paper. What else would Murdoch sell? What about the loss-making Times Newspaper Group? How radical would any changes have to be to cauterise the toxicity of the Murdoch brand? And what did that mean for the staff and their careers? Their mortgages, children, school fees and professional future? To this extent the closing of the *News of the World* was an effective example of shock and awe tactics, instilling psychological terror among the citizens of Fleet Street.

The resultant access of acute personal anxiety had an impact on many journalists, regardless of whether they had worked for News International or not – though given the number of UK papers Murdoch owned, the chances that they had or did were quite high. If Murdoch withdrew from UK publishing, the knock-on effects for the whole sector could be dire: fewer opportunities to move or rise up the chain and the threat of competition and undercutting for existing jobs in an already shrinking industry, challenged by unpaid bloggers and free-to-view journalism. At the time I sympathised, but as this level of reasoning carried over to the following year, it seemed more and more like partisan special pleading and undermined the much vaunted claim that Fleet Street was the watchdog of the nation's liberty.

If there's any remaining doubt that by this time News International had gained a position of monopolistic power, this widespread anxiety of journalists should allay it. Murdoch's company so dominated the news world that friends in unrelated business magazines felt threatened. The arguments ran (and still run) like this: from 'How would you feel if you couldn't make your mortgage payments?' to 'How would you feel if he sold *The Times* to a Russian oligarch?' Whether they liked or loathed Murdoch's politics or business practices, the majority of media people I spoke to during that time were like victims of a Stockholm Syndrome: they relied on Murdoch for all his faults. From being their captor and bully he had now become their protection against a cruel unknowable world.

As Upton Sinclair once remarked: 'It's difficult to get a man to understand something, when his salary depends on his not understanding it.'

The real outside threat that people talked about, but none could counter, was the precipitous decline in advertising revenues in traditional print newspapers and magazines. With internet access now reaching 90 per cent of the British population (one of the highest penetrations in the world) an increasing number of readers were going online to get their news and entertainment. In 2008 the media analyst Claire Enders had predicted the print ad market would decline by a fifth, with newspaper display ads down 21 per cent and classifieds down 19 per cent. This same crisis was the context of the 2010 conference I spoke at where (apart from the consensus between Tory advisers and News International journalists that the BBC should be shrunk) the main topic was the new *Times* and *Sunday Times* paywalls and whether they would work.

The 'problem of free' – and how to get people to pay for journalistic content while they could get it for nothing online – was having the same effect on news publishing that Napster and digital file-sharing had on the music industry years before: destroying the business model. This is the real context of James Murdoch's 2009 MacTaggart lecture, *The Absence of Trust*. James's attack on Britain's public service broadcaster was really a demonstration of the crisis in the commercial sector. His grandfather, Keith Murdoch, opposed the formation the Australian Broadcasting Corporation (ABC) in the thirties; his father Rupert had attacked both ABC and the BBC throughout his career, now James was following in the patriarchal tradition and characterising the BBC as 'chilling' and a threat to freedom – at least his freedom to make a fat profit.

Of course the family copy of *Nineteen Eighty-Four* was unshelved again and the Orwellian threat of authoritarianism revisited – an even more spurious argument on this occasion as James had spent a large part of his News Corp career flattering the Chinese communist government (see Chapter 8). His words were hardly measured:

> *There is a land-grab, pure and simple, going on – and in the interests of a free society it should be sternly resisted. The land grab is spear-headed by the BBC. The scale and scope of its current activities and future ambitions is chilling.*

(MURDOCH, 2009)

In retrospect, the speech did mark the beginning of land-grab – by News Corp. The suggestion that public service broadcasting was 'crowding out' private innovation was like a virtual equivalent of land enclosures of the eighteenth century: expropriating the 'commons' for a private profit. Under intense pressure to generate digital revenues for News International papers, the first port of call was to demolish a competitor – in this case the BBC's successful online news service: 'it is essential for the future of independent digital journalism that a fair price can be charged for news' (ibid.).

Deciding the fair price for news is harder than you think and as we'll see, the history of papers is quite counterintuitive in this regard. However, if the rational analysis was lacking in James's speech, the political logic wasn't; within a few months of gaining power in 2010, the Tory-led coalition government would literally decimate public service broadcasting in the UK, shrinking the BBC's budget by 16 per cent overnight. And before we get lost in the commercial arguments about fair prices and competition, which jar somewhat with News Corp's ability to circumvent monopoly law, anti-competitive pricing and mounting allegations sabotage and piracy against rivals, one crucial factor has been overlooked in the younger Murdoch's techno-libertarianism. Accurate information is fundamental to a democracy. Like education or law, a free-to-view source of news has underpinned the civil societies of most Western societies. In short, an element of news (though certainly not all or indeed the majority of it) constitutes a public good which cannot just be ruled by the profit motive. This may distort part of the market – just as socialised healthcare has a 'chilling' effect on private provision – but is not the same as 'chilling' free speech.

When I pointed this out at the conference a senior *Times* journalist replied plaintively: 'What do you want me to do – work for nothing?' (British–American Project, 2010). The complaint seems valid, until you consider that many services are delivered free at the point of use and yet the deliverers get paid. Teachers, doctors, priests and police officers don't starve. Scientific researchers adhere to the free exchange of ideas without living in complete penury. This is true of 'for-profit' institutions too. Many journalists working in commercial TV and free newspapers get compensated handsomely for work that is free at the point of use to the consumer. The counterintuitive truth about newspaper publishing through most of the twentieth century is that most of the content has not been paid for directly by the consumers.

As Clay Shirky has repeatedly explained, readers rarely pay the salaries of journalists. With cover prices for *The Times* at 10p on Mondays (during its predatory pricing era) or the *Sun on Sunday* at 50p, it's a simple economic fact that sales revenues from subscriptions to most publications barely account for print and distribution costs, averaging around only a fifth of newspaper income. What the modern commercial newspaper has done is assemble a mixture of diverse elements – crosswords, parliamentary reports, crime stories, horoscopes, sport, promotions, sleaze, foreign reportage, lifestyle and sex tips, political editorials, photojournalism, soft porn – and then bundled them together in different versions to gain enough readers to make their advertising revenues cover staff costs and profits.

It's the advertisers who pay for content. Of course, circulation figures are important for the advertisers and increasingly they want tight profiling of demographics for their products and brands. The crisis in newsprint both here and in the US does not come directly from the decline of readership (which has been falling year-on-year since the sixties) but the devastation of traditional advertising models. US newspaper advertising has fallen every year since 2006. In 2009 it fell by nearly 30 per cent, exacerbated by the continuing global economic crisis. But even in 2012 when the US started growing again, with its car industry recovering and Wall Street stocks rallying, newspaper advertising fell 7.3 per cent to $24 billion. This was easily outstripped by one single organisation, Google, whose advertising revenue for 2011 was $38 billion.

Misunderstanding the nature of the problem in the news market leads to some bizarre and counterproductive solutions. Attacking the BBC or the internet for providing stuff for free or trying to substitute lost income with paywalls or monthly subscriptions (with the exception of dedicated financial news services like the *Financial Times*) has done little to offset the decline of the traditional revenues. This is massive technological, commercial and eventually a social shift to be explored in the penultimate chapter.

Much of the Stockholm Syndrome in Fleet Street caused by Murdoch – the journalists' co-dependent fear and admiration for their monopoly captor, their anger about the investigation of phone hacking and police bribes, an intense irritation with the proceedings of the Leveson Inquiry – can be explained by this cold wind blowing in from cyberspace. The irony is that many of those who talk about preserving loss-making papers such as *The Times*, often celebrate the effects of disruptive technology and social change when it either benefits them or hurts others.

These same journalists, leader writers and columnists who talk about the need to preserve a Murdoch subsidy for their jobs, had criticised the print unions for their Luddite attitudes, restrictive practices and aversion to innovation. These same people still urge other parts of the media – music, photography, film, TV – to live with the effects of the digital revolution, even if it means a loss of jobs, salary or status, while deploring the same for themselves. They berate other industries or public services for not supplanting labour with technology; health care doesn't need so many carers, as Murdoch recently suggested, new software can replace many teachers in schools. Those who praise innovation and 'creative destruction' elsewhere are often the most reluctant to see the writing on the wall when it comes to their own jobs. Who are the Luddites now?

For Brooks, despite all of Murdoch's assurances of protecting his top news executive in the UK, the writing was on the wall as soon as the *News of the World* logo was unscrewed from the Wapping gatehouse.

WEDGE ISSUES

Just as it would be hard to write about American politics over the first decade of the millennium without invoking the influence of Murdoch's Fox News network, it is impossible to understand the history of Britain in the eighties without referring to Murdoch's Fleet Street tabloids – particularly the daily *Sun*.

Though hard to imagine in retrospect, the epoch-making election of Margaret Thatcher in 1979 wasn't so obviously momentous at the time. This was the first election I was old enough to vote in and – apart from the novelty of a female political leader – most of my punk-influenced friends, bored by the yo-yos of the two party system, were inclined to vote against the outgoing Labour government. For the wider electorate Labour seemed incapable, like the previous Tory administrations of Edward Heath, of reversing the industrial decline that had led Britain to be called the 'sick man of Europe'. The Labour Party itself was riven by factionalism – old style corporatists at war with left-wing entryists and an increasingly disaffected group of social democrats who would soon break away and form the SDP. Out of protest, hope or mere speculation, many left-wing intellectuals and centrist independents voted for Margaret Thatcher, from Harold Pinter to Harry Evans.

At this point the *Sun* was just taking over from the *Daily Mirror* in terms of readership. It had already manufactured an urban myth that the incumbent Labour Prime Minister Jim Callaghan had said 'Crisis? What crisis?' on a foreign trip during the industrial troubles which were billed as a 'winter of discontent'. But by now it had mastered a spirit of populist exasperation that governed the appeal on the front page of the *Sun* on the eve of the election, which by all accounts Murdoch dictated himself:

Figure 5.1 Sun, *May 1979*

The roots of the Sun are planted deep among the working class.

We are proud to have a working class leadership. The LARGEST working class readership of any daily paper.

We are equally proud of the fact that we have more young people readers than any of our contemporaries.

Both young people and traditionally Labour supporters tend to be idealists. And The Sun is an idealistic newspaper.

We firmly believe in that system of government which offers the greatest good to the greatest number of people.

That is precisely why, on this momentous occasion, we firmly advise our readers to VOTE TORY

This talk of working class 'idealism' is new – influenced by what Murdoch had learned in the US, where he had been based for six years, and whose *New York Post* had turned political coverage in the financial and cultural capital into personal exposures and knockabout attacks. Ronald Reagan would be elected the year after Thatcher and it was around the same time – when Larry Lamb left the editorship of his daily tabloid – that Murdoch would perfect the British equivalent of the rhetoric of American right-wing talk radio and the rising tide of shock-jocks: *Sun*speak.

The roots of modern American right-wing populism go back to the fifties and Senator Joseph McCarthy's use of radio talk shows to decry the Washington elites and smear them for being complicit with communism. One of McCarthy's most dedicated followers (for a while) was Richard Milhous Nixon and he turned the trade in anti-establishment rhetoric into a TV phenomenon in his famous 'Checkers' speech of 1952. To divert attention from a slush fund scandal in his election campaign, Nixon addressed millions of television viewers with an emotional, almost evangelical, appeal to the values of what he would later call the hard-working 'silent majority'. In what would be a typical manoeuvre for the rest of his career, Nixon made the political personal by constantly bringing up his own humble background and lifestyle, in which his wife Pat wore plain 'cloth coats' instead of the Democratic Party establishment, whose wives wore mink.

In his book *Rupert Murdoch: An Investigation into Political Power*, David McKnight argues that Nixon, more than Thatcher or Reagan, is really Murdoch's political model. First he dismisses the prevalent notion that money-making is his main focus and goal: 'For Murdoch, politics is equally as important as business. Being a political insider and an activist is supremely important to his personality and his outlook.' But while from his student days through the first two decades of his career Murdoch had vacillated between various parties and political mentors his ideology was crystallised by his late thirties. It was a meeting with the American president that hypostasised it. As David Marr goes on to explain in the *Monthly*:

> *Visiting Washington in 1972, the young tycoon fell under the spell of Richard Nixon and was never the same again. The flip-flops ended. He had once sung Fidel Castro's praises, cultivated crusty old Arthur Calwell and used his new national broadsheet, the* Australian, *to demand 'Black Jack' McEwan succeed the drowned Harold Holt. Crazy stuff. He had swung his UK titles behind Labour and his Australian papers behind the rising Gough Whitlam. Then he went to Washington and turned hard right. Nixon – and later Ronald Reagan, Murdoch's enduring love – gave him the politics he's pursued and the rhetoric he's used ever since.*

(MARR, 2012)

It's worth a quick detour to grasp the fundamental tenets of Nixonian politics. In the sixties, after the crushing defeat of Republican challenger Barry Goldwater in 1964 and President Lyndon B. Johnson's landmark civil rights legislation, Nixon came to rely on a 'Southern Strategy'. The route to electoral victory was no longer through the old Republican centrists on the coasts or Midwest. A vast pool of voters, formerly Democrat, were now disaffected by cultural change. They were god-fearing, gun-toting and – to say the least – wary of the consequences of racial desegregation. Nixonian political strategy, devised to a large extent by Pat Buchanan and a certain Roger Ailes (who would run Murdoch's Fox News Network thirty years later) was based around the concept of 'positive polarisation', targeting the white blue-collar voters in the south, appealing to their resentment and disaffection by focusing on contentious areas of cultural identity – wedge issues such as gun ownership, religious affiliation, sexuality and race. The result would haunt America and eventually cause near civil war in the Republican Party as the country ended up in the cultural polarisation, and political gridlock, of the Blue states versus the Red states and finally the insurrectionary 'Tea Party' movement.

I lived in America in the early eighties and, despite the recent history of Vietnam and the civil unrest of the sixties, the political polarisation had not yet frozen into hard attitudes it displays today. I was taught by liberals but lived with centrist Republicans, visited Mormons and stayed with a leading Republican attorney, Howard Liebengood, who had been a key advisor during the congressional investigations into Nixon during the Watergate hearings. Despite the massive upheavals of the civil rights movement, desegregation and the Vietnam War protests, party allegiance in the US was more fluid than I was used to. Democrats and Republicans would not only date each other, but cross the divides of the House and Senate with surprising ease.

When I returned to Britain in the early eighties, my homeland seemed deeply polarised by contrast: a country in which Tory and Labour supporters would rarely mix socially, let alone date each other. This remained my experience through the eighties and only began to heal sometime in the following decade, thanks to the more ameliorative governments of Major and Blair. When, in the late nineties, I started visiting America regularly again, the political temperament of the two countries seemed to have precisely reversed. America now appeared to me as divided as Britain a decade before: Republicans and Democrats would barely talk to each other, let alone date each other. If, as Michael Wolff suggests, Murdoch and his Fox News Network helped polarise America into a 'two-nation state', perhaps he had a trial run with Britain first.

It's certainly possible to see a British version of the 'Southern Strategy' in the politics of Thatcher. It was a psephological cliché that Thatcher's route to a permanent majority in parliament was in attracting the skilled or semi-skilled manual workers of London, the Midlands and the South-East. By concentrating on these she could forget the Labour strongholds the North, Wales and Scotland. Learned from the US, this strategy of focusing on the swing votes of Basildon or Ohio would be very divisive for national coherence, if not for marginal electoral success. Many Thatcherite policies, which entailed deindustrialisation of the coal and steel areas of the North, or the shipbuilding centres of the Clyde and the Tyne, were predicated on losing votes there, but getting them elsewhere. In this respect Murdoch's *Sun*speak, like the shock-jock talk of Rush Limbaugh, Sean Hannity or Glenn Beck, perfectly targeted the disaffections of the southern English male working-class voter: the 'cheeky chappy' at home with his pint, the breasts of his Page Three girl, his football and pools coupons.

True, the *Sun* and *News of the World* still enjoyed baiting the remnants of the upper classes, particularly if their wealth came from celebrity or nobility; but the anger and disgust was more commonly focused on strangers outside or the lumpenproletariat below, having children in their teens, living on benefits, indulging in drug use and drink-related crime. Despite Murdoch's background, Irish, Scots, Liverpudlians and the Welsh were often lumped into this antipathy. Immigrants came in for special treatment too, especially since Thatcher had blown her Powellite dog-whistle by talking of the country being 'swamped' by immigrants during her election campaign; so too old enemies like the French and the Germans (as Thatcher once said, most of the problems during her lifetime had come from 'mainland Europe'). Underneath the varied rhetoric was a consistent thread which played to the anxieties of blue-collar males, though the irony is not accidental; it was precisely the white working-class manual labourer who was suffering most with structural changes in employment, deregulation and globalisation. The *Sun* distracted this core constituency away from their real economic interests with cultural wedge issues such as race, region, ethnicity and sexuality.

The variants of *Sun*speak and its ability to frame political issues through a form of linguistic programming is worthy of a book in itself. We'll see it in many of the famous key headlines over the next few pages and the logical fallacies and rhetorical tricks of 'The *Sun* Says' leaders. The barbed ideology permeates every level of discourse, right down to subtle shifts in grammar and vocabulary and is not unique to Murdoch's tabloids by any means. An amusing satiric style guide to the *Daily Mail* has more examples of semantic slippage, pointing out how the paper describes how ordinary people 'receive' benefits, while the lower classes 'claim' them and immigrants 'demand' them. When individuals are given government money this is called a 'hand-out'; for a company or corporation it is an 'incentive'. It survives today in the propaganda of Islamophobia, most prevalent in Richard Peppiatt's old paper the *Daily Star*, but also the stock-in-trade of Richard Desmond's *Daily Express*. While in most foreign conflicts or terrorist incidents across the world the combatants are described by personal, ethnic or political tags, for any incident involving the 1.3 billion of the world's population who believe in the various forms of Islam, they are invariably described as 'Muslims'.

In 1981 this confection of resentment and xenophobia needed a new voice and Murdoch soon found someone to express it when he appointed Kelvin MacKenzie to replace Larry Lamb. MacKenzie's political persuasion is best summed up in a comment recorded in Chippindale and Horrie's book *Stick it Up Your Punter!* (the title a play on one of MacKenzie's famous 'Argie Bashing' *Sun* headlines of 1982 – 'Stick it up your Junta'):

> *You just don't understand the readers, do you, eh? He's the bloke you see in the pub, a right old fascist, wants to send the wogs back, buy his poxy council house, he's afraid of the unions, afraid of the Russians, hates the queers and the weirdos and drug dealers. He doesn't want to hear about that stuff [serious news].*

(Chippindale and Horrie, 1990)

Read that again. MacKenzie's sentiments are very different from the nationalist, nativist and xenophobic statements of the generation before. There's a level of self-awareness here. MacKenzie knows he's winding people up; his language is calculated to offend. It's ironic, post-modern and reactionary in the purest sense. There's no programme or a positive set of beliefs, only a set of provocations. In other words, in the language of today's more interactive online discourse, MacKenzie is *trolling* and his transgressions pay a perverse tribute to the achievements of race relations legislation, the legalisation of homosexuality and the rise of workers' rights. Even MacKenzie's most famous headline – 'Gotcha' – was stolen from the title of a BBC television play by the left-wing writer Barrie Keeffe. Like American shock-jocks, *Sun*speak deliberately seeks to inflame by subverting the norms of liberal discourse.

Under MacKenzie's editorship the *Sun*'s tabloid rhetoric reached to its perfect pitch: screaming – as the 4 May 1982 'Gotcha' front page typifies. By appearing to celebrate the sinking of the Argentinian cruiser General Belgrano by a British submarine before the Falkland Island conflict escalated into all-out war, the headline caused an outcry and it was changed to 'Did 1,200 Argies drown?' after it was established that there had been a large number of Argentine sailors killed.

Figure 5.2 Sun, *4 May 1982*

Later, MacKenzie would still revel in its scandalous success: '"Gotcha" was mine, which I'm very proud about. The fact that the enemy were killed to my mind was a bloody good thing and I've never had a moment's loss of sleep over it.' There's more than a little 'protest too much' in this bullish defence. For all his working-class cred, MacKenzie is dependent on offending liberal opinion – *épater la bourgeoisie*. That's the secret of trolling and its original definition (on Usenet) as a form of information interference; it seems to display an opinion, but often it's only a counter opinion, a form of abreaction, designed to stymie the opponent in circumlocutions or emotional outbursts. MacKenzie still confounds his critics to this day with these slippery rhetorical tactics. As Roy Greenslade, the regular *Guardian* columnist who worked with MacKenzie during his editorship, claims:

> *He is a genuine one-off, a complex mixture of unreconstructed chauvinist, unapologetic xenophobe, unacceptable bully, right-wing ranter and self-deprecating comedian. Oddly, in spite of the somewhat negative characteristics, it's the latter which tends to overshadow the rest. You can laugh with him and at him.*
>
> (GREENSLADE, 2007)

If only the choice was that simple. From most accounts of the *Sun* under MacKenzie's leadership, he seemed to be laughing at other people and targeting them with ridicule; according to Chippindale and Horrie (1990), bullying and verbal abuse was rife. MacKenzie constantly berated the more senior journalists as 'old farts' and conducted campaigns against employees who were too liberal or who didn't agree with him. This culture is not unique to the *Sun*: Peppiatt described similar routine humiliations and baiting while working at the *Daily Star* twenty years later, but it seems to be a recurring feature in many of Murdoch's tabloid papers, from the Sydney *Mirror* to the *New York Post*. Under Rebekah Brooks's editorship at the *News of the World* one of the junior staff was forced to dress like Harry Potter all the time, even during the traumatic 9/11 attacks on the World Trade Center. When he complained to the news editor Greg Miskiw how humiliating this was, he was memorably told: 'This is what we do, we go out and destroy other people's lives' (Burden, 2008). (Miskiw signed the £105,000-a-year contract *News of the World* paid to the private detective Glenn Mulcaire and worked under both Brooks and Andy Coulson. He was arrested by detectives from Operation Weeting on 10 August 2011.)

If internally the *Sun* was managed by mockery and fear, the paper vigorously enforced the same techniques externally on whatever politicians, celebrities or groups of people it didn't like. The *Sun* rightly has a reputation for brilliant wit in the occasional headline, but it's a knockabout form of comedy, with a vicious edge that is close to the knuckle. Even the completely fallacious 'Freddie Starr Ate My Hamster' hangs in that strange liminal region between ridiculousness, ridicule and cruelty.

Figure 5.3 *Sun, 13 March 1986*

Often, the headlines went beyond the knuckle right up to the elbow. In 1988, when the TV chat-show host Russell Harty was dying from hepatitis, reporters from the *News of the World* posed as junior doctors in order to see his medical records and installed photographers in a flat in front of his hotel room to snap the dying man. The paper was convinced Harty was dying of AIDS and had conducted a long campaign against the TV host because of his homosexuality. At Harty's funeral, the playwright Alan Bennett spoke out against the paper's hounding of his friend: 'The gutter press finished him.' MacKenzie's *Sun* reacted with a calculated and cruel obloquy:

> *Stress did not kill Russell Harty. The truth is that he died from a sexually transmitted disease.*
>
> *The press didn't give it to him. He caught it from his own choice. And by paying young rent boys he broke the law.*
>
> *Some — like ageing bachelor Mr Bennett — can see no harm in that. He has no family.*
>
> *But what if it had been YOUR son Harty had bedded?*

Not only does this compound a smear with cowardice (the dead can't sue) it marks News International's disturbing record of homophobia. It's been a key element of the *New York Post* which used to allege AIDS could be caught by kissing, a disease whose real aetiology was denied for many years by *The Sunday Times*. This attitude clearly comes from the top. Murdoch himself has gone on record about his dislike for 'poofters' over the years ('Who's Afraid of Rupert Murdoch?', 1981; Wolff, 2008). Brooks would carry this tradition when she caught the openly gay MP Chris Bryant — who had got her to publicly admit before a parliamentary select committee that she had paid police — leaving a reception at the Labour Party Conference the following year. She asked him, 'Oh, Mr Bryant, it's after dark — shouldn't you be on Clapham Common?' (Murphy, 2011). Her soon-to-be ex-husband Ross Kemp retorted 'Shut up, you homophobic cow.' News International tabloids proceeded to 'monster' Bryant for years ahead.

AD PERSONAM

Back in the eighties, various parliamentary committees had looked into the rising tide of unethical journalism: the honey traps, stings and intrusions into privacy, but any recommendations or private member bills usually got blocked by senior Tories. Norman Tebbit warned of any measures that would 'dilute the free press', though in the case of Thatcher's policies, this kind of free press often meant getting a free ride. But the *Sun*'s reaction to the Hillsborough stadium disaster took the default ridicule to a much darker place.

The *Sun*'s coverage of the tragedy in which 96 Liverpool football fans were crushed to death due to bad stadium management and crowd policing is one of the most notorious in British press history. MacKenzie calumniated the innocent victims by falsely claiming that other Liverpool fans had urinated on the police and rescue workers and robbed their own dead; more Southern strategy, more divide and rule class warfare between the have-nots and have-less. Though MacKenzie has rightly been reviled for his toxic take on the tragedy, it now transpires, thanks to papers released for an official inquiry into the disaster, that this line came from the top: Margaret Thatcher.

By the late eighties a string of press outrages forced the government to commission a report into press standards and investigate whether the Press Council (formed after the previous threat of statutory regulation in 1953 and 1962) was competent to deal with media excesses, especially intrusion and privacy. The Home Office committee was led by Sir David Calcutt to look at the law of privacy, the right of reply and what kind of sanctions could be created.

The *Sun*'s response to this inquiry was personally drafted by Murdoch on the twentieth anniversary of his purchase in 1989 and once again he sounds the revolutionary anti-establishment note:

> *The Establishment does not like the Sun. Never has*
>
> *We are so popular they fear our success, since they do not understand the ordinary working man and woman.*
>
> *There is a growing band of people in positions of influence and privilege who want OUR newspaper to suit THEIR private convenience. They wish to conceal from readers' eyes anything that they find annoying or embarrassing.*
>
> *LIVING LIES AND HYPOCRISY ON HIGH CAN HAVE NO PLACE IN OUR SOCIETY*
>
> *IT IS THE STRUGGLE OF ALL THOSE CONCERNED FOR FREEDOM IN BRITAIN.*

The Calcutt Committee published its report in June 1990, concluding that the press should regulate itself through a voluntary body and a full code of conduct. If this system of self-policing failed to work within a year and half, an official tribunal, consisting of a judge and two lay members appointed by the Home Secretary, would be established with the right to regulate complaints. Eager to avoid that statutory oversight, the Press Complaints Commission was established by the major Fleet Street editors in 1991. Since the Leveson Inquiry it's now become apparent that this toothless organisation wasn't even a self-regulator, let alone a regulator, dominated as it was by the interests of newspaper proprietors. Murdoch, as owner of more than a third of the national press, had a powerful say in its conclusions. But rather than tone down its coverage during the period of the Calcutt review, the press went to war with the politicians.

This time, it was even more personal. When, after another tabloid excess, the Conservative minister for culture David Mellor warned the papers they were still under review and 'drinking in the last chance saloon', the response was lethal. The next year the *Sun* ran the story of Mellor's extra-marital affair with the actress Antonia de Sancha, based on illegally recorded conversations, added a fabricated detail that he made love wearing a Chelsea F.C. shirt and alleged the minister had sucked his lover's toes. When Mellor resigned a few months later, the *Sun*'s headline was typically cruel and funny: 'FROM TOE JOB TO NO JOB'.

In his witness statement to the Leveson Inquiry in June 2012, Mellor brought new testimony from Thatcher's circle (like Woodrow Wyatt in his diaries) of the dominance achieved by Murdoch in this era. It's worth quoting his written witness statement at length:

> *I was responsible for media policy, including press regulation, for much of the period from 1983–1992, at the Home Office and at the Department of National Heritage. I was a close witness to the arrangements whereby Rupert Murdoch became the most powerful press baron in the history of the United Kingdom. Murdoch's undeniable love for newspapers made him a buyer when others weren't, while his straightforward right wing populist opinions made him a soulmate for Mrs Thatcher, who at that time, the early 80s, didn't have that many. She was therefore ready to bend the rules to allow him to establish a commanding position over the UK print media, and to take on a position of political influence which was to remain unbroken for more than a quarter of a century ... Whatever benefits Murdoch brought to Mrs Thatcher personally, the Tory party generally, or the UK national interest, he had a huge downside. There's no doubt that he coarsened British newspapers, especially his two red-tops, and dragged other red-tops down with him ... Britain as an entity really doesn't matter to him, which is why the amount of power he had for so long is so regrettable, and the way that he and his minions have chosen to exercise it, often so deplorable. The downside of Murdoch soon became apparent, but there was never any serious prospect of any Government doing anything about the excesses of the tabloids. I spoke of the tabloid press 'drinking in the last chance saloon', but it was more bravado than anything else. And as soon as they had my head on a pole, the chance of anything being done, always minimal, became non-existent.*

> (MELLOR, 2012)

By now the *Sun* seemed to operate with impunity and the humour was beginning to grate. Britain's politics seemed to be controlled by the tabloids and their campaign of personal destruction against any public figure who challenged them or the agenda of their proprietor and editor. Another famous headline of 1992 was the revelation (through the theft of private divorce papers from a solicitor's office) that the leader of the Liberal Democrats, Paddy Ashdown, had had an affair with his secretary five years earlier. Though Ashdown's marriage survived, the Liberal Democrats failed to make any breakthrough in the April election. It's unlikely that the front page splash had any effect on Ashdown's electoral chances, but as Liberal Democrat leaders Vince Cable and Nick Clegg agreed twenty years later, when News International threatened to 'do over' a political party, it was a threat any British politician would take extremely seriously.

Figure 5.4 Sun, *6 April 1992*

The other telling thing about the hatchet jobs on Mellor and Ashdown is not the blatant commercial and political leverage, but the illegal means by which the scoops were achieved: an illicit recording of a conversation; the burglary of private papers from a solicitor's office. As we now know, the dark arts of surveillance and espionage had begun to permeate Fleet Street from the late eighties, with News International in particular gaining competitive advantage by employing a small network of ex-police officers and private investigators.

There's much more to be said about these dark arts and how the investigatory powers descended into theft, blackmail, police corruption and – in the case of the private detective Daniel Morgan – to one of the most significant unexplained murders in the last twenty-five years. Compared to that, the attack on Kinnock on the eve of the 1992 election and the self-congratulatory crowing the day afterwards seems almost innocent.

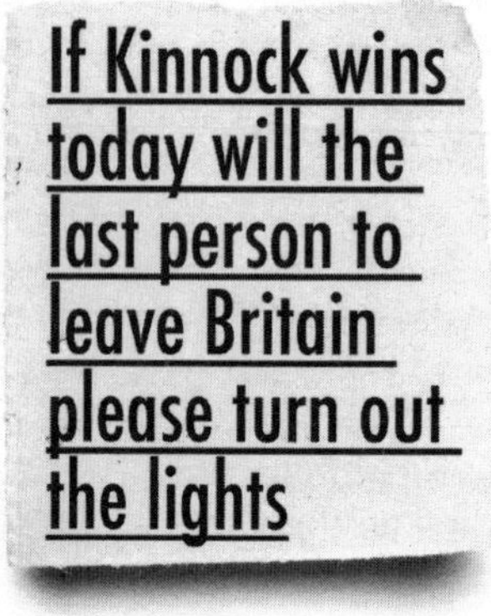

If Kinnock wins today will the last person to leave Britain please turn out the lights

Figure 5.6 Sun, *11 April 1992*

Figure 5.5 Sun, *9 April 1992*

Behind the famous election day cover, page three of the *Sun* showed a picture of an overweight old woman in a swimsuit with the caption – 'Here's what Page Three will look like under Labour'. This is not the subversive humour of the fool or comedian who punctures the pretensions of the power. This is the bullying ridicule of the powerful, of an organisation that feels entitled to mock its enemies without fearing any consequences. Whether the *Sun*'s coverage actually swung the close election contest between John Major and Neil Kinnock at the last moment is unlikely. That it felt it could attack politicians with impunity and thereby shape the political landscape is obvious. And the swinging had little to do with reasoned persuasion.

To what extent can we pin the blame for this coarsened almost brutalised discourse on Rupert Murdoch himself? According to his Leveson testimony, he rang MacKenzie the morning of the 'It's the Sun Wot Won It' to give his editor one of his regular bollockings.

However, it is reported that when Murdoch heard the news that John Major had been re-elected he was on the lot at Twentieth Century Fox and said two words: 'We won'; the 'we' probably didn't refer to the government. MacKenzie stayed at the helm and after a currency crisis a few months later told the newly re-elected Major that he had 'a bucket of shit on my desk, Prime Minister, and I'm going to pour it all over you.' At the Leveson Inquiry Murdoch himself said that 'If you want to know what I think read the *Sun*' – which rather undermined all his other claims not to meddle in his newspapers. Just as the editorial content of the daily tabloid matched Murdoch's political beliefs, the *Sun*'s highly targeted mockery of political figures, like its own tone of targeted mockery towards employees, is surely a reflection of the ethos set by the owner.

This is true of most British tabloids which – unlike the broadsheets – are determined almost wholly by editors and sub-editors, according to the columnist and editor, Deborah Orr. In the quality papers much of the reporting or opinion pieces are writer-led and whether in the *Wall Street Journal* or *The Times*, it's hard to force a well-known columnist or journalist to march in lock-step with the leader writers. The talent gets to call its own shots – at least in the short term.

By contrast, rather like the all-powerful director of an auteur movie, the editor of a tabloid gets to set the scene and make the final cut. Michael Wolff, who spent many hours with Murdoch as his biographer, contends:

> *Rupert gives his broadsheet editors far more latitude than his tabloid ones. If you want to know what Rupert Murdoch really thinks, then read* The Sun *and the* New York Post *...* The Sun *reflects what Rupert thinks on every major issue.*
>
> (Neil, 1996b)

Murdoch affectionately called MacKenzie 'my little Hitler' but the *Sun*'s dictator had to answer to another master. As Andrew Neil relates, Murdoch would subject MacKenzie to hour-long expletive-laden tongue-lashings on the phone at least once a week, even though he was running a paper which netted his proprietor £70 to £90 million a year. At the Leveson Inquiry, MacKenzie himself said that his proprietor would call him every day. Eventually, after twelve years of what MacKenzie would call Rupert's 'bollockings' even the thick-skinned *Sun* editor had enough. MacKenzie left in 1993.

However, though their contents may not be 'dictated', the broadsheets aren't completely free from the more subtle internalised forms of (self) censorship. Even when Murdoch is not directly involved in the day-to-day running of a paper his editors, in Neil's words, still wonder how to please the '*Sun* King' (ibid.). MacKenzie's successor at the *Sun*, David Yelland admitted in an article about the dangers of addiction, alcoholism and his divorce:

> *All Murdoch editors, what they do is this: they go on a journey where they end up agreeing with everything Rupert says. But you don't admit to yourself that you're being influenced. Most Murdoch editors wake up in the morning, switch on the radio, hear that something has happened and think, 'What would Rupert think about this?' It's like a mantra inside your head. It's like a prism. You look at the world through Rupert's eyes.*
>
> (Groskop, 2010)

The imprisoned editor might be held in a velvet prison of privilege and remuneration, but he's still captive.

Given these personal statements, there can be little doubt that the vitriol of *Sun*speak originally came from the top. There is just too much countervailing evidence to believe Murdoch's statement, made before Parliament, that he doesn't interfere in his papers. The formative tone of the *Sun* is no accident and Murdoch himself has averred many times that the *Sun* is his most personal vision of what a paper should be, along with the *New York Post*. This vituperative personal tone was also glimpsed in Murdoch's Leveson Inquiry testimony during which, despite showing humility and deference to the court, he managed to calumniate Gordon Brown, Andrew Neil and Sir Harold Evans in little asides. But whether Murdoch sanctioned the excesses of the *Sun* or the *News of the World* is a different matter. Just as it is incredible to assert that he had no idea of the personalised attacks and intrusive means deployed by his tabloids in the UK, it is entirely credible that – as Murdoch's focus turned overseas and to the skies of pay-TV – his employees took some of his principles to excess, thus leading to the criminality of the last decade.

While one can completely believe that, as a private person, Murdoch can be charming, loyal and kind – as a public person his impact has been somewhat different. The effect of his tabloid titles, both locally on Fleet Street and in terms of the larger national culture, is indisputable. As Murdoch once told his biographer: 'The English respond very positively to a kick in the head' (Wolff, 2012). English readers seemed to enjoy the violence too, done to their laws, their politicians and public language.

6

10 July 2011
Hard Times

The day the last edition of the *News of the World* was published, the paper's mast-head was unscrewed from the Wapping gatehouse and for the first time in thirty years, Rupert Murdoch's hold on the British press looked precarious – and lop-sided. The nice symmetry of the four quadrants had gone. News International was suddenly tilted in favour of its upmarket titles, *The Times* and *The Sunday Times*, and away from its mass tabloid base. Balance would be re-established when the *Sun on Sunday* was launched seventh months later and even on the day *News of the World* closed, commentators had noted the internet domain name had been quietly registered days before: News International is nothing if not forward-looking. But with the breakage of the old order the sudden rupture brought forth new possibilities, not just about what the future would hold, but how different the past could have been.

Figure 6.1 News of the World, *last edition*

A tabloid re-engineering of public rhetoric discourse is one thing, but as Murdoch discovered back in Australia, true influence requires a backchannel, a means to address politicians (or indeed often to employ politicians) through the insider language of the broadsheet opinion columns. That's one of the reasons why Murdoch founded and funded the loss-making *Australian* in the sixties, which in turn led to the political clout to release funds to buy the *News of the World*. Despite owning the two most popular papers at the beginning of the eighties, Murdoch lacked such an upmarket political house organ in the UK, until the Times Newspapers Group became available.

DEFINITIVE ARTICLE

The Times of London is – in printers' rules – the only newspaper to get a capitalised definitive article and has a symbolic status as the first truly independent newspaper of the modern age, one which Abraham Lincoln once described as more powerful than anything except perhaps the Mississippi. After the death of Lord Thomson who had created the Times Newspapers Group (which includes the famous supplements) and years of damaging industrial disputes with the press room union chapels and journalist unions, his son Ken Thomson announced that the board wanted to sell. Rather than create a London-based version of the *Australian*, Murdoch made a bid for the historic paper of record.

However, there was one apparently insuperable hurdle: the governing law, the Fair Trade Act of 1973, laid down that every newspaper transfer had to be approved by the Monopolies and Mergers Commission. Lord Thomson had to go through the needle of the MMC when he merged *The Sunday Times* with the daily *Times* – and that was with only 6 per cent of the national press. Since Murdoch already owned 28 per cent of British newspapers, his bid shouldn't have stood a snowball's chance in hell of surviving an investigation.

Murdoch's bid for Times Newspapers Ltd would be a watershed in British journalism and indeed in the political future of the nation and the tortuous history of this era has been explored many times – most notably in Harold Evans's *Good Times, Bad Times*, which is about to go into its fourth edition. The open culture war of the tabloids disguised a much more covert and bitter battle for the heart of the British establishment. *The Times*, after all, though loss-making throughout most of the seventies, was still considered the in-house journal of professional and political classes: the paper of record, the place to announce court circulars, notable marriages, births and deaths. It was also held up as the example of a true model of editorial independence guaranteed, not by the subsidy of a proprietor or political party, but by its own revenues.

Clearly, that model was failing, even thirty years ago before the digital revolution, but still *The Times* was a profound symbol of seriousness, separation of editorial from comment and historical longevity.

For Murdoch, acquisition of this paper could have been either sentimental, revenge, commercial instinct – or perhaps all of the above. This was after all the paper formerly owned by Lord Northcliffe who had done so much to promote his father's career and mythically establish him in Australia as the 'Journalist who won the War'. Moreover, since Murdoch had been snubbed by the establishment for raking over the ashes of the Profumo affair, taking over their favourite newspaper could also be a sweet form of retribution. He had been resident in the US at this point for longer than he'd ever lived in London. Owning *The Times* would both secure his legacy in Britain and allow him to trash anyone who threatened it. It would also give him a monopoly share of the market, massive economies of scale and – with a careful timed strike of blitzkrieg modernisation – liberate millions in cash which could be leveraged into further acquisitions overseas.

While *The Times* was losing millions a year, *The Sunday Times* had been – until a long shutdown due to strike action in 1980 – extremely profitable; it also had a deserved reputation as a leading advocate of investigative journalism through its Insight team. *The Sunday Times* was not originally a sister paper to its daily namesake; indeed, they had no relation to each other until both were amalgamated under the ownership of Lord Thomson in 1966. A famously hands-off proprietor, Thomson let both his newspapers continue their separate editorial traditions: *The Times* conservative, fusty, old-school but reliable; *The Sunday Times* modern, culturally liberal and challenging. By taking over them both, Murdoch could revenge himself both on the old establishment that had shunned him and the newer sixties establishment that had mocked him.

Furthermore, his animosity to the form of investigative journalism *The Sunday Times* had pioneered under Evans should not be underestimated. As an admirer of Nixon, Murdoch was appalled by the contribution of Woodward and Bernstein to his favourite President's downfall and antagonistic to the Liberal elites who covered the scandal, represented by the Grahame family (who owned the *Washington Post*) or the Sulzberger family at the *New York Times*. Though Murdoch hadn't yet the firepower to take on these bastions of the 'establishment' in the US, he could wreak revenge by proxy in the UK.

There was also money to be made. A proper union agreement on reasonable staffing and modernisation would have transformed the cost base of even the loss-making daily. The profits of *The Sunday Times* could cover *The Times*'s losses if Murdoch could get the unions to agree to the use of the computers the Thomson management had installed and had tried to introduce into editorial and advertising typesetting for years. There was also a highly valuable property in Gray's Inn Road and a lucrative tranche of shares in Reuters. Both in political and commercial terms the bid made sense. The only problem was … it was completely illegal.

British competition law and anti-monopoly legislation had been applied to the newspaper industry in 1966 after an extensive report by Lord Shawcross. The legislation acknowledged two central truths of market-based liberal democracies: first, that monopoly economic power distorts the competition for products, and second, that any kind of social monoculture smothers the creative competition for ideas. For years this acceptance of liberal pluralism had gained cross-party support; indeed, it could be considered the mainstay of Britishness for two hundred years.

It would take a revolution to supplant that tradition and by 1981 the vanguard of that revolution was at work. Its leader was Margaret Thatcher and as Danton to her Robespierre, or perhaps Trotsky to her Lenin, Murdoch emerges in retrospect as the prime ideologue. Acres of print have been expended on this particular battle for the heart of British public life. For anyone of the baby boom generation who had an interest in how politics was conducted and reported, the struggle for the Times Newspapers Group would be the first real Rubicon which, once crossed, would transform the political landscape forever. From this point flows both the content and form of most of the public intellectual arguments for the last thirty years. The radical conservatism of Thatcher would be made permanent through the acquisition of the country's premier newspaper of note and the future of British politics – through New Labour to the 2010 coalition – would be sealed.

But now the arguments about the past are over…

CHEQUERS

It was only in March 2012 when Thatcher's private papers for this period were released that the behind the scenes real struggle for media power came to be seen in its proper light. By early 1981, with unprecedented post-war unemployment heading towards three million and large parts of the country's manufacturing base collapsing, Thatcher was polling as the most unpopular prime minister in recent history, though Labour was also deeply divided and polling for the mooted breakaway Social Democratic Party showed it attracting massive support from disaffected Tory voters. The real challenge Thatcher faced at that time wasn't from the unions, other political parties, nor indeed the recurrent riots on Britain's streets, but from the 'wets' in her own Cabinet and simmering revolt on the backbenches. (Thatcher would finally be ousted nine years later not by the ballot box and the electorate, but by a coup from inside the Conservative Party itself, which has a ruthless way of dealing with its leaders.) The support of the upmarket papers, especially a Conservative icon like *The Times* was crucial to her survival in 1981.

Murdoch arrived on the scene like a knight on a white horse. From his years in America he could bring the 'positive polarisation' tactics of Nixon to bear, as well as key contacts with Reagan's inner circle. Whatever the populist strategy of the tabloids, the sharper ideological struggle among opinion formers and politicians would now be Reaganite in tone: a ramping up of Cold War rhetoric which attacked 'communism' in the Soviet Union while implicitly (often explicitly) targeting the 'enemies within' promulgating 'Socialism' at home.

I remember this time vividly, as I was an exchange student in the US and as part of our briefing by the English-Speaking Union before we left, we were told by some senior politician or Lord (whose name I can't remember) that after the Soviet invasion of Afghanistan the Anglo-American Alliance was faced with the biggest challenge since World War II. A recently published book won as a school prize, *A History of the World* by Hugh Thomas (who had formerly written a brilliant account of the Spanish Civil War), also spoke in portentous apocalyptic tones about the end of détente, comparing the confrontation between the West and the Soviets with Pericles of Athens facing Darius the Persian.

Though the attack on the repressive regimes in the Warsaw Pact was justified, this emerging language would brook no nuances. To be for freedom also meant subscription to monetarist theory of money supply and a Hayekian acceptance that all government intervention was a road to serfdom. And so the neoconservative movement came of age, riding on an escalation in the arms race and using fears of foreign attack to negate domestic dissent. This was not necessarily a cynical ploy; the escalation in the arms race in the late seventies and early eighties and the Soviet invasion of Afghanistan was genuinely construed at the time as an existential struggle. Against the possibility of apocalypse or communist domination, the niceties of media pluralism and competition law look rather more dispensable. At the same time a neo-liberal belief in deregulated markets was happily conscripted into the struggle. These two planks, strong government overseas, minimal government at home, were the mainstays of the transatlantic philosophy of Reagan and Thatcher, with Murdoch as one of the prime facilitators and interlocutors.

We can see this movement happening in the recently released notes of a secret meeting between Murdoch and Thatcher at Chequers on 4 January 1980. Both the Conservative Party and the official *Times* history of the era had denied such a direct behind the scenes meeting for thirty years, with the paper of record apparently airbrushing out this inconvenient fact about its own history. On the surface, the notes by Thatcher's press secretary Bernard Ingham are innocuous. What is recorded – and this may well be an airbrush in itself – was that the Australian-born newspaper proprietor merely briefed the prime minister on his and the other competing bids and promised to introduce her to the key players and thinkers in Reagan's administration (something he subsequently did at a White House dinner that May).

What such an account overlooks – apart from the gross censorship of history – is the appearance that the process was fixed. The British government and cabinet were legally bound to review Murdoch's bid in the light of parliamentary legislation. In a commercial acquisition like this, that oversight has a quasi-judicial function. To take advice from only one of several bidders in a commercial auction could have opened the whole process to judicial appeal had it been revealed at the time. No wonder the note about the meeting was marked 'in commercial confidence'.

The Murdoch–Thatcher summit, as it appears in this scant record, was of course only the final phase of a complex choreography of lobbying which had gone on behind the scenes. Woodrow Wyatt, friends to both parties, is quite explicit about the bigger picture in his memoirs:

> I had all the rules bent for him [Murdoch] over the Sunday Times and the Times when he bought them … Through Margaret I got it arranged that the deal didn't go to the Monopolies Commission which almost certainly would have blocked it.

> (Curtis, 1998–2000)

Thatcher's support was key, though it needed some deft back-room manoeuvres. As Wyatt suggests, there must have been multiple conversations before the meeting to provide a get-out clause to evade monopoly scrutiny. The crucial terms in the Ingham note is Murdoch's mention of the newspaper's economic viability in the short term. This was to be the get-out clause.

One technicality allowed a newspaper bid to be excluded from a Monopoly and Mergers referral: a loss-making newspaper could not be expected to survive the four-month long investigation, so the newspaper in question needed to be a 'going concern'. As Bruce Page points out, this potential loophole was subject to intense parliamentary debate in 1966 during the original Times Newspapers Group merger, when MPs realised that creative accounting could make a newspaper appear not to be a going concern to escape referral. However, it was a tough call: the legislation specifically spoke of the viability of individual newspapers, not a whole newspaper group like Times Newspapers Ltd. Though *The Times* had been loss-making for several years, *The Sunday Times* was extremely profitable. Its results in the previous year had been adversely affected by industrial disputes, but it remained Britain's leading Sunday 'quality' paper with a 1.5 million circulation the year before and when the paper reappeared after a year-long strike, the circulation was even higher.

To get round this would require not only extensive political lobbying, but some creative accounting by members of the Times board who wanted to sell to Murdoch. As Evans points out in a chapter of *Good Times, Bad Times* called 'Biffen's Missing Millions' this is exactly what happened after the Murdoch–Thatcher summit. The minister in charge of the bid, John Biffen, was shown figures that suggested *The Sunday Times* was unviable too, only 24 hours before he made his statement to the house. When he did so, Labour opposition MPs and even some Conservatives, called the 'going concern' argument a 'phoney pistol' and the fact there were other bids proves the immediate threat of closure just wasn't there.

There was one additional hurdle. During the original merger in 1966 the Monopolies committee had only reluctantly allowed Lord Thomson to take over both *The Times* and *The Sunday Times* under strict conditions guaranteeing the papers' independence. If that was a stricture for someone owning only 6 per cent of the market, the hurdle surely had to be higher for Murdoch who was on his way to a technical monopoly in 1981, with 27 per cent of the UK's newspapers (and a much larger percentage of circulation). However, much like the attempted takeover of LWT in the late sixties, and BSkyB in 2011, Murdoch made written assurances of non-interference. They would not last long as he later conceded: 'They're not worth the paper they're written on' (Evans, 2011, pp. 489–90).

In retrospect, the approval of the Times Newspapers Group takeover appears no more legal than the recording of private conversations that would later tarnish Conservative culture minister David Mellor's career or the theft of solicitor's papers that would attempt to do the same for the Liberal Democrat leader Paddy Ashdown. The lawlessness which would break out in the systematic gutter criminality of *News of the World* and the *Sun* had its precedent in the way its proprietor glided and slid through the highest corridors of power.

CHECK MATE

The Times Newspapers bid was not just a watershed for British political life; it would transform the fortunes of Murdoch. Up until then he had been an interesting but not exceptional figure in the English-speaking world. In the early documentaries about him from 1968 and 1969 (available on Adam Curtis's blog, The Medium and the Message) he appears as part of a 'room at the top', early sixties jet-set celebrated in James Bond films at the time or retrospectively in the television drama series about advertising executives, *Mad Men*. Buccaneering, jocular and unpretentious, you can see him making coffee in some bedsit and admitting, rather coyly, to the camera:

> *Of course one enjoys the feeling of power… We have more responsibility*
> *than power I think. The newspaper can create great controversies, stir up a*
> *[unintelligible] in the community, discussion, throw light on injustices – just*
> *as it can do the opposite. It can hide things, and be a great power for evil.*

It's worth repeating this: *It can hide things, and be a great power for evil.* In his late thirties Murdoch still had an insight into the power of repression, the 'anti-news' agenda of brokerage and non-disclosure, which rapidly parlays itself into favour seeking or even blackmail. He had already shown some adeptness at this himself in Canberra with McEwen's government and the Whitlam dismissal where he kept two hot political stories secret. By their very nature, suppressed news stories are hard to uncover – unknown unknowns are unfathomable – but the record now shows that Murdoch was engaged in a thirty-year repression of the truth about his meeting with Thatcher in 1981.

As for other repressed stories during Murdoch's career: there is Chris Patten's account at the Leveson Inquiry of how his book on his time as Governor General of Hong Kong before its handover to China was not printed by Murdoch's HarperCollins press because it might offend the Chinese government. In more recent times the cases are more numerous: Neville Thurlbeck claims he had to spike a *News of the World* story about an A-list celebrity on Murdoch's insistence; the blogger Guido Fawkes's allegation that the *Sun* paid £20,000 for a photo of Conservative foreign secretary William Hague's special advisor in a gay bar which it never published; and of course, the admission by News International of intentional email deletion and destruction of evidence whilst under instruction from the courts to preserve all records relevant to the phone-hacking civil suits brought in 2010. There are also the reported remarks of the biographer, Michael Wolff, who recalls Murdoch often says about political figures 'Oh we have a picture of him' – implying a cache of incriminating evidence held over politicians to match the famed files of FBI Director, J. Edgar Hoover.

As Murdoch said: newspapers 'can hide things, and be a great power for evil'. Back in 1969 Murdoch also had a prophetic insight into the need for pluralism:

> *I think the important thing is that there be plenty of newspapers with plenty*
> *of different people controlling them, so there's a variety of viewpoints, so that*
> *there's a choice for the public. This is the freedom of the press that is needed.*

('WHO'S AFRAID OF RUPERT MURDOCH?', 1981)

But by 1981, Murdoch himself would ensure that one person controlled a third of all Britain's press and approaching 40 per cent of its readership. Is this just shameless hypocrisy and dissimulation? Or did something change?

To watch David Dimbleby's *Panorama* interview 'Who's Afraid of Rupert Murdoch?', broadcast a week after he had taken over Times Newspapers, is to see a very different Murdoch: driven, steely and no longer diffident or reticent, but recalcitrant – almost imperious. The difference between the two Murdochs is the difference between the meritocratic optimism of the sixties and the ideological polarisation of the eighties. Much more than a decade separates them.

True, it probably didn't help Murdoch's demeanour that he had just sat through a penetrating forty-minute documentary about his personal and professional history and analysis of his claim that he would 'Save Times Newspapers'. The documentary lays out both for and against in an accessible and forthright manner which makes one long for BBC journalism in the seventies. Evidence of Murdoch's past behaviours is all here as is, for today's viewers, intimations of things to come.

The *Panorama* documentary destroys the 'wild colonial boy' myth by filming the substantial colonnaded mansion Murdoch was brought up in. While it praises his success in launching the high-quality national the *Australian* (funded with millions from the more popular regional papers) it also points out the paper had been through eight editors in its first sixteen years. There's an interview with the 'most brilliant of them', Adrian Deamer, who described how whenever Murdoch would come back from overseas he'd go through all the back editions and lead political stories and challenge his editor: 'Why did you do that?' His paper's relentless campaign against Gough Whitlam in the mid-seventies is also traced and footage shows Murdoch's hands-on role with editors, restlessly pacing the newsroom, heading into an editor's office, pulling copy out of his hands. Murdoch even admits in a pre-recorded interview: 'When I'm around I interfere too much.'

Thus we have another blow to demolish Murdoch's claims before the DCMS select committee in July 2011 that he was a 'hands-off' proprietor. His 1981 admission to Panorama didn't bode well for his simultaneous and much heralded guarantee of freedom from proprietorial interference for *The Times*. In perhaps the most trenchant comment of all at the time, the *Observer*'s Conor Cruise O'Brien predicted:

> *Murdoch's personality and the concentration of power that he represents are more important than any guarantees. It's perhaps the biggest concentration of newspaper power ever. And Mr Murdoch's track record shows he expects, and gets, uncritical subservience from the newspapers he owns, I don't think genuine quality newspapers can continue for very long under those conditions.*

('WHO'S AFRAID OF RUPERT MURDOCH?', 1981)

Murdoch's tight-lipped response to those charges was a mixture of typical tabloid ad hominem – his critics are 'self-interested' – and a new, more American trope: 'they don't seem to like success'. It's an odd and slightly jarring juxtaposition, perhaps owing to the Ayn Rand fetish of elitism that was then endemic in the American right. Then, having identified himself as part of a successful elite, Murdoch somersaults and accuses the BBC of elitism – a vendetta he would pursue for the next thirty years. His language becomes more extreme and McCarthy-esque: he talks about rooting out communists, Trotskyists and 'left-wingers'. There's a sense of purpose and ruthlessness entirely missing from a decade before. It's as if he knows now is the time and the West is facing the final battle with enemies within and without. He's dressed himself in the feathers of a culture wars conservative and cold war hawk.

Certainly it is this ideological edge both on foreign affairs and monetarist dogma which finally forced Harold Evans out of the editorship of *The Times* a year later, despite the fact his presence and independence was seen as one of the key tests of Murdoch's good faith. Evans, who had led a rival buy-out for Times Newspapers by its management and journalists, had been persuaded by Murdoch to stay and oversee the resuscitation of the daily. In retrospect, this looks like a ploy by Murdoch to provide legitimacy for the deal. Once he had the power, Murdoch dropped the niceties:

> *During their first visits to the building, Murdoch and his associates made clear their hostility to* Sunday Times *journalism and their contempt for those who practised it. The journalists collectively were stigmatised as lead-swinging, expense-padding, layabout Trotskyites. Each of these epithets was uttered in my hearing by senior Murdoch executives. The political label was especially emphatic, wholly removed though it was from reality.*
>
> (DAVIES, 2008, P. 296)

Murdoch was a deeply politicised proprietor during one of the most divisive times in British twentieth-century politics. Despite an attempt to keep up the appearances of the guarantees, the urge to control and propagandise was uncontainable: a penchant for rule-breaking that would set the scene for a culture of future lawbreaking. As Evans has written in the preface to the new edition of his book:

> *The experiences I describe in* Good Times, Bad Times *have turned out to be eerily emblematic. The dark and vengeful undertow I sensed and then experienced in the last weeks of my relationship with Murdoch correctly reflected something morally out of joint with the way he ran his company.*
>
> (EVANS, 2011)

Though *The Times*'s daily circulation recovered to over 300,000, its much vaunted political independence did not last many months. The general manager, Gerald Long, rebuked the editorial staff for publishing figures which suggested the recession wasn't over. Though the paper supported the deployment of Cruise and Pershing missiles to the UK, Murdoch sent for a chief leader writer demanding the anti-Soviet rhetoric be amped up.

The editorial board had bad memories of the thirties when an editor suppressed news that might upset Hitler and the German leadership. Murdoch himself has averred that the job of a free press is to eschew the kind of crass propaganda found in *Pravda* – but this is exactly what was being demanded in the name of anti-Soviet political rhetoric. The final straw for Evans was when Murdoch tried to bypass the promised editorial independence by secretly transferring the Times Newspaper titles to his News International subsidiary, which had no legal obligation to respect the guarantees. Evans got wind of this sleight of hand and published it in his paper, but there was now open warfare between the editor and proprietor. Murdoch demanded cost saving redundancies of senior editorial staff: Evans refused to comply and quit, leaving for the US soon after.

Over the next nine years Murdoch's quality papers would do sterling service for Thatcher, lambasting enemies in the Church, Europe, the old 'wet' wing of the Conservative Party, the European Community and the BBC. *The Sunday Times*, apart from discrediting itself in 1983 by claiming to have an English-language exclusive in the publication of Adolf Hitler's newly discovered diaries would also back off an investigation of Thatcher's deliberately leaking against her own Cabinet colleagues during the Westland crisis. The same paper would target political enemies in classic smear fashion – such as the absurd allegation that the Labour Party leader Michael Foot was a KGB spy. It would also target other journalists, notably the Thames TV documentary team who made *Death on the Rock*, exposing the inconsistencies of the official account of how the SAS shot dead three IRA members in Gibraltar. During the subsequent commercial TV licence renewal, Murdoch would hound Thames TV itself to the point of extinction.

The Times would be less obviously tabloid in its character assassinations and commercial–political vendettas, but still provided tepid criticisms of Thatcher's repeated abrogations of Cabinet government over that time. It would, in general, go along with the private briefings of Bernard Ingham, who was the source of the internal attacks on Defence Secretary Michael Heseltine during the Cabinet battle over the future of the Westland Helicopter manufacturer and perhaps the inventor of the role of press secretary as internal party whip and enforcer.

The origins of 'spin' and ministerial tactic of destroying colleagues and purveying policy through behind the scenes gossip, go back to this Thatcher era. New Labour would deploy the same tactics of selective leaks against unruly ministers, a massive increase in 'government information' expenditure, thus sealing the rise of the communications expert as the prime political fixer, but it was in the Thatcher era that this became the norm.

The Times, like most other broadsheet papers, did neither the British press nor the Conservative Party many favours in the long run. As John Stuart Mill observed, the censorship of dissident ideas hurts the orthodox more than the heterodox. Apart from a sense of entitlement and immunity in senior Tories that ended eventually in corruption investigations and criminal charges for perjury (Jeffrey Archer, Jonathan Aitken, Neil Hamilton) the echo chamber of opinion that surrounded Thatcher is in a large part responsible for the excesses of executive power in the late eighties. The effective use of the lobby suppressed dissent, leading to a putsch of all Thatcher's Cabinet rivals and eventually a disastrous lack of a succession strategy. The over-reach of the Poll Tax and the eventual 'defenestration' of Thatcher herself, followed by thirteen years of civil war and wilderness for the Conservative Party, are part of its unintended consequences. When David Cameron finally took over the leadership in 2005, he promised an end to such division and with his main guru Steve Hilton planned to 'win without the *Sun*': but within two years the leadership of the Conservative Party was once again dealing with Murdoch and his son.

As for *The Times* itself, Murdoch's breaking of the guarantees led to the exodus of several senior journalists who left to found the *Independent* in 1986. The new paper was soon targeted, and nearly destroyed, by a deliberate cover price war by *The Times* in the early nineties. The Office of Fair Trade found News International guilty of anti-competitive activity and predatory pricing in 1999 and put the company on notice. Though still employing many excellent journalists, *The Times* no longer has a special reputation for probity and factual accuracy compared with a journal like the *Financial Times*. Though it still has some of the best columnists in the business and its coverage of the hacking scandal was (eventually) excellent in the circumstances, some of the illegal practices endemic in the tabloid stable at Wapping did infect the paper of record – the outing and silencing of an anonymous award-winning police blogger, Nightjack, by hacking his email being the most glaring example (see Chapter 11). The fact that it was run by the same proprietor as the *Sun* and *News of the World* would lead to some almost insurmountable conflicts of interest. As late as July 2012, *The Times* had to issue an apology to former prime minister Gordon Brown, after rushing in to defend the *Sun* over the publication of his son's medical records.

Yet the biggest casualty of this era almost goes unnoticed. It's only foreign newspaper journalists who can see the damage wrought. By accident of history, the major American newspapers have still clung on to those principles of independence, of separating news and comment, double sourcing stories and making sure the subjects are given a chance to respond and comment. British journalism has almost entirely lost these standards. I have a brief but memorable experience of this, having written occasionally for periodicals and newspapers here and – in the process of writing this book – covered the Leveson Inquiry and hacking scandal for *Newsweek* and the Daily Beast.

Even in the brief online pieces I've written for the US publisher, every fact has to be substantiated and not from a secondary source such as another newspaper or media outlet. I'm told to look at original court records, garner statements from eyewitnesses, talk directly to police and other authorities and they must go on the record to be verifiable. Unnamed sources are allowable but must be multiply verified. Partisan points of view are not enough. And no article can be based on one unattributed source. This process has come as a culture shock for me.

The default unnamed single source tracks exactly the lobby system of private briefing and unattributed assertion. The tabloids may be famed for making up entire interviews with celebrities, but look at most British broadsheet newspapers, from the right or left, and check out how many times the source isn't named ('It is believed that…', 'sources say…', 'A close friend confides…'). This pusillanimity shown by the press on this issue extends across the political spectrum, from the once reliable *Telegraph* to the *Observer* which – especially in the run up to the Iraq invasion – seemed to fill its pages with spin and insinuation. We've forgotten the important barriers that separate fact from opinion and the divergence of our eleven national dailies front pages just reminds us how selective and biased news coverage is. It's certainly not all down to Murdoch – indeed, the rise of radical propagandising left-wing journalism in the seventies may in some ways have predated his style of overt conservative polemic. No matter who started it, the end effect is the same – truth has been a casualty of the culture wars.

British civil society has survived this abject polarisation of the press because we still have – just – a relatively objective broadcast news system. In the US, despite the print journalists who still cling to basic standards in the *New York Times*, *Washington Post* or *Wall Street Journal*, its broadcast news has given itself over to tabloid partiality. As we shall see, Murdoch had an important part to play in both phenomena.

THE VELVET PRISON

The build-up of News International's monopoly in the British press set all the preconditions that would erupt thirty years later: illegal intrusions into privacy, character assassination in the tabloids and behind the scenes political lobbying at the most senior level to break the norms and bypass or change legislation. All these would come back to haunt News Corp in 2011 as well as the dozens of journalists, broadcasters, opinion formers, lobbyists, lawmakers and lawbreakers who were implicated in this extensive co-option of Britain's media and political classes. Norman Fowler, a cabinet minister in Thatcher's government, recalled recently how this came from the top:

> *A friend of mine who became chairman of a media company in the 1980s found that the appointment brought with it one unexpected privilege. Periodically he was invited into Downing Street for a private talk with the prime minister, Margaret Thatcher. At one such meeting the issue of Murdoch arose. 'Why are you so opposed to Rupert?' the Iron Lady asked. 'He is going to get us in.'*

(FOWLER, 2012)

Before she was ousted from office, Thatcher had one more chance to repay Murdoch's subservience to her party line, both ideologically on the need for deregulation and privatisation and specifically for his support during the almost terminal Westland crisis. In 1989 she allowed Sky, a moribund satellite channel based in Brussels that Murdoch had bought for £1 in 1983, to broadcast direct to users in the UK in competition to the recently launched British Satellite Broadcasting Company (BSB), set up by a consortia of ITV channels and the Pearson Group, which had beaten Murdoch for a satellite broadcast licence in 1986 on the basis it would be sole broadcaster. When both Sky and BSB found themselves in financial trouble in 1990 (Sky alone wrote-off £235 million losses that June) Thatcher waived through a merger between both satellite companies; and thus BSkyB was born, with Murdoch holding a controlling interest.

Once again, there were many who thought such a monopoly should have been referred to the Monopolies and Mergers Commission, but satellite broadcasting was so new it hadn't attracted any relevant legislation and besides, the existential threat would have probably worked again as it had with Times Newspapers: if Murdoch doesn't buy it, it won't work. If Murdoch doesn't pay, who will?

This counterfactual can never be answered. However, history shows that there were other viable bidders for Times Newspapers, just as there was another satellite cable channel in the UK. As Tony Judt said of communism and the captive mind, it is precisely this inability to conceive of any alternatives that characterises the totalitarian mindset. For the many great journalists, producers and staff who currently work for BSkyB or the Times Newspapers – indeed for the press and broadcasting as a whole – the belief that their businesses couldn't survive without News Corp subsidy is actually a telling indication of the pernicious effects of monopoly and reliance on one proprietor and one corporation. Their fear that there was and is 'no alternative' amounts to another indication of a Stockholm Syndrome: the captive mind in its velvet prison identifies with and depends on its captor.

RINSE AND REPEAT

Twenty years later, after years of losses, having been regularly promoted in News International newspapers and acquiring key sports and film rights, BSkyB would finally become an extremely profitable concern, with annual revenues over £3 billion and projected to rise 6 per cent year-on-year. On this score alone it proves that – for all his faults – Murdoch was a man of vision when it came to broadcasting and one who was willing to take considerable financial risks in pursuit of innovation. Not all of BSkyB's dominance can be put down to the monopoly position: James Murdoch certainly deserves some credit for chairing the organisation and creating a broad platform of channels tied in with broadband access, and Sky News – though not to everyone's taste – has a reputation for insightful news coverage (for example some brilliant dispatches from Libya in 2011). But then again, the company was only 39 per cent owned by News Corp and exists in a tightly regulated Ofcom framework with its 'plurality' test.

James's decision to demand the dismantling of Ofcom and seek to take over the whole of BSkyB smacks of a reversion to the darker side of the family legacy – the insider rather than the outsider, someone who trades power surreptitiously behind the scenes rather than expose it to cleansing daylight. Just as with previous acquisitions by his father a generation earlier, the satellite takeover could have been unlawful: in breach of competition law and the principle of news plurality. Once again, just as in the Rupert–Maggie rapprochement of the early eighties, a Murdoch ended up in a dance with the leader of the Conservative Party, in this case David Cameron.

Thirty years on, history would repeat itself: first time in secrecy, the second time in scandal.

Cameron ran for the leadership of the Conservative Party in 2005 as a modernised, socially liberal Tory and under the guidance of his strategist Steve Hilton, tried to detoxify the 'nasty Tory' legacy of the nineties. Part of this strategy was to explicitly 'win without the *Sun*', and frame Cameron as a less polarising figure than his predecessors, more as a post-partisan 'heir to Blair'. The strategy was nearly derailed on the eve of the Conservative Party conference in 2005 with the allegations of drug taking against George Osborne, Cameron's campaign manager. But then Andy Coulson, as editor of *News of the World*, ran his successful spoiler which took the heat from the incipient scandal and Cameron was duly elected. Coulson's colleague and friend, Rebekah Brooks, sent one of her senior editorial writers to join the new leader's speech writing staff.

In 2008, in his first major speech as News Corp senior executive, James Murdoch called for Ofcom's powers to be removed and the BBC diminished. That summer Cameron was flown out to meet Murdoch, accompanied by Rebekah Brooks, Matthew Freud and his wife Elisabeth Murdoch. The meeting must have gone well, for on 3 November that year the Tory Party leader wrote a full-page article for the *Sun* 'Bloated BBC out of touch with the viewers'. A year later, in July 2009, the secondary attack on Ofcom emerged as Cameron called for a 'bonfire of the quangos'. A month later, during his famous Edinburgh International Television Festival speech, James also demanded that the BBC be downsized and Ofcom to be diminished. What *Private Eye* called the 'Murdoch Mating Dance' became more intense. Shadow Culture Secretary Jeremy Hunt began uncannily echoing James's lecture from 28 August in a piece for the *Sun* newspaper on 19 September, in which the Conservative broadcasting spokesman seemed toe-to-toe with the media proprietor in every step complaining about the 'chilling' effect on the market of the BBC, the need to shrink its licence fee and get rid of the BBC trust.

Two weeks later the *Sun*, now under the direct control of James, reversed twelve years of Labour support. At the general election in 2010, all News International papers told their readership to vote Conservative. It was only when Cameron was finally in 10 Downing Street (and with Murdoch as one of the first visitors) that James finally launched his £8 billion bid for the remaining share of BSkyB in June 2010.

The BSkyB bid would be just as contentious as the Times Newspapers Group takeover three decades earlier and more commercially important by a factor of ten. However, though the government was once again supposed to be operating a quasi-judicial process, the volume of contact between News Corp and senior ministers was much more rampant. In the first six months of power, when the BSkyB bid was launched, there were over 60 meetings between senior News Corp or News International executives and the prime minister, chancellor, culture minister and education minister alone, and new ones are coming to light all the time. Given the millions in lobbying fees News Corp had devoted to the Rubicon process, there must have been hundreds of other communications at lower levels.

To make a proper comparison with Murdoch's meeting with Thatcher in January 1981, we could just look back at the brief period around Christmas 2010 as the BSkyB bid was rocked with scandal when Vince Cable was replaced by Jeremy Hunt. On three separate occasions in the months preceding, James Murdoch and Rebekah Brooks had stayed as a guest of the prime minister at his official residence in Chequers. Brooks and Cameron would text each other once or twice a week to organise meetings. In November Brooks had also spent a weekend with Osborne at the chancellor's official residence, Dorneywood, accompanied by Coulson, still then Number 10's head of communications.

The interpenetration of News Corp and the highest reaches of the government are all evident in one dramatic day on the morning of 21 December 2010. The day started with the European Commission in Brussels approving the bid around noon. James Murdoch called Jeremy Hunt immediately and the culture secretary texted back to apologise for missing the call and to celebrate the good news: 'Great and congrats on Brussels. Just Ofcom to go!' They agreed to talk at 4 p.m.

But just after two o'clock the same afternoon the BBC's business editor, Robert Peston, revealed that there was more to the *Daily Telegraph* sting than had previously been publicised and that Vince Cable had also told the undercover journalists that he had 'declared war' on Murdoch and boasted: 'His whole empire is now under attack.' News Corp issued a statement saying they were shocked and dismayed, just before 4 p.m. when Jeremy Hunt and James Murdoch are documented as having a phone conversation.

As soon as he was off the phone to James Murdoch, Hunt sent a text to George Osborne: 'Just been called by James M. His lawyers are meeting now & saying it calls into question legitimacy of whole process from beginning "acute bias", etc.' Two minutes later he emailed Andy Coulson at Number 10: 'Could we chat about this? I am seriously worried Vince Cable will do real damage to coalition with his comments.'

Fifty minutes later there had clearly been discussions between the prime minister, his press officer and the chancellor because George Osborne texted back: 'I hope you like the solution.' The solution to Cable's clear bias against the BSkyB bid had been to strip him of his responsibility for it and to hand it to someone with clear bias in favour of the bid – Jeremy Hunt. As a *Daily Mail* leader said in May 2012 when these communications were revealed: 'It's extremely hard to avoid the conclusion that the sole intention of Mr Hunt and Mr Osborne (who must surely now be called before Leveson himself) was to keep Mr Murdoch happy.'

Two days later at a pre-Christmas dinner, Cameron met Brooks and James Murdoch at a dinner party with fifteen guests when they discussed the bid. Brooks met Cameron again on Boxing Day. Though all parties claimed 'nothing inappropriate' was said about the $16 billion takeover, the volume of meetings make a mockery of the whole 'quasi-judicial' process. Where was the media co-alition that opposed the bid? Where was the BBC, Channel 4 and most of the other major newspaper groups in Fleet Street?

Compared to the riot of contacts, drinks, texts, emails and phone calls, Murdoch's secret meeting with Thatcher thirty years over seems sober, diplomatic and above board – even though it was likewise in defiance of competition law and dealing with market-sensitive information. At least Murdoch and Thatcher seem to have known the narrow boundaries of deniability when dealing with due legal process. But their heirs had no such compunction and very little restraint. The level of interpenetration of political, personal and financial instincts between Cameron, Osborne and Hunt, and James Murdoch, Brooks and Coulson, is dazzling. News Corporation almost merits Tom Watson's description of it in his book, *Dial M for Murdoch*, as a 'shadow state'.

As Thatcher's Children and self-styled Heirs to Blair wined and dined the Murdoch family that winter of 2010, Britain was the closest it's been to being run by unaccountable press barons for a hundred years.

7

11 July 2011

Sky's the Limit

It's to the credit of the remaining independence of *The Times* that once the phone-hacking story broke the newspaper began to cover it fairly fully (as did the *Wall Street Journal*) and also one of the signs – like spring in the arctic – of the icy corporate façade of denials breaking.

Police to interview Brooks as Murdoch takes control

Figure 7.1 The Times, *11 July 2011*

Hacking: the 'smoking gun' emails

Figure 7.2 Daily Telegraph, *11 July 2011*

For ten years there had been a drip drip drip of information about phone hacking which had been largely ignored or derided. Politicians who incurred News International disfavour – like Labour MP Chris Bryant to whom Rebekah Brooks had inadvertently confessed the *Sun* made illegal payments to police – found themselves 'monstered' and abused in the company's tabloids. Lawyers like Mark Lewis who pursued civil phone hacking cases were challenged over their probity, ousted from their law firms and even put under surveillance by private detectives hired by News

International. Journalists who tried to follow the story were publicly castigated as politically motivated by the likes of the Mayor of London Boris Johnson, who in late 2010 described the bubbling scandal as a 'load of codswallop cooked up by the Labour Party'. The investigative work of the *Guardian* was dismissed by no one less than Baroness Buscombe, the chair of the Press Complaints Commission.

With the flood of revelations, first about the hacking of Milly Dowler's phone and then more and more new victims, the private fear of News International was turning into revulsion. Suddenly public celebrities, politicians and other journalists could speak up without fear of being blacklisted or hounded by legal suits. The company's former invincibility, its power to chill or frame the debate even without realising it, evaporated overnight and thirty years of hurt finally found expression.

THE BIG LEAP

One clear sign of this lost immunity was the decision of the new Labour leader, Ed Miliband, to thrust himself into the crisis and take a partisan stand. According to a senior Labour Party source (Senior Labour Party source, 2012) the opposition were briefed a few weeks in advance of Nick Davies and Amelia Hill's scoop about the forthcoming phone-hacking revelations by senior News International executives. (The Dowlers themselves had been informed by the police in April that their daughter's phone had been hacked.) The Labour Party was given an explicit deal in return for the advance warning: 'you can have Andy, but not Rebekah'. At this point News International still thought it could control the news agenda and thereby the course of events: Andy Coulson, Rebekah Brooks's long-serving deputy and successor at *News of the World*, was to be the sacrificial offering to appease the public disgust: the CEO of News International was still untouchable.

In what was, at the time, one of the riskiest moves in his brief tenure as opposition party leader, Miliband defied the threats of News International and, during Parliamentary questions, demanded to know why 220 *News of the World* staff should lose their jobs while their chief executive, Brooks, should keep hers.

The fact that the Labour Party should now distance itself from Brooks and News International was significant in itself. Tony Blair had engaged in a long courtship of Murdoch in the nineties and Brooks herself had become a friend, partying with Tony when Cherie was away, while simultaneously cultivating his internal rival Gordon Brown, mainly through a close friendship with his wife. (The supreme networker, Brooks was becoming best friends with the Conservative party leader Cameron at the same time.) Brooks famously joined Elisabeth Murdoch at a 'sleepover' at the prime minister's country residence Chequers with Sarah Brown in 2008. Despite the forced exposure of his four-year-old son's cystic fibrosis in the *Sun*, Gordon Brown even turned up to her wedding to Charlie Brooks in 2009.

The reaction in Wapping to Miliband's stance was pure fury. Tom Newton Dunn, the *Sun*'s political editor, allegedly threatened 'You made it personal about Rebekah. Now we'll make it personal about you' (News International, 2012). Days later personal stories about senior Labour Party figures began appearing in the tabloids. This had become the modus operandi of News International under Brooks: a charm offensive combined with the threat of public humiliation. Once again, the old politics of personal destruction were wheeled out to bring an errant politician to heel. But it no longer worked. With their obvious motivations now undermining their credibility, the News International attack dogs lacked both bark and bite.

For the first time in decades, the narrative of News International was no longer in the hands of its headline and leader writers. During the Leveson Inquiry ten months later, Murdoch would admit that the closure of the *News of the World* was a 'panicked move'. It was on this Sunday in July, having flown in the previous day that Murdoch told a scrum of photographers and camera crews outside a Mayfair restaurant that his priority was to protect 'that one' – i.e. Brooks. Someone who used his papers regularly to trash personal reputations rather poignantly put the personal reputation of one of his employees above his oldest newspapers. Even more perversely, by doing so, the man who used to own the news found it running away from him again and again.

The next day it emerged that five senior police investigators had been targeted by the *News of the World* in 2006 after Scotland Yard began its initial investigation into phone hacking. The famous question of Juvenal – *'quis custodiet ipsos custodes?'* – 'who watches the watchmen?' or 'who polices the police?' – was finally answered: Murdoch's Sunday tabloid.

The levels of surveillance and intrusion seemed to creep into the highest reaches of the British state. Robert Peston from the BBC revealed police had been handed emails that suggested *News of the World* had paid royal protection officers for private phone numbers and personal details of the royal family. In a BBC interview that day the former prime minister Gordon Brown alleged multiple intrusions into his privacy, attempting to access his voicemail, his bank and legal accounts and his family's medical records. He also claimed that a private investigator used a serving police officer to trawl the police national computer for information about him. The liberal spectre of state surveillance – a major theme since the War on Terror – had completely overlooked the dangers of the threat from private corporate interests.

According to Michael Wolff, the crisis was leading to a 'headless chicken' time at News Corp's New York HQ on the Avenue of the Americas: 'I think Rupert Murdoch for one of the first times in his life has absolutely no idea what he should do,' Wolff tweeted. More lethal allegations were now coming to the surface: a suggestion in the *Daily Mirror* that victims of the 9/11 Trade Center attacks had also been targeted by phone hacking (which has never been substantiated) brought the company close to an American scandal to match the British one. Citizens for Responsibility and Ethics in Washington called for a Congressional Inquiry. More allegations of payments to British police officers brought the US corporation ever closer to a Department of Justice investigation under the Foreign Corrupt Practices Act 1977 (FCPA), which makes it illegal for US companies to bribe foreign officials. News Corp stock fell 7 per cent.

Most catastrophic of all the criminality at the heart of Murdoch's tabloid newspaper operations was the effect on the key corporate objective of the decade. Whoever came up with the codename Rubicon (enough, as Anthony Barnett has said, to 'make a classicist shudder') certainly understood how News Corp's takeover of Britain's pay-TV giant would be a watershed for the media empire, let alone the future of British democracy (for the long-term implications see Chapter 11).

By this point in its history, the world's third largest media conglomerate had transformed itself from a publishing company to one mainly reliant on broadcasting and entertainment. At the end of the first decade of the twenty-first century newspaper and book publishing accounted for less than 20 per cent of News Corp's profits and though they had been great cash cows in the eighties (and still wielded great political influence) the whole News International subsidiary only accounted for 3 per cent of revenues. The future was all in pay-TV and digital services and as a monopoly satellite broadcaster in the UK and a growing European brand, the acquisition of BSkyB was not only a huge boost to News Corp's revenues. Capitalised at around $60 billion, News Corp's future growth was very much predicated on gaining full control of the $20 billion BSkyB asset.

Caesarean ambitions apart, the name Rubicon was probably chosen to mark the big leap forward in News Corp's long-term digital strategy, in the investment into high-definition and interactive services and as Britain's fourth largest provider of broadband access. Having moved from print to analogue broadcasting, James had promised to lead the company forward into the wired-up age of online dominance. Besides being one of his father's cherished long-term ambitions, total ownership of BSkyB was also the prize that could convince any rivals on the News Corp board of James's claim to his father's throne.

Had the Conservatives been in power with an absolute majority perhaps

News Corp could have brazened things out despite the hacking scandal. As Murdoch's written depositions to the Leveson Inquiry later revealed, the bid had been gestating for at least four years and the whole courtship of Cameron had been predicated on its realisation. We've already seen in the previous chapter how the Conservative's policies towards Ofcom and the BBC closely tracked the demands of News Corp from 2007 to the point – on the morning after Gordon Brown's conference speech in 2009 – when the *Sun* switched supported to the Conservatives.

Only now is the extent of the personal lobbying becoming clear. As I write, evidence of even more meetings has emerged and it turns out that James Murdoch met with Cameron at least 14 times between January 2006 and January 2010. Meanwhile, between the election of the coalition government in May 2010 and the breaking of the phone-hacking scandal in July 2011 there were more than sixty meetings between ministers and either Murdoch, James, Brooks or James Harding, editor of *The Times*. These are only the meetings logged by Downing Street and this already amounts to a meeting a week. Then there are the other points of contact, especially between senior News International editors and lobbyists like Frédéric Michel, who seems to have wined, dined, texted and played tennis with most of the special advisors in Whitehall. As a former senior News International journalist told me, by the time of the 2010 General election 'the Court of Murdoch and the Court of Cameron were almost totally enmeshed' (Senior News International source, 2012).

Of course News International had lobbied New Labour for years, especially during the 2003 Communications Act. They had key allies on the Labour side but their crucial miscalculation seems to be that they never planned for any sort of coalition government and their connections with the Liberal Democrats were either poor or non-existent. Indeed, News International had led the fray to 'Get Clegg' after he bounced up in the polls in the first-ever televised leadership campaign during the 2010 election. It could be argued that the independence of the Lib Dems from News Corp influence was the saving grace which made the Leveson Inquiry, and all the subsequent disclosure, possible.

It's hard to escape the conclusion that the key reason for News International's repudiation of Gordon Brown, despite Murdoch's personal friendship with the prime minister, was because he seemed less likely to waive through the BSkyB bid without reference to the regulator or Monopolies and Mergers committee. The remorseless campaign News International – particularly the *Sun* – pursued against Brown was a reminder that the 'bucket of shit' editorial policy Kelvin MacKenzie deployed against Major was still an option.

Surely Miliband could see this: Labour fared badly in the polls without the support of Murdoch's papers. It doesn't really matter if it was down to Murdoch's uncanny ability to pick winners or his ideological leverage to help make them, either way opposing the country's biggest media conglomerate would be risky and even downright dangerous. Nevertheless, that weekend Miliband broke the long Labour truce with News International and called for the BskyB bid to be postponed at least until the criminal investigations were completed. Three days later he would add:

> I think that we've got to look at the situation whereby one person can own more than 20% of the newspaper market, the Sky platform and Sky News. I think it's unhealthy because that amount of power in one person's hands has clearly led to abuses of power within his organisation. If you want to minimise the abuses of power then that kind of concentration of power is frankly quite dangerous.

> (HELM ET AL., 2011)

On the BBC, the deputy prime minister Nick Clegg was actually ahead of the opposition leader and came out publicly against the bid:

> At the moment you can only apply this test of plurality … when you've got a business transaction which you've got to examine. I don't see why that text isn't applied all the time … whether its fitness and properness test, whether it's the plurality test, it's being applied at the moment in a very snapshot way…

> (BBC NEWS, 2011)

Indeed the snapshot was very random. The BSkyB takeover had bypassed the plurality test by promising to spin off Sky News, but news itself is a product of a wider culture, not only of politics, but various forms of expression and communication. Dissidents under Soviet rule understood this and samizdat literature circulated not only underground news but poetry, philosophy, cultural criticism, entertainment and even sports coverage. The danger of a state or commercial monopoly is not just a matter of partisan headlines. If one company becomes the main commissioner of books, newspapers, TV shows, sports and celebrity coverage (not to mention politician's biographies) the whole sphere of free expression becomes chilled and returns us to a pre-modern world of patronage. The Murdochs might make excellent Medicis, but the free market was supposed to bring commercial independence and diversity.

On this day, 11 July 2012, News Corp's years of lobbying and planning were about to go up in smoke. In a manoeuvre designed to postpone but preserve the takeover, News Corp would offer to refer the bid to the Competition Commission the next day – something the whole corporate policy previously was at pains to avoid. Ostensibly it was a canny move to kick the issue into the long grass for another year – perhaps long enough for the scandal to blow over – and in another era would no doubt have succeeded. But not in the new regime: with Miliband's change in stance from postponement of the bid to calling for it to be dropped and the support of Clegg, Murdoch was – for the first time since the late seventies – vulnerable to a chaotic and unpredictable democratic political process. Parliament was in one of its paroxysms and an emergency parliamentary debate on the BSkyB bid was set for two days' time, on 13 July.

Having fallen from grace, the House of Murdoch was now also falling from power.

RUBICON ONE

Twenty-five years earlier, in the first Rubicon moment, Murdoch had sacked 3,000 staff at his existing central London HQ (mainly members of the Society of Graphical and Allied Trades (SOGAT) print union) and moved his four major national newspapers to a new fifteen-acre site in Wapping, whose new presses were now manned by members of the electrician's union, the EETPU. This was a break – paralleled in large swathes of Britain's industrial base – away from both mechanical assembly line production and the associated power of organised labour and free collective bargaining. Though SOGAT was unloved by many (particularly by journalists and editors who had encountered restrictive practices), this violent rupture with trade unionism brought thousands of sympathetic union members onto the streets. The Wapping works were picketed for the next two years, with protestors trying to prevent strike breakers entering the plant or the trucks of the Dutch transport firm TNT leaving it. One night in January 1987, an estimated 10,000 pickets clashed with over a thousand police.

As with the other conflicts in Thatcher's Britain, the traumas of deindustrialisation led to outright civil strife on the streets, but unlike other confrontations – most notably the miners' strike three years previously which took place in the manufacturing heartlands in the north – Wapping became the most tumultuous industrial dispute leading to public disorder in the nation's capital. The other great public order events in London in the eighties – the riots in Notting Hill, Southall, Lewisham, Brixton and Tottenham – had been triggered by heavy-handed policing mixed with racism and youth unemployment: social disorder was an unintended consequence of bad policy. But the protracted dispute at News International's new headquarters was driven by strategy: the conflict wasn't an accident – it was planned. This would have consequences for both the private security and public policing around Wapping for years to come.

Murdoch has claimed that he never had the direct support of government over the move to Wapping, though we know now thanks to the Thatcher archives that there was a lot of mutual agreement about reducing union power in their discussions about the Times Newspapers Group. It's highly unlikely that the consequences of this policy had not been thought through and Murdoch admitted as much when he told the *Independent* in 2006: 'We knew there would be a lot of police protection.' That protective relationship formed in the crucible of the Wapping Dispute would intensify over thirty years, until the Metropolitan Police and News International became so entwined that parts of the tabloid press thought they could operate with impunity. Even when Goodman and Mulcaire were sentenced in 2007, senior executives behaved as if they were 'too big to jail' and the failure of the Metropolitan Police to fully investigate phone hacking at the company would cause several senior officers to resign in short order (see Chapter 10).

For Murdoch and News Corp there were even more pressing commercial imperatives at the time. As we shall see in the next chapter, Murdoch was embarking on a huge US adventure and needed to boost his profits in the UK to do so. The new offset printing presses he had smuggled in (though still not top of the range) combined with computer typesetting would generate great efficiency savings compared to the old hot metal linotype process. Situated outside the inconvenient and congested roads of EC1, Wapping HQ also drastically reduced transport and distribution costs. Murdoch wasn't the first to move his newspaper base from Central London, any more than he was the first to challenge the printers' unions with new technology (Eddie Shah had confronted them at his Warrington print works three years before) but the relocation of the two biggest tabloids and the Times Newspapers Group from Bouverie Street and Gray's Inn Road represented nearly half the entire readership of Britain's papers.

In a few years, Fleet Street had gone from a synecdoche to an antique metaphor. For News International it was a hugely profitable move. The company's profits rose almost fourfold in just two years, from £40 million in 1985 to £150 million in 1987.

Depending on political outlook the Wapping revolution can be seen in three classic ways: the violent betrayal of organised labour, in which capital and the state colluded to tear up the post-war social democratic contract; or a long overdue moment of innovation and job creation, breaking with the corporatist grip of unions power on democratic politics; or – as a combination of both – a necessary moment of breakage with inefficient labour practices, but achieved with unnecessarily brutality and without regard to the long-term consequences. While the private gains mounted, the social costs would be picked up by the tax payer – vastly inflated policing bills, social disruption and long-term problems of unemployment.

In all three accounts, however, there is an undeniable congruence: Thatch-erite beliefs in neo-liberal markets weren't just espoused by Murdoch's news-papers, they were embedded in their means of production. During this period, Murdoch would pull out all the stops to defend Thatcher. Harold Evans had already left *The Times* – and almost came to fisticuffs with his proprietor be-cause of Murdoch's editorial insistence on monetarist dogma and anti-Soviet propaganda. The great crusading investigative *Sunday Times* gave Thatcher cov-er during the Westland crisis. And while the broadsheets failed to investigate the sale of Britain's last remaining helicopter manufacturer to a US company, the *Sun* was less subtle: it ran a picture of the opposing minister, Michael He-seltine, on its front pages with the headline 'You LIAR'. (Only later was it revealed that Murdoch himself was a non-executive director of the American company bidding for the helicopter maker.)

During this era – the moment of News Corp's greatest expansion – Murdoch's editorial writers espoused deregulation and downsizing while he and his manage-ment capitalised on the competitive advantage. There was a brutality about the way News International comported itself, which had something in common with the company's long-term enemy, the Unions. As Peter Mandelson said during the Leveson Inquiry: 'Like the trades unions of old, [the Press] want to operate above the law. And like the trades unions, when you try to apply the law, they shout from the rooftops about basic freedoms and fundamental rights.' True to his uni-versity admiration for Lenin, Murdoch returned to his Marxist materialist roots and proved that base determines superstructure and economics underpins ideology.

CREATIVE DESTRUCTION

I lived across the Thames from Wapping in the eighties and wailing police si-rens could be heard across the river, where trade unionists handed out flyers by Greenwich railway station. Hundreds of police and protestors were injured in nightly demonstrations and over 1,200 arrested. Wapping, like the miners' strike, showed Britain at its most divided since the thirties, but with a subtle difference. As a police helicopter hovered above the docks of East London that night the new equipment started to print a *Times* supplement, the backdrop was different from the valleys of South Wales or the Yorkshire moors.

That this struggle should have taken place in the run-down docklands area of London, symbol of Britain's decayed industrial past and its potential post-industrial future, only adds to Wapping's iconic status. For the generation coming to age in Thatcher's Britain, the unionist past – the guaranteed jobs, the apprenticeships, the knowledge of who you were and what you would do for life – was fast becoming an inconceivable privilege. In an era of mass unemployment, the closed shops and restrictive practices of the print unions appeared self-interested, exclusive and part of the past. Meanwhile the new global horizon could be glimpsed in the scaffolding and cranes on the skyline.

The Wapping dispute took place against the backdrop of the docklands, a vast redevelopment zone which would turn London's former docks into an extension of the financial City and symbolise the increasing reliance over the next three decades on financial services as a source of national wealth. It's hard to remember quite how parlous Britain's economic position was by the late seventies. Having had to be bailed out by the International Monetary Fund (IMF), the country was known for its declining industrial base and decaying Victorian infrastructure. Productive energies were so depleted that one of the few feature films made in the UK in 1979 (and released in 1980) was *The Long Good Friday*, which explored the relative decline of Britain compared to both the US and nationalist movements such as the IRA, through the get-rich-quick gangsterism underpinning the renewal of the docks. Murdoch's Wapping move coincided with an even bigger move – the 'Big Bang' of deregulation, electronic trading and a series of global acquisitions and mergers in the City of London, which led to a sudden explosion east. As I wrote in a book at the time, *A Shout in the Street*:

> *If you really want to see the future of London in the making, you would do well to take a road back to the east.*
>
> *The red brick road round the Isle of Dogs is the long red road of redevelopment. Laid out in the early eighties, it was the inaugural act of the new Development Corporation, and the first sign that the docks, made obsolete by the growth of containerization; were now open for another kind of business. And they soon moved in – the builders, the property speculators, to be followed by the financial headquarter spreading out from the booming square mile of the City. Soon the London marathon was run round this road: and the lean hungry joggers, like the lean hungry businesses, seemed to express not only the renovation of the Docklands, but the revitalization of the British economy. When she visited it during the 1987 election campaign, and rode on its light railway, Prime Minister Margaret Thatcher claimed it as*

her dream colony, her vision of what the new enterprise culture should be like. And what an urban vision that was – sandblasted brick combined with Big Bang hi-tech. The billboards hiding the marked lots showed corporate tower shimmering over the dock-water, with this legend beneath: 'Canary Wharf – It will look like Venice, but work like New York'

Whatever your opinion of this vast urban 'renewal' scheme, no one can help being impressed by its phenomenal energy and shattering force. Come back in a month or so and you'll scarcely recognize the landscape: bricks, girders and glass seem to be spewed out of the ground. Beneath the whirr of the Docklands model trains, the chatter of props from the Docklands model planes, signs say DANGER: DEEP EXCAVATION or THS IS A HARD HAT ZONE. And that's what it is, a place for hard hats, hard heads, hard cash. It's not just new building you can smell here, but the new designs, new industries, new lifestyles of a global culture. Indeed it could be business district in New York, or it could be Venice. It could be Hong Kong or Bogota.

(JUKES, 1991)

One of the first significant principalities in this new multipolar and borderless world of finance and information would be what I call 'Newscorp Nation'. The relocation as News International's print plant to the periphery of this new zone is no accident. From his business trajectory from Adelaide, through London, to New York, Murdoch has emphatically identified himself with the forces of global deregulation, followed their deep currents, surfed and occasionally crashed on their eddies and flows, but here he was riding high. As Murdoch told the *Independent* in 2006, the Wapping dispute was in many ways the high point of his career in 'political economy': 'It was an ugly period, but it was wonderful.'

Ugly but wonderful: innovation and conflict, social disruption and transformation, this is the creative destruction of modern markets in which – as Marx and Engels described in the *Communist Manifesto* – 'all that is solid melts into air'. With his roots in colonialism and an Oxford degree in philosophy, politics and economics, Murdoch became a pivotal player in an era which saw Britain lurch violently away from its manufacturing base towards a service-based economy, increasingly reliant on information and knowledge, in which financial services, virtual markets, advertising, PR, design, entertainment and news would become bigger sectors of the economy than steel, coal or shipping. Within a few years there would be more people employed in telesales than agriculture. Murdoch's terse expression of wonder at all this tumult echoes Marx's encomium to the bourgeoisie (rather brilliantly changed to 'capitalism' by John Lanchester in the *London Review of Books*).

> *Capitalism cannot exist without constantly revolutionising the instruments of production, and thereby the means of production, and with them the whole relations of society. Constant revolutionising of production, uninterrupted disturbance of all social conditions, everlasting uncertainty and agitation distinguish the capitalist epoch from all earlier ones. All old-established national industries have been destroyed or are daily being destroyed.*
>
> *In place of the old wants, satisfied by the productions of the country, we find new wants, requiring for their satisfaction the products of distant lands and climes.*
>
> *Commercial crises put on trial, each time more threateningly, the existence of the entire capitalist society. In these crises a great part not only of the existing products, but also of the previously created productive forces, are periodically destroyed.*
>
> (LANCHESTER, 2012)

(Even the word capitalism doesn't do justice to this phenomenon; this was an era of top-down, finance driven investment of a few global players. International monopoly capitalism would be a better description.)

Ultimately, it is this emotional apprehension of that 'wonderful moment' of disruption which unites the anti-establishment radical in Murdoch with the conservative hegemon and makes him a representative of an epoch, a real-life Citizen Kane of the second half of the twentieth century. The anarchist tradition is there in the legacy of Mikhail Bakunin, who once averred 'Revolution requires extensive and widespread destruction, a fecund and renovating destruction, since in this way and only this way are new worlds born' (Bakunin, 1971). But the Thatcherite revolution is also contained in it, as the rallying cry of 'creative destruction' was adopted, via Joseph Schumpeter, as the neo-liberal justification for ferocious downsizing and the predatory mergers and acquisitions of the eighties (see Chapter 8).

For all his myriad contradictions, Murdoch is entirely consistent with the unambiguous trends of the last century.

Tony Blair once described dealing with Murdoch as 'riding the tiger' but the same is true of Murdoch's own engagement with capitalism: there's no guarantee that any company which seeks to ride these disruptive energies will always benefit and the titanic forces that helped to create News Corp as a family dynasty would begin to consume it. That belief in the unmitigated good of unfettered Reaganomics and global financial wizardry – physically represented by the banking district around Canary Wharf – now looks as outdated as the post-modern architecture. Wapping itself would soon fade into myth and reality as the fifteen-acre site was put up for sale in 2011 and sold in spring 2012 to make way for a residential development.

SATELLITE BUCCANEER

One indication of the executive nomadism of Murdoch's life is that, for all the epochal changes during the Wapping dispute, his mind was actually focused on forces thousands of miles away from the street-level battles. By 1986, with his market power in British newspapers producing profits of hundreds of millions of pounds a year, Murdoch was lifting his eyes both upward and outward: outward to the US where thanks to Reagan he was a rapid entry citizen and upward to the new infotainment horizons of satellite broadcasting and pay-TV. Having created the first popular tabloid of the television age with the *Sun*, Murdoch realised quickly that it was a means to an end: why rely on television to promote your products when you could go into television yourself?

In the thirties Keith Murdoch had seen in the US the importance of cross-ownership of radio stations for a newspaper business; in the sixties his son had attempted to buy chunks of TV stations in Australia and the UK. But now Murdoch had a strategic vision of this new media future based on something much more global and broad ranging than mast based signals. Satellite communications, first imagined by Arthur C. Clarke, had made global news coverage a reality. In the eighties satellites were still mainly used as a form of communication between terrestrial stations. Murdoch spotted a new possibility, however: direct broadcast satellite services which would directly communicate to the consumer through their own satellite dishes. Freed from the national restrictions of land-based broadcasting, this kind of communication was only limited by the curvature of the earth.

Unlike most other would-be satellite pioneers in the UK, Murdoch already had the loyal consumer base. Management had calculated in 1981 that if the daily four million newspaper readers of the *Sun* and *News of the World* could be converted into pay-TV viewers, then they would pay much higher premiums – especially for sport. The company's revenues could be increased tenfold. Without losing circulation (and with near zero advertising costs) a pay-TV station could be marketed to that captive audience, creating a virtual circle of cross promotion and subsidisation potentially more lucrative than the famous 'license to print money' commercial stations already enjoyed.

It was an insight of technological and consumer genius. Murdoch didn't need to buy stakes in LWT or destroy Thames TV anymore, he could supersede the old land-based masts. Whether or not Murdoch's intervention in satellite broadcast was the beginning of a new monopoly or – as the blogger Paul Staines (aka Guido Fawkes) recently informed me – a great moment for pluralism and freedom of choice can be left aside for a moment. There's no doubt it was a visionary insight and one which the media mogul pursued with great tenacity, at a cost of billions of dollars over the next decade and near bankruptcy for News Corp.

In 1983, for only £1 plus debts, News Corporation acquired an ailing satellite channel called SATV which mainly broadcast feeds to cable companies. Murdoch renamed it the Sky Channel early the following year. For five years the company lay in abeyance, biding its time. Then in 1987, as the Independent Broadcasting Authority (IBA) opened for licences for direct broadcast, Murdoch put in his bid. But his existing holdings in papers put him again in danger of competition law and the IBA awarded a direct satellite licence to British Satellite Broadcasting, a consortium of ITV companies and Pearson. But Murdoch was ready with his own 'spoiler': Sky TV was launched as four channels on the Astra 1A satellite orbiting at 19.2° east: Sky Channel, Eurosport, Sky Movies and Sky News.

Sky would be the main thrust of Murdoch's UK strategy throughout the nineties, only paralleled by his slow establishment of a fourth TV Network in the US, which required US citizenship to follow through. Having triumphed in the Fleet Street ground war, News International's editors were deputised to lead an air campaign. Both Andrew Neil and Kelvin MacKenzie were enticed away from their editorships of the *Sun* and *Sunday Times* by the bright lights of the TV studio. As Chippindale and Horrie put it: 'Throughout News Corp., resources and talented executives were being moved out of mass-market-papers and into mass-market television ... As the *Sun* began to sink below the horizon, the Sky satellite began to shine more bright' (1990). The TV dominance of the tabloids would be replaced by tabloid TV.

MONOPOLOGY

It's part of the Murdoch paradox, especially given his libertarian beliefs, that Sky's fortunes at the time relied once again on the role of the regulator – though in this case, by reverse. The licence won by Murdoch's rivals, BSB, was actually restrictive, limiting the number of channels BSB could broadcast and insisting on high-tech specifications for the satellite receiving dishes were much more ambitious and expensive. Though based in the UK (near Isleworth where it is still headquartered) Sky was actually transmitting from a Belgium registered satellite and came under the purview of the more lenient Cable Authority. Murdoch exploited the bureaucratic red tape that hindered his rivals. And he had important support in high places; despite protests from most people in the broadcasting industry, Thatcher's government didn't close the legal loophole which Sky had snuck through. Rather like Queen Elizabeth I with her penchant for 'privateers', Thatcher admired many free market adventurers who pushed the boundaries.

It was a risky move which could have gone badly wrong. Both Sky and BSB haemorrhaged cash and within a year the two satellite companies were struggling with their debts and cash losses. In a parting shot, before her own defenestration by the Conservative Party, Thatcher allowed Sky and BSkyB to merge. Thanks to News Corp's centralised ownership the fifty–fifty split left Murdoch with a controlling interest of 39 per cent compared to the BSB stakeholders. Meanwhile his old enemy the BBC, under the directorship of Marmaduke Hussey (a former employee of Murdoch's at *The Times*), helped him acquire rights for the broadcast of English football away from ITV.

All this was taking place in an era of rapid technical innovation and the success of direct broadcast satellites was – rather like the explosion of personal computers around the same time – dictated by social trends towards personalisation, 'me-TV' and a kind of narrowcasting which few experts predicted at the time. Murdoch's great gamble would take years to pay off and only did so on the back of an even bigger social and technological movement, when computing and broadcast TV underwent the great 'convergence' of the digital age and the activity of the consumer – their power to search, download, save and control programming – undermined the whole mass media broadcasting paradigm of the twentieth century.

For all his inventiveness and investment, Murdoch also had a unique insight into the loopholes in competition law and cross-ownership from his experience across three continents and various changing national governments. The great thing for him, in terms of this revolution in technology and patterns of consumption, was that regulation was very slow to catch up to his various interlocking projects. The advent of the internal combustion engine had created the same loopholes a hundred years ago, which allowed Standard Oil to develop various upstream and downstream forms of integration in the oil business that landed it monopoly power across whole swathes of the East Coast, until trust-busting legislation broke it up.

A similar monopoly control shaped the movie industry in the mid-twentieth century, until trust-busting legislation limited cross-ownership of both studios and cinema chains. In the early days of the information age, Murdoch understood that controlling the carrier is more important that whatever raw material you're delivering: refined news or crude entertainment. How you get to market is more relevant than what you take to market: content is not king, distribution is.

It took years of legislation to break the monopoly powers accrued in oil distribution or Hollywood films. It wasn't until Claire Enders analysed the consequences of News Corp's complete ownership of BSkyB in late 2010 that the potential monopoly problems in the British media market were exposed – and this was almost too late. By that time News Corp, at least in the UK, had become the Standard Oil of the information age.

One example of the problems of monopoly for fair competition is the cross-promotion which Murdoch soon exploited in News International. With four million readers, the *Sun* was an ideal vehicle to target potential subscribers to Sky; sometimes through the tradition means of advertising, but also through stealth marketing of the 'advertorial'. The British satirical magazine *Private Eye* has been running a regular column since 1990 called 'I-Sky' documenting the obvious plugs for the satellite broadcaster in the comment and news sections of the tabloid. When, in May 2012, Murdoch said to Lord Justice Leveson (more than once) 'we have never pushed our commercial interests in our newspapers' the magazine let rip:

> So said Rupert Murdoch at the Leveson inquiry, speaking under oath. We must assume that either the DPP will prosecute him for perjury ... or that incidents recorded in the Eye over the last 25 years have been complete coincidences.
>
> Such as the series of pieces examining the complex problem of deregulating television under headlines such as 'Smash The ITV Cartel' which we noted began appearing in Murdoch's mid-market title Today at the time Mrs Thatcher was chairing a cabinet sub-committee on broadcasting in 1987.
>
> Or the appearance of a puff-piece for Disney in the Sunday Times at the exact point, in 1988, when Sky TV was doing a deal with the company, negotiated by Sunday Times editor Andrew Neil, who was employed at the same time as executive chairman of Sky. Neil also recruited one Jonathan Miller to write a 'Behind the Screens' column, which peddled some extremely Murdochian views of the TV industry in the early 1990s, without disclosing to readers that his previous job was as director of public affairs for Sky.

(PRIVATE EYE, ISSUE 1313)

(I remember Jonathan Miller's vituperative attacks on public broadcasting; it felt like partisanship at the time, masquerading as journalism. But I had no idea that he was paid to be a zealot.) The *Private Eye* article then goes on to list just a few of the more egregious cross-promotional plugs such as a 36-page supplement on digital television in the upmarket *Times* on the very day Sky Digital launched in 1998; or a *Sun* tirade against a rise in the BBC licence the next year which pointed out:

> Our parent company, News Corporation, bet the ranch on Sky – the entire company's future rested on its success. In the process, millions of Brits were given more choice, 24-hour news, the best movies and the best in sports. Now, a few years later, Sky Digital customers are to be asked to pay £24 to help its main rival, the BBC, catch up. What sort of a country is this?

This 1998 op-ed is nearly identical to James Murdoch's MacTaggart lecture a decade later and the essential argument has not changed: an anti-establishment line used to create a new media establishment; a celebration of pluralism deployed to justify a dominant market share. There should be a new word for this: *monopology*.

Private Eye shows the monopologists at work for the next decade, both in the downmarket tabloids and the supposed independent upmarket titles. *Private Eye* concludes:

> Since the I-Sky column (aka I-BSkyB and Plugged In) launched in 1990, Lord Gnome has run hundreds of examples of plugs for Murdoch businesses – not just Sky, but his film and web interests too – masquerading as news items in papers he publishes.
>
> On the very two days on which Rupert was in the witness box at the Leveson inquiry last week, the Sun carried an anti-Beeb story, 'BBC slated on 'Olympic social cleaning claim', a gratuitous plug for Sky in a photo story about a policeman road-testing a motorised scooter with a speech bubble 'Must remember to Sky Plus the Grand Prix', and the claim that Kasabian singer Tom Meighan had boasted that 'We've got satellite TV on the tour bus so we can watch footie on Fox Soccer.'

Yet still the monopologists continue to maintain that the merger of Sky and BSB advanced the cause of pluralism. Guido Fawkes told me that Britain only had three broadcasters when BSkyB came along (there were actually already four) and somehow forgot that the formation of the company reduced the number of satellite broadcasters by 50 per cent.

There's little doubt that BSkyB was a commercial triumph: it went on to become the most lucrative broadcaster in the UK due to some major innovations in sports rights and digital technology. But was this really a triumph for pluralism? As for those libertarians who cite BSkyB as an exemplar of the superiority of the free market model compared to the 'state socialism' of the BBC, they're obviously overlooking an inconvenient fact: Murdoch was hardly winning a simple market battle with his competitors. Under Thatcher's government he was clearly a beneficiary of government favouritism. The 1990 Broadcasting Act had a controversial loophole which exempted Sky as a non-UK service. This 'picking winners' – exactly the kind of corporatism Thatcher and Murdoch claimed to hate. Though his buccaneering spirit had been admired in the court of Thatcher since the beginning of the decade with the takeover of The Times Group, Murdoch sailed very close to the wind even as her administration drew to a close.

For all the success of getting Sky off the ground direct satellite broadcasting would soon create a huge headache for Murdoch. Unlike subscription cable, with its hard-wired hook-ups to individual users, a satellite signal can be received by anyone with a dish in the line of sight. Old terrestrial broadcasters had solved this problem by going 'free to air' and funding their free broadcast either through advertising or some state subvention. Murdoch's pay-TV model only worked if it could achieve 'conditional access' – in other words, a way of making people pay for premium material, usually through the encryption of the original transmission and decryption through a smart card in a set-top box.

To form the basis of this revenue gathering system, Murdoch turned to a company based in Israel, National Datacom Services, founded by ten scientists from the Weizmann Institute in 1988. The start-up had developed a smart card based on the technology developed by the Israeli cryptographer Adi Shamir, and Murdoch chose their product to control his worldwide pay-TV services. However, National Datacom Services was riven by board factions, accusations of illegality and even phone tapping. The company was bought by News Corp in 1992 for $15 million, renamed NDS, and headquartered in Staines not far from the BSkyB base.

Many threads would converge in the fascinating history of NDS (best documented by the investigative work of Neil Chenoweth at the *Australian Financial Review*). Over the next two decades, NDS would take the piracy problem to a new dimension and combine the allegations of anti-competitive behaviour at News Corp with another potential hacking story that could still dwarf the *News of the World* scandal in terms of commercial cost and international scope. Even more significantly, at least in terms of the human cost of the Wapping dispute, it would unearth connections between senior News Corp staff and two notorious murders in the London quarter of a century ago (see Chapter 10).

MONOCULTURE

This long history of anti-state rhetoric and deep-state collusion came to head with the Rubicon process – James Murdoch's bid to achieve his father's dream of total control of UK broadcasting. The explicit aim, as reiterated by Hunt's memo to Cameron in November 2010 (only revealed through Leveson Inquiry disclosure in the summer of 2012) was to launch Wapping Two in the acres of land recently acquired round the BSkyB base in Isleworth and to create the same kind of hegemony in broadcasting he had achieved in print. The hubris of the Rubicon project, not only in the way News Corp wielded its massive legal and lobbying clout, but also in the attempt to nobble its public service rival, the BBC, provides – in retrospect – the underlying framework to the whole hacking scandal and vigorous corporate cover up.

Everything was done to keep the BSkyB bid separate from the hacking scandal; this explains the doubling down on the 'rogue reporter' defence for five years, despite mounting evidence to the contrary. As the crisis reached a crescendo over these two weeks in July, the backstop position was the 'rogue newspaper' defence and hence the sudden closure of *News of the World*. The unexpected arrest of the CEO of the whole London publishing subsidiary, Rebekah Brooks, removed the last firewall before James Murdoch himself. But then an ever bigger threat emerged across the Atlantic. As corrupt payments to officials became part of the alleged criminality at Wapping, the US Department of Justice took an interest, since American legislation forbids US companies from corrupting officers in other countries (see Chapter 8). The News Corp headquarters in New York was now in the firing line.

None of this means that either the Murdochs or News Corp are evil incarnate. When it comes to the criminal allegations against News International, the abuse of power flows from the monopoly position within the British press.

In economic terms, monopoly is a special problem which all but the most extreme libertarians acknowledge is one of the limitations of laissez faire capitalism: price efficiency and discovery go out of the window without real competition. As Adam Smith (the economist, not Hunt's special advisor) had pointed out 300 years ago, monopolies often form where there is legal or governmental restriction – a natural issue in broadcasting because of licensing of the common goods of the broadcast spectrum. Monopolies can also arise by mergers, horizontally within a sector or vertically through the supply chain. In this case, legislation is not the problem it's the solution, as witnessed by the trust-busting Sherman Act in the US in the late nineteenth century, which allowed the Supreme Courts to begin to break up the monopoly of Standard Oil in the early twentieth century.

When it comes to modern media monopolies, which intrude in the realm of information, the economic problem rapidly becomes a social and political one. Dominant news organisations not only have the power to affect our rational choice of their products, they also impinge on the public's perception of political choices and therefore vitiate the democratic process. The consequences of this go well beyond price signalling or a commodity scarcity; a media monopoly can both dominate the market and influence legislation designed to fix market failures. Though not unique to media conglomerates (modal monopolies in the banking system have created similar feedback loops), the News Corp story is an historic object lesson in the combined abuse of economic *and* political power. As new media monopolies – from Facebook and Google to Amazon – form before our eyes, the lesson it provides is even more salutary for the future.

Many free market thinkers will, however, defend News Corp's commercial monopoly in the UK as some kind of counterweight to the state monopoly represented by the BBC. They (as Hunt did in his memo) argue that though the public service broadcaster's £3 billion licence fee income is dwindling to a half of the revenues of BSkyB, the BBC's TV and radio stations reach many more people than the commercial satellite channel. They effectively elide an ideological argument with an economic one. Not only is the public service broadcaster biased to the left in its news coverage, but its very existence, funded by the compulsory tax of the licence fee, smacks of the suppression of free choice imposed by state socialism.

Some rhetorical legerdemain is going on in this argument, though it doesn't necessarily discredit the central thesis. Most governments impose compulsory tariffs, such as the driving licence and road tax, which are vital to the smooth working of physical communications and do not indicate a far left authoritarian regime. As culture secretary James Hunt pointed out in his Leveson testimony, the BBC is not 'state sponsored', but run at arm's length by charter – though the ability of successive governments from Thatcher through Blair to Cameron to undermine senior management and affect its budget somewhat contradicts that. The BBC is not technically an economic monopoly either because it's a non-profit making organisation – though that wouldn't prevent the social and cultural effects of over centralised media power. Besides, as a libertarian argument, the idea that the 'BBC did it first' is hardly a compelling justification for market dominance. Free enterprise is supposed to be the antidote to the road to serfdom and centralisation of power, not an excuse for 'It's my time for monopoly too'.

With the theoretical arguments so convoluted and confused, perhaps the best assessment of the value of public service broadcasting is evidence-based; an empirical evaluation of what collective provision delivers compared to an unfettered free market. At a third of the cost of BSkyB for consumers, the BBC – a bit like Britain's socialised healthcare system – claims great 'value for money' in terms of news coverage, entertainment and cultural creativity. On news coverage alone: despite many recent cuts the corporation's news and current affairs coverage has international profile and authority which Sky News is a long way from matching in news gathering and foreign bureaux. As for investing in national talent, whether through in-house traineeships or production of science documentaries, pop and orchestral music, local radio, radio drama, reading programmes, adult education, children's programming, coverage of politics and Parliament, this is something that BSkyB, for all its qualities, does not yet even pretend to touch.

However, none of these proven successes necessarily means the BBC will *a priori* advance pluralism any more than News Corp. Indeed, my criticism of the BBC (which I have made publicly at some risk to my career as a television dramatist) is the internal lack of pluralism and accountability when it comes to its internal structure and diversity of programming.

With some historical irony, my essay 'Why Britain can't do The Wire' would have been music to the ears of News Corp lobbyists when it was published by *Prospect* magazine and then promoted by the *Guardian* in late 2009, especially when it was summarised: the critically acclaimed US television drama could not be made here. We have writing talent in abundance, but its output is controlled by a stifling monopoly – the BBC. The piece was about the relative rise of quality US TV drama compared to the UK, which used to dominate the field. Rather than a decline in directing, writing or acting talent I found that the key problem was institutional and structural: diversity and innovation was being squeezed out by a heavily centralised and controlling hierarchy. In 1994, I wrote a tribute to Dennis Potter in the *New Statesman* about the decline of the single authored play on British television. The most obvious cause of this decline was the concentration of commissioning into a few hands. Despite the growth of the independent sector, just four men decided what millions would watch. The difference between 1994 and 2009 was startling. Instead of being the responsibility of four network controllers, most drama was commissioned by one person.

Thirty years previously, before the rise of the channel controllers and during the corporation's golden age, individual producers had much more autonomy. The internal pluralism was high and the overarching hierarchy of the organisation was much smaller and less focused on controlling content. Like any bureaucracy, the BBC is in constant need of reform to make it concentrate on delivery and evidence-based assessments of that. Like most public sector reforms, the supposed restructuring has more than often seen an increase in managers and consultants, at a cost to the consumer.

There are of course many other ways to fund public service broadcasting apart from the licence fee and there is no reason a single hierarchy should dominate the distribution of revenues. One of the huge oversights of the BBC's governance is that principles of pluralism are not written into the corporation's structure as well as its mission statement. For all the problems of the BBC, the comparison with News Corp only proves one thing: a corporate bureaucracy can be as bad as a public service one. Murdoch can't excuse News Corp's failings merely by claiming two wrongs make a right and the BBC (or ABC) started it.

The criticism of the BBC by James Murdoch, swiftly followed by Cameron and Hunt, was opportunistic. They complained that the broadcaster was not commercial enough and then that it was too commercial. A win-win for them and a lose-lose for the BBC. However, the long-term devaluation, through the libertarian rhetoric of Murdoch's newspapers, of any notion of a public service ethos, has inevitably had its effect.

The BBC has intellectually doffed its hat to the libertarian argument and conceded the principle in the last twenty years of reforms, mainly initiated by John Birt. Though he did a great job of protecting the BBC and expanding its news and current affairs coverage during the time of Thatcher, the chasing of audience ratings, the 'change management' turmoil and jargon (called 'Birtspeak' by *Private Eye*) and the paying of private sector fees and salaries to staff: all these can be seen as a category confusion, the invasion of corporate commercial practices in a company that was protected from the whims of the market.

By the late noughties, when Murdoch and Cameron let off their warning broadsides, the BBC had become the worst of both worlds – a state monopoly with a private corporate ethos. Despite these rectifiable errors, the BBC is – like the National Health Service – still democratically supported by an overwhelming proportion of British tax payers in recent opinion polls.

If we are to believe that buying a copy of a newspaper is some kind of analogy for democracy, as Murdoch told the Leveson Inquiry, then the BBC has been approved by its listeners and viewers for nearly a century. Of the dozens of governments it has survived since 1921, none of them have campaigned on a manifesto promise to destroy it. We now know that a key part of James Murdoch's Rubicon process was to nobble his main opposition and reduce the BBC budget by 40 per cent (Senior BBC source, 2012). Thanks to the intervention of the Liberal Democrat coalition partners, the effective cut ended up being 16 per cent – a small victory perhaps for back-room lobbying, but not for democracy; neither reduction was in the Liberal Democrat or Conservative party manifesto.

None of this invalidates BSkyB's claim to its own audience. One of the paradoxes of the whole collision between the hacking and the BSkyB bid is that this happened during a time when the satellite broadcaster was expanding its UK production and finally staking a valid claim to be a contributor to the country's cultural pluralism. Under James's leadership (and let us not forget the strictures of Ofcom regulation) BSkyB was rolling out high-definition TV, new arts, drama and comedy strands, as well as a strong broadband complement. BSkyB has – empirically – begun to demonstrate its worth as a commercial broadcaster and a national treasure. The fact it got targeted in a dynastic succession, and caught in the illegality at News International, should not stop anyone appreciating what it has achieved.

Combined with proper regulation and a diversified ownership, BSkyB shows what the Murdochs' acumen can achieve when they're kept honest by a variety of forces. It also goes some way to show that, if you really believe in competition, then you need competing models of broadcasting too – not the monoculture of something entirely state run or commercially driven.

NOT FIT

The Murdochs' favourite author, George Orwell, was inspired by his wartime experience at the BBC World Service (funded at that time by the Foreign Office) for his depiction of media totalitarianism. Big Brother showed how dangerous a state monopoly of speech could be for civil debate and civil society in the twentieth century. But we don't have many models for how a corporate monopoly would look like in the twenty-first – until now.

When the House of Commons Select Culture, Media and Sport committee finally issued its final report into News International and Phone Hacking on 1 May 2012, it was this aspect of corporate governance the committee emphasised in its damning conclusion:

> On the basis of the facts and evidence before the Committee, we conclude that, if at all relevant times Rupert Murdoch did not take steps to become fully informed about phone-hacking, he turned a blind eye and exhibited wilful blindness to what was going on in his companies and publications. This culture, we consider, permeated from the top throughout the organisation and speaks volumes about the lack of effective corporate governance at News Corporation and News International. We conclude, therefore, that Rupert Murdoch is not a fit person to exercise the stewardship of a major international company.
>
> (Great Britain. Parliament. House of Commons, 2012b)

The 'not fit' language was a bomb lobbed at Murdoch's BSkyB holdings and a reference to the 'fit and proper person' test of the broadcasting regulator, Ofcom, which by then had begun its investigation (Operation Apple) into News Corp's status. However, the 'not fit' descriptors had also been used in the past by the Office of Fair Trading when evaluating Murdoch's long-dead foe, Robert

Maxwell. Meanwhile the 'wilful blindness' phraseology was just as damaging to the parent company, News Corp; it is the precise formula describing the duty of senior executives to actively seek out malpractice, which came into force after the Enron scandal.

At the time, in the British press at least, this conclusion was deemed to be highly partisan, beyond the remit of the committee's brief and undermining the wider consensus that Colin Myler (former *News of the World* editor), Tom Crone (top legal advisor) and Les Hinton (former CEO at News International) had misled Parliament. Conservative members of the committee took to the airwaves to denounce the highly partisan conclusion (though the Liberal Democrat MP Adrian Saunders had voted for it).

Of the sixty or so people so far arrested in the police investigations into News International only a handful have been charged, most notably Brooks and Coulson, and there are still more arrests and hundreds of potential charges to come. Criminal trials on phone hacking, police bribes and attempts to pervert the course of justice are expected to last until 2015, right up until the planned next general election in the UK. The Metropolitan Police have budgeted £40 million to carry on their three major investigations until the same time. As those criminal allegations are examined in open court over the next two or three years, the select committee's 'not fit' conclusion may well seem self-evident in the years to come, if not erring on the side of caution. By that time News Corp could furnish historians with an example of how a corporate bureaucracy can be as dysfunctional as any government one.

8

13 July 2011

News Corp Nation

It was a momentous day for Parliament, a rare instance – outside wartime – of complete unanimity among the three major parties as the House of Commons debated the BSkyB takeover: every member of Parliament who spoke excoriated News International for the phone-hacking scandal and agreed the News Corp bid should be dropped. In Prime Minister's Questions, David Cameron acknowledged that the revelation of the hacking of Milly Dowler's phone had unleashed a 'firestorm'. The opposition leader Ed Miliband concurred and pressed home his advantage: Rebekah Brooks should resign. It was no longer possible to separate the BSkyB bid from the wrongdoing exposed at News International. The owners of News Corp should 'recognise the House has changed' and have 'stopped the business of mergers, and got on with the business with cleaning its own stables'.

The writing was on the wall for Project Rubicon. Even before the House of Commons debate began, News Corp pre-emptively withdrew its bid for 100 per cent of Britain's biggest broadcaster. James Murdoch's claim to succession was abandoned with a cost of around £100 million in legal and break fees and a gaping hole in the long-term corporate strategy for dominance in the digital age. A combination of tenacious investigative journalism, political campaigning,

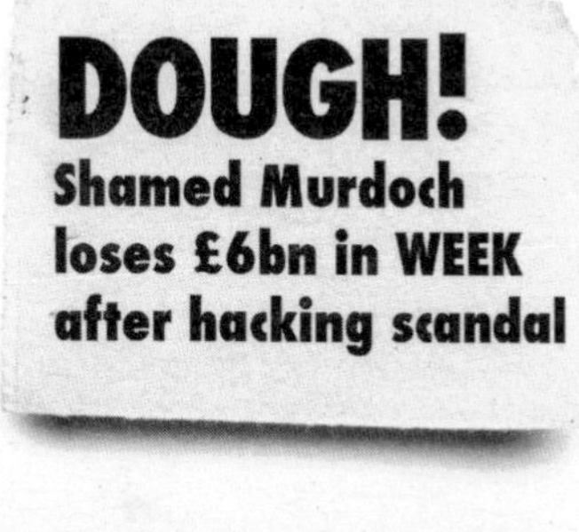
DOUGH!

Shamed Murdoch loses £6bn in WEEK after hacking scandal

Figure 8.1 Daily Mirror, *13 July 2011*

legal revelation and finally 'people pressure' exercised online through advertising boycotts and petitions, had stymied the greatest threat to media plurality and political transparency in post-war Britain.

CAESAREAN BIRTH

It would take another ten months for the truth to emerge about the intense volume of background lobbying that had gone into the bid. As part of his evidence – and in what looked like a permanent burning of bridges with his erstwhile supporters in the Conservative Party – Murdoch lodged over 160 emails between Europe's senior News Corp lobbyist, Frédéric Michel, and the Special Advisor (spad) to the culture minister, Adam Smith. They showed an intimacy between the corporation and the department supposed to be overseeing the proposed takeover in a 'quasi-judicial' way. Smith promptly resigned. More evidence of the volume of interaction between Hunt's office and News Corp which, in total, amounted to over 1,000 phone calls, texts and emails surfaced when Smith and Michel appeared before Lord Justice Leveson in May. Meanwhile, Smith admitted, his department had had virtually no contact with the coalition of media companies that opposed the bid (including the BBC, the *Guardian*, the *Daily Telegraph* and the *Daily Mail*) as it tried to judge a merger which would have radically changed the landscape of British broadcasting.

Robert Jay QC, counsel to the Inquiry, called the regular email, calls and texts from Hunt's office a 'running commentary' for News Corp. One of the most potentially damaging emails revealed that Smith sent Michel advance notice of Hunt's decision at 3:25 a.m. the night before it was announced to Parliament. This was market-sensitive information and according to newspaper reports has since attracted the interest of Britain's financial regulator, the FSA. Under pressure, Smith conceded that Hunt had been 'favourable' to New Corp's bid.

One of the most important disclosures of the whole Leveson process to date had been the scale of the ambition behind the BSkyB bid. This was revealed in a draft memorandum written by Hunt to Cameron in November 2010 after Hunt had been in conversation with James Murdoch: 'James Murdoch is pretty furious with Vince's referral to Ofcom...' In an illuminating insight into the combustible mix of family dynamics and corporate hubris in News Corp, Hunt then went on to explain how James wanted to emulate his father's bold Wapping move in the eighties, which revolutionised Fleet Street:

> *The U.K. has the chance to lead the way on this as we did in the 80s with the Wapping move but if we block it our media sector will suffer for years. In the*

> *end I am sure sensible controls can be put into any merger to ensure there is plu-*
> *rality but I think it would be totally wrong to cave into the Mark Thompson/*
> *Channel 4/Guardian line that this represents a substantial change of control*
> *given that we all know Sky is controlled by News Corp now anyway.*
>
> (MICHEL AND SMITH, 2011)

Not only did the memorandum contradict what Hunt had said in Parliament ('I made absolutely no interventions seeking to influence a quasi-judicial decision that was at that time the responsibility of the Secretary of State for Business' (Great Britain. Parliament. House of Commons, 2012a)) it also revealed the un-reliability of News Corp's assurances about the BSkyB bid. To counter the media coalition's claims that the takeover would give the company a cross-platform mo-nopoly, News Corp explicitly denied it was going to 'bundle' its print, broad-cast and digital products. But after a conversation that day with James Murdoch, Hunt revealed to the prime minister that this was indeed News Corp's plan all along. The secretary of state for culture does not seem shocked by this change of plan, indeed he actively approves it. A few months later, Hunt would accept News Corp's 'undertakings in lieu' in which it promised to spin off Sky News into a separate company, thereby obviating any need for an Ofcom news 'plu-rality' test. Later the next year the culture secretary would take this promise at face value, even though Hunt's memo reveals he knew News Corp had not been honest with the public about its real aims. He also ignored the long history of the Murdoch family when it came to government agreements, going back to the attempted takeover of LWT and particularly the guarantees for *The Times* which Murdoch himself had later said were not worth the paper they were written on.

As revealed in that memo, Hunt's main line of defence for the takeover was that a News Corp digital hegemony would advance the interests of the Brit-ish media sector. This betrays either stunning ignorance or shameful mendacity. True, the classic neo-liberal defence of national monopoly has been the argument that companies need to converge to compete globally and that a lack of competi-tion at home could mean more competition in the global market. Such a rationale is often deployed to justify market dominance in the banking, aerospace or phar-maceutical industries – with mixed results. But there's a salient error in Hunt's defence of News Corp as a representative of the British media sector.

News Corp is a US, not a British, company. The Murdochs are American citizens, whose wealth is ultimately held in a trust in Australia. Whoever benefit-ted from this combination of a print and broadcast monopoly it would not be the British taxpayer. Meanwhile, any nationally-based competitor would be radi-cally out-matched and outgunned. The long-term national interests of the media sector here would have withered in the shade of such an empire.

News International's domination of Fleet Street led to many abuses of power – surveillance, privacy intrusion, bribes and lawbreaking. If the company had achieved an equivalent dominance in TV and the digital domain, there would have been no checks and balances. Already powerful enough to intimidate prime ministers and senior police officers, the merger would have made News Corp – in other words the Murdoch family – de facto the most powerful institution in the country. Britain would have been ruled by an unaccountable foreign dynasty, reversing hundreds of years of parliamentary reform.

In retrospect the code name for the BSkyB takeover (perhaps borrowed from Tom Holland's *Rubicon*, a riveting and popular account of the destruction of the Roman Republic) was all too apt. Julius Caesar's *'discrimen'* before the small river near Ravenna before he marched on Rome in 49 AD to end the republic and re-place it with autocracy. As a result of crossing that Rubicon 'a thousand years of civic self-government were brought to an end, and not for another thousand, and more, would it become a living reality today' (Holland, 2003). The Murdoch imperium would never be so vast or long-lived, but had this particular Rubicon been crossed, the republic of letters and ideas, the autonomy and diversity of our media, would have surely – if the Fleet Street example is anything to go by – viti-ated by dynastic power for a generation or more.

It was such a close run thing. Before civil society congratulates itself, we should remember that we only got through by the skin of our teeth. Hunt planned to rubber-stamp the bid on 18 July 2011 – i.e. in five days' time according to the chapter timeline. Evidence presented at the Leveson Inquiry later revealed that during the first ten days of the hacking scandal, even after Brooks resigned, the News Corp lobbyists were still in deep conversation with aides to the prime minister and the chancellor and the culture secretary, and still trying to save the Rubicon process.

For the long-term health of the press, politics and the police – the three pil-lars of society who failed their duties during the early phase of the hacking scan-dal – an important announcement was made this day, 13 July 2012, which would have long-lasting ramifications. During the debate on the BskyB bid, Prime Min-ister David Cameron announced the formation of the Leveson Inquiry.

Various inquiries had been mooted in the first week after the Milly Dowler story broke, but they were vague. Often public inquiries and Royal Commissions are seen as ways of defusing a contentious issue in protracted legalities: nothing makes a scandal more tedious than having lawyers debate it in the dowdy atmo-sphere of the Royal Courts of Justice. But Cameron announced something much more far-reaching and incisive on this day in 6 July: a tribunal of inquiry with teeth, led by the respected appeal court judge Lord Justice Brian Leveson.

This judge-led inquiry, instituted under the 2005 Inquiries Act, would be held in public, with the power to compel witnesses and take written and oral evidence under oath. According to its terms of reference, the Inquiry would not only examine the hacking scandal, News International and the relationship between the press and the public. It wouldn't just consider the worrying relationship between the police and the press (which somehow had allowed industrial crime breaking to remain hidden and unpunished for years); the Leveson Inquiry would also conduct a much wider examination of the relationship between press and politicians.

For reasons now obvious in retrospect, it is reported that Cameron wasn't initially keen on this wider remit; only the strong stance of Deputy Prime Minister Nick Clegg and Leader of the Opposition Ed Miliband succeeded in getting those terms of reference through. Neither, however, were the real innovators in the underpinning of the Leveson Inquiry. The groundwork for this had all been done by the Hacked Off campaign, set up only weeks before the scandal exploded by the former journalist and academic Brian Cathcart and Martin Moore of the Media Standards Trust. With an advisory committee that included the former Liberal Democrat MP, Dr Evan Harris, Labour MP Tom Watson and the lawyer Mark Lewis, this was both a broad alliance from centre to left of the political spectrum and one deeply informed by years of dealing with the implicit corruption of the original phone hacking and its subsequent cover-up. Their platform for a major examination of the interconnections between the media and political classes had also won the backing of the parents of Milly Dowler – whose moral authority was hard to ignore.

DRAINING THE SWAMP

Meanwhile, a more immediate threat for News Corp was drifting across the Atlantic, like volcanic dust caught in the jet stream. There were mutterings of discontent from various members of the Bancroft family, former owners of Dow Jones & Company, publishers of the *Wall Street Journal*, who sold out to News Corp in 2007. Christopher Bancroft, who used to control 13 per cent of Dow Jones shares, claimed that if he had known then what he knew now, the sale 'would have been more problematic for me. I probably would have held out'.

Disaffected scions of rival dynasties are nothing new to Murdoch, but the allegation that there were attempts to hack a 9/11 victim would, if ever substantiated, have been as potentially as dangerous in his adoptive homeland as the Milly Dowler story was in the UK. Al Qaeda's attack on the World Trade Center and the near 3,000 deaths it caused had become a sacred symbol of national sacrifice and grief in the US; had News Corp intruded on that it could have been fatal to the corporation. The mere rumour alone caused angry family members of victims of the 9/11 attacks to call for a US investigation into whether *News of the World* journalists sought to hack the phones of their lost love ones or their grieving families.

Three Democratic senators, Jay Rockefeller of West Virginia and Chair of the Commerce Committee, Barbara Boxer of California and Frank Lautenberg of New Jersey, home to many of the families of 9/11 victims, now joined in the attack. Each wrote to the Attorney General and the head of the SEC, asking both to investigate whether News Corp violated FCPA laws by bribing officials. Rockefeller called for an FBI probe into whether phone hacking affected US citizens, telling his reporters that his 'bet' was that 'we'll find some criminal stuff'. The calls for investigation strengthened considerably when the Chair of the House Homeland Security Committee, Republican representative Peter King, also asked the Department of Justice to investigate allegations of bribery and wiretapping. News Corp had just abandoned a $16 billion bid in the face of legislative hostility. If charges were brought against it under US law, where executives proven guilty of certain kinds of financial malfeasance are regularly punished with jail time, the consequences could be even more serious.

The Foreign Corrupt Practices Act was enacted in 1977, but it has only been in the last few years that cases had been vigorously prosecuted. About 70 companies were under investigation in mid-2011 and, if made the subject of a probe, News Corp would join the likes of Avon, Goldman Sachs and Hewlett-Packard. Of the approximately 50 companies charged so far most have been penalised by fines – around $2.5 billion dollars to date – though senior executives can potentially face criminal charges and prison sentences. However, the Justice Department also offers incentives for co-operation, with a reduction of fines if a company suspected of FCPA violations vigorously pursues its own internal investigations and willingly produces evidence.

On the same day it dropped the BSkyB bid, News Corp began to set up the Management and Standards Committee (MSC) reporting to Joel Klein, a prominent New York City lawyer and as luck would have it a former deputy US attorney general in the Anti-Trust Division. Around this time the Justice Department made contact with senior News Corp executives and the independent directors hired several senior FCPA lawyers, so it's hard to separate the creation of the MSC from the 'co-operation' expected by the FBI to forestall higher penalties – as US corporations typically do in this situation. With over a hundred staff from the law firm Linklaters, PricewaterhouseCoopers and forensic IT consultants from Stroz Friedberg, this unit of News Corp would cost some £50 million in the first year. It was this unit which discovered the print out, in fact the single remaining copy, of email correspondence to James Murdoch from 2008 which had informed him of the extent of phone hacking at *News of the World*, including the incriminating 'For Neville' email which blew the 'rogue reporter' defence, because it contained transcripts of messages of voicemails Glenn Mulcaire had intercepted and apparently shared with other journalists beyond Clive Goodman. This email would make it hard for James to maintain his innocence and keep his reputation as an effective CEO. Either he had read it and was part of the cover-up or he hadn't and was incompetent. When push came to shove before the parliamentary sub-committee, James chose to be a fool rather than a knave.

For the next year, in a sealed-off, secured second floor of the Thomas More complex at Wapping, the London arm of MSC would work in tandem with a dozen dedicated police investigators and trawl through Data Pool 3 – a backup of some 300 million News International emails which had accidentally escaped the company's campaign of wholesale deletion. Emails containing terms that could be associated with improper or unlawful conduct, like 'copper', 'bribe' or 'payment', would then be checked against related phone records and expense claims. Evidence thus produced would then be vetted (to protect journalistic sources) and then handed over to the Elveden or Weeting teams. Though at first this arrangement could look like a fig leaf to save News International's blushes, in fact, it worked to the police's advantage, freeing them from the obligation of obtaining 'production orders' which would have raised complications of journalistic privilege and protection of sources. At least two dozen further arrests have come from this source since the MSC was formed. By the spring of 2012, it was reported that thousands of emails related to police bribes and other payments of state officials had been sent to the FBI. Meanwhile, investigators had shown an interest in alleged illegal activity by News Corp subsidiaries in Russia, by executives associated with a SkyItalia subsidiary currently on trial in Sicily and allegations of smart card piracy at the News Corp subsidiary NDS (see Chapter 9). The Securities and Exchange Commission (SEC) was also reported to have been actively pursuing several of their own investigations.

As of early summer 2012, none of these US investigations have led to any prosecutions. While pundits have asserted that the US regulators and investigators are biding their time until after the upcoming US general election in the autumn, legal experts on FCPA have repeatedly explained:

> …because News Corp. is likely in cooperation mode and because the company has an incentive to learn this information itself, News Corp. will likely

> *conduct a targeted world-wide review of its operations. Such a review*
> *takes time and often costs tens of millions of dollars in professional fees and*
> *expenses. Because of these dynamics, it is typical for FCPA scrutiny –*
> *from the point of investigation to the point of enforcement action – to last*
> *between 2–4 years.*
>
> (FCPA PROFESSOR, 2011)

Whatever the eventual effect of these investigations on News International's parent company in the US, the creation of the MSC has had a profound impact in England, particularly on the *New of the World*'s sister daily paper the *Sun*. Data Pool 3 has led to the arrest of a dozen senior journalists and editors under suspicion of corrupt payments to public officials.

Guto Harri, the former BBC journalist who, after being pipped to the post by Andy Coulson as head of communications for the Conservatives in 2007, worked as Head of External Affairs for the Mayor of London, said he took a job heading up communications for News International in 2012 to counter the 'hysteria' about the company: 'I cannot think of any company in history – and this does go to the very top from the man himself in New York – that spends millions of pounds employing people to trawl the bowels of their own servers in order to find evidence to hand over to the police to actually convict their own staff,' he told the *Guardian*: 'They are being extremely robust and arguably brutal about cleansing up the past, and they are not only disciplining people internally, they are handing over evidence to the police' (Mulholland, 2012).

Amid these loud and well remunerated claims for a new era of transparency and accountability, it should be remembered that it took the nightmare scenario of criminal investigations in the US before News Corp finally showed real resolve to confront past wrongdoing in London.

JUNK

After the divisive relocation of his British papers to Wapping in 1986, Murdoch's focus turned to his US Empire which by the late eighties represented approximately 70 per cent of his company's assets. In a *Newsnight* documentary of the time (also archived on Adam Curtis's blog, The Medium and the Message) the then journalist (and now novelist) Robert Harris explored how the Wapping conflict funded Murdoch's transatlantic growth and the evolution of News International into News Corp.

Harris interviewed John Reidy, vice president of the famous 'junk bond' US investment bank Drexel Burnham Lambert, who explained how the Wapping move increased the value of the British papers by over 300 per cent and led to a jump in the value of the stock of Murdoch's holding company. This allowed the corporation to borrow even more – sometimes by a factor of ten – against the new earnings. Most of this was used to expand into the US. Or as Tony Dubbins, General Secretary of the National Graphical Association, told Harris: 'So we have British workers being put in the quite invidious position of are being forced to lose their jobs to fund his investments in America' (Harris, 1986b).

The trade unionist's insight is also underlined by the pioneering financial journalist who has followed the complex investments flows of News Corp, Neil Chenoweth:

> *Murdoch had never been able to afford his great move in 1985–6 to buy Twentieth Century Fox, the Metromedia television stations and launch Fox Network. To pay for it, he moved his British newspapers to Wapping, and triggered a year of violent industrial confrontation.*

> (CHENOWETH, 2001, P. 87)

Given the relative size of the markets, Murdoch's transatlantic leap was merely following the money, just as he had done nearly twenty years earlier when he expanded from Australia to the UK. But instead of being a transitional phase, his moment of growth and dislocation, funded on rising stock prices and expanding debt, became the constant heartbeat of the new corporation, expressing the existential premise of grow or die.

An early adopter of the Anglo-Saxon model deregulation and globalisation of the finance markets, Murdoch could exploit the difference between national currencies, tax regimes, technological development and labour market relations in a form of international arbitrage. From the Australian project of News Ltd, through the lateral invasion of News International, to the borderless hegemony of News Corp, globalisation went from being an external condition to an internalised governing principle. True to his distrust of the 'establishment', the wild colonial boy now became a founding member of a new post-colonial elite.

In this multinational corporate domain there is no loyalty to any nation state: ultimate sovereignty lies – by law – in maximising shareholder value. If those shareholders are dominated by specialised arrangements that ensure that the chair and CEO's 12 per cent of the shares gives him 43 per cent of the vote, along with his family which leads to majority control, then the corporate structure conceals a dynastic imperium.

Behold the birth of News Corp Nation, a fluid series of legal agreements, special investment instruments, credit agreements and family loyalty which, though headquartered in New York, is accountable everywhere and nowhere, like a medieval kingdom boosted into geostationary orbit.

The bulk of Murdoch's increased cash and fresh debt would go into television, mainly into setting up the Fox Network through the purchase of six Metromedia TV stations. However – and this is what makes him distinct from the new media moguls at the end of the end of the twentieth century – Murdoch still kept in touch with his press baron past and though his newspaper holdings constitute a shrinking proportion of News Corp's revenues, he has increased them in number to 200 publications worldwide today.

Nonetheless, for all his continuing love of newsprint, Murdoch's newspaper adventures in the US have been relatively unsuccessful. Once he'd settled down in New York in 1974, his first big venture, the *National Star*, was really just plagiaristic homage to the *National Enquirer*, the celebrity 'strange but true' magazine that parodies the news and yet sold four million copies a week at the time. Murdoch's *Star* failed to make any inroads in that market and so he concentrated on his home patch of New York, buying the *New York Post* for $30 million and the *New York Magazine* for $26 million in 1976. So great was the perceived threat of Murdoch's newspaper domination of the city that *Time Magazine* ran a picture of King Kong on the cover with the headline: 'Extra! Aussie Press Lord Terrifies New York'.

It was a jokey headline and the implementation of the Murdoch strategy in US publishing would veer between the comic and grotesque. Although heavily influenced by the Nixonian rhetoric of the 'anti-establishment' New Right, Murdoch nonetheless never really had a strong policy base in Washington, as he did with *The Times* in London and the *Australian* in Canberra, and the reliance on tabloid tactics backfired. The *New York Post* followed the same strategy as the *Sun* – buy cheap, make ruthless cuts and efficiency savings while driving sales through ever more lurid shock-horror headlines – but the paper continued to lose millions, despite the Son of Sam summer and regular celebrity and political hatchet jobs on its infamous Page Six.

Murdoch's tabloid experience in New York confounds H. L. Mencken's oft-cited observation that 'Nobody ever went broke underestimating the taste of the American public.' With the *New York Post* Murdoch did: he drove it too far down-market and managed to limbo dance under the low standards of the tabloid press. Lessons Murdoch had learned years before on Fleet Street were lost in translation. Sales picked up, but advertising didn't. Unlike the UK, the big retail chains and brands didn't want to be associated with the increasingly crass and tabloid *New York Post* – which says something about the differentials between New Yorkers and Britons. Though it turns out to be apocryphal, an anecdote of the time had the chief executive of the upmarket department store Bloomingdale's, Marvin Traub, explaining to Murdoch that: 'Your readers are our shoplifters.'

Importing key staff from Australia and Britain, the paper encouraged what a *New York Times* editor called 'mean, ugly, violent journalism' and after the Summer of Sam hysteria, was described in the scholarly *Columbia Journalism Review* as 'a force for evil'. But to be fair to the *Post* – fairer than it ever was to its targets – the paper also managed to emulate some of the better humorous traditions of the *Sun* with no less than five of the top ten tabloid headlines in *New York Magazine*'s 35th anniversary edition, including the 1982 headline: 'HEADLESS BODY IN TOPLESS BAR'. Though loss-making financially, the *Post* still had strategic political value and was a useful instrument to wield in the city's politics, most notably when Murdoch gave his personal support to Ed Koch in his successful mayoral campaigns of 1977, 1981 and 1985 and then to Koch's successor Rudy Giuliani.

By the late eighties however, Murdoch's tabloid newspaper strategy was beginning to conflict with his pay-TV ambitions. News Ltd had already acquired some important regional papers in the *San Antonio Herald* and *Boston Herald* in 1982 and then the *Chicago Sun Times* in 1983, but when he launched the Fox Network in 1986, he would run afoul of the more stringent American rules severely limiting both foreign and cross-ownership of US media. A fast-tracked award of citizenship through a special act of Congress solved the first problem and an unprecedented two-year waiver forestalled the second, but in 1988 Murdoch would have to sell the *New York Post* when he bought WNYW-TV, the base from which he would launch his Fox Network.

It was a brief interregnum and just as he had during the acquisition of *The Times*, Murdoch would use his local political leverage effectively. The *Post* struggled for the next five years and was soon threatened with closure. Thanks to intensive lobbying of the Federal Communications Commission by numerous political officials, including Democratic governor of New York, Mario Cuomo, Murdoch was granted a permanent waiver from the cross-ownership rules and allowed to reacquire the *New York Post*.

In the late nineties, the *New York Post* changed its tone in line with what was happening in other tabloids like the *Sun*. The brutal shock-jockery was moderated somewhat (perhaps because it was already catered for elsewhere) and the paper pursued the kind of obsession with celebrity which had boomed after the death of Princess Diana. Page Six was re-launched as a gossip column, more akin to the *Sun*'s show business Bizarre column, alma mater to Piers Morgan, Rebekah Brooks and Andy Coulson. Now The Page is rarely found before page ten and is usually a double-page spread, complete with colour advertising from upmarket brands and stores like Bloomingdale's.

Whatever clout Murdoch achieved by owning the *New York Post* which justified the loss of millions over the years, the political effect was limited and local. Until the purchase of the *Wall Street Journal* in 2006, there was nothing in the US as yet to match the double whammy Murdoch had in London – the pugilistic populism of the *Sun* combined with the establishment kudos of *The Times*.

ON THE RECORD

One of the reasons the US newspaper market was ill-suited to Murdoch's brand of lateral invasion was the country's lack of national titles and a smart route to parachute in and corner a market. Historically the distances between the far flung US states were too vast to allow overnight delivery and by the time electronic transmission made nationwide publishing possible, a stable oligarchy of newspaper ownership had formed around the *Washington Post*, *New York Times*, *Wall Street Journal* and *Chicago Tribune* – each a kind of national institution. The race to the bottom of the yellow press had been exhausted by the late nineteenth century when Joseph Pulitzer moved away from his initial blatant partisanship to the – albeit unachievable – concept of 'objective journalism'. That tradition of reportage would influence fiction writers such as Ernest Hemingway in the twenties and thirties and would lead Henry Luce to set a similar tone in *Time*, *Fortune* and *Life* magazines. Under these pressures, the newspaper industry began to compete for higher standards of style and accuracy and above all scooping each other about the 'Beltway' – the inside track of Washington politics.

The competition between the *New York Times* and *Washington Post*, for example, to expose the excesses of the Nixon administration, led to revelation of the foreign policy debacle of Vietnam in the Pentagon Papers as well as the domestic dysfunction of Watergate. Since then, for the last forty years, Woodward and Bernstein's Watergate articles have remained the model for American investigative journalism – loads of phone time and worn shoe leather to slowly substantiate leads provided by a 'source' in their case, the allusive and elusive 'Deep Throat'. The model has its problems, especially the cost of lengthy investigations given a massive drop in advertising revenues and the as yet unresolved issue of how to monetise online print, but it is still in stark contrast to its British counterpart: our best current examples are the 'Fake Sheikh' entrapment of celebrities, sports stars and corrupt politicians in illicit sex or drug taking; or the undercover reporters from the *Telegraph* who caught Vince Cable boasting. Most of this, however, has been focused on the politics of personal destruction – 'playing the man' rather than playing the ball – have become the default mode of British journalism, with the ad hominem fallacies behind it infecting even the quality papers. This is still not true for US print journalism, which still retains some separation of fact and comment. Sleaze re-emerged in US reporting with the online publication of the Drudge Report, which first exposed Bill Clinton's liaison with Monica Lewinsky in 1998, and on TV, in cable news coverage warped by the partisan tendentiousness of Fox News.

Two factors kept the political economy of American print journalism healthy. Captive regional readerships provided stable revenue and circulation to support well-staffed newsrooms. But it wasn't just economics. There was (and still is) a robust core ethic and belief in American print journalism that has made it more immune to tabloid debasement over the years. The founding fathers of the US, having fought a revolutionary war partly in defence of enlightenment dissent, enshrined freedom of speech and open discourse in the First Amendment of their constitution. As Harold Evans declared, long before he moved there, America has embedded freedom of information both in civil law and government behaviour. The First Amendment enshrines freedom of speech in the US constitution, while the 1952 Defamation Act protects American journalists from being sued for libel if their story is based on an official statement 'by or on behalf of any government department, officer of state, local authority or chief officer of police'. Freedom of information acts also oblige politicians and bureaucrats to release documents that reveal their activities when requested – which reduces the need for personal 'gotchas' and entrapment. Compared to America, Evans said at the Leveson Inquiry, the British press is only 'half free'.

As I wrote previously, I have witnessed these differences first hand, initially from living in the US and becoming a consumer of its newspapers, and more recently from my brief experience of writing for *Newsweek* and the Daily Beast, which required multiple sourcing, a balance of partisan perspectives and generally giving parties concerned a chance to comment and respond. It's a difference you can see between both national traditions, regardless of the political allegiance of the paper or its proprietor. Compare the number of facts and citations, for example, in an average (Murdoch owned) *Wall Street Journal* piece compared to one in the (Guardian Trust owned) *Observer*. The *Wall Street Journal* will be predicated on 'reporting' facts, quotations and (preferably) named sources. The *Observer* will more often than not contain many more speculations and opinions per paragraph and – anathema to most serious US journalism – often taking one unnamed source as the basis for the whole argument. Over the years the distinction between news and comment has been blurred in most of British reportage.

In explaining the relative decline of British journalism compared to the US there may be some parallels with our relative decline in TV drama (explored in my *Prospect* essay 'Why Britain can't do The Wire?'). Just as the debasement of the tabloid end of the market has ended up infecting broadsheet newspapers, the soap style of cheap kitchen sink TV drama has percolated through most of British television, even its once admired quality products. Though Brits like to pride themselves on their refined tastes compared with brash US commercialism, the truth is that 'soaps' – often thought of as an uniquely American creation of downmarket populism – are only seen on daytime TV in the UK. In Britain, soaps are at the centre of the prime-time schedules, just as tabloid values are at the front of its news-stands. In the case of British journalism, this downward spiral of cost-cutting while trying to increase audience share led to criminality and ethical failure.

Though they can often be dull, without international breadth or a tabloid zeal for imaginative design, American newspapers are much more likely to be reliable 'papers of record' for any future historian who wanted to reconstruct the political machinations of Congressional politics or fracking for natural gas in the Appalachians. British journalists still think they excel in getting the truth with their ruthlessness, but you could equally argue that the ends of disclosure would be more readily served, with administrators and lawmakers more likely to open up, without the constant 'gotchas'. And there's little doubt that 'spin' forms the heart of British political journalism from the off the record meetings of the 'lobby system' to the private unattributed briefings. In comparison, the open system of live televised White House briefings provides just as much access and infinitely more accountability.

I've seen the chilling effect of the British gotcha system of political coverage when a friend of mine, Samantha Power, a Pulitzer Prize-winning writer, arrived in Britain in April 2008 to launch her book *Chasing the Flame*. Power had followed her ground-breaking book about genocide, *A Problem from Hell*, with a biography of Sergio Vieira de Mello, the UN High Commissioner for Human Rights and United Nations Special Representative in Iraq who was killed along with other members of his staff in a Baghdad bombing in 2003.

By coincidence, Power's long-planned book launch coincided with the protracted and increasingly fractious primary contest for the Democratic presidential nomination. As a foreign policy advisor to Barack Obama, Power was intensively quizzed about the state of the primary race on the British media and had dozens of interviews in the couple of days she was in London. We met to watch the Texas primaries one evening and she was exhausted; her main concern was that she'd said something about US policy in Iraq during a BBC

World Service *Hard Talk* interview which might cause some consternation back home. She had no idea that another interview, with a journalist from the *Scotsman*, would cause much more grief. She had interrupted the interview to take a call from a colleague involved in some fracas with the competing campaign of Senator Hillary Clinton. Quizzed by the journalist in what she thought was completely off the record conversation, Power called Hillary a 'monster'. However, the tape was still running.

Though the remarks weren't allegedly in the first version of the *Scotsman* piece, a rewrite foregrounded the 'monster' comment. It took several days for the interview to be published, but the following 'Monstergate' scandal caused Power to resign from the Obama campaign. She and Hillary eventually rebuilt their relationship and worked closely together in government, especially over the successful Libya intervention. But at the time, that one unguarded remark, which in the US would be deemed unusable in journalistic terms, appeared to have destroyed the political future of one of America's best thinkers on human rights, genocide and diplomatic and military intervention. It proved to Power that there's 'no over there' anymore when it comes to international media: it proved to me that the obsession with ad hominem scoops was making the British system less transparent and leading to less overall disclosure.

To many, British journalism, the Monstergate story – as with the whole monstering phenomenon of Fleet Street journalism – is a sign of the rude health of a system that discloses stories that French or American newspapers might ignore or repress. However, does the obsession with the personal faux pas or private sexual lives of our public figures actually aid the democratic process? Logically, the politics of personal destruction is fairly meaningless, since the fact someone has had an affair or said one or two stupid things, does not invalidate all their other arguments or their contribution to public life. In short, our national newspapers are completely reliant on the joint ad hominem and ad personam fallacies – that what someone has said or done before invalidates what they do or say now. Some may argue this has been a cleansing force in Fleet Street for thirty years; the balance of evidence amassed here suggests the converse.

It's worth noting that these principles only really apply to American print journalism. When it comes to comparisons between British and American broadcast journalism, the positions are nearly completely reversed with the BBC setting a standard of practice which has brought out the best in its domestic competitors, such as ITN and Sky News, and providing both the CNN International and Al Jazeera bases in London with a pool of highly trained production, documentary and news-gathering staff.

There can be unintended consequences, however, of professional standards and best practice, especially when news begins to merge with entertainment in a global village, which confuses gossip with knowledge. In *Stick it up your Punter!*, Chippindale and Horrie argued that the *Sun* found a successful niche in the UK with celebrity and sport-obsessed fun, inflammatory fare that couldn't be found in the tightly regulated regime of TV news coverage. The same could be true – in reverse – of New Corp's failure to create a populist press in the US; the public appetite for sensationalism and scandal was already satisfied by the shock-jock radio tradition. But a failure in one area opens up opportunities in another.

Murdoch's great US innovation was not in tabloidising the newspapers, it was in a more far reaching revolution: the tabloidisation of cable television and the creation of Fox News.

CORPORATE RAIDS

Murdoch's American escapades do not receive the same detailed attention in this book as his British adventures. Like his background in Australia, the US story of the last two decades acts more as a bookend. There are several reasons for this: first and foremost, News Corporation's activities in both countries have not (at least as yet) revealed anything like a scandal to match the revelation of phone hacking in the UK, police bribes or the backchannels to government during the biggest bid in media history. The US stands as a counter-example for what went wrong in Britain.

In political terms, Murdoch never developed the intimacy with presidents that he achieved with successive prime ministers. Though, in his secret meeting with Thatcher in January 1981 over the Times Group, Murdoch offered to introduce her to key thinkers in Reagan's circle, but his privileged US political clout seems to have ended with Reagan, who approved Murdoch's cross-ownership of TV stations and fast tracked his citizenship. There were no regular meetings with George Bush Senior, or Bill Clinton, or George W. Bush; indeed, Murdoch claims to have never met the latter and Obama famously refused to take a meeting with Murdoch to gain his endorsement in 2008. The lack of concentration of media power means that Murdoch can be more easily ignored and less able to theoretically intimidate politicians and change legislation.

This is not to say he didn't try and often succeed. In the mid-eighties he managed to get the Reagan-appointed head of the Federal Communications Commission (FCC) to waive cross-ownership laws so he could acquire TV stations. In the nineties he would court the New Right generation of politicians, giving Newt Gingrich a major book deal and helping Gingrich's rival Bill Kristol set up the Washington-based *Weekly Standard*. When Time Warner refused to carry Fox News on its New York cable system, Rudy Giuliani helped Murdoch rush his appeal to the federal courts. The same modus operandi of political support in return for favourable treatment obtained; but unlike Britain or Australia, Murdoch was one among many and his new allies didn't get the top job in the White House.

Perhaps the simple core of the American counter-example is the fact Murdoch owns no more than 10 per cent of any US media market, a stark contrast to the 43 per cent of British newspaper readership or the largest broadcaster in terms of revenues, BSkyB. According to Claire Enders, most media markets end up as stable oligopolies, with five or six players in competition, none with more than 20 per cent of the market. We can see the results in the big personalities that dominate US media, many of whom would gather at Herb Allen's Sun Valley ranch for an annual media summit. Murdoch would form strategic alliances there, and often strategic rivalries with, in close succession, Ted Turner, Michael Eisner, John Malone, Sumner Redstone, Bill Gates, Barry Diller, Charlie Ergen, among others. His UK rivals, such as Conrad Black or Robert Maxwell – fade in comparison.

The other reason the US career receives less detailed attention here is because, time after time, there is a sense that all Murdoch's wheeling and dealing is just a recapitulation of what he had already learned in Australia and Britain. These deals and procedures are, in absolute financial terms, vastly greater, but in terms of his trajectory and previous history, relatively smaller in scale. Just as Bruce Page's *The Murdoch Archipelago* is an exhaustive and ink-stained chronicle of Murdoch's Australian and press background, Neil Chenoweth's *Virtual Murdoch* is a comprehensive, breath-taking, but occasionally baffling and breathless account of his launch in satellite TV and broadcast media at the end of the twentieth century. The canvas, the polity and commercial landscape of the US, is much broader. But somehow the figure Murdoch cuts against it, smaller and less vivid.

One innovation nevertheless stands out during the eighties and nineties: Murdoch's use of leverage. The great leap forward begins with Murdoch's bid for a chain of six city TV stations called Metromedia, the basis for a fifth national network to rival the big four for the first time in forty years. Originally, Murdoch had been on the lookout for an existing cable channel and around 1984 was focused on Ted Turner's CNN. But instead, Murdoch purchased Twentieth Century Fox studios in 1985 and then moved on the Metromedia as a distribution channel, even if the total cost of $2.7 billion was well beyond his company's reach in terms of conventional bank borrowing – fifteen times more than the lending limits of Murdoch's company. The deal would have been impossible except for two factors: the globalisation of News Corp and Murdoch's crucial alliance with one of the Wall Street figures of the eighties.

This was the era of the leveraged buyout and the corporate raiders, a frenzy of aggressive mergers and acquisitions, which provides the narrative backdrop for Oliver Stone's 1986 film *Wall Street*. Companies could be bought, sold, re-structured or liquidated by a small number of players deploying powerful new financial instruments, most important of which was the 'junk bond' a form of high yield debt which looks like an investment but which is really a speculative bridging loan. Murdoch had forged a crucial alliance with Michael Milken, the pioneer of junk bonds at Drexel Burnham Lambert, who organised the famous 'Predators' Ball' for would-be corporate raiders. They agreed a $1.6 billion junk bond issue to finance the Metromedia acquisition, but that still left Murdoch only half way to the $3 billion dollars he needed.

Another factor would come into play, which News Corp has deployed to great effect ever since – the paradox of globalisation. The company already stretched around the world and the complex bureaucratic differences in national taxation and regulation across Murdoch's empire could actually be turned to its advantage. By a strange quirk of international accounting, low-grade non-invest-ment stock could be counted as equity under Australian law. In other words, a $1.6 billion Milken loan could be transferred from the liabilities side of the bal-ance sheet to the asset side, therefore increasing the apparent value of Murdoch's holding and allowing yet more borrowing. In the bizarre logic of modern finance debt becomes its opposite, outgoings become income. Once again, Murdoch's acumen and opportunistic brilliance came to the fore as he used regulation to his benefit, spinning national red tape into global gold.

International arbitrage of this kind has been a staple for News Corp ever since; though Murdoch complains about government intervention and bureau-cracy, few modern businessmen have actually been so dependent on it. But the junk bond issue was less successful. The terms of the deal would later turn puni-tive for the media mogul. Around that time, in 1988, Milken was indicted on 98 counts of racketeering and fraud, including insider trading, stock parking and profiting from illegal trading. It was one of the first times that Racketeer Influ-enced and Corrupt Organizations Act (RICO), enacted to deal with the Mafia and other forms of organised crime, had been deployed against an individual who was not part of a criminal organisation. Milken pled guilty to six lesser charges and was initially sentenced to ten years imprisonment, eventually reduced to two years. There would also be an even enduring legacy of this era. Milken's high-yield junk bonds became a core component of the collateralised debt obligations (CDOs) that extended the shadow banking system to the point of collapse in 2008 and would lead to the longest global recession since the thirties.

Murdoch was one of the first to experience the dangers of these strange new hybrids of debt when he suffered his own devastating credit crunch. Within three years of creating the basis for the Fox Network he was caught in the global debt squeeze and was a few days away from going broke. All the new share issues and loan had left him in an impasse: Murdoch was running out of other people's money. The crisis came to a head on 6 December 1990 when Murdoch needed to reschedule $7.6 billion of debt held by 146 institutions around the world. Suddenly he hit the brick wall of the Pittsburgh National bank, which was a recalling a $10 million loan.

News Corp didn't have the cash and a default would have sent the share price crashing, leading to further defaults and decades of litigation as the labyrinthine corporate holdings of News Corp were liquidated. According to his biographer, William Shawcross, Murdoch tried to plead with the loan officer who demanded immediate repayment: '"We can't. You know what that means. We'd go out of business." The loan officer said, "That's right." "You're telling us to liquidate our company?" And he said, "Yes"' (Shawcross, 1992).

Somehow Murdoch managed to survive this ordeal and restructure his debt. Chenoweth outlines some of the highly imaginative accounting procedures, intra-company loans and share issues behind this Houdini act, but the persistence and will to survive is impressive. Barry Diller, who has both worked with Murdoch and against him, explains 'Rupert Murdoch at his best is probably when cornered or when he does have great adversity going against him. And maybe it's his moment of greatest pleasure' (Frontline, 1995). Some of it skirted on the edge of legality and the Australian Securities Commission wrote a highly critical draft report in 1993 on the way one News Corp subsidiary, Queensland Press, paid a premium of almost 100 Australian dollars in an off-market transaction to another subsidiary. Like Milken, some of Murdoch's transactions sailed close to the law. Unlike Milken, Murdoch survived both the parlous personal credit crunch and subsequent investigation.

DEBT AND TRANSFIGURATION

Murdoch's debt crisis and near-death experience in the early nineties explains the ramped up animosity his British papers showed towards a Labour victory in 1992, even though they quickly turned on the Conservative victor, John Major. During the 1992 general election campaign the Labour Party announced that, if it won, new cross-media ownership rules would be introduced. As Shawcross explains 'no other company in Britain stood to lose so much from a Labour victory in 1992 as News Corporation'. Murdoch would have been forced to choose between his dominant newspapers or his newly launched BSkyB station. It's unsurprising then that not one of their five national newspapers, read by ten million, deviated from an anti-Labour Party message in the run up to the general election, with the *Sun* reaching its apogee – or nadir – of personalised attack.

What then happened to John Major, the one British prime minister who didn't play the game with Murdoch during News International's thirty-year dominance of Fleet Street, would have a long-term chilling effect on British politics and laid the seeds for many of the abuses to come. Having boasted the *Sun* won the election for Major, its editor Kelvin MacKenzie threatened to 'pour a bucket of shit' over the Prime Minister every day after the fiasco of Britain's forced exit from the European Exchange Rate Mechanism (though the precise wording of that conversation has been disputed by Major). Whether the papers were merely reflecting widespread public disillusion with Major's government, or actively fomenting dissent, the effect of News International's campaign against Major was to send a shiver down the spine of any serious politician who thought of getting on the wrong side of Murdoch's UK papers in the years ahead – though they could be accused of a certain spinelessness in this regard. Not since the first three decades of the twentieth century, when the press barons Northcliffe, Beaverbrook and Rothermere were successively (and occasionally simultaneously) at the height of their political influence, had there been a demonstration of press power; and now there was a salient difference: 'power without responsibility' could be wielded by one proprietor alone. As Nicholas Coleridge put it in 1993:

> *The fiefdoms of Beaverbrook, Northcliffe and Hearst, often invoked as the zenith of proprietorial omnipotence, were in fact smaller by every criteria than the enormous, geographically diffuse, multi-lingual empires of the latest newspaper tycoons ... none dominated so many world markets simultaneously as does Rupert Murdoch in Britain, the far east and Australia.*

> (COLERIDGE, 1993, P. 2)

But was it Murdoch who drove this strategy in the nineties? Or did his proconsuls in this part of the Murdoch empire get out of hand? In light of the distractions of the bursting of his junk bond bubble, it's an open question how much attention Murdoch was really paying to the consequences of his UK hegemony. Juggling figures and shares at a hundred points across the globe, Murdoch was more than anything exercised by financial wizardry. Calls to his editors over content seem to have declined. His papers must have been less significant as channels of information or news and more vital as streams of revenue, tax breaks or debt repayments. For this part of Murdoch's career, as he struggled under a financial cosh, the conventional opinion that Murdoch is always motivated by the bottom line – a plimsoll line well underwater in the early nineties – is much more plausible.

In the background, a new generation was also rising up to threaten Murdoch. This wasn't the domain of old-school bosses in belt and braces, rolling up their sleeves with print-inked fingers, fighting inveterate wars of capital versus labour. The wired up generation wore jeans and T-shirts. Their top entrepreneurs like Bill Gates and Steve Jobs, were geeks, hippies and high school dropouts. Out of the blue those 'dang libruls' and hippies had created a new lucrative world of personal computing and online interaction. Part of Murdoch's slow makeover in this era – something which will become more apparent with his marriage to Wendi Deng – is a response to the fact the press baron was going the way of the dinosaur and the mass media mogul had to reinvent his bearing and his dreams.

A revolution was taking over the whole media sector, mainly due to the convergence of technology and formats in the digital age. If photos, moving images, music and text could all be produced and manipulated in binary format, then all the sectorial divisions begin to melt away. Within the next few years, industries that had built up over a century – chemical photographic processing, vinyl record manufacture – would disappear almost entirely. Distribution services like video rentals would bloom and die in less than a decade. The convergence in the technology created a parallel convergence of ownership. In 1986 there were 50 major media corporations in newspapers, television, books, movies and music. Thanks to the rash of mergers and acquisitions after deregulation that number was halved by 1990. With the growth of digital content at the beginning of the new millennium, US media was dominated by five cross-platform companies: Time Warner, Disney, Viacom, Bertelsmann of Germany and News Corporation.

It's a staggering statistic and hard to parallel in any other industry except for finance; 95 per cent of the media disappeared with power and ownership concentrated in the remaining 5 per cent. The information economy might have promised a democratisation of the means of production, distribution and exchange, but it delivered a global oligopoly in media and one that shows no signs of abating (see Chapter 9).

In the face of the information revolution, Murdoch wasn't lucky to grow, but amazingly fortunate just to survive. Whether by design or inertia, News Corp still remains pre-eminent in print, even though publishing provides a diminishing fraction of its revenues. In addition to several new newspapers, the corporation acquired Triangle Publications and William Collins in the late eighties, and folded the latter a year later with Harper & Row to create HarperCollins. (Another story here of broken promises.) Almost by accident, as a side-line to his accelerated broadcasting mergers, Murdoch became one of largest publishers in the world.

But is growth the same as dominance? There's something to the argument that as his business interests mushroomed, the Murdoch imprimatur became blurred like a monarch's face on an old coin. In the case of HarperCollins, for example, there is the occasional moment of distinctive intervention: the *Suppressio veri* of Murdoch's reluctance to publish the memoir of former Governor of Hong Kong, Chris Patten's *East and West* out of fear of offending the Chinese government. (Patten gives a full account of this episode in his Leveson Inquiry testimony.) Perhaps there is also the legacy of the *suggestio falsi* – i.e. the positive censorship achieved by commissioning the work of pet politicians; for example the $4.5 million advance HarperCollins paid for Gingrich's *To Renew America*, most of which was never recouped from sales. And in the case of Gingrich the investment never recouped itself politically either – Murdoch's ability to pick presidential winners never matched his ability to pick prime ministers – though the House Leader did help draw up a provision which gave tax breaks to broadcasters like News Corp (Wilson, 1996, pp. 30–34). But these few books seem to be the exception to HarperCollins' otherwise independent backlist: 'taking the Murdoch Shilling' would mean that Nelson Mandela could be considered a News Corp stooge.

Compared to the importance of News International in the UK, the political influence on News Corp's publishing acquisitions in most of the world is almost too diffuse to be detected. Except for Fox News, the same is true for most of the broadcasting acquisitions. As he expanded through these mega media mergers, Murdoch was becoming more attenuated and indistinguishable from his corporate competitors: who would know the political affiliations of Viacom? How does Bertelsmann deal with climate change? What does Time Warner think about abortion? It's a ridiculous question. Their commercial strategies trump any ideological priorities, they follow the audience when it comes to content. These corporations may have a brand, but they have no personality in that individual sense Murdoch still tries to impose on News Corp. But this desire for political distinctness is nearly a losing battle. It would end in a decade with *Hello!* magazine pictures of the mogul purified, blandified, dressed in white on the banks of the Jordan at the baptism of his two new children, flanked by Princess Rania and Nicole Kidman (with Tony Blair conveniently cropped out), smiling benignly like some baffled Buddha.

FOXED

For all the presumption that the Information Revolution would lead to a Knowledge Economy, that a wider dispersal of the means of communication would lead to a deeper understanding of the world, the convergence of digital media underlines Marshall McLuhan's dictum that 'the medium is the message'. That's what new network and computing media really concentrate on, the means of communication and not the ends: noise to signal ratios, network protocols, formats for sharing data. The founder of information theory, Claude Shannon, explicitly stated this in 1943 when he said: 'The "meaning" of a message is generally irrelevant' (Gleick, 2011, p. 219). The revolution would take place in the means of signal processing, the ease of reproduction rather than production, the network effects of file sharing and distribution on the internet, not in semantics. The significance of this data is almost irrelevant, or at least cannot be computed, which explains how amateur porn and Lolcats have been some of the great innovations of the information age. In other words, the plethora of data in the information age does not necessarily lead to 'knowledge'.

Much of the 'knowledge' economy is purely valueless distribution of data and this can be seen in the corporate strategy of media companies. As Chenoweth points out in *Virtual Murdoch* the corporate mantra that 'content is king' turns out to be bullshit: 'At the turn of the twentieth century, appearance dictated substance, form controlled content, distribution determined programming' (Chenoweth, 2001, p. 131).

In the case of News Corp, its distribution systems expanded much faster than any concept of the content that would fill them: movie channels, music channels, children's channels, sports channels; Latin, Chinese, Italian, German networks. It's a model that might be the dream of the foreign sales agent and scheduler, not the newspaper man who wants the latest political gossip in order to fell a foe or protect a friend. It's hard to find the ideological statement in *Titanic* or Murdoch's short-lived purchase of the Los Angeles Dodgers in 1997 (or attempted purchase of Manchester United the year after) – according to Michael Wolff, Murdoch hates sports. This is all about achieving vertical economies of scale in broadcasting rights. Like the classic Paul Newman movie, *The Hustler*, which shows a pool player exploited by the gambling and agent system in the sport, we're in an arena where the game is not actually the game – the side bets are everything.

One of the people who had the greatest insight into this merry-go-round of cash and access is Roger Ailes: 'Money is something you use to trade to get distribution. Everybody knows it. Anyone who has the nerve can play that game. This is capitalism and one of the things that has helped to make this country great' (Chenoweth, 2001, p. 147). (Ailes seems to have overlooked that many of the avatars of this untrammelled high finance capitalism, such as Ivan Boesky and Michael Milken, spent time in jail.) Murdoch might have encountered Ailes through his connections to Nixon's circle, but by the time Ailes was working on Giuliani's campaign for Mayor in the early nineties they definitely had met and then Murdoch would recruit him from NBC to run his Fox News.

Ailes became a television producer at the moment the political significance of the new medium was first realised, as Nixon's sweaty, unshaven appearance against clean-cut John F. Kennedy in the televised presidential debates in 1960 was deemed crucial to JFK's electoral victory that November. Six years later, Ailes worked as a media adviser for Nixon during the successful presidential campaign of 1968 and went on to consult in the next three Republican presidential campaigns, for Reagan and George Bush Senior, before retiring from direct political campaigning in 1992 to work for NBC. Four years later, Murdoch hired Ailes and some 89 other NBC employees, to set up the Fox News Network. Again, distribution was key. In an inversion of the normal rights of carriage, in which channels pay producers for content, Murdoch paid the cable networks over $275 million to carry Fox News.

Some of the old Murdoch reappears in the battle to promulgate Fox News – a willingness to wield political influence to increase his market share and market share to wield political influence. Most of the infighting happened in his home turf of New York, which witnessed a re-run of Murdoch's long-running feud with Ted Turner. Turner was allied with Time Warner whose New York network had 77 cable channels on the dial in those days, and 30 applications for a vacant slot. Fox News was one of the applicants and they were refused. News Corp went to war. In a manner which will seem reminiscent of governmental interactions in the UK, Murdoch called Giuliani about the matter on 20 September 1996 and this was followed by over 25 conversations and at least two private meetings between News Corp officials and senior Giuliani aides.

Eric Alterman, who worked at Ailes's former channel, takes up the story in an article for the *Nation*:

> *While Murdoch's* New York Post *had been four-square in Rudy's corner during his 1989 and 1993 mayoral races, the intensity of the connection did not become clear to me until 1996, when Murdoch launched Fox News. I was working at MSNBC at the time and did not know that Roger Ailes had actually run Rudy's failed 1989 campaign. But even so, when Time Warner at first refused to carry Fox, I could not help wondering why Giuliani felt that having a second all-news cable network in Manhattan was akin to preventing Armageddon.*

(ALTERMAN, 2011)

Giuliani castigated Time Warner and threatened to revoke their licence. When that failed, he offered a free public channel to Fox News until that arrangement was thrown out by a federal judge in 1997 and later, by an appeal court.

Murdoch's ties with Giuliani are the closest thing the US has to the media-political nexus in the UK, As Wayne Barrett has documented: 'The Rudy–Rupert relationship is in fact as close as we come in America to understanding the hubbub now consuming the U.K. It is a tale of transactional journalism that goes to the heart of everything long wrong in the Murdoch empire, where politicians are acquired as frequently as businesses, and mergers occur at personal as well as corporate levels' (Barrett, 2011). Eventually Time Warner caved into the pressure and gave Fox News its New York outlet – but though this was another Murdoch triumph over the politicians, the key player was actually Ailes.

It took almost a decade, but under Ailes's guidance Fox News achieved for American cable news what the *Sun* had for the British tabloids: it became the dominant 24-hour news channel by 2010, with the top dozen slots among cable news watchers. The impact of Fox News on the American media scene and the multiple misrepresentations, distorted debate and false dilemmas it has produced since 1996 would require a book – in fact several books, with several volumes. One thing is for sure, it has irrevocably changed the tone of 24-hour news to something combative, partisan and highly profitable.

Fox News is an object lesson in post-modern propaganda through its 'talking points' and confusion of news and editorial, and it turns shock-jock *Sun*-speak into a truly Orwellian 24-hour wall-to-wall immersive illusion. Some of its tactics appal, manipulating news footage to make a sparsely attended Tea Party event look crowded or randomly putting up D for Democrat graphics accompanying any Republican caught in a sex scandal. At the time of writing this chapter, here's a more subtle piece of anti-news reporting plucked from the airwaves:

> *Fox Blames Obama For Change In Gas Prices From January 2009*
> *To Now.*
>
> *On at least six occasions in the past week, Fox News has pushed the talking point that gasoline prices have almost doubled (increasing 83% or 90% or 91%) since Obama took office in January 2009. The claim was also promoted this week by the Drudge Report and CNSNews, as well as the Senate Republican Conference. Fox falsely suggested that Obama's energy policies are to blame for the increase in prices, without explaining that prices were low in January 2009 because the recession slashed demand.*

(FITZSIMMONS ET AL., 2012)

The blog Media Matters – which has an extensive library of Fox News misrepresentations and manipulations – amply demonstrates how, having twisted the statistics, the cable news channels anchors blatantly incited Republican politicians to blame Obama for the price rise, all the while openly expressing the hope it will be 'enough to derail his election'. Such a level of bias and misreporting would not be tolerated on British television; on the other hand, Britain still has a proper broadcast regulator, despite all the best efforts of James Murdoch to destroy it.

Fox News and all it stands for is, however, primarily the brainchild of Ailes, now a senior News Corp executive and according to reports, the one person Murdoch is scared of on his own board. Given Ailes's background in Nixonian politics and shock-jock rhetoric, one could legitimately put the Murdoch/Ailes influence the other way round – as we saw in Chapter 5 *Sun*speak and Murdoch's Southern strategy could more rightly be said to be something he imported from the US, rather than vice versa. This could also explain the enormous amount of deference the CEO of News Corp accords to the Fox News founder. In 2004, Ailes was reported to have scotched the claim to the succession from Murdoch's oldest son, Lachlan, who retired hurt from New York to concentrate on News Ltd's interests in Australia. Murdoch's son-in-law Matthew Freud lambasted Ailes and Fox News in a strategic interview with the *New York Times*: 'I am by no means alone within the family or the company in being ashamed and sickened by Roger Ailes's horrendous and sustained disregard of the journalistic standards that News Corporation, its founder and every other global media business aspires to' (Carr and Arango, 2010). Murdoch himself was berated for Fox News's 'destructiveness' by Steve Jobs before he died (Isaacson, 2011, p. 508). But Ailes seems to be untouchable and is paid more than anyone on the News Corp board, including the Chairman. The power relation doesn't follow the ostensible executive flow chart. By outfoxing his boss, in many ways, Ailes has out-Murdoched Murdoch.

Until the hacking scandal and the 'Not Fit' pronouncement of the DCMS parliamentary sub-committee, Murdoch has achieved neither the success nor the notoriety he has in Britain. He is, according to Alterman, still 'an honoured figure in both the media and the New York social whirl'. In 1997, after the testy Time Warner/Fox News fight during which Ted Turner compared Murdoch to Hitler, Murdoch was awarded the Humanitarian of the Year award by the United Jewish Appeal. As he told William Shawcross: 'They were so outraged that they gave me a great dinner, with Henry Kissinger making me Humanitarian of the Year, purely to stick their finger in Ted Turner's eye.' Outside of New York and Los Angeles, however, his name is not so recognisable. Part of the reason why the scandal has not captivated the media's attention in the US as much it has Britain, is that Murdoch has only captured a small fraction of it.

However, there is one lasting legacy to Murdoch's US holdings which – just as the Times Newspapers Group takeover sealed his monopoly over the British press for a generation – could spell long-term trouble for American broadcast news. Since the Fairness Doctrine was dropped by the FCC in 1987, after it was criticised in a stinging report by the same Reagan appointee who waived the cross-ownership laws for Murdoch, there is no longer any burden on broadcasters to provide adequate coverage of public issues and to ensure that coverage fairly represents opposing views. Without it, Fox News can still (mis)represent itself as a 'fair and balanced' news organisation, rather than a partisan noise machine. Without any restrictions on what is true or false, Fox News presenters can still cast doubt on Obama's parentage or portray him as a secret Muslim/Communist/Nazi (delete as applicable). Still, Ailes insists the Channel's coverage is 'fair and balanced'. All this was foreseen by James Fallows in the *Atlantic* magazine when Murdoch was lobbying the FCC for wider cross-ownership in 2003:

> *Sooner or later Murdoch's outlets, especially Fox News, will be more straightforward about their political identity—and they are likely to bring the rest of the press with them. There will be liberal papers, radio shows, TV programs, and Web sites for liberals, and conservative ones for conservatives. This result will hardly be new. Frankly partisan media have never ceased to be the rule in modern Europe. Our journalistic culture may soon enough resemble that of early nineteenth-century America, in which party-owned newspapers presented selective versions of the truth. ... An age of more purely commercial, more openly partisan media leaves out some of the functions that news was until recently expected to perform: giving a broad public some common source of information for making political decisions, and telling people about trends and events they didn't already know they were interested in. One way or another, self-governing societies must figure out the suitable commercial channels through which the information necessary for democratic decisions can be spread. That's not exactly Murdoch's problem, though he helped make it the world's.*

(FALLOWS, 2003)

Though this may please Republican Tea Party supporters, it gives them no moral defence from a far left cable news channel taking to the airwaves in the future and promoting communist propaganda, under the label of 'fair and balanced'. The libertarian right often talk about their struggle as freedom from tyranny and cite the founding fathers in their aversion to any kind of government influence. However, Jefferson or Hamilton would soon spot the difference between real defenders of the public interest of liberty, rather than those who would sacrifice the principle to private interests.

The fact that Murdoch is the bankroller rather than the genius behind Fox News does not free him from blame for its excesses, any more than he can be ethically exculpated from the cover-up of phone hacking by his London News International executives. As head of Corporate Governance, he should be exercising oversight. Eric Alterman again, this time writing in *American Progress*:

> One could fill entire libraries with the crimes against journalistic ethics practiced by Murdoch properties over the decades. But rather than get into the actions of his employees, let's keep the focus on Murdoch himself.
>
> When Glenn Beck—then of Fox—called President Barack Obama a 'racist' with a 'deep-seated hatred for white people or the white culture,' Murdoch endorsed his views, insisting that Obama 'did make a very racist comment about, you know, blacks and whites and so on, and which he said in his campaign he would be completely above. And, you know, that was something which, perhaps, shouldn't have been said about the president, but if you actually assess what he [Beck] was talking about, he was right.'
>
> (ALTERMAN, 2012)

It was perhaps an understandable political calculation that Murdoch, urged by his children to support Obama, still decided to back the losing Republican candidate for president in 2008, John McCain. But Murdoch's defence of Fox News and Glenn Beck's statement that Obama hated both his white mother and white grandparents is not easy to excuse. Expediency has slipped into support for the dog-whistles of 'anti-anti-racism' (i.e. racism) – a jarring contradiction since two of Murdoch's children are half Chinese and two of his grandchildren have an African father, just like Obama.

CHINATOWN

The perversity of Murdoch helping to promote the xenophobia of the Tea Party while he heads a multi-national, multi-racial family in a migratory jet-set life, is another of the paradoxes of the News Corp Nation he now inhabits. This Scottish descended, Australian-born, British backed, American citizen, with his Chinese wife, half-Chinese children and other mixed ancestry grandchildren scattered across the hemispheres, more often than not channels the turmoil of globalisation into a fear of strangers. A practising internationalist, he plays on nationalist sentiment, encouraging nativism in the US, anti-immigrant rhetoric in Australia, anti-EU coverage in Britain, anti-English independence in Scotland. The man who flies above all borders tries to erect ever bigger barriers in people's minds. Murdoch has taken British imperial divide and rule to heart, until he is radically divided from himself.

That bifurcation became potentially costly in 1979 when the Australian Broadcasting Tribunal held an extensive hearing before renewing News Ltd's television licenses, to assess whether Murdoch was still a resident Australian for tax and regulatory purposes. Though he'd lived abroad for ten years Rupert protested:

> *I carry an Australian passport. My children are Australian. I pay my taxes in Australia. I have a home in Australia. It has all my personal belongings in it. It is lived in by no one but myself ... I certainly intend to come back to the country and certainly when my children are old enough to leave home I trust I will in fact put them through Australian universities. I chose to have them with me. I think it is very important, more important than proving some point at the moment by separating them and breaking up the family.*
>
> (CHENOWETH, 2001)

None of these promises came to pass. In 1985, when setting up Fox Network, the FCC gave Murdoch a two-year waiver of cross-ownership rules so he could own both television stations and newspapers in New York, Chicago and Boston. But Section 310 of the 1934 Communications Act, however, which forbade 'alien' companies owning more than 25 per cent of US television station, was not so easy to get around. There was only one solution to this. With help from Reagan, Murdoch replaced his Australian citizenship with an American one and was sworn in during a private session in the judge's chambers rather than with the hoi polloi in the courtroom, declaring: 'I am very proud and grateful to be sworn in as an American citizen.'

Call it treachery, call it commercial expedience, but there's a personal compartmentalisation underway in these two mutually exclusive declarations, which cannot at all be comfortable to live with and requires an element of self-denial to convincingly sustain. Murdoch's fissured loyalties become even more evident in the late nineties as News Corp tried to expand beyond the English-speaking world, especially with his disastrous courtship of the Chinese government. Here was the self-confessed libertarian conducting a fire-sale of his beliefs for the authoritarian Chinese Communist party.

Bruce Dover, who from 1992 to 1998 was News Corp's representative in China, sees more in common between the libertarian businessman and Chinese communism than at first meets the eye. Both organisations are run in an authoritarian way, with an organisation chart that 'would have Murdoch at the top and under him a single straight line to everyone else' (Dover, 2008). Add to that an obsession with loyalty, dynastic succession and a burgeoning surveillance apparatus in the News International headquarters, the affinities between the Murdoch family and the Chinese authorities look less surprising after all.

News Corp's Chinese adventures are a sorry example of political appeasement for commercial gain which ended up losing Murdoch both financial and moral capital. He set up Star TV in Hong Kong in order to broadcast direct satellite to the Chinese mainland and in order to persuade the Chinese government to allow his satellite dishes, he kowtowed to every demand, dropping the BBC's uncensored news from his satellite and trying to spike the memoirs of Chris Patten, the last British colonial governor of Hong Kong. Beyond negative censorship, Murdoch also deployed his classic positive censorship, paying a large advice to Deng Xiaoping's daughter for a hagiography of her father. The Chinese satellite ban remained in place and Star TV's key audience and revenue earners remained out of reach, losing the company $200 million a year.

Soon after he met Wendi Deng in December 1998 Murdoch was finally granted an audience with Jiang Zemin, then China's party chief, to get the satellite ban lifted. Not only did Murdoch speak out against the Dalai Lama, the exiled spiritual leader of China's restive Tibetan population, he also put $60 million into a venture of Zemin's son. Two years later Murdoch sent out James to court the Chinese. The junior Murdoch was quickly conscripted into the Chinese propaganda campaign against the Falun Gong movement, describing them as a 'dangerous' and 'apocalyptic cult' that 'clearly does not have the success of China at heart' – which of course James Murdoch clearly did. James also criticised the Western press for their negative coverage of the People's Republic and their support for pro-democracy agitators in Hong Kong. Perhaps the family copy of Orwell's Nineteen Eighty-Four had been mislaid on this trip. Certainly, the vernacular adopted by James Murdoch at the time somewhat compromises the later talk about the 'chilling' effect of 'state sponsored' media like the BBC. Indeed, James sponsored state television by setting up loss-making TV channel, Phoenix, in consortium CCTV– one of the most government controlled media organisations in the world (Goldmann, 2002). All this was forgotten during James's indictment of the 'chilling effect' of 'state sponsored' media then seven years later. It's hard to decide whether the Orwellian rhetoric of James's MacTaggart lecture is just mendacity, expedience or some major inherited dissociative disorder.

James was just following his father's footsteps, though – for grabbing the crown of News Corp required showing the same political elasticity as its current

Chair and CEO. During one of his spats with Ted Turner at the National Press club in 1996 (during which he called the CNN network a hive of 'left-wing bias') Murdoch wheeled out what he considered his best wares (interestingly enough *The Times* newspaper, *The X-Files* and *The Simpsons*) before launching into an attack which, given the manic Chinese diplomacy then underway, was the most breathtakingly disingenuous: 'We do, however, draw the line at professional wrestling and brown-nosing foreign dictators. You'll have to turn to one of Ted's channels for that. I'm reminded of something Disraeli once said to a colleague in Parliament: "Honorable sir, it's true that I am a low, mean snake. But you, sir, could walk beneath me wearing a top hat"' (Turner, 1996). The irony bypass, which first emerged in the decades before Murdoch's claim to be a meritocrat outsider despite his privileged background, was now being stretched to breaking point across the world.

GLOBAL VILLAGE NEWS

News Corp Nation is one of the most significant enclaves in what, following Marshall McLuhan, we now call the Global Village: a world of 24-hour news and immediate international communications. In the eighties it was observed how Sub-Saharan nomads would delay their northward annual migration to catch the last episode of *Dallas* on satellite TV. A friend of mine who recently travelled deep into the Amazon saw a group of tribal people dancing in a circle by the river: when she asked why they were dancing, they told her translator they were trying to summon the internet. The 'village' metaphor thereby expresses the proximity and intimacy of global communication. But on further inspection there is much more to it than that.

When McLuhan coined the term Global Village he was well aware of the alternative possibility – the Global City. This had been imagined by St Augustine, a visionary City of God that combined the messianic promise of Jerusalem with the Hellenic values of civility, urbanity and citizenship represented by Athens. In a global city you have to deal with otherness as well as intimacy; there is a distinction between our private selves and our public face. In a global city, you are constantly confronting strangers, from other tribes and nations and establishing rules of the road to negotiate your differences. In a global city, mobility and lack of presumption are everything. Public discourse, as represented by the agora or Acropolis, has to leap over particular identities and speak to a more abstract universal of the citizen.

In a global village, by contrast, the talk would be all gossip and scandal, obsessed with the private lives of celebrities and public figures. In a global village, everyone would know everyone else's business and that tyranny of intimacy would imprison us in the fixed identities of our caste, class, family and past. In a global village, conformity would be enforced through shame and punishment, with miscreants from the group held up for ridicule and contempt. In a global village, mobility would be reduced and the private sphere would be open to constant intrusion of spies and rumour mongers. In a global village, the narcissism of differences would be amplified, this group against that group, that quarter against this, this household against that. In a global village, universal communications would not make us citizens but denizens, sub-urban, wired up and fascinated by the spectacle of our neighbours from hell.

Fox News, like *News of the World*, are products of the global village – not the global city.

REBIRTH

Something broke around this time. For almost half a century, Murdoch had been living an increasingly itinerant life. During the fifties and sixties his far flung Australian outlets were thousands of miles apart and required hours in transit. This jet-set vagrancy intensified to hemispheric proportions with his arrival in London in 1969, a 25-hour flight from home. The move to New York in the seventies and brief spell in LA in the nineties didn't diminish the air travel, but created more global circumnavigation. Wolff describes the travel as a 'kind of monomania that, from an early age, fascinates and disturbs other people'. It certainly, by all reports, disturbed his second wife Anna Murdoch who had assumed the rootlessness would diminish as Murdoch approached his seventies. But to give up this outsider status would have meant the refutation of a core principle and perhaps mark the onset of the end, for many men of Murdoch's generation who devoted themselves to their work, retirement has led not to relaxation but a swift demise. But there was another option. As Chenoweth surmises: 'Over half a century the course of Murdoch's odyssey would be marked regularly by the painful moment when he jettisoned cargo: people and ideas and places he had outgrown' (Chenoweth, 2001, p. 35). In 1998, this would lead to one of the most painful changes of all – the end of his 32-year-long marriage to Anna and a potentially divisive rift in the family fortunes when he married Wendi Deng in 2001.

I'm not going to add to gossip about Murdoch's divorce and remarriage, except where it impinges on the culture and ethos of News Corp and News International. There's enough conjecture in the public domain and – as so often with the Murdoch family – personal loyalty or antipathy blurs the real historic issues. Politically, however, his marriage to Deng does seem to have changed Murdoch's ideological fervour. After being diagnosed with slow growing prostate cancer in 2000, he changed his diet and lifestyle. A millennial Murdoch was born.

Though the media mogul never shed his mix of Conservative libertarian beliefs, his new wife, 38 years his junior, brought him into contact with a younger generation of politicians and celebrities who were more socially liberal. The combined effect of this was to dull some of the sharper macho rhetoric of the papers he still controlled, like the *Sun* and *New York Post*. News Corp became more 'feminised' – at least on a superficial level – as he promoted female writers and editors such as book editor Judith Regan, and Rebekah Brooks, albeit with unfortunate consequences for both. As he went through his second divorce, Murdoch's daughter from his first marriage, Pru, became a closer confidante. Meanwhile the reported rupture with his second daughter, Elisabeth, caused much distress. The family stress of the demise of a long marriage and his prostate cancer, not to mention the continuing high-risk deal flows (in this case an abortive attempt to set up an American version of Sky, ASkyB), seem to have settled his mood, ground down the edges and turned Murdoch into something more abstract and other-worldly.

Without falling into the celebrity coverage traps of unknowable personal disclosures, it does seem that illness and divorce, while they gave Murdoch a new lease of energy and life, had also made him more aware of his mortality. Whether the result was personal humility can again only be answered by a tiny number of people, possibly only Murdoch himself. But the events of the new century clearly did lead to a renewed focus by the media mogul on his legacy.

How would he be remembered? The Rockefellers, Carnegies and Pulitzers had endowed foundations which, though funded through rapacious careers of accumulation, gave something back to the future and rebranded them for posterity. What would the Murdoch legacy be? Great crusading newspapers that survived the turmoil of technological change? Or a vast entertainment business devoted to movies, music and pay-TV? And what of the family future in News Corp, the global empire he'd built up over fifty years? Would it stay in the family? Could a Murdoch still run it? Or would all the accumulated capital and reputation be squandered by the squabbling children?

9

15 July 2011
Freudian Communications

With the resignation of Rebekah Brooks, the current CEO of News International, on Friday 15 July 2011, swiftly followed by her predecessor Les Hinton, who had moved on to become the publisher of Dow Jones and executive in charge of the *Wall Street Journal*, the last firewalls protecting the Murdoch family had fallen. These were significant losses: Hinton had been one of Murdoch's longest serving lieutenants, with a fifty-year history going back to the early days in Australian newspapers; Brooks had been so close to the Murdoch family that she was often described as part of it. *The Daily Telegraph* reported that Elisabeth Murdoch, once a close friend of Brooks's, had said 'Rebekah fucked the company' at a book party the previous weekend. But the divisions went far deeper; according to Michael Wolff who tweeted that the account was 'incomplete' what she had really said '*James* and Rebekah fucked the company.'

Again Murdoch's hand was forced and he was behind events. He had only accepted Brooks's resignation when Saudi Prince Al-Waleed bin Talal, one of the largest independent shareholders of News Corp, told BBC *Newsnight* that she had to go. Hinton was Brooks's former mentor and had oversight of News International until 2009 when hacking was rife, but had denied it in testimony before Parliament: Brooks's exit inevitably would mean his.

News Corp was still in firefighting mode, responding to events rather than pre-empting them. Making another prescient comparison with Watergate, Carl Bernstein predicted 'we are the beginning, not the end, of the seismic event' and stressed the importance of the US holdings and that the danger of the allegation that *News of the World* tried to hack 9/11 victims. With the bombshells landing ever closer to its corporate HQ in New York, News Corp suddenly woke up to the seriousness of the situation and hired a new PR firm, Edelman, whose clients include Starbucks and Burger King. On this Friday, Murdoch embarked on a new strategy of apology rather than denial, meeting with the Dowler family. The account of that meeting by the family's lawyer, Mark Lewis, is revealing: Murdoch told the family that this was 'the worst day of my life', and that his 101-year-old mother, Dame Elisabeth Murdoch, would be ashamed of him, 'He had his head in his hands,' Lewis recalled. 'He brought up his father and said he was a great journalist, and the British people never forgave him for what he exposed about Gallipoli' (Ellison, 2011). There's a hundred years of post-colonial resentment, newspaper history and family psychology, encapsulated in that sentence.

An ad campaign over the weekend was even pithier: 'We Are Sorry'.

> *We are sorry.*
>
> *The News of the World was in the business of holding others to account. It failed when it came to itself.*
>
> *We are sorry for the serious wrongdoing that occurred.*
>
> *We are deeply sorry for the hurt suffered by the individuals affected.*
>
> *We regret not acting faster to sort things out.*
>
> *I realise that simply apologising is not enough.*
>
> *Our business was founded on the idea that a free and open press should be a positive force in society. We need to live up to this.*
>
> *In the coming days, as we take further concrete steps to resolve these issues and make amends for the damage they have caused, you will hear more from us.*

(FINANCIAL TIMES, 2011)

It was an abrupt change of tone, though. Only the day before Murdoch had called the *Wall Street Journal* to tell his subsidiary that News Corp had handled the crisis 'extremely well in every way possible', making just 'minor mistakes'. He still thought the reputational damage in Britain was recoverable – 'We have a reputation of great good works in this country,' he told the *Wall Street Journal*, but the unpredictable unfolding crisis was denting even his famed resilience: 'I'm tired.'

Murdoch's weary ire was particularly focused on former prime minister Gordon Brown who had coined the phrase a 'criminal media nexus' in a speech to the House of Commons and alleged both the *News of the World* and *The Sunday Times* had obtained information about him illegally: 'Some of the things that have been said in Parliament, some of which are total lies,' Murdoch told his paper. Gordon Brown 'got it completely wrong' even though 'the Browns were always friends of ours'.

With the exception of the news that Tony Blair was the baptismal godfather to Murdoch's daughter, Grace, in 2010, the fact that Brown and Murdoch had been friends was one of the most unlikely revelations of the whole scandal, especially given the way News International had attacked Brown and his supporters during the internecine struggle over succession only five years before and then supported David Cameron during the election. The combination of both political betrayal and personal animus would inform Murdoch's appearance before the Leveson Inquiry in April 2012, where he claimed he had a conversation with Brown soon after the *Sun* declared support for the Conservatives and that Brown had 'declared war' on his company in 2009. Murdoch added the barb that the former prime minister was angry because he was 'mentally unstable' – a damaging rumour that had circulated on the blogosphere before Brown failed to get re-elected two years earlier. Brown would have his revenge though, in Court 73, a couple of months later.

Brown then went on to vehemently deny Murdoch's oral evidence about the call when he declared war on Murdoch. Supported by five affidavits and logs of all his outgoing and incoming calls, Brown said 'This call did not happen. The threat was not made. I couldn't be unbalanced on a call that I didn't have'. Brown claimed 'the only conversation they had was a year later, and that was about Afghanistan'. The oral evidence was backed up by written affidavits by five members of staff who listened into the conversation.

Given their political differences, the previous rapport between Brown and Murdoch might be hard to fathom: Blair always appeared more centrist and willing to trim to tabloid opinion. But this is an appearance. The New Labour project, which rested on a form of triangulation on social issues like law and order, was predicated on the need to quell the antagonism of the tabloids and it was very much a joint project with all its founders. On the personal level, the connection was thought to have first been between Brown's wife Sarah and Wendi Deng, who joined Brooks and Elisabeth Murdoch at the famous pyjama party organised by Sarah at Chequers in 2008. During her testimony to Lord Justice Leveson, Brooks claimed she had been friends with Sarah since the late nineties, guiding her throughout her courtship, engagement and then marriage to the then chancellor and prime minister-to-be. But looking again, the closeness between Gordon Brown and Murdoch is really not so hard to fathom.

Brown is the 'son of the manse', whose father was a preacher, as was Murdoch's grandfather: Murdoch had always valued his Scottish non-conformist roots. Both men are reported to have the same gruff, high minded but slightly awkward manner. Moreover, Brown is nothing if not thoughtful and serious and Murdoch has a declared aversion to PR types and smooth operators. Murdoch would have also admired Brown's relative lack of privilege and his deep-seated belief in self-help and self-improvement.

Murdoch actually backed Brown to succeed Blair and by his own account reluctantly followed his son James's succession strategy which led to Brown being brutally dumped by the *Sun* on the day of his party conference speech. Murdoch senior disparaged the method, but had already signed off on the big strategy. The business – most importantly the family business – trumped everything else.

In the most emotionally charged part of his appearance, Brown also dealt with Brooks and the *Sun*'s revelation of his son's cystic fibrosis on the front page of the tabloid within days of it being diagnosed in 2006. Brown 'absolutely' denied he had given Brooks permission to reprint details of Fraser Brown's condition. Brown claimed he was presented with a 'fait accompli' by Brooks and that no parent would willingly divulge such confidential material about their child, especially since he was only four months old at the time, and other relatives – who could be directly affected by an inherited illness like this – had not been told.

Brown effectively accused Brooks of lying under oath about him and the charge was laden with more than the usual freight of political betrayal, because these were two people he obviously once considered as friends. But friendships were expendable when it came to the family business, as even Hinton and Brooks had just discovered on 15 July.

COMPETING FOR THE CROWN

Family and politics, blood versus business: you can see the impact of these two forces in Murdoch's boyish shame in front of Bob and Sally Dowler as he apologised to them and then announced that somehow this was the worst day of *his* life. An oppressive of generational duty turns Murdoch into the victim, just as his father was the victim of British snobbery nearly a century ago. His mother would be mortified and yet his dad had never been forgiven for telling the truth about Gallipoli: the insiderdom/outsiderdom dynamo derives from this. You can never let go, but you can never be at home; a corporate dynasty driven by an attempt to hang on to the inherited ties that almost strangle you, while enjoying and fearing the mobility and competition that dissolves them like an acid.

In the late eighties Murdoch once said 'I'm a great believer in nepotism' (Chenoweth, 2001, p. 107) and yet – as Blair reminded us at Leveson – bits of Murdoch are meritocratic, anti-establishment and always prone to mock 'toffs' and their inherited wealth. Nevertheless, in an article describing the complicated arrangements which followed Murdoch's traumatic divorce from Anna, the *Atlantic* reported in 2002:

> *Whether or not News Corp is an empire, functionally it is a dynasty ...*
> *Lachlan, thirty-two, is the deputy chief of operations at News Corp.*
> *James, who will turn thirty-one late this year, runs the Star satellite*
> *business in Asia. For several years Murdoch has been indicating that*
> *one of the sons—probably Lachlan but perhaps James, depending on*
> *how he does in the next few years at Star—or both jointly will succeed*
> *him at News Corp.*

(FALLOWS, 2003)

Forget for a moment the obvious patriarchy – only one of the two male children could possibly replace their father as Chair and CEO – the double bind of this conditional commercial love has awkward implications. Like Keith before him, Murdoch both cajoles and punishes his offspring. He regards them highly enough to want them to inherit, but suspects they might not be good enough and forces them to compete to win their legacy. The sons are doubly overshadowed, with an external compulsion determining their fate and an inner drive that might, just might, prove they are worthy. To expect your children to compete for your crown is Lear-like in its callous neediness.

Thus Murdoch passes on the poisoned chalice bequeathed to him by his father under the watchful disapproving eye of his mother, the pressure of success and the anticipation of failure; only with Lachlan and James it is supercharged into a male sibling rivalry which Murdoch, as the sole male heir, never had to deal with. It's divide and rule all over again, embedded deep within the family psyche. Though they're apparently competing with each other, the sons are in fact competing with Murdoch. This punitive arrangement suits the patriarch more than his heirs. No wonder James installed a full-scale model of Darth Vader on the executive floor at Wapping when he arrived there. The shadow of the 'dark father' dominates, even in jest.

Though Murdoch is reported to be attentive to all his children, call them 'darling' and asking how they are doing, he would have been kinder as a father to have provided for his children financially and then explicitly written them out of any commercial succession plans. That way they could have fared for themselves professionally and proved themselves on their own grounds. Elisabeth, implicitly excluded from the News Corp chairmanship in 2002, followed this path and – having worked her way up running a TV company in the US and then at Sky operating under Sam Chisholm – left the family empire and set up the Shine Entertainment group. But even independence has its price and Murdoch – unable to leave anything out of his ambit – brought Elisabeth back into the fold by buying the Shine group for nearly $700 million, with a promise to install Elisabeth on the board.

All this might seem like more biographical fetishism, but in the case of the Murdochs – unlike the tabloid obsession with biographical melodrama – it's relevant because of the public interest. Millions of families suffer from similar issues of inheritance and there are probably several hundred where the monetary stakes are just as high and the dysfunction worse. Indeed, as he proved through his takeover of the *Wall Street Journal* from the divided Bancroft family, Murdoch has a canny insight into the petty squabbles and divisions as expanding generations compete for the family spoils. Why this matters here – why it matters to you and me – is the impact such a family dynamic has had on our politics and media.

Beyond Murdoch's own ambitions, that insider/outsider dialectic which has driven his lateral invasions across the world, we have to consider the impossible ambitions it bequeaths to his heirs and how they led to the overreach of the Rubicon process. Having seen his older brother Lachlan fail at the succession, ousted from New York by other board members and retreating to Australia, James understands the challenge. The rebellious son, who founded a hip-hop label, tried his hand as a satirical cartoonist, before taking on the role of his father's ambassador to the Communist Dynasties in China, knows the real obstacle that he has to overcome. He has to surpass his father merely to equal him. This leads to the hungry hubris of the BSkyB bid, the remorseless lobbying around it which would embarrass a government and the desperate cover-up of phone hacking that would end in the courts. James had no choice: like Alexander the Great invading India only to expire there, the horizon is the only place where the pressures of the past can be escaped. It sounds like hyperbole and speculation, but it's in that notorious memo Jeremy Hunt wrote to the prime minister David Cameron after a long conversation with James in November 2010: James has his eyes set on a huge vision, an integrated cross-platform publishing and broadcast business around the BSkyB hub, which would launch News Corp into the digital future; it would be like his father did at Wapping, only bigger. It was planned as his Rubicon, if no one else's.

The Murdoch family will no doubt enter the realm of myth in the many depictions in drama and fiction yet to come. Murdoch has often been compared with King Lear, demanding his children compete for his affections, but given the short-lived tragedy of James's Rubicon and even better mythic prototype might be Icarus, who was encouraged by his father Daedalus to try out his new invention: wings made of wax. Despite his father's admonitions about aspiring too high, Icarus knew he had to prove himself and flew too close to the sun. The *Sun* and the *News of the World* would likewise bring James crashing to the ground.

The Murdochs' tragic flaws deserve their own unique narrative mythos, if only because they compel us so completely. Murdoch's distaste for 'toffs', the royal family and other dynasties has been reiterated over half a century with such venom, can only be explained by an unresolved psychological split. Murdoch is still competing with his own inheritance, angrily at war with himself, a condition he encourages his children to heal but which ends up wounding them too. This is part of the secret of Murdoch's success: an inner conflict that we all recognise so well in our own families and hungrily buy into, as readers and watchers, consumers and commentators, thus helping him extend the conflict further into the public domain, until the psychological flaw has become bodied in our collective history.

At the heart of our elevation of Murdoch, and of course his canny response to it, is a lack of boundaries, an inability to accept the painful difference between private affection and public accolade. Running through the internal and external legacy of the Murdoch project is a confusion between the personal and the professional, the familiar and the strange, a constantly contested borderline which is echoed in his treatment of public figures whose private failings provide the fodder for his papers and material for our fantasies: voyeurism posing as moral outrage, ridicule turned into mass entertainment. Given this tortured ambiguity it's no surprise that Murdoch's best-selling and oldest established paper should end up illegally invading private agony on an industrial scale. It's a grim kind of poetic justice that only stepping over that ultimate boundary and the wanton intrusion on the grief of the parents of a murdered schoolgirl, could finally force Murdoch to atone for how invasive his empire had become, to his mother, his children, to himself.

But then again, his father was never forgiven for Gallipoli. Back to work.

DEAL – NO DEAL

Before we can understand the new generation of Murdochs, they have to be seen against the new kind of politics that arrived in in Britain in the twenty-first century.

The primacy of public relations and media coverage was self-evident to the three architects of New Labour, Blair, Brown and Peter Mandelson, after eighteen years in opposition, much of it vitiated by corrosive coverage from News International. The expected Labour victory of 1992, which the *Sun* claimed to have snatched away from them at the last moment, was etched on the memory of a generation of Labour supporters. Though nowhere as prolonged or contentious as the 'hanging chads' fiasco during the 2000 US presidential election, the trauma for the centre left was almost as big. In this case it was not the Supreme Court that turned victory into defeat, but the *Sun*, the biggest selling paper at Wapping, with four million buyers and eight million readers. Something had to be done.

In 1994, when the sudden death of John Smith left a vacancy at the head of the Labour Party, it was quite clear that, though Brown was the more experienced, his close ally and colleague Blair was more telegenic, and his easy Southern patois with a hint of the glottal stop would be less problematic to the swing votes in southern England, compared to Brown's Scottish brogue and often awkward seriousness. When Blair won the leadership of the Labour Party that year, the courting of – or at least the neutralisation of – the Murdoch effect was a high priority. As Blair told Piers Morgan: 'Piers, I had to court … It is better to be riding the tiger's back than let him rip your throat out. Look what Murdoch did to Kinnock' (Morgan, 2005, p. 147). There was a face-to-face meeting with Murdoch soon after Blair won the party vote and in 1995 Blair circumnavigated the world to address News Corp. To the amusement of the Royal Courts of Justice, Murdoch confirmed before Lord Justice Leveson that he'd used an animal metaphor to describe the courtship: porcupines making love, slowly and carefully.

As we've seen it's not unprecedented for Murdoch to form alliances with centre left leaders. He'd done exactly this for the Australian Labor Party over several decades, from Gough Whitlam to Bob Hawke and Paul Keating had explicitly guided the new generation of British labour politicians how to deal with him. Whatever the personal rapprochement between Murdoch and Blair, the signal to New Labour's rising apparatchiks was loud and clear. Lower down the food chain, lobbyists and correspondents would walk through the revolving doors of remunerative columns, book deals and policy discussions about crime, foreign policy and of course media regulation. The *Sun* finally reversed two decades of Tory support in 1997 to back Labour during the election.

So traumatic had been the years of defeat – especially after the false hope of 1992 – that even though Blair won by a landslide in May 1997, right up till the last minute there were plans to form an alliance with Paddy Ashdown and the Liberal Democrats. In this light, the courtship of Murdoch made paranoid sense: do anything for victory. The question isn't why Labour courted News International but why – given an unassailable majority and the honeymoon period of good will – it still carried on doing so. It had the power to renege on any implicit deal with its former enemy. Was it lack of ruthlessness which stopped them pushing through the cross-ownership rules? Or did they fear that an onslaught could still unsettle the government in the same way it had for John

Major? Or maybe it was just a simple question of keeping their (unspoken) word? Or is it something more complex and surprising: were New Labour's leaders somehow persuaded by News Corp's arguments, just as Murdoch was increasingly beguiled by theirs?

We also know that Murdoch had always enjoyed debating with the left, something which represented his student days, and his support for Blair coincided a late efflorescence of youthfulness after his marriage to Wendi Deng. It was Wendi, after all, who asked Blair to be the godfather to her daughter Grace as she was baptised on the banks of the River Jordan. Had some strange new synthesis overtaken the vituperative polarisation between right and left which had dominated Murdoch's career for so many years?

In his assured performance at the Leveson Inquiry, Blair denied any explicit deal was done – but revealed the implicit deal. New Labour quietly dropped the cross-ownership rules which would have made Murdoch sell his BSkyB stake, or sell some of his newspapers. That was the tacit precondition for the support of News International, a force that Blair readily admitted was too big to combat – even with the largest majority in living memory – unless he wanted to sacrifice all his other reforms in healthcare and education. Taking on the press would mean 'a long protracted battle that will shove everything else aside'.

That was an admission enough in itself. For all the reasonableness of Blair's presentation, the recognition of these brute, stark realities of power underpinned his whole approach to the media, and the Murdoch press in particular. He called it a 'working relationship with powerful people' and described the newspapers as 'instruments for political power'. In a surprising admission Blair also conceded the 'politician manqué' in Murdoch. Though he'd initially believed, like many others, that the mogul only deployed his political clout to aid his commercial interests, years of familiarity had revealed the opposite and Blair conceded the ideological agenda came first. Though he was friendly with Murdoch, Blair claimed that real friendship was only possible once he left office ('you can't have personal relationships based on power'): he also made the astute observation about the complexity of Murdoch which meant there were elements of his ideological matrix he could tap: Murdoch was not an 'identikit conservative' but bits of him were 'anti-establishment and meritocratic'.

Clearly stung by the accusation that New Labour had been pliable to News Corp's demands, Blair's written evidence to the Inquiry contained a litany of deals it hadn't done during his tenure: New Labour raised the BBC licence fee and allowed an extension in their number of channels, despite many objections from News Corp. Though the Communications Act of 2002 changed the terms governing cross-media ownership to allow News Corp to purchase Channel 5 if it wished, the rules explicitly forbade it from taking a controlling interest in the main commercial channel ITV (a rule that James Murdoch would test at some expense in 2008). Labour also intervened – after some delay – to try to stop the predatory price dumping of *The Times* which cost other broadsheets in terms of circulation and to prevent the purchase of the world's biggest football team, Manchester United.

On the other hand, anyone looking at a balance sheet of News Corp's assets would see that it survived thirteen years of Labour government fairly intact, with its dominance of Fleet Street consolidated and BSkyB in the ascendant with an ever increasing share of broadcast revenues and even more sports and film rights. Whatever Blair said about there being no 'deal', the relationship between his government and News Corp looks profoundly *transactional*. Murdoch, Hinton and then Brooks remained loyal to Blair till the end of his term in 2007. During that time he admitted to meeting Rupert at least three or four times a year and his lieutenants even more regularly.

An example of the nitty-gritty of quid pro quo that obtained under Blair can be found in the memo of a meeting released in 2008 through a freedom of information request. Within a year of Blair entering Number 10, Murdoch wanted to meet to discuss a new brainchild of his – British Interactive Broadcasting – a kind of walled garden of online access and retail which was the vogue in the late nineties. All the powerful players in Blair's government turned up to discuss the matter with the mogul in January 1998: Blair's chief of staff, Jonathan Powell; James Purnell, then a Downing Street special adviser on the media; and Blair's powerful press secretary, Alastair Campbell.

Murdoch – an avowed anti-European who would often debate with the prime minister about the role of the EU – objected to an investigation by the European Competition Minister into the new interactive scheme:

> *The competition commissioner, [Karel] Van Miert, had come up a long list of complaints and the project was being delayed at huge cost. Sky's own investment was very significant (£800m so far) and the success of the venture was crucial to their overall plans for developing digital services.*

> (HENCKE AND EVANS, 2008)

Blair spoke up in favour of Murdoch and claimed 'it was important that the UK remained at the cutting edge of developing this kind of media product'. In a line of reasoning that prefigured the one Jeremy Hunt used to lobby David Cameron about the Rubicon process in November 2010, Blair used the 'global competition' argument and somehow convinced others (and himself) that the success of

BSkyB – controlled by a US registered corporation – was in the national interest. As the *Guardian* explained:

> *The prime minister envisaged Europe being dominated by four or five big media groups – with Sky as one – competing against each other, adding 'that meant genuine cross-border competition, not a heavy regulatory approach from the commission'.*

(IBID., 2008)

This encapsulates the great failure of understanding that vitiated New Labour's dealings with News Corp throughout the years ahead. Despite trenchant comparisons at the Leveson Inquiry between the power Murdoch had accumulated in the press through the Times Newspapers Group takeover in 1981 and James's attempt to establish the same kind of broadcasting dominance with the BSkyB bid, Blair still maintained that 'ownership' was less of an issue than the advent of the 'feral press' and the confusion of news and comment. He seemed to miss the whole point; if the hacking saga and its cover-up revealed anything, it was precisely the monopoly power of News Corp which politicians feared too much to challenge and led to obvious crimes the police didn't dare investigate.

Instead, Blair – as most British governments have done for the last three decades – reverted to the 'globalisation' defence. Given borderless commerce and the frictionless movement of capital (if not labour), corporations were judged not on their national impact but their international competitiveness. The limitation of this model is that, as the banking system catastrophically demonstrated in 2008, companies become so big they are beyond any national accountability or democratic control. In the modal monopoly in finance this led to 'moral hazard' – high risk taking with toxic derivatives because the banks knew they would be bailed out. The moral hazard of News International was less financial than political; its purchase on the country wasn't so much that it could close the cash machines, but it could make or break political careers and was beyond the law: less 'big to fail' and once again 'too big to jail'.

SULTANS OF SPIN

Another legacy of the exceptional media power of News International under New Labour was an obsession with presentation and propaganda – the domination of political 'spin'; briefing anonymously against internal rivals to a chosen coterie of reporters. This was not, of course, a late nineties invention. Thatcher had undergone a massive personal and vocal make-over in the run-up to the 1979 election, and then deployed her press spokesman, Bernard Ingham, to perform precisely the same set of lobby briefings against competing ministers. Bill Clinton, especially through his turbulent second term, had come increasingly to rely on spin doctors rather than policy substance. Media trained and media obsessed personalities were even more central to New Labour, with both Alastair Campbell and Peter Mandelson highly adept and interventionist in the press and on TV, while central to the policy decisions.

The importance of PR and the optics of media presentation model would imprint itself on a younger generation of politicians coming up the ladder, particularly those like Cameron and Osborne in the Conservative Party who considered Blair a political 'master' of presentation – even while they disprized 'spin'. Osborne and Cameron specifically hired Andy Coulson to be their 'Alastair Campbell' after Coulson resigned as *News of the World* editor in 2007. As for their Peter Mandelson, with his background in PR and television, the consummate performer at this level would be none other than Cameron himself.

Blair's fall from grace – his support for George W. Bush's Iraq invasion – cannot be directly attributed to his News Corp friendships, even though he spoke to Murdoch three times in the run-up to the invasion in March 2003. The whole transatlantic post-war alliance between Britain and the US was at stake, summarised in the principle that 'it's better to be wrong with the US than right with Europe', though Murdoch might have some influence here: Blair told Lord Justice Leveson that 'few people' knew America as well as Murdoch (a claim many Americans might dispute). The fact that all News Corp's newspapers had come out in favour of the invasion would have been a powerful persuader, but so too had the *New York Times* and the *Observer*.

More than anything, the fiasco of the Iraq invasion and the propaganda surrounding it betray an even more worrying phenomenon that of the cosiness of one British prime minister and one powerful media mogul. As Nick Davies shows in *Flat Earth News*, the interpenetration of media and politics, of reportage and partisan opinion, had formed a circular loop of self-confirmation.

Based on some flimsy and ultimately spurious intelligence, most of the Anglo-Saxon press and media became an echo chamber, repeating and amplifying its own half-baked whispers into a chorus of stupidity and misinformation, especially about the presence of Weapons of Mass Destruction in Saddam Hussein's arsenal. Though this was exploited and manipulated for political purposes, those who think it had been a conscious conspiracy should just ask themselves this: why didn't Bush just plant WMDs in the desert to justify the invasion post-hoc? He didn't because both the British and American governments did something worse than consciously lie to us; instead they began to believe their own publicity. The self-delusion, the 'conspiracy' of voices hyperventilating the same toxic air, is much more ominous for the future than any conscious attempt to mislead public opinion.

For Britain specifically, an obsession with presentation and spin was behind the 'dodgy dossier' the government produced on Iraqi weapon readiness on the eve of the invasion. Questioned by a BBC report that quoted some unknown insider source, the media battle that ensued led to the identification of the whistleblower, weapons expert Dr David Kelly, who committed suicide a few days later. Kelly's death led to the formation of the Hutton Inquiry in August 2003, which cleared the government of any wrong-doing, but criticised the BBC instead, leading to the resignation of the BBC's director general, Greg Dyke.

Nine years later, the same room, Court 73 of the Royal Courts of Justice, would host the Leveson Inquiry, which would not give politicians such an easy ride.

Ultimately Blair paid the price for the Iraq fiasco, with his popularity plummeting as the disaster of the post-invasion unfolded. For all his reasonableness and charm, he still reverted to the ultimate 'faith' argument, unprompted, in his oral testimony at Leveson. The invasion was right because he 'believed' in it; and he believed in it because it was 'right'. This lapse into the dogmas of belief – and its imperviousness to debate – made Blair a charismatic leader, but ultimately unable to distinguish between the political and personal. The tyranny of intimacy – and the cosiness between members of the international elite in business and politics – could never be broken by him.

POLITICS FOR BEAUTIFUL PEOPLE

Before the pall of terrorism fell over it, the early sheen of the Blair effect would impress a whole generation of political players and rising media stars – a glittering 'Cool Britannia' and 'Notting Hill' era where culture, celebrity and politics seemed to elide under the young telegenic new prime minister. There was a new paradigm in the economy, booming under credit expansion and rising property prices; there also seemed to be a new paradigm in politics, where the old class struggles and bitterness of the Thatcher years seemed to have been forgotten in the populist youth and accessibility of Tony Blair.

If politics used to be show business for ugly people, these were the Beautiful People, who combined media power and PR clout to create new brand of celebrity politics.

This was the world that Rebekah Brooks (then Wade) and Matthew Freud were ushered into and where they formed their connections first with New Labour and then the Conservatives under David Cameron. Whereas someone who wanted to succeed in politics in a previous generation might have worked for a trade union, policy think tank or attended the bar, the rising stars of the late nineties were all media trained in publishing and broadcasting or savvy about PR. To a certain extent you can't blame them; the skills required to command a chapel meeting or fund-raising dinner, let alone the oratory need to still the hustings in a large hall, were increasingly obsolete in the 30-second sound bite of 24-hour news. Compression, affect, the subliminal emotional messages of voice tone, gesture and bearing, these have become descants of public discourse over a generation.

When one looks at the preconceptions of the third generation of Murdochs, prepared to take power at the dawn of the twenty-first century, the more interesting Freud is not Sigmund – founder of psychoanalysis – but his great grandson, Matthew Freud, founder of Freud Communications and the powerful PR titan who married Elisabeth Murdoch at the beginning of the decade. It was Matthew Freud who established the kernel of what would become known as the Chipping Norton set, a small group of powerful political and media players with weekend homes within a dozen miles or so of the small town in North Oxfordshire. Freud had retreated to China Corner, a family home on the Blenheim Palace estate over a decade before, when the news of his affair with one of his clients, Elisabeth Murdoch, who then worked for BSkyB, had led to the break-up of both their previous marriages. During what was reported to be a tempestuous off-on relationship Elisabeth became pregnant with Freud's child and Brooks, a rising star of the News International stable, was a frequent visitor. When the couple reconciled, Brooks attended Elisabeth's bridal shower and then the small private wedding of some 70 guests in 2001 with her then boyfriend and husband-to-be, the British soap opera actor, Ross Kemp.

For all the psychological speculations about Brooks being Murdoch's favourite, a so-called 'impostor daughter', the core relationship was with Elisabeth and it was through his daughter, rather than against her, that Brooks garnered the loyalty and affection of the ageing media mogul. By that point, both Freud and Brooks had become relatively important players in the triumphant New Labour administration: Freud through his friendship with Mandelson, the business minister was a key advisor on Labour's Millennium Dome project for a theme park in docklands; Brooks was mentored by Blair's powerful Communications Director and enforcer, the ex-tabloid journalist, Alastair Campbell.

Mandelson and Campbell occupy an important part of the New Labour philosophy for both were really schooled in media before politics: Mandelson through LWT and his role as a producer on *Weekend World*, the Sunday politics programme which became – more than any of the day newspapers a key agenda setting current affairs analysis of the eighties for the cognoscenti – and Campbell through the populist tabloid school as he rose to become political editor of the *Daily Mirror*.

Freud's clients, apart from Sky TV where he met Elisabeth, were mainly celebrities and television presenters such as Paula Yates, Angus Deayton, Zoë Ball and Geri Halliwell. He eventually moved on to multinational companies such as Pepsi, KFC, Asda, Nike, the drinks giant Diageo and large projects like the London 2012 Olympics. But in his early days 'St Matthew of the Shadows' was a celebrity publicist and the tabloid papers his main arena. As Max Clifford realised when he front-paged the spurious allegation that his client Freddy Starr ate a hamster, a 'light' scandal could be even more effective positive puff and there's nothing better than rumours of a false but illusory affair between two clients to provide a perfect 'double whammy' – acres of speculation and full-colour photos – two profiles raised and no harm done. Whether as editor of the show-business column on the *Sun*, or in her various editorial roles after that, Brooks would have found Freud a brilliant resource – and vice versa. In the celebrity obsessed world after the death of Diana, the synergy between PR and the press was drawing ever closer.

Just as the obsession with royal celebrity led to Princess Diana's death, pursued by paparazzi on motorbikes, the tabloid obsession with victims would encourage Brooks's employees at *News of the World* to hack the phone of Milly Dowler, as seven reporters and photographers were sent to pursue the phantom of a teenager who was already lying dead, murdered by Levi Bellfield.

So much has been written in such a personalised and occasionally misogynistic tone about Brooks – her looks, her hair, her 'relationship' with Murdoch and other senior figures – that it would be pointless to reiterate them here and fall into the trap she made to Robert Jay QC in the Royal Courts when many of these 'gossipy' and 'personal' issues were raised: 'We're not in a tabloid newsroom now, are we?'

What is worth observing, however, is that for the former CEO of News International, the political was always personal. Her astonishing networking skills led to friendships not only with three successive competing prime ministers, but also with a raft of celebrities, senior police officers like Andy Hayman and John Yates, and important lawmakers like the former Director of Public Prosecutions Lord MacDonald. Even expected enemies like Murdoch's biographer Michael Wolff found her a fun person to share time and gossip with and the gnarled tough New York executives at News Corp's HQ in Manhattan spoke of her with misty eyes according to Wolff. Even Gordon Brown turned up at Brooks's wedding to

Charlie Brooks in 2009, despite his son's cystic fibrosis having been broken to his dismay by the *Sun* under her editorship. At the height of the hacking crisis, when Brooks was forced to resign from News International in the days that closed *News of the World*, her testimony to the Leveson Inquiry revealed Blair and Cameron sent her personal messages of condolence. To this day, most her former employers, employees and friends, defend her with fierce loyalty.

An element of aggressive victimhood is the basis of Brooks's defence. Now that she has been charged with three counts of conspiracy to pervert the course of justice her lawyer's main case seems to be that Brooks can't get a fair trial and is a victim of a witch-hunt. There are investigations into alleged phone hacking and corruption of public officials still underway as I write and contempt of court rules make it unwise to explore the prosecutors' charges until pleas are in and any possible trial is over. However, the charms of her personality politics are still relevant to real politics to this extent; to get on the wrong side of Brookes was clearly a very different proposition

Along with Labour MP Chris Bryant, Tom Watson's published account of being 'monstered' by Brooks's tabloids in his book, *Dial M for Murdoch* (co-written with the *Independent* journalist Martin Hickman) while surprisingly dispassionate as a third-person account, is still scarily compelling. Having been one of the signatories to a letter on 5 September 2006 asking Blair to stand down as prime minister, Watson came into the sights of the daily tabloid Brooks's was editing. Brooks, by then a personal friend of Blair, began a personal campaign to discredit him. On 7 September, the *Sun* called him the ringleader of the 'plotting gang of weasels'. At the Labour Party conference the following month, Watson was told by the *Sun*'s political editor, George Pascoe-Watson: 'My editor will pursue you for the rest of your life. She will never forgive you for what you did to her Tony' (Watson and Hickman, 2012, p. 27).

For the next four years Watson was subject to a campaign of harassment so intense that he began to doubt his own sanity. People broke into his garage and attempted to read paperwork. He was followed by private detectives. The intimidation reached a fever pitch when the Damian McBride scandal erupted.

This was Britain's first big scandal of the blogosphere and concerned two men: a Number 10 aide, Damian McBride, and the founder of the LabourList website, Derek Draper, who had exchanged emails discussing setting up another website to be named Red Rag which could disseminate false personal and sexual rumours about the private lives of some Conservative Party politicians. The emails, sent from the Downing Street Press Office, were somehow acquired by Paul Staines, author of the Guido Fawkes blog, who passed them on to the *Daily Telegraph* where they were published on 11 April 2009. Though

Watson claims he knew nothing about the Red Rag plot, his name was allegedly mentioned in a CC list and three days later the *Sun* went for the kill in a column by Fergus Shanahan:

> *There is another unsavoury creature lurking in the shadows who should join McBride on the dole – and he's not a civil servant like McBride but a minister appointed by Brown. Treacherous Tom Watson – a tub of lard who is known without affection at Westminster as 'Two Dinners' Tommy – is suspected of being up in this to his bloated and bulging neck.'* Under the headline 'Mad Dog was trained to maul', the *Sun's* political writer Trevor Kavanagh accused 'hatchet man Tom Watson' of being among the plotters … Wade also texted someone very close to Brown personally urging him to sack Watson.

> (IBID., 2012, P. 29)

Though Watson successfully sued the *Sun* for defamation, the constant onslaught from the tabloids wore down his resilience and he was resigned to leaving politics. It's only his interest in film and culture that led him to join the DCMS select committee, where he would eventually have such a fateful impact on the hacking scandal.

In his draft statement to the Leveson Inquiry, even the formidable Alastair Campbell talked of the 'bullying culture' at *News International*: 'I recall Rebekah Brooks telling me that as far as she was concerned, with Tom Watson it was personal, and we won't stop until we get him.' In passages which were not included in his final witness statement, Campbell claimed he was even subject to 'threatening text and phone messages from both Rebekah and the offices of James Murdoch' when he pointed out that the phone-hacking scandal could cause problems with Andy Coulson's appointment as Cameron's press supremo. You can laugh at Campbell – previously famed for yelling down the phone at other journalists – complaining of bullying, or you can think again. If even Campbell felt intimidated, one can only imagine how this felt for an ordinary member of the public.

For all this, Brooks was promoted to the most senior roles in Fleet Street, as CEO of the biggest newspaper group. The elevation of those values of bullying and monstering wasn't just the fault of News Corp nor the Murdochs: a whole culture was complicit. As Watson and Hickman point out, during Coulson's tenure the *News of the World* won the 'Sunday Newspaper of the Year' award on three consecutive occasions. The Sunday tabloid was celebrated as 'an incredible sledgehammer of a production', even though the judges must have been aware that this sledgehammer often broke through many of the moral or legal bounds of privacy. The celebration of this brute, personalised and highly vindictive kind of press was given the assent and approval of the senior figures in the industry. As John Lloyd pointed out in the *Financial Times* even the quality press was complicit: 'That we mostly passed by on the other side, often with a humorous shrug, is a shame that envelops all of British journalism' (Lloyd, 2012).

Brooks and her close friend and colleague Coulson were now the leading duo on Fleet Street, with a power not only within the industry but upon the whole political sphere; however, it's their association with the next prime minister-in-waiting, David Cameron, which would be the most intense and dangerous of all.

THE YOUNG PRETENDER

Even Cameron's biographer, James Hanning, is not certain when Cameron was drawn into the charmed magic circle of the Chipping Norton set, but unlike any of the previous prime ministers that coincide with Murdoch's media presence, his background was already in media: Cameron was head of public affairs at Carlton TV in the late nineties and remained a consultant there even when becoming an MP. His professional connection would have probably introduced him to Elisabeth Murdoch at Sky TV, Matthew Freud at his powerful PR agency or indeed Rebekah Brooks at the *Sun* or *News of the World*.

In 2001, Cameron became the Conservative Member of Parliament for the constituency of Whitney, which includes the town of Chipping Norton. Five years later, when he came virtually out of the blue to become a challenger for the Conservative Party leadership after the party's third successive general election defeat, Cameron seemed to have the big guns of the media on his side. The only real hiccup in his campaign – the alleged sex and drugs scandal that claimed guilt by association with his campaign manager George Osborne – was effectively neutralised by a *News of the World* spoiler. Cameron's press chief at the time was explicitly renouncing the world of spin: 'we're not going to deviate from things just to get a headline in the Sunday paper'. However, Francis Elliott and James Hanning reveal just how deeply involved with the PR media world Cameron still was after giving the victory speech when he won the Conservative leadership ballot:

> It was only after the speech that the reality of his victory began to dawn. Among those calling to congratulate him were the News of the World *editor Andy Coulson, obligingly ringing to suggest possible names of the new head of communications that he would undoubtedly need. Another was Matthew Freud, with an invitation to him and George Osborne for dinner at China Corner, his house on the Blenheim estate. Suddenly he*

really was the man to know. He had arrived at the Royal Academy in a
taxi; he left in the official car of the leader of the Opposition.

(ELLIOTT AND HANNING, 2012, P. 304)

According to Hanning, Brooks joined Cameron and Freud for that promised dinner on the Blenheim estate. Cameron's leadership was no more distanced from the *Sun* than the planet Mercury.

Nonetheless, at this point Murdoch himself – now developing a friendship with Blair and Brown – was not willing to jump ship and overtly back the new Tory leader. When interviewed by Charlie Rose in July 2006 about what he thought about Cameron, Murdoch replied rebarbatively: 'Not much. He's bright. He's quick. He's totally inexperienced.' Murdoch told the *New Yorker* later that year that Cameron 'behaves as if he doesn't believe in anything other than trying to construct what he believes will be the right public image. He's a PR guy.'

Apart from the dinner at China Corner, the first public record of the Brooks/Cameron connection can be found in the House of Commons Register of Members' Interests, which details how Brooks invited Samantha and David Cameron to a lavish World Cup Party hosted by David and Victoria Beckham in 2006. In the summer of 2008 Matthew Freud paid some $50,000 to fly Cameron and his wife Samantha around the coasts of Greece and Turkey to meet Murdoch on his yacht, *Rosehearty*, and then sail around the Aegean with Freud and Elisabeth Murdoch. Throughout, Brooks was on hand to ease the introductions.

By now the larger Rubicon process was beginning to hum in the background, after James Murdoch became chair of BSkyB in 2007. By all accounts, it was an aggressive courtship. A source close to Cameron is known to regale friends with the story of the time he asked the prime minister's wife, Samantha Cameron, how she and her husband distinguish their real friends from those who have just latched onto them because of their power and celebrity. 'Well, there's x and there's y and there's z,' Samantha Cameron replies in the tale. 'And then there's Rebekah…' As I was told by a senior Tory while writing a profile of Brooks for the Daily Beast 'The Woman Who Could Bring Down Cameron': 'She courted him like crazy as soon as he became leader. It was all one way.' A former News International insider maintains the personal and political were one and the same for Brooks: 'She liked to be close to power. It was very personal, but also about power in its purest sense—advancing the interests of the company.'

News Corp's interests were clear-cut: the desire to initiate a Wapping Two in Isleworth and combine complete ownership of BSkyB with the paper holdings at News International to create a powerful cross-platform player for the digital age. Though the BSkyB bid was run from the holding company, News Corp, News

International had a role to play. In the first year of Cameron's leadership, News International still backed Blair and Murdoch was inclined to hedge his bets and personal connections by backing Brown as he became prime minister in 2007. A twin-track strategy is at work here – or even a disagreement between the generations – as James and Brookes tried to persuade Murdoch to change allegiance.

According to Wolff, the employment of Coulson as director of communications for the Conservative Party in 2007 was a key part of the plan. Hanning and Elliot describe the process in their biography of Cameron: once again Brooks is the key player, proposing Coulson and eliciting the support of William Hague (who wrote the well remunerated columns for Coulson at *News of the World*) and George Osborne, who had been only lightly monstered by the Sunday tabloid:

> '*Cameron was told [his new media boss] should be someone acceptable to News International,*' someone involved in Coulson's recruitment told [Simon] Walters [of the Mail on Sunday]. '*The company was also desperate to find something for Andy after he took the rap when the phone hacking first became a scandal. The approach was along the lines of "If you find something for Andy, we will return the favour".*'

(IBID., 2012)

However it took another two tortured years before the *Sun* dumped Brown. Part of this was Murdoch's antipathy to Cameron's Etonian background and time in PR for rival commercial TV company Carlton Communications. But by all reports Murdoch felt it was time the younger generation got to run the show. And so the policy dance began.

Shall I repeat it? I think it bears repeating. In April 2008 James announced he wanted to do away with the regulator Ofcom, which regulates broadcasting in the UK. In July 2009, Cameron agreed. James Murdoch gave his MacTaggart lecture in August 2009, which is swiftly followed in September with Jeremy Hunt repeating the same lines. At the end of the month the *Sun* reversed 12 years of support for the Labour Party and reprised its famous line from Labour's defeat in 1992 – 'It's the Sun Wot Won It' – with the new line 'The Sun Says: Labour's Lost it'.

By the time of the general election in 2010, Brooks had divorced the Labour-supporting actor Ross Kemp and married another old Etonian, Charlie Brooks, and settled in his family farm in the hamlet of Sarsden, four miles away from Cameron's constituency home in Dean. A couple of miles further away is the home of TV motoring presenter Jeremy Clarkson, perhaps Britain's closest equivalent to a shock-jock. Twenty minutes further away by car was the converted barn owned by Steve Hilton, Cameron's strategic advisor until 2012. So too is Burford Priory, a mansion so chic and capacious Clarkson calls it 'France', where Elisabeth Murdoch lives with Matthew Freud. The tight network of media and political interests had crystallised into a distinct geographical matrix. The combined Courts of Cameron and Murdoch now had a local habitation and a name.

Over the next seven months, the prime minister and the chancellor George Osborne would have nearly 40 meetings with Senior News International executives. Brooks was Cameron's guest at Chequers twice in 2010, a rare accolade even for members of the Cabinet. Unlike Cameron's supposedly old 'school chum' Charlie (they were in different houses at Eton and four academic years apart) Brooks would be invited to Cameron's 40th birthday party, reserved for his oldest friends. Cameron would also meet her socially three times that Christmas. Meanwhile, James Murdoch was invited to Chequers in November and also met socially over the Christmas period. As Brooks appeared in May 2012 before the Leveson Inquiry, more meetings and a voluminous text and email correspondence came to light. In Cameron's evidence, it emerged that Brooks sent the leader of the Conservative Party 43 personal text messages in just two months of the data preserved as a back-up of her phone on News International's computers.

On the eve of the general election in spring of 2010, Paul McMullan – the former *News of the World* investigative journalist who had helped to blow the whistle on the hacking scandal in the *New York Times* – was tasked by the *Guardian* to get a front page shot which could demonstrate the power of the Chipping Norton set: Brooks out riding with Cameron. Local publicans, riders and dog walkers had told him the group could be caught some weekend mornings around dawn. 'That was the shot that might have changed the whole election,' McMullan told me, 'It could have encapsulated the idea that David Cameron was molded by the Murdochs' (McMullan, 2012).

Though McMullan never got his front page photo, the phantom image of the prime minister-to-be and Murdoch's most trusted deputy hacking through the British countryside, became even more powerful as a metaphor for the cosy relationship when, two years later, it emerged through the Leveson Inquiry that Brooks had been loaned the use of a retired Metropolitan Police horse. The prime minister was forced to answer questions about this concede (during a press conference during an important EU summit) that he probably rode the mare in question, Raisa, who was returned to the Met in early 2010, allegedly in poor condition.

The 'Horsegate' revelations caused much hilarity, with the *Daily Telegraph* running one of the funniest live blogs ever, filled with various equine puns. Though far from fatal, it was another damaging blow against Cameron's attempt to distance himself from the scandal and even worse, it undermined his attempt to shed the image of upper-class privilege, undoing five years of carefully planned PR. As for the image of him out riding with the Queen of Fleet Street on a knackered old police horse: this wasn't the tabloid staple of personal destruction. It spoke to an older tradition of pamphleteering, a satirical cartoon worthy of Hogarth or Gillray. 'Horsegate' was then followed by 'LOLgate' a few months later when Brooks revealed in her own testimony to Leveson that Cameron used to sign off their regular text message communications with LOL, thinking it meant 'lots of love' before she corrected him that it meant 'laugh out loud'.

The British media laughed out loud for several weeks, a slowly erosive ridicule which would leave Cameron dropping in opinion polls but still soldiering on; a death by a thousand paper cuts which – as John Major proved in comparison with Thatcher – can actually be worse than the sudden kill.

The Leveson Inquiry, although set up by Cameron with strong powers and a wide remit, had since gone from being an inquiry into the ethics, culture and practices of the press, into a kind of trial of the culture of his administration and leadership. Cameron's close personal connections with Brooks and his even closer personal connections with Coulson, encapsulated the problem. While the public might not follow all back channel nods and winks in terms of the BSkyB bid, the prospect of two of Cameron's closest confidantes facing trial could yet cause the coalition government to collapse prematurely.

When he finally appeared before the Leveson Inquiry in June 10, British Prime Minister David Cameron admitted that politicians had got 'too close' to the press. That point was made uncomfortably clear in a text message, from Brooks when she was editor of Murdoch's *Sun*, which was subpoenaed from News International by the Inquiry. Sent in October 2009, just after the *Sun* had switched its support to Cameron's Conservative party, Brooks wrote: 'Rooting for you tomorrow not just as a proud friend but because professionally we're in this together!' Then she signed off, 'Speech of your life? Yes he Cam!'

The last rejoinder – a parody of Obama's 'Yes we can' slogan from the 2008 Presidential elections – was a theme followed through by the *Sun* right on the eve of election, with an Obama style coloured outline of Cameron dominating the front page with the line 'Our Only Hope'. When Cameron was quizzed by the Inquiry as to what the text meant, he looked excruciatingly embarrassed and replied that, while he and Brooks were indeed 'friends', he and the *Sun* were 'pushing the same agenda'.

Before the line of questioning had even arrived at this point, Cameron was refuting the allegation made by former prime minister Gordon Brown, that there had been any kind of 'grand bargain' of Tory support for News Corp's BSkyB in return in return for switching support from Brown's Labour government to

Cameron's Tories. But Jay honed in on a series of meetings in the summer of 2009, when the *Sun* switched to supporting Cameron's bid to be the next prime minister and Conservative policy towards the BBC and broadcasting regulation seemed to chime more with the demands famously made by Murdoch in his Mac-Taggart lecture in 2009. Cameron made a vigorous defence of his own independent policy-making – and angrily insisted he hadn't done any kind of deal. When Jay suggested there could be a 'perception' of such a concordat, Cameron pushed back, saying that vague perceptions of 'winks and nods' could easily decline into a 'trial for witchcraft'.

Meanwhile the extent of Matthew Freud's hand in the formation of the Chipping Norton set and his involvement in the creation of Cameron as prime ministerial material, may never be known, but one thing is for sure: it's over. While Freud once allegedly exchanged high fives with Cameron during Brooks's marriage celebrations, the truly effective PR man is always a magician behind the scenes and the exposure of the technique ruins the magic of the trick. TV satellite vans now park in the quiet country lanes and any cosy behind-the-scenes private meetings and parties are subject to the cruel winds of public scrutiny. As a senior PR titan explained to my colleague Mike Giglio while researching an article for the Daily Beast: 'The Chipping Norton set has exploded … I mean his [Freud's] parties were mythical. But could David Cameron turn up at his party now? Don't think so. Could Ed Miliband? I don't think so…'

Politics is always about conflict: negotiating it, forming alliances against your instincts, seeking ways beyond violence to hammer out a compromise: war by other means. For the post-partisan heirs to Blair, who wanted to make politics a showplace for beautiful people, things turned very ugly indeed.

THE DYNASTY FAILS

It is not just a coincidence that the whole hacking scandal came to light because the *News of the World*'s royal correspondent was caught trying to hack the phones of the royal household. Many tabloids, both in the UK and abroad, have used the glamour (and occasional squalor) of the Windsor family as a basis for their sales. Few, however, have been led by a man with such pronounced anti-royal sentiments. Though he would have been offered them, Murdoch has never accepted a 'gong' – honour, knighthood or a peerage. He has remained consistent in his dislike of other family dynasties and any kind of inherited privilege – except, of course, his own.

The whole structure of Murdoch's $50 billion corporation is vested in the concept of nepotism. Again, Wolff puts the case across most vividly: 'Inside

News Corp., you treat the Murdochs like they are the royal family—or the way the British royal family was regarded before Rupert Murdoch's tabloids came along and destroyed their mystique.' But the gift of birth-right limits the possibility of self-authorship: the children's power is always borrowed power and with an even more privileged international background than their father, their hopes of equalling the example he posed were vanishingly small. In the end, having Rupert Murdoch as a father is radically different from being Rupert Murdoch.

For the third generation of Murdochs, ferried around in helicopters, SUVs and private jets, ushered into the VIP private enclosures at pop concerts and sports events, attending parties awash with oysters and champagne, surrounded by politicians and celebrities looking to them for preferment, employment or merely a chance to shine on their stage, the world must resemble nothing so much as a court, a shifting masque of acolytes and favourites. Though it may not suit the Murdochs, fortunately the rest of the country doesn't live in the eighteenth century – or not quite – where wealth can be transferred automatically into political power. Even if a national government was cowed by the combined threats and promises of News Corp, there is still some residual democracy in modern corporations.

A corporation is specifically not a dynasty; it is based on the idea of the joint-stock corporation, a basically egalitarian method of sharing risk. In the complex arrangements of News Corp, the difference between A and B stock give the Murdoch family 40 per cent of the voting rights with only 10 per cent of the share. It's hardly a democracy, but it is an important signalling mechanism.

At the Annual General Meeting of News Corp shareholders in Los Angeles in November 2011, the independent shareholders let their displeasure with the dynastic idea be known. After subtracting the shares controlled by Murdoch, 67 per cent of the votes went against James Murdoch and 64 per cent against his older brother Lachlan remaining on the board. While Murdoch's role as both Chair and CEO was uncontroversial, the resounding judgement on James Murdoch was a vote of no confidence after his handling of the hacking scandal. The vote against Lachlan was something else: an indictment of the idea of family succession.

For the dynastic politics of News Corp, the wreckage of James Murdoch's Rubicon process would be far more disastrous than his older brother's attempt to win the crown in 2005. On this momentous day in July 2011, when Brooks and Hinton left the company to which they had devoted their lives, the *New York Times* reported that Murdoch was blaming his son for the debacle. Within months James would drop his chairmanship of News International and BSkyB and return to New York to concentrate on his 'TV interests' with little support from other members of the board. Elisabeth Murdoch refused to play the corporate game of thrones and declined to join the board in New York. This left the then 81-year-old Chairman and CEO exposed. For all his executive power, Murdoch could not now ensure it would be passed on intact to his children. Though News Corp would survive, and the Murdoch family remain one of the wealthiest and best known in the world, the dynastic succession at the world's third largest media conglomerate was effectively over.

A year later, on Saturday 21 July 2012, News International staff were told by email that Murdoch had resigned from directorships of the *Sun*, *The Times* and *The Sunday Times* and had stepped down from the board of the News International Group, Times Newspaper Holdings and News Corp investments in the UK. The email, from the CEO of News International Tom Mockridge, maintained Murdoch 'remains fully committed to our business as chairman'.

I contacted three of the leading campaigners that evening. 'This is clearly corporate lawyers in New York trying to insulate themselves from more revelations in the UK,' Tom Watson told me. 'There are more waves of misery to come. ... But the few remaining executives in the UK will be feeling abandoned.' Mark Lewis, the campaigning lawyer agreed: 'Although surprising, it was inevitable that the board of News Corp would call a halt to the family control of the print media in the UK when that was harming the running of an international company ... It was time for a change.' Lewis added, 'People are left having to clear up the mess made on his watch.'

The co-founder of the Hacked Off campaign, Brian Cathcart, was more cautious: 'Until something actually happens, it's hard to know what's going on in Murdoch's head,' he told me. 'He's always been something of a business Houdini.' But Cathcart also thought this was a salutary day for Fleet Street. 'From the point of view of people who work in newspapers in London, Murdoch has been very good to them,' Cathcart said. 'He effectively created the *Sun* and saved *The Times*. He has a long history of investing in journalism here.'

After a year of scandals and arrests and with more years of misery ahead, it looked like the long goodbye was gathering momentum. It was almost a Saigon moment, with the feeling that the Murdoch helicopters were on the roof of the embassy and the end of an era in Fleet Street.

10

16–17 July 2011
Criminal Media Nexus

It was a good cop/bad cop routine. While News Corp lobbyists wined and dined key players in their Rubicon process, News International knew how to brutalise any opponents if need be. Whether this double act was consciously formulated and the right hand knew what the left hand was doing or just evolved, the *News of the World* became the equivalent of corporate enforcers or secret police, complete with the paraphernalia of surveillance: blagging, bugging and public shaming for non-compliance.

It's hard to believe that, after fifty years involved in political machination and skulduggery, Rupert Murdoch didn't know the source of so many stories in his best-selling papers. However, once the hacking scandal was exposed from 2006 onwards there was a conscious act of repression, cutting the corpus callosum that connected the hemispheres of News Corp's cerebral cortex. Les Hinton's move to the US and then the extensive 'email deletion' policy were all part of what Murdoch himself admitted in the Royal Courts of Justice was 'a cover-up', but amnesia and denial were hardly new to the company. As Neil Chenoweth put it years before: 'The danger in all this mystery is that News Corporation is a company, that at any time, could choke on its own secrets' (Chenoweth, 2001, p. xv).

Many comparisons with *The Godfather* have been made about the Murdoch family, but this seems the most apposite: in both narratives the sins of the father come back to haunt the progeny and the ethos Murdoch created resurfaced at the last moment to sink the new culture his son had planned. Nevertheless, the Murdochs were hardly the main victims of this saga – there was more collateral damage to come.

DECOMMISSIONED

In a stunning twist to the hacking scandal, two days before the Murdochs were due to appear before parliament, Britain's most senior police officer, Metropolitan Police Commissioner Sir Paul Stephenson, resigned.

Figure 10.1 Daily Mail, *18 July 2012*

Forced out
Met Police Commissioner resigns over links to News of the World Journalist

Figure 10.2 The Times, *18 July 2012*

Three days previously Operation Weeting had arrested Neil Wallis, a former executive editor of *News of the World*, famed as the 'Wolfman' of Fleet Street, who Stephenson had hired as a PR consultant when taking office in 2009 for nearly £30,000 a year; Chamy Media continued to provide advice to the Met until 2010, a few months before Operation Weeting was set up. Having only returned to Scotland Yard a few years previously, Stephenson inherited the close connections between News International and the Met; it was actually Dick Fedorcio, Scotland Yard's communications chief, who had hired Wallis and whose press office was dominated by former employees of News International. (Fedorico resigned in advance of a critical disciplinary investigation in March 2012.) This weekend *The Sunday Times* revealed that Stephenson had received hospitality of around £12,000 from a spa when recovering from cancer that he had not declared on the police register, which was also represented by Wallis's PR company, Chamy Media. Once again, it was not so much that Stephenson had set up or furthered this network of favours and interests, but he got caught in the flashlight of public exposure and his position became impossible.

If there was a perception that News International had a cosy deal with the police, then two other senior police officers deserved much closer inspection: the officer tasked to look at the original hacking inquiry in 2006 during Operation Caryatid, Andy Hayman, and his successor Assistant Commissioner John Yates who cursorily looked at the new evidence in 2009. Hayman had retired to take up a post as a columnist for *The Times* at News International, but Yates was still in place and he had dismissed the *Guardian*'s allegations about the extent of phone hacking in 2009 – all of which turned out to be true – within a few hours of reading its new report. Both officers had appeared before Parliament denying any negligence or collusion (Yates in 2009, Hayman in 2011). Two days after Stephenson's resignation, Yates would also resign.

During the Leveson Inquiry in March 2012 both Yates and Hayman had to answer for their extensive meetings, many at expensive London restaurants fuelled with alcohol, with the News International executives they were supposed to be investigating. The intimacy was startling. Yates was close friends with Wallis, so was Hayman. There were numerous expensive drinks and meals with him and other journalists and editors, including Andy Coulson and Rebekah Brooks, at the most fashionable London eateries, including Soho House and the Ivy Club. The *News of the World*'s crime editor, Lucy Panton, used Fedorico's computer to file a story while her news editor sent an email telling her to call in the favours: 'John Yates could be crucial here. Have you spoken to him? Really need an excl [exclusive] splash [front page] line so time to call in all those bottles of champagne…' (Morgan and Marsden, 2012). Their children were looked after too: Wallis's daughter got a job at the Met; Fedorcio's son a work placement scheme at the *Sun*.

In return for exclusive tip-offs about raids in advance, News International provided extensive, often adulatory, coverage especially of the dynamic 'Yates of the Yard'. The perception of another cosy clique, this time at the top tier of Britain's police, was seen by some as an explanation to why the phone-hacking scandal had not been investigated properly for the last five years. News International was so deeply embedded in the Metropolitan Police, their interests seemed to be converging. To be fair to the police though, they were only following the example set by their political masters.

In his resignation statement on Sunday 17 July, Stephenson made exactly this point. His proximity to *News International* was no worse than the higher ups. The politicians vigorously pursued News Corp connections: why was what he had done wrong, while what they had done was right?

> *Now let me turn to the reported displeasure of the Prime Minister and the Home Secretary of the relationship with Mr Wallis. The reasons for not having told them are two fold. Firstly, I repeat my earlier comments of having at the time no reason for considering the contractual relationship to be a matter of concern. Unlike Mr Coulson, Mr Wallis had not resigned from News of the World or, to the best of my knowledge been in any way associated with the original phone hacking investigation.*

(TELEGRAPH, 2011C)

The BBC's correspondent Robert Peston quickly got the message: 'Stephenson was saying that his employment of Wallis was less controversial than David Cameron's employment of Coulson' – especially since Coulson had resigned from his editorship in the wake of the Goodman–Mulcaire trial. The message wasn't lost on the opposition either and Labour Shadow Home Secretary, Yvette Cooper, tried to go for the kill:

> *It is striking that Sir Paul has taken responsibility and answered questions about the appointment of the Deputy Editor of the News of the World whereas the Prime Minister still refuses to recognise his misjudgement and answer questions on the appointment of the Editor of the News of the World at the time of the initial phone hacking investigation.*
>
> *People will wonder at why different rules apply for the Prime Minister and the Met, especially when as Sir Paul said himself, unlike Andy Coulson, Neil Wallis had not been forced to resign from the News of the World.*
>
> *It is also a very serious concern that the Met Commissioner felt unable to tell the Prime Minister and the Home Secretary about this operational issue with Neil Wallis because of the Prime Minister's relationship with Andy Coulson.*

(LABOUR PARTY, 2011)

In less than two weeks the phone-hacking scandal had instigated eight arrests, closed Britain's oldest newspaper, led to the resignation of the CEO of News International and her predecessor and now two senior Met officials were out. The bombshells were landing higher and higher up the political hierarchy. Could they now damage the prime minister? He was a close friend of Brooks and, only six months earlier, Coulson was part of his inner circle of government. Even Iain Dale, a pioneering *Conservative* blogger began to think the unthinkable: could Cameron be next?

> *I can't believe I am even writing this, but it is no longer an impossibility to imagine this scandal bringing down the Prime Minister or even the government. OK, some of you reading this may think that last sentence is a deranged ranting, and you may be right. Indeed, I hope you are. But Sir Paul Stephenson launched a thinly veiled attack on David Cameron in his resignation statement and the Prime Minister is already on the ropes about the propriety of his relationship with Andy Coulson.*

> (Dale, 2011)

Perhaps it was the prime minister's slowly eroding Teflon coat or the time lag of public opinion, but Cameron would survive the next year. Rather than a sudden kill, the calamity of his close relationship with Brooks and James Murdoch would be drawn-out and debilitating, casting a shadow over the probity of his closest Cabinet colleagues, George Osborne and Jeremy Hunt, both of whom got entangled in the BSkyB bid. More dangerous still, Coulson, would provide a direct link from the heart of government to some dark and disturbing parts of the London criminal demimonde where the victims suffered something much worse than phone hacking.

THE MURDER OF DANIEL MORGAN

Of all the many 'falls' in the fall of the House of Murdoch, Coulson's is one of the most precipitous. Apart from editing the country's most successful Sunday paper, his recruitment to head up communications for the Conservative Party in 2007 was celebrated in Tory ranks, with Matthew d'Ancona writing in the *Sunday Telegraph*: 'This is an unalloyed coup for the Tories, as Mr Coulson is one of the most formidable journalists of his generation, combining a sharp tabloid eye with a keen political intellect' (d'Ancona, 2007). When the *New York Times* refuted the 'rogue reporter' defence in 2010, the prominent conservative blogger Iain Dale wrote 'Coulson's Accusers Can Go to Hell':

Andy Coulson is bloody good at his job. That's why the likes of The
Guardian, *Alastair Campbell, Prescott and Johnson are doing their best
to jump on the back of the New York Times story about an ex* News of
the World *journalist who was sacked by the paper for persistent drug and
alcohol problems. You don't think he might have a grudge, do you? They
all want Coulson's scalp. Well, sod 'em … Coulson took responsibility for
the episode at the time and resigned. What do they want him to do – resign
a second time from a job which has nothing to do his previous incarnation?*

(Dale, 2010)

Coulson had famously been given a 'second chance' by Cameron after his resignation from the *News of the World* and as if to show this generosity was a virtu-
ous circle, two years previously Coulson had himself given a 'second chance' to
someone else who had fallen from grace. He hired Jonathan Rees, private investigator, on his release from prison after serving five years for conspiring to fit up
an innocent woman with cocaine in a child custody case. Rees was actually heard
planning that crime while the police were investigating another – the bloody
murder of his business partner in South London a decade earlier.

Coulson's direct connection to a second private investigator thereby took
the criminal associations of senior News International management well beyond privacy intrusion. As a 'close ally of the Prime Minister' admitted to
the *Guardian*, senior Tories knew some things but not others – 'hacking yes,
axe murder no'.

The axe murder in question was that of Daniel Morgan who has – in
the words of the authors of *Dial M for Murdoch* – one of the Britain's biggest
unsolved crimes (Watson and Hickman, 2012, pp. 107–10, 167–81). Daniel's
case has undergone no less than five separate police investigations over the
last quarter century at a cost of between £20 to £40 million but still with
no resolution for his brother, mother or children. The most recent murder
trial of Rees and his associates collapsed in technicalities and the backlog of
three quarters of a million pieces of paperwork as recently as March 2011.
Daniel's family now accept that the entangled and knotted history of his case
may now never be solved in a way to satisfy any criminal courts, but they still
want a public inquiry at least to separate some threads, many of which suggest extensive police corruption in South London and what Gordon Brown
called a 'criminal media nexus'.

Daniel's Southern Investigations was a small but successful private security company that investigated car theft by organised gangs. Work would
also often take him on travels abroad to investigate corporate fraud. As he got

busier, Daniel formed a partnership with Rees in the mid-eighties. However, tensions soon built up. According to his brother, Alastair Morgan, Daniel had always avoided jobs involving cash transits and fell out with Rees when he undertook such a job and a large amount of cash went missing (Morgan, 2012). By spring 1987, Daniel was even more concerned. The private detective told his brother how he'd discovered a network of corrupt police officers in London, led by a senior officer. A colleague of Daniel's now claims Daniel planned to sell this story of police corruption to a newspaper and was negotiating with the *News of the World*. Under Parliamentary privilege, the MP Tom Watson alleged that Daniel approached the tabloid's crime reporter Alec Marunchak, who offered him £40,000 for the story. Marunchak has vehemently denied this.

On 10 March 1987, half an hour after he was seen drinking with Rees at the Golden Lion pub in Sydenham, Daniel was found dead in the pub car park next to his BMW with a large fatal axe wound to the back of his head. His trouser pockets were ripped and notes that he had earlier been seen writing were missing. Gone too was his watch, although Daniel's wallet, containing a large sum of money, was still in his jacket pocket.

One of the first detectives assigned to the murder case, Detective Sergeant Sid Fillery stationed at Catford police station, turned out to have been moonlighting for Southern Investigations. In April, Fillery, Rees and two other police officers were arrested on suspicion of murder, along with Rees's brothers-in-law Glenn and Garry Vian. All were then released without charge. By the time the inquest into Daniel's death took place the following year, Fillery had retired from the police and replaced Daniel as Rees's partner in Southern Investigations. The coroner heard claims that police officers were involved in the murder and had tampered with evidence and interfered with witnesses; Hampshire police then launched their own investigation. In 1988 they arrested Rees and charged him with the murder, but charges were dropped again soon because of a lack of evidence.

Meanwhile, Rees was pursuing a lucrative career working for Fleet Street and soon was claiming the *News of the World* alone paid him more than £150,000 a year. All this emerged through the surveillance of Southern Investigation in a third secret police inquiry into the unsolved murder. But the third inquiry was interrupted when Rees was overheard planning to plant cocaine on a mother in a custody battle. Rees was arrested and in December 2000 sentenced for seven years imprisonment for attempting to pervert the course of justice.

While Rees was in prison, a fourth inquiry was launched in 2002–2003, led by David Cook. As his wife, Jacqui Hames, a former police officer, explained to the Leveson Inquiry, News International – who had unbeknownst to the police employed Rees extensively before his imprisonment, took an acute and disturbing interest in the case. Hames broke down as she told Lord Justice Leveson how her family was followed and their phones were hacked in a *News of the World* operation she claimed was led by Marunchak. Coincidentally, Marunchak, with a Ukrainian background, was also revealed in 2011 to have had a side line as translator for Scotland Yard for 21 years.

Marunchak's boss, Brooks, then editor of *News of the World*, was confronted about this surveillance both by Scotland Yard's chief press officer, Fedorcio, and Cook himself. On both occasions Brooks said the surveillance was only initiated because she believed Cook and Hames were having an affair. This was an 'absolutely pathetic' justification according to Hames who went on to explain: 'We had by then been married for four years, had been together for 11 years and had two children!' Hames contends that the real reason was to scupper the police inquiries: 'I believe that the real reason for the *News of the World* placing us under surveillance was that suspects in the Daniel Morgan murder inquiry were using their association with a powerful and well-resourced newspaper to try to intimidate us and so attempt to subvert the investigation' (Hames, 2012).

After his release from prison in 2005, Rees began to work almost exclusively for *News of the World* where his main point of contact is reported to have been Marunchak. The relationship was alleged to have been so close that Marunchak registered his company at the same address.

By the time Coulson's connections to Rees emerged, the former editor was Director of Communications for the Conservative Party and the private investigator could not be named because of a new murder trial that had begun in 2008 and would continue for another three years. When Coulson entered Number 10 Downing Street in May 2010, the *Guardian* editor, Alan Rusbridger, made a personal call to a Cameron senior staff member to warn him of Coulson's connection to Rees. It took until March 2011, when the case collapsed through failed disclosure and doubts about two supergrasses, for the truth to be made public. Nick Davies, who described Fillery and Rees as building an 'empire of corruption', wrote with Vikram Dodd in the *Guardian*:

> Rees, now aged 56, worked regularly for the Daily Mirror and the Sunday Mirror as well as for the News of the World. His numerous targets included members of the royal family whose bank accounts he penetrated; political figures including Peter Mandelson and Alastair Campbell; rock stars such as Eric Clapton, Mick Jagger and George

> *Michael; the Olympic athlete Linford Christie and former England football Gary Lineker; TV presenters Richard Madeley and Judy Finnigan; and people associated with tabloid story topics, including the daughter of the former miners leader Arthur Scargill and the family of the Yorkshire Ripper, Peter Sutcliffe.*
>
> *Jonathan Rees paid a network of corrupt police officers who sold him confidential records. He boasted of other corrupt contacts in banks and government organisations; hired specialists to 'blag' confidential data from targets' current accounts, phone records and car registration; allegedly used 'Trojan horse' emails to extract information from computers; and – according to two sources – commissioned burglaries to obtain material for journalists.*
>
> (DAVIES AND DODD, 2011)

Looking back on Jonathan Rees's proven criminal acts and allegations they dwarf the activities of Glenn Mulcaire; yet, for reasons of their own, the Operation Weeting team has excluded a large quantity of Rees's material from their investigation. Just as the rogue reporter defence was never credible, the known facts about Rees prove that Mulcaire was not the sole private investigator hired by News International, let alone other Fleet Street papers. But the press's reliance of covert and illicit sources of material has made them masters of selective disclosure – happy to reveal other people's secrets, adamant about keeping their own. News International may have been the market leader in this kind of criminal activity, but certainly – as both Steve Whittamore and Rees demonstrate – not alone.

For the family of Daniel Morgan, however, a quarter of a century has passed with no resolution and none in sight. Alastair Morgan is still campaigning for some kind of justice for his brother and seeks a full judicial inquiry, hopefully to reach some kind of conclusion while his mother is still alive. He still remembers one of his last meetings with Daniel at his office. Rees came in and took Daniel outside for a 'private word'. When Daniel returned ten minutes later, he walked up to the window. Alastair asked if anything was the matter and Daniel replied, concerned but not frightened: 'Bent officers. They're all over the place down here.' He then mentioned to his brother the name of a police officer at the heart of the corruption in the South London police. Alastair has wracked his brains many times to remember the name – it was very bland and unmemorable. He has heard several names since which sound familiar and though he wishes he could be sure what Daniel said, the passage of time has clouded his memory.

TV PIRATES

From the grim used-car lots and pub car parks of South London, the taint of complicity in the bond forged between the police and News International during the Wapping conflict would continue into the blue skies of satellite broadcasting and the new frontiers of cybercrime.

We're back to the problematic News Corp subsidiary NDS, which created a proprietary conditional access system for of BSkyB in the late eighties, based around a smart card in a set-top box. The first case of phone hacking concerning a News Corp subsidiary was around NDS when Israeli tax inspectors raided the company's Jerusalem HQ and discovered illegally wiretapped conversations of senior executives. That legal difficulty almost prevented News Corp from taking over the company, but Neil Chenoweth claims this problem was overcome soon after a meeting between Tony Blair and Rupert Murdoch in March 1998, followed by Benjamin Netanyahu and Tony Blair the day after. The Israeli authorities dropped the case soon after the Blair/Netanyahu summit and Murdoch's takeover of NDS went ahead (Chenoweth, 2001, pp. 294–5).

After its move to the UK, NDS became one of the leading manufacturers of conditional access services. Their main competitors included Nagra in Switzerland, Viaccess and Canal Plus Technologies in France (later sold to Nagra) and Irdeto in South Africa and the Netherlands, but having proved itself much more secure than rival services, NDS had a dominant 75 per cent share of the conditional access market by 2001.

Most information security companies employ 'white hat' hackers who try to test the security of their own product by attempting to crack the source code of smart card microchips and there is a clear line between that and 'black hat' hacking, in which codes are broken and disseminated to access services free. However, this was precisely the allegation put by the BBC's flagship current affairs program, *Panorama*, in March 2012 and was heralded by several legal warnings from News Corp (which backfired and perversely gave the programme more publicity). 'Murdoch's TV Pirates' alleged that NDS had hacked and distributed the proprietary code of the pay-TV access cards of a rival broadcaster, ITV Digital, which closed in 2002 due to massive losses, partly incurred by piracy. The following morning, the *Independent* provided detailed allegations that an Italian hacker, who had cracked and pirated rival satellite channels in Italy, was paid through News International (though NDS is not a defendant in the ongoing legal action). Soon after, the *Financial Review* in Australia followed up with claims that similar dirty tricks had crippled an Australian pay-TV channel that News Corp was in the process of acquiring.

Allegations about NDS hacking its rivals are nothing new: the company was sued in California for $1 billion by rival smart-card manufacturer Nagrastar and its parent company EchoStar for hacking their access cards and by Canal Plus for passing on these details to pirates. Most of these cases were either settled out of court or by News Corp acquiring the litigating partner in a takeover. However, BBC journalists interviewed several witnesses who claimed that NDS distributed the hacks of rival companies mainly through an online site called The House of Ill Compute. Lee Gibling, the former owner of the site, told the BBC that he was paid directly by NDS's head of security to finance the site, promote it and share the codes. Gibling claimed his point of contact was a former senior police detective called Ray Adams, who had joined NDS in 1993 and rapidly became an expert on the problems of hacking in the industry.

More evidence to substantiate these claims arrived when Chenoweth, of *Virtual Murdoch* fame, uploaded a cache of 14,400 emails that purported to come from the mail folder of Adams. A legal take-down notice from NDS's lawyers suggested they were genuine. Though the files lack the all-important attachments such as images and invoices, some of the language seems to confirm the claims of other witnesses that NDS was using hacking to gain an unfair competitive advantage over its rivals. One example copied to Adams on 21 November 1999 at 1:39 p.m. exclaims 'Yes the Ondigital hack is working fine…' There also appear to be unexplained payments to Surrey Police.

If any of these computer-hacking allegations have any substance, they may be even more significant than the phone hacking. As Chernoweth told me in an interview for the Daily Beast:

> *The phone hacking in Britain revealed intrusions into personal privacy, and caused reputational and succession damage to News Corp. But the costs will be only a few hundred million dollars. What you have here is an issue which caused five separate different lawsuits in the past against News Corp. from global corporations each claiming billions of dollars. I would estimate this is at least 50 times bigger than phone hacking.*

(JUKES, 2012A)

In 2002, Adams was cited by plaintiffs in a billion-dollar piracy lawsuit launched by Canal Plus in California and he retired to a large three-story house opposite a golf course in Windsor. Eventually, Canal Plus exited the case when its Italian arm was bought by News Corp to create SkyItalia. In 2008 a Californian jury found in EchoStar's favour over the piracy allegations but awarded only nominal damages. The subsequent appeal process went all the way up to the Supreme Court, which upheld the allegations that NDS had violated antipiracy laws, but still refused to reverse a previous ruling that EchoStar should cover the $19 million legal costs incurred by NDS. In Italy, Nagrastar is still locked in litigation with Sky Italia over hacking allegations.

In July 2012, the executive in charge of SkyItalia, Tom Mockridge, replaced Brooks as chief executive of News International when she resigned over the phone-hacking scandal. In September 2011 *Financial Review* reported NDS was being put up for sale to 'distance' it from News Corp. In March 2012 – a few days after the planned first broadcast of the *Panorama* documentary – NDS was sold to Cisco for $5 billion.

News Corp pushed back against the press firestorm launched by the *Panorama* investigation, accusing the BBC of 'gross misrepresentation of NDS' role as a high-quality and leading provider of technology and services to the pay-TV industry' and claimed it was helping to track both hackers and pirates. However, neither it nor NDS appears to have launched any kind of defamation action against the broadcaster or the *Australian Financial Review*.

ANOTHER NOTORIOUS MURDER

It is not the first time that Adams's name has surfaced in connection with scandal. In 1987 he was subject of an internal corruption investigation, Operation Russell, soon after he took over the Met's Criminal Intelligence Branch (CIB) at the age of 45, the second youngest officer in Scotland Yard to be appointed commander; CIB dealt with high-value informants as well as internal investigations into police corruption and has been rite of passage for many Metropolitan police high flyers. Both Andy Hayman and John Yates rose through the ranks of CIB.

Operation Russell investigated Adams's time as a detective in South London and his alleged connections with an infamous gangster, Kenneth Noye, who had killed an officer investigating the famous Brinks-Mat gold bullion robbery. Adams's colleague, DC Alan Holmes, was found dead with gunshot wounds the day after he was interviewed by investigators about Adams and Noye. The inquiry concluded Adams's behaviour was 'highly questionable and unprofessional' though it failed to level any charges.

However, it is Adams's connection to yet another death, the notorious racist killing of Stephen Lawrence six years later, that would bring him back into the limelight. In 1993, 19-year-old Stephen Lawrence was stabbed to death in Eltham, a British National Party stronghold in South East London, by a gang of young men yelling racial taunts. The police investigation, how-ever, paid little heed to the question of a racial motive. Officers responding apparently failed to give Stephen proper medical attention and treated his friend Duwayne Brooks as a suspect rather than a witness. Police also failed to take proper forensic evidence or interview several well-known figures in the area, although they were named by eyewitnesses as having been involved in the stabbing.

The Lawrence case eventually developed into a cause célèbre, leading to a public inquiry that found there was a problem of 'institutional racism' within the Metropolitan Police. Lawyers for the Lawrence family, however, suggest-ed that police corruption had played a part; Clifford Norris, the father of one of the suspects and a well-known criminal, was also a police informant and claimed to be a friend of Noye. During the murder investigation, Command-er Ray Adams contacted the family of the victim through their lawyers offer-ing to act as a liaison. The Lawrence family claimed that Adams's connections to Noye and thereby to Norris, the father of one of the prime suspects, was a 'channel of influence'. It took nineteen years to finally convict David Norris for Stephen Lawrence's murder. He was sentenced in January 2012.

Adams, who denied all allegations of interference with the original mur-der investigation, was questioned during the public inquiry and although his testimony was accepted, the inquiry found that Adams's involvement in the case, which was nothing to do with Criminal Intelligence, had 'strange fea-tures'. In 1993, the year of Stephen's murder, Adams was also the target of another internal anti-corruption investigation, Operation Othona, a secret four-year investigation into corruption in the Metropolitan Police, which again failed to come up with any criminal charges. Adams retired soon after, citing a back problem.

Now Adams's private sector career began and he was soon recruited by NDS, where he rapidly became an expert on the problems of pay-TV se-curity and avidly recruited smart card hackers. When the *Panorama* BBC investigative journalists interviewed Adams, especially regarding his ap-proach to computer hackers who had compromised pay-TV encryption keys and pirated the access cards, Adams claimed he used them merely to test and improve the company's own security. So successful was NDS security that it became the basis for News Corp's wider group 'Operational Security' under the leadership of Reuven Hasak, a former director of Shin Bet, Israel's inter-nal security organisation.

Historically, Operational Security reports directly to the office of the chairman of News Corp – none other than Murdoch himself.

As more details about Adams appeared in the press and on TV in March 2012, the mother of Stephen Lawrence, Doreen Lawrence, demanded that a public inquiry should be re-opened to look at allegations that secret investigations into Adams had been withheld from the public inquiry. Six weeks later Scotland Yard was considering keeping its internal report secret and at the end of May 2012 declared that an internal review showed no evidence of corruption. On the same day Home Office Secretary Theresa May over-ruled them and ordered a new inquiry headed by a Mark Ellison QC, who secured the first convictions of Stephen's murderers in early 2012.

The links between senior News Corp employees and the cover-up of two of the most notorious murders in recent British history are circumstantial and one of them is still subject to judicial review. One can only hope that Alastair Morgan eventually gets the public inquiry in his brother's murder for which he has long campaigned. But in case all the links between police corruption and News International seem far-fetched and conspiratorial, there is one on-going investigation which has already arrested dozens of journalists and public officials: Operation Elveden.

REDEMPTIONS

By Day 13 of the hacking scandal, I was already beginning to cover the non-stop tumult of events in a regular series of 'diaries' for the progressive blog Daily Kos, which I was calling 'Fall of the House of Murdoch'. I had just published my sixth diary in the series (there are now nearly fifty) when someone in the comments section broke an important newsflash. I updated my diary immediately.

> IMPORTANT UPDATE; 13.20 BST – thanks to CEE-BS: The Metropolitan Police have announced they have arrested a 43 year old woman in relation to phone hacking. Rebekah Brooks (nee Wade) is 43. The arrest of the Chief Executive of News International an important development. She's been charged with both phone interception and corruption…

For many people, the arrest of Rebekah Brooks was the first sign that the Metropolitan Police, having lost two senior officers because of their apparent closeness to News International, were doing everything they could to restore their reputation and pursue the criminal allegations all the way to the top. The arrest of Brooks brought the police investigation into the heart of the family circle.

According to Michael Wolff, who spent time with Brooks for his official Murdoch biography, she received seven calls from James Murdoch in one day. Brooks's arrest was doubly significant in the long run because – like Coulson – she was not only arrested on suspicion of phone hacking but the more serious suspicion of corrupting public officials.

At the time of writing there have been over thirty arrests as part of the Operation Elveden inquiry into illegal payments to public officials, including: seven senior *Sun* journalists, the defence editor Virginia Wheeler, deputy editor Geoff Webster, picture editor John Edwards, chief reporter John Kay, chief foreign correspondent Nick Parker, news editor John Sturgis and the royal editor, Duncan Larcombe, who testified under oath to the Leveson Inquiry in January 2012 when asked about police bribes: 'I have never paid them, nor been asked to by my employers.' None of those arrested so far have yet been charged (see Appendix 2 Arrests).

On 27 February 2012, the day after Murdoch had launched the *Sun on Sunday* to rally his demoralised Wapping troops, Deputy Assistant Commissioner Sue Akers, arrived at Court 73 to update Lord Justice Leveson on the progress of her investigations. Having seen these police operations described a couple of weeks earlier by Trevor Kavanagh, the former political editor of the *Sun*, as a 'witch-hunt' and by the former *Sun* star columnist, Richard Littlejohn, that it was an operation 'like Nazi Germany or Communist East Berlin under the Stasi' Akers sat in her police uniform, hand clasped in front of her, and revealed that there was corruption in the daily tabloid *Sun* to match that of his defunct Sunday *News of the World*. She talked of payments to 'a wide range of public officials' in 'all areas of public life'. There appeared to be, she said, 'a culture at the *Sun* of illegal payments' with systems to hide the identities of the officials being paid. One government official received £80,000 in alleged corrupt payments over a number of years and a *Sun* journalist had paid out a total of more than £150,000 to various sources.

The calm but intense demeanour of the DAC, reportedly a source of inspiration for Helen Mirren's character in the *Prime Suspect* TV drama series, made the hyperbole of Kavanagh and Littlejohn sound absurd and hysterical in comparison.

Even more striking was the contrast between Akers and the last senior officer who looked into the phone-hacking allegations, Yates. He had been quizzed by counsel to the Leveson Inquiry over a video link from Bahrain a few days before. Counsel to the Inquiry, Robert Jay QC, honed in on a period in 2009 when Nick Davies's ground-breaking *Guardian* article had blown apart the rogue reporter defence. Yates had concluded within eight hours that there was nothing in it that represented new evidence and therefore no need to reopen the investigation. In his slow relentless manner, Jay then went through Yates's diary of the time, particularly the 'gifts and hospitality' registry compiled by Scotland Yard. Compared with an impressive collection of expensive dinners, football matches and long lunches with News International journalists, Yates's diary tersely recorded: 'Meeting with Nick Davies, *Guardian*, 30 minutes only.'

On 24 July 2012 eight former *News of the World* employees were charged with nineteen counts of phone hacking based on the evidence gleaned by Sue Aker's team. The list amounted to an indictment of Fleet Street's finest: Stuart Kuttner was managing editor of the *News of the World* for twenty-two years, until he retired in 2009; James Weatherup, Ian Edmondson and Greg Miskiw were senior reporters and assistant editors; Neville Thurlbeck was the chief reporter; and the former private investigator Glenn Mulcaire faced four additional charges. The most high-profile charges were against former editors Rebekah Brooks, whose trial for perverting the course of justice was due in court two months later, and Andy Coulson, already facing charges of perjury in Scotland.

Though the nineteen charges related to a number of high-profile figures, from celebrities such as Angelina Jolie and Brad Pitt, Jude Law and Sienna Miller, and Sir Paul McCartney, to senior British politicians such as the former deputy prime minister John Prescott and the former home secretary Charles Clarke, the most emotive charges related to the murdered teenager Milly Dowler.

Soon after the Crown Prosecution Service announced its decision Brooks made the following statement through her lawyers: 'I am not guilty of these charges. I did not authorise, nor was I aware of, phone hacking under my editorship ... The charge concerning Milly Dowler is particularly upsetting not only as it is untrue but also because I have spent my journalistic career campaigning for victims of crime. I will vigorously defend these allegations.'

II

18 July 2011
Elusive Electrons

This was the day that, according to the Secretary of State Jeremy Hunt, the $16 billion News Corp bid for BSkyB would have been given government approval. Instead – in defiance of the best laid corporate plans – News Corp had to make a rather different statement.

Murdoch Says News Corp. Will Recover

Figure 11.1 Wall Street Journal, *18 July 2011*

On 18 July, News Corp publically announced a revamped and fully independent Management and Standards Committee which would do so much to expose the corruption of officials at the *Sun* in months to come. Under the independent chairmanship of Lord Grabiner it was to be run by former *Telegraph* managing editor Will Lewis, former legal advisor to Chelsea football club, Simon Greenberg, and another News Corp lawyer, Jeff Palker. The committee would report to the former assistant attorney general Joel Klein in New York, who in turn would report to Viet Dinh, another former assistant attorney general on the News Corp board and godfather to one of Lachlan's children.

Meanwhile, News Corp had another strategy to keep investors happy: the spare cash left over from the failed BSkyB bid could be used to restore the losses on the stock market. On 12 July the company announced a $5 billion share buy-back plan and NWSA's share price started rebounding. This would be doubled to $10 billion ten months later. Murdoch had previously rejected repurchases, so the buy-back represented a triumph for Chief Operating Officer Chase Carey, more share-holder friendly and focused on the pay-TV business. It was also another sign of a shift in culture for the corporation, which had to eschew the past on many fronts, in this case the billion-dollar acquisitions of the eighties.

REVERSE ENGINEERING

Two other bits of breaking news this day spoke to the future of the media rather than the past. The first was a prank, when the LulzSec collective hacked News International's website and redirected traffic to a mocked-up page of the *Sun*.

Media moguls body discovered

Rupert Murdoch, the controversial media mogul, has reportedly been found dead in his garden, police announce.

Figure 11.2 Fake Sun *page created by LulzSec, 18 July 2011*

The hack was like a virtual form of the foam pie which would be hurled at Murdoch (and ably fended away by Wendi Deng) when he appeared before the Parliamentary Select Committee in Portcullis House the next day. Both were a diversion from the real debate about what had gone wrong with the Murdoch empire and how most of our institutions had failed to cope with it. But compared to the protest of the pie thrower, LulzSec's online vandalism made a new point about the asymmetry of the digital domain. 'Hacktivists' can act at a distance and with apparent impunity compared with, say a protestor in the seventies, who would have a hard time defacing all the print copies of a daily tabloid.

LulzSec's puerile display was no better than the hacking and outing of Nightjack by a journalist from *The Times* – though the *Sun*'s blog was shut down for only a few hours, unlike Richard Horton's, which is silent for good. Yet it was something else LulzSec claimed to have done which inadvertently had the most impact. The group tweeted that they had hacked Brooks's password combination and was 'sitting on their [the *Sun*'s] emails' which they would release the next day. That never happened. But a very strange incident soon did. That evening the *Guardian* reported that a laptop had been recovered from a bin near Brooks's London base in Chelsea Harbour. Commenting on this at any length could be prejudicial to current court proceedings but the LulzSec hack vividly demonstrates a wider theme: the panicked reaction to the never-to-materialise threat of Wikileaks-style intrusion into corporate secrets shows how News International executives have demonstrated a poor grasp of the possibilities of new technology and the digital domain and what it could entail for the future of newspapers, free speech and the wider politics of personal privacy.

My brief personal experience of working for News International's multimedia division in the mid-nineties confirms this. I worked happily away for a year on the dialogue, drama and basic design of an immersive interactive game set and filmed in the code breaking centre of Bletchley Park, which challenged users to crack the Enigma code during various phases of World War II, from the bombing of Coventry, the Atlantic U-Boat campaign, to the war against Japan. News Multimedia was run by a great creative team, who in turn hired a brilliantly inventive Israeli company called Zapa to do the graphics and computer interactions. However, the strategic vision seemed to be missing at a management level, with executives coming and going every few months. The division produced several award-winning DVD-ROMs, but it was peremptorily closed before the Enigma game was finished, though a million or so pounds had already been invested in it.

Of course, such ad hoc decisions are part and parcel of a freelancer's life and characteristic of many bureaucracies, especially in the fast moving digital domain. But this brief experience of managerial insouciance might explain why News Corp has failed to create any great innovations in new media, and has positively destroyed some – the purchase of Myspace by James Murdoch being one of the most costly. News Corp bought the leading social networking site at the time for $580 million in July 2005, the same year that James's elder brother Lachlan abruptly resigned as the company's deputy chief operating officer. For all this vast financial investment, however, nothing seemed to change in the online social networking and music sharing site and Myspace was quickly surpassed by Facebook, with its cleaner design, growing applications and add-ons. Just before the hacking scandal erupted in 2011, News Corp sold Myspace for one twentieth of the purchase price, $35 million. The next year, Facebook's IPO valued the company at around $100 billion.

It was not all failure and James Murdoch made a canny decision to acquire an internet provider to boost BSkyB's broadband services and the data from the millions of MySpace users would be a great marketing resource. Beyond the marketing though and despite a new generation of management, at some profound level, the leadership of News Corp just don't get the basics of the digital domain.

Though News International is staffed by tenacious journalists, fantastic networkers and a legal brain or two, the structure of the parent corporation, a steep hierarchy focused on the personality of one man, is very cumbersome and repels eccentricity and autonomy. Such a structure worked well in the assembly line process of printing and analogue TV production, where information could be more tightly controlled. But in the digital domain data moves around with the uncertainty of quantum physics, leaving management either in the dark or intervening in the wrong things at the wrong time.

A lack of understanding of this new networked world has been part of News International's downfall. If senior executives had understood the basics of computing, their 'email deletion' policy would have been more effective. Data is actually very difficult to delete and unless overwritten apparently erased files can be easily reconstructed. With News International's various back-up facilities, outsourced to servers in India, the chances that its data were still stored somewhere were very high – as the MSC soon proved when they discovered the 300 million emails of Data Pool 3, which have provided much of the evidence for Operation Elveden's investigation into corrupt payments to police and other public officials.

It's also possible to see the backlash that erupted against Murdoch's media empire during the phone-hacking scandal as the revenge of interactive media over the passive mass media of the past. The viral online campaigns by Avaaz and 38 Degrees that spurred the boycott that closed the *News of the World* and sourced over 100,000 signatures to get the BSkyB bid referred, are both examples of a parallel network rather than linear command process. That network transmitted the Milly Dowler story before it even made the front page of the *Guardian*. Through this rapid reaction system, the distribution of breaking news and the commentary upon it is no longer controlled by TV pundits, leader writers or indeed libel lawyers.

News Corp may be a $50 billion conglomerate, but it's small compared to the (as yet) unenclosed commons of the internet. Unlike the tiered gardens and crystal palaces of the BBC or Times Online – some charging for entrance and some not – the wild woolly fringes of cyberspace are still a place for free speech and, more importantly, free assembly. Individuals – as we have seen – have had a hard time taking on the world's third largest media corporation: their lawyers and leader writers (and occasionally their private detectives) can shut us down in an instant. But thanks to the adventitious connections of social networking, we could comprehend them before they could apprehend us.

The long-term legacy of the wired up world is that (as Wikileaks has proved) the communications of the powerful lose their privileged status. Despite non-disclosure orders or confidentiality agreements, leaks can be replicated and distributed instantaneously. Once out, they are hard to get back in: a file can be copied endlessly and stored in the global cloud. Importantly, the computable nature of text also makes it easy to find the damning quote or damaging discrepancy through a quick database search. Thanks to Full Fact's searchable Leveson Inquiry, we now have such a database: a glittering trail of text messages, emails and phone logs that we can study at our leisure. In the past, paper-based bureaucracies could steal our secrets and yet preserve their own in hard copy. But unlike atoms, the pesky electrons of the information age move through institutional barriers like neutrinos through the core of the earth. The power relations between the top of the pyramid and the base, between the core and periphery, have been melted as thoroughly as classic visual perspective was by Cubism. We don't know what up or down is anymore: everything is at the centre of everywhere.

Or at least that's the theory.

STAKEKNIFE

Operation Tuleta – investigating computer hacking – is the third prong of the Metropolitan Police's investigation into the alleged crimes of News International, and of all the three major investigations, the most secretive. Email hacking has already been tacitly admitted by News International in the first tranche of legal settlements they made in February 2012, with concessions that a journalist had hacked the emails of Sienna Miller and Christopher Shipman the son of the mass murderer Harold Shipman. With another 200 private legal claims in the offing as of early summer 2012, many more instances of computer hacking at News International could well come to light and we already know this wasn't just confided to the now defunct Sunday tabloid (see 'Nightjack' below).

One perpetrator of email hacking has already come to the attention of the police. We know of at least four private investigators employed by News International through the hacking scandal: Glenn Mulcaire with his expertise in phone hacking; Steve Whittamore and his talent for blagging or buying his way into confidential databases; Jonathan Rees and his connection with corrupt police officers; and Derek Webb, an expert in surveillance. Now a fifth private investigator, Philip Campbell Smith, comes into the story. A BBC *Panorama* documentary alleged that Smith was hired by Jonathan Rees, Daniel Morgan's former partner at Southern Investigations. This happened in 2006, soon after Rees himself was rehired by Coulson after years in prison. Rees was once again working directly with Marunchak, the senior *News of the World* editor then running the Dublin office (when he wasn't moonlighting as a translator for the Metropolitan Police).

Smith was allegedly ordered to target an army intelligence officer, Ian Hurst, who had worked at the Force Research Unit in Northern Ireland, as a handler for informants. Smith is reported to have hacked Hurst's computer with a Trojan Horse virus, and managed to extract email messages concerning two of Hurst's most high-risk Provisional IRA informants, including Freddie Scappaticci, codenamed Stakeknife. These emails were then forwarded to the Dublin offices of *News of the World*.

When Hurst discovered the security breach – potentially fatal to his informants – he approached Smith and got him to admit on tape how he'd hacked his computer: 'I sent you an email that you opened, and that's it. It's in.' In his oral testimony at the Leveson Inquiry Hurst alleged that as well as hacking his emails, Smith had taken passwords, pin codes and even his wife's CV: 'he more or less charted the events from the middle of June 2006 – he states for a three-month period, and all the documents he could access via the back door Trojan: emails, the hard drive, social media … the type of Trojan which is deployed by newspapers or private detectives isn't that sophisticated' (Hurst, 2011). Smith also alleges he was in contact with Coulson during this time, when Cameron's former press supremo was still editor of the Sunday tabloid.

According to the *Guardian*, Smith was not the only News International employee using computing hacking and Hurst is far from being one of the most high-profile targets:

> Smith is understood to be under investigation by a Scotland Yard inquiry, Operation Kalmyk, which is examining allegations that email hacking may have been used against several dozen targets … Met officers are known to have approached leading members of the Labour party as possible victims, including Gordon Brown, the former No 10 communi-

*cations chief Alastair Campbell, the former Northern Ireland secretary
Peter Hain, and Tom Watson, the backbench Labour MP who has been
particularly vocal in the phone-hacking scandal. If any of the Labour figures
were targets, it is not known who carried out the hacking and for whom.*

(DODD AND DAVIES, 2012)

Operation Kalmyk is closely related to Operation Tuleta which, according to Sue Akers, has made so far just one arrest. Given the potential victims of email hacking already named – a former prime minister, the former Northern Ireland minister, a former Number 10 head of communication – the security implications are far reaching. Many scoops and scandals have also come from intercepted emails in the last ten years. As Tom Watson has prophesied many times, this issue 'could potentially dwarf' the scandal of Milly Dowler: 'Email hacking could be worse than phone-hacking.'

In his ill-timed speech of 1993 which antagonised the Chinese government, Murdoch praised the way new technology was eroding national borders and claimed that it was a threat to totalitarian regimes across the world. His inspiration for the speech was the work Peter Huber, a libertarian thinker who had rewritten *Nineteen Eighty-Four* to give it a happy ending, showing the citizens of dystopia using the all-pervasive media to turn the tables on their government. Instead of passively consuming the diktats of Big Brother, the heroes of Huber's revisionistic reworking actively create their own meanings and share them through the technology. Huber suggested that we would all change from Winston Smiths, rewriting history for our oppressors, to Dan Rathers, making history for ourselves. In another speech in Melbourne in 1994, Murdoch continued on this theme and talked of the twenty-first century inaugurating a 'Century of Networking'. He was right, of course, but without seeing what networking would mean for hierarchies like News Corp.

Though slow to implement in his own company, Murdoch was an early adopter of a kind of 'techno-libertarian' rhetoric, which boosts the advent of new technology as a way of liberating individuals from the constraints of the state. At the heart of this argument is the fallacy of 'technologism' – the simple idea that society as determined by technical inventions when, more often than not, the opposite is true. The Gothic arch, for example, was invented 400 years before it became the key feature of cathedral making in Western Europe. Before soaring arches could become the mainstay of ecclesiastic architecture in Europe, the technology required the cultural and political aspirations of the late medieval period as a precondition. Likewise, the invention of steam or discovery of electro magnetism only came about through increased division of labour, the sharing of research and a society which invested both surplus cash and kudos in scientific and technical innovation.

For these discoveries to be turned into railroads or city lighting required even more investment, social organisation and of course a pool of consumers. Even then, the development of any technology is not necessarily 'liberating' – as witnessed by the Soviet exploitation of electrification and collectivisation or the Nazi use of the railroads in the Final Solution. There's nothing inherently socially progressive or morally desirable about technology: it's not an end but a means.

The same ambivalence is true of social media and internet communication. Facebook is a secret policeman's wet dream, as it gives up in one electronic swoop a suspect's whole social network. Twitter has been taken up by the Basij militia in Iran, even though they smashed the computers of the students in Tehran during the failed Green Revolution. Anders Breivik schooled himself in Islamophobia through online sites, before he killed eight people with a bomb in Oslo and then shot dead 69 young people on Utøya Island. Technology is a tool, to be used by one social group for or against another, to enlighten or inflame, to spy or to divulge.

NIGHTJACK

In his written witness statement to the Leveson Inquiry Hurst alleged police collusion in the failure to alert him to what had happened. 'I strongly feel that the matter was "swept under the carpet",' he wrote. 'I am also absolutely certain that there were strong links between certain newspapers and former and current officers of the Metropolitan Police Service.' None of Hurst's allegations has been proved and before the police are made the villains of this kind of cyber intrusion, we should remember the case of the police officer who became a victim of it.

The police officer in question was previously known as Jack Night, whose vivid, insightful writing on policing in modern Britain won the first ever Orwell Prize for a blog in April 2009. The Nightjack blog described crime and everyday life in the generic urban environments of 'Smallmarket' and 'Bigtown' and was, by necessity, written under a pseudonym because of the sensitive nature of Jack Night's police work.

However, within a month or so of winning the prize, DC Richard Horton of the Lancashire Police received a phone call from a *Times* reporter asking him to confirm he was Jack Night. The reporter claimed to have already talked to Horton's employers and that the newspaper planned to publish his real identity anyway. As Horton wrote soon after, 'This was easily the worst afternoon of my life.'

Horton tried to stop the outing of his real identity and placed an interim injunction on *The Times*. Minutes later he called the professional standards department of his constabulary and informed them of his authorship of the blog. His lawyers argued in the high court that the proposed article was a breach of confidence and wrongful disclosure of public information. But the newspaper's legal team contended that Nightjack was identified by details in the public domain. Justice David Eady, in *The Times*'s favour, added that no blogger could have a 'reasonable expectation' of anonymity in the circumstances. The case caused an outcry in 2009, not only because a valuable voice was lost, but because it was also a landmark ruling about privacy: 'blogging is essentially a public rather than a private activity'. *The Times* article was published, Horton was disciplined by Lancashire Police and the excellent Nightjack blog deleted. One up for free speech, it seems, or at least the free speech of *The Times*.

It's worth noting that Horton's lawyers, Daniel Tench and Hugh Tomlinson QC, specifically raised in court the issue of how Nightjack had been exposed and *The Times* were explicitly asked if they had hacked Horton's emails; as Horton told me, 'in the face of their repeated denials we were forced to proceed on the basis that they had not' (Horton, 2012).

Two years later, in written testimony before the on-going Leveson Inquiry, a lawyer for News International admitted an isolated case of email hacking at *The Times*. On the witness stand, the newspaper's editor, James Harding, confirmed the hacking of an email account by a junior reporter in 2009, but said the reporter had been disciplined and subsequently left the paper:

> There was an incident where the newsroom was concerned that a reporter had gained unauthorised access to an email account. When it was brought to my attention, the journalist faced disciplinary action. The reporter believed he was seeking to gain information in the public interest but we took the view he had fallen short of what was expected of a Times journalist. He was issued with a formal written warning for professional misconduct.
>
> (HARDING, 2011)

However, Harding failed to mention that the article – written by media correspondent Patrick Foster – was still published and available online and the fact that Jack Night had been so desperate to preserve his anonymity he'd fought it through the courts.

What happened next is largely down to the work of the *New Statesman*'s legal blogger, David Allen Green, who had been shortlisted for the Orwell Prize in 2010, the year after Nightjack, who had then been on the judging panel. Green has campaigned tirelessly for the rights of free speech on the internet and led the way in his forensic investigation of the Nightjack case.

Having written up the case on his blog, Green was called to the Leveson Inquiry soon after to explain that the hacking in question probably concerned the outing of Richard Horton and that the *Times*'s defence, that it had worked Horton's identity out from material in the public domain, was a bit of reverse engineering. They already knew what details to look for because they already knew who Nightjack was.

Harding was recalled to the witness stand and testified that his reporter had not deduced Nightjack's identity from publicly available details but by hacking the blogger's Hotmail account. In one of the testiest exchanges so far in the public inquiry, Lord Justice Leveson rebuked the *Times*'s veteran legal manager, Alastair Brett, over the way *The Times* had misled the high court. Horton has now lodged a civil case against the paper seeking aggravated damages for alleged breach of confidence, misuse of private information and deceit.

I spoke to a senior leader writer at *The Times* who was present during the initial decision to identify the police blogger before the email hacking was known about. He said the decision to out Nightjack had been taken in the 'public interest' because Horton was a paid public official and victims of crime could be identified in his blog (Senior *Times* journalist, 2012). I pointed out the logic fail here: the disclosure of Jack Night's real identity made the identification of victims even more likely. The other defence as Horton was a paid official and there was a public interest in knowing who he was. David Aaronovitch, a well-respected *Times* columnist, put the same case to me: the rule of journalism is 'disclosure, disclosure, disclosure'.

There's much merit to this: the feral press performing the cleansing role by forcing out the secrets of state and exposing the hypocrisies of individuals. But there's also a major flaw: the *Times*'s journalist and lawyer failed to disclose the nefarious means of disclosure – email hacking – and under the 1990 Computer Misuse Act, there is no 'public interest' defence for this. More importantly the Nightjack case revealed a crucial distinction between the right to free speech and the freedom of the press. In this case, Horton's right to free expression (which had to be exercised anonymously) was in direct conflict with the 'freedom of the press'.

In his first appearance before Leveson, *The Times* editor, James Harding, deployed again the classic (eighteenth-century) defence that any kind of legal regulation – a 'Leveson Act' – would chill 'free speech': 'We don't want a country in which the government, the state, regulates the papers … we don't want to be in a position where the prime minister decides what goes in newspapers' (O'Carroll, 2012b). As so often with these sub-Orwellian versions of the free speech debate, a totalitarian chimera is evoked as a smokescreen over the reality. Many corporations are more powerful than many national states and when it comes to the arrayed legal and administrative firepower of News International, they are much more powerful than one celebrated but anonymous writer. Murdoch has spoken disparagingly about 'bloggers' but if we're really going to celebrate the virtues of free speech we can see in the Nightjack case an individual silenced, not by the state, but by a large corporation, with its array of legal and editorial support.

David Aaronovitch argues this is an unintended outcome – and a rare one-off case. Green disagrees: 'If this is true, one has to wonder what was happening elsewhere in News International,' he told me, 'The management and legal failures similar to those which occurred in respect of Nightjack and similar unlawful invasions of privacy are unlikely to have been detected in other titles' (Green, 2012). Free speech is a human right, an individual right, and corporations are not 'people'. But time and again through the hacking scandal we have seen large media companies invoke free speech in disclosing personal details of other individuals while claiming the privilege of non-disclosure for themselves.

IN MEMORIAM

On this day, 18 July 2012, the day before the Murdochs and former Met Commissioner Sir Paul Stephenson were due to appear before Parliament, the former *News of the World* show business report, Sean Hoare, was found dead in his home in Watford, north of London. He had been ill for some time and the police reported no 'suspicious circumstances'.

NoW whistleblower found dead

Figure 11.3 Guardian, *18 July 2011*

Hoare suffered from long-term drink and drug addiction and a later inquest concluded that irreversible liver failure was the direct cause of his death; but the hacking scandal had been an indirect factor. He was one of the first whistleblowers to connect the hacking scandal to the higher management of News International in the *New York Times* expose of 2010, for which he was rewarded by being interviewed under caution as a suspect by the police. Hoare had stopped drinking a year before after being diagnosed with liver disease, but the publicity and pressure of the hacking scandal led to a relapse.

Though journalists sometimes take extreme risks in their reporting, they often rely on whistle-blowers whose evidence can leave them even more exposed. The role of the 'insider' who risks all to expose malpractice or corruption in his or her profession has been celebrated in the film of the same name. Everyone knows the 'Woodstein' duo, but they would never have exposed the Watergate scandal without 'Deep Throat' (identified after his death as FBI deputy director general W. Mark Felt), or forgotten heroines of Watergate, such as Margaret Mitchell and Debbie Sloan. Indeed, as disciplines such as finance and scientific research become more specialised and arcane and the means of communication became less and less and remote, the role of self-reporting whistle-blowers becomes more important: figures like Sherron Watkins who blew the whistle about account irregularities at Enron, or auditor Cynthia Cooper about the $3.8 billion fraud at WorldCom, or Leyla Wydler during the billion dollar Ponzi scheme run by Allen Stanford at the Stanford International Bank (Press, 2012, pp. 131–42). Paradoxically, the intense specialisation of other professions means that journalism has to do the reverse.

In another article in the *New York Times*, published just a week before he died, Sean Hoare, the former *News of the World* journalist, explained the principle of 'pinging' whereby a target – celebrity, politician, whoever – could be geographically located by merely knowing their mobile phone number. This was allegedly demonstrated to him by the *News of the World* news desk editor, Greg Miskiw, the same man who had come up with the infamous line: 'That is what we do – we go out and destroy other people's lives.'

ELECTRIFICATION OF THE WORD

At the high water mark of his career at the age of 80, just before the hacking scandal exploded, Murdoch's career had straddled three great eras of social and technological change in the history of modern media.

Born the son of a press baron in the heyday of mechanical reproduction Murdoch had been schooled in the old industrial workflows of Fleet Street: hot metal, rolling print presses, unionised labour with long apprenticeships, the logistics of railway haulage and newsagent sales. This kind of assembly line production extended to workers of both hand and brain: the copy tasters who trawled the wires for good stories, the journalists who hit the pavements with their notebooks, chatting to police officers in bars, doorstepping eyewitnesses, writing shorthand in court and then submitting their work to the typists, the sub-editors, the editors and the typesetters. It was a linear sequence where – more or less – everyone knew their place.

Though this was Murdoch's inheritance in the fifties, he could foresee that newspapers weren't secure and were threatened by electronic media. His father had already tried to buy radio stations and force the early ABC national network to use his news service for their broadcast news bulletins. From the late fifties onwards the electronic mass media were the growth areas, with television news and entertainment – though often editorially still led by the papers – rapidly stealing their readership, advertising revenues and political clout. Unlike newspapers, which had to be physically delivered and actively engaged with, the distribution of radio and TV was seamless and passive, like wallpaper. The consumption of television, apart from being visual and passive, could be a family or social event, unlike the solitary act of newspaper reading. For many thinkers and commentators, the mass media of the era seemed to be creating a uniform mass, passive and easily led, the lonely herd bewitched by the spectacle of consumer society.

Murdoch tried to buy into this brave new world of broadcasting both in the UK and Australia, but for over thirty years failed to find a secure foothold. He blamed this on elites – the liberal establishment of public service broadcasters like the BBC, or the public school cliques who ran their cosy cartels of commercial broadcasting. It would take until the late eighties, with the rise of direct satellite broadcasting and the establishment of the Fox Network, before Murdoch found a permanent place in broadcasting. To achieve that feat he had to lose his citizenship and almost lose everything else due to a disastrous amount of debt. And even so, waiting in the wings was a third huge revolution which could undo all he'd done so far.

In the early days of the electronic revolution, while the mass media was just beginning to hold sway, the mathematician Alan Turing had dreamt up its replacement. In a theoretical paper written in 1936 Turing laid down the theoretical properties of the modern computer, a few years before he helped build one at the British signals intelligence centre at Bletchley Park. Turing's imaginary Universal Machine would use digital code to process all of its instructions. In effect, it translated every other kind of motion or process in a computable number (hence the term computer) and as such it could emulate all other machines. Today we see the effects of this in miniature, as our smart phones become switchboards, music players, gramophones, radios, cameras, map readers, typewriters, recording studios, arcade games, guitar tuners, compasses, microphones, notepads, TV sets... (and that's just on mine).

Murdoch exploited computers in newspaper typesetting, but he still missed the social dimension of this third wave of media. He saw new technology as another form of automation, wherein capital could reduce labour costs and so dispensed with 6,000 print workers overnight at Wapping. Soon faxes and word-processing workstations meant that he could strip out a whole layer of white-collar administration in his newsrooms too. But Murdoch was still – as most people were – seeing the new technology through the prism of the old hierarchies.

In his classic late sixties vision of the future, *2001: A Space Odyssey*, Stanley Kubrick had imagined mankind's ultimate tool in the form of a mainframe computer named HAL – the initials of IBM transposed one letter up the alphabet. The vision of an all-powerful centralised artificial intelligence obsessed both science fiction and theoretical research for the next two decades, but completely missed the real innovation taking place. With Moore's Law, formulated in the mid sixties, accurately predicting a doubling of processing and memory storage every two years, computers didn't become bigger and more impersonal, but smaller, ubiquitous and personal.

Personal computing would quickly transform media production. By the mid-nineties, for not much more than the cost of a new TV, people could own a mini Turing machine which could function as a print shop, recording studio, film laboratory or video editing suite. The barriers to entry, which meant only massive capital investment could buy you a newspaper or a television station, were rapidly eroding. Rather than being passive consumers of mass media, more and more people could become active producers of it.

Right away, this began to cause problems for various sectors of the media industry, from tape manufacturers and record companies to video hire shops and film processing labs. But a revolution in the means of production was not enough to replace the old mass media. You might be able to produce your own book or recordings, but how could anyone find them? What was needed was a parallel revolution in the means of distribution and exchange.

Murdoch might have presaged the 'Networking Century' in his 1994 speech, but he saliently failed to capitalise on it, unlike the 30-year-old entrepreneur Jeff Bezos who, in the same year, stumbled across an amazing statistic: four years after the first World Wide Web browser was invented, the internet had been growing at the rate of 2,300 per cent a year.

When Bezos started Amazon.com in 1996, only 16 million people were active users of the web. A year later that doubled to 36 million. Internet take-up continued to rise and soon fuelled the speculative rush of the dot-com boom, which was to make new media worth $600 billion more than old media by 1998. The bubble burst on the dot-com boom, just as railway companies had crashed in the mid-nineteenth century, but that didn't stop the trend. At the time of writing, a quarter of the world's population, 1.7 billion people, are online; Facebook has been capitalised for $100 billion in its first IPO and Apple's stock value, at $500 billion, is bigger than the entire US retail sector, and worth more than Poland.

For creativity and communication, the upside of the internet is the network effect. Though online piracy and the lack of approved commissioning structures may create problems for well-remunerated authors at the top of the old industrial hierarchy, the vast majority of rock bands, writers, short-filmmakers, humourists, poets or cartoonists no longer have to go through the filter of publishing and distribution companies to find a market. Though peer-to-peer distribution has yet to replace the marketing operations of large corporations, the trends are there too. In 2011 three out of the top ten best-selling Kindle books on Amazon were self-published. Ten million people use Twitter in the UK, more than the nine million who daily purchase newspapers. What had previously been an assembly line chain of command and value is beset by disruptive and apparently random variables. For most media, what William Goldman once said so memorably about the film industry, is true throughout the business: 'No one knows anything.'

The traditional independent newspaper industry may be gutted by this and so too its dwindling employees, but that does not necessarily mean journalism itself is withering or that readers are become less literary and informed. Though newspapers vaunt themselves as watchdogs over state officials or errant corporations many of the actual functions of traditional newspapers and magazines are very different: they serve as arbiters of taste when it comes to books, fashion or film; as sources of information on the weather, stock market movements, electoral returns, births and deaths, and as forums for self-expression such as a letter page or agony aunt column. Many of these functions can be fulfilled more easily and quickly online, either through expert data sources (used by the papers anyway) or through peer-to-peer forums. Just think how much more successful online dating sites are – used by 25 per cent of the US population – compared with lonely hearts columns. As Steve Myers writes at Poynter:

> *These disruptors don't replace investigative reporting, but they replace the other 95% of what made professional news organizations important. This is not sharing cat pictures, this is stuff that matters. People can read the health section in their newspaper and get drip-fed badly researched advice about how to live a healthy life, or they can visit the NIH or the Mayo Clinic online, or create an account on one of the many bulletin boards about anything from fitness to dealing with cancer.*

(MYERS, 2012)

On his blog the software developer Stijn Debrouwere explains how online sites are 'nibbling away' at journalism, using the example of listings and review magazines:

> *We used to peruse the entertainment section of our favourite magazine for movie reviews and recommendations. Now most of us use IMDB or the recommendation engines behind Amazon and Netflix*
>
> *Same thing for music: people still find new music through Pitchfork or Rolling Stone, but services like Spotify and Rdio actually replace music journalism for many. More music and less bullshit. Better recommendations and you can start listening right away.*

(DEBROUWERE, 2012)

(Appropriately enough, you'll only find intelligent discussions of this online, rather than in the newspapers, who are naturally wary and preternaturally dismissive of the potential of blogs and web-based journalism.) In a comment to the post, Michel Huber makes an even better point:

> *...could it be that those sites are actually nibbling away the pieces that are actually NOT journalism? In my definition, journalism has much more to do with providing useful ways to reduce complexity than with just producing content. And while all that content may have been vital for the economic survival of traditional media, it didn't – at least not always – fulfil the core tasks of sound journalistic practice. So the main task remains to develop new formats in which journalism can thrive.*

(IBID.)

So little of modern journalism, particularly British journalism, is actually investigative and 'telling truth to power'; the mass tabloid market is more concerned with scoops about celebrity love lives or with vast tracts of it given over to sports or PR. For the broadsheets, there are great swathes of eristic opinion. Much of it is very well written and informative, but if it can't find a market without the subsidy of advertising, these comment pieces are just vanity publishing, albeit with an editor's imprimatur. Columnists are pictured on the masthead of many newspapers because they are deemed to add monetary value, but if people won't pay for that added value then the whole equation is bankrupt. The paywall experiment currently utilised by the *New York Times* is sometimes deemed a great success – but of the American newspaper site's visitors only 1 per cent actually pay subscriptions. As Howard Owens explains in the *Columbia Journalism Review*, paywalls won't work; they won't pay for reporting staff; they are driven by the wrong people; and they just delay the final reckoning for print journalists. The usual justification for paywalls is the objection to readers getting stuff for 'free': 'Journalism is expensive, therefore people should pay for it.' But, as we've seen, the consumers of the independent newspaper never paid for journalism. Subscriptions only covered a fraction of production costs. Commercial newspapers were – like commercial TV or free sheets - financed by bundling content together with advertising. That physical bundling has been torn to shreds by the elusive electrons of the internet.

Based on a bureaucratic model, most newspapers and media companies acted as 'gatekeepers': an op-ed in the *New York Times*, an appearance on BBC *Question Time*, a rave review in the *Sunday Times*, these are deemed to be a quasi-official stamp of approval, a sign you've 'arrived'. Social media work by another principle – the principle of 'gate-opening' – with low barriers to entry, there's little to stop you making it to market. Publication itself is no imprimatur; each article needs its own marketing, using word of mouth or cross linkage to reach its audience. The net result is a media world that is much wider, but experienced as something much shallower for those used to commanding the mastheads of the old regimes. The hierarchies provided a captive audience and linear path to work your way up the ladder. Now success is as elusive as those electrons. Things happen from left field or not at all.

This was certainly my experience of blogging in the US which informed and enthused the writing of this book. It started five years ago, when I became involved in the Obama campaign, which itself revealed the possibilities of online advocacy, research, fundraising and what is called 'citizen journalism'. The prime political blog is Daily Kos which, though it has 'front pagers' chosen (and sometimes paid) by the site's founder, also has a recommended list of articles or 'diaries' which are voted up by users until they virtually cross over to the front page (a form of collective editorship I suppose). I had joined Daily Kos back in 2004 under the highly imagine user name 'Brit', but it was only during the Murdoch scandal last year that my diaries gained regular attention. They would be voted to the top of the recommended list and be met with hundreds of comments, many of them more informative than the piece itself. The commenters would add sources and snippets of information, put together arguments, mine data from stock price movements, legal records, post facts, figures, images, graphs, YouTube videos, timelines and historical data; composing – as it were – an instantaneous collective broadsheet. (It was these diaries which out of the blue attracted the attention of Tina Brown and led to me becoming a regular contributor to *Newsweek*/Daily Beast.) By no design or linear plan, I moved into the mainstream.

All of which, of course, incurs the understandable irritation of trained professionals who have spent years working their way through regional and local newspapers to the studios and news rooms of the main stream national media. They think the concept of the citizen journalist is as ludicrous and dangerous as the citizen brain surgeon. Yet journalism didn't originate in some hyper specialist training. Daniel Defoe, Émile Zola, Thomas Paine, Karl Marx and George Orwell did not go through a three-year long journalism course. Their craft of writing began by writing daily 'journals', a principle probably closer to Daily Kos than the *Daily Star*. They exercised their free speech from a personal informed basis to describe what they saw in the world around them and argued passionately about perceived injustices or to advance some kind of remedy. They had no specialised training but were seen as exemplars of an active citizen – interested in how things are and eager to express an opinion.

I suspect that, if most professional journalists looked at their careers, they would actually find that the source of their success is not some specific technical knowledge or long studied for qualification. Experience is their expertise and their mystery is their mastery of fact, argument and language. Of course there are many skills involved in being a good journalist, beyond just writing: knowing the laws of defamation, contempt of court, laws of secret recording and protection of sources – but these are usually double-checked by lawyers. There is also the importance of objectivity – news shouldn't be suppressed just because it doesn't fit with your political persuasions and untrained journalists are more likely to lapse into the partisan and tendentious. But this is a different kind of professionalism compared to the doctor who cannot refuse a patient because she doesn't like her, or a lawyer who cannot refuse to take on a client. There are professional standards when it comes to law or medicine which can be tested by the evidence of outcomes. No such measure applies to journalism and even if it did, J.S. Mill's principle that conformity and heterodoxy are more dangerous than mere error applies here. If this story of this book tells you anything it's that monopoly breeds abuse and lack of diversity leads to collective malfunction.

Perhaps the key virtue of journalism, the element that makes foreign correspondents still mythic heroes despite all that's happened, is their very humanity, the fact that all of us can imagine becoming that witness or messenger with an urgent story to tell. That's why so many great reporters and commentators apart from Orwell or Zola – Alexander Herzen, Charles Dickens, Jack London, Ernest Hemingway, Isaak Babel, George Orwell, Truman Capote, Ryszard Kapuściński – switched between journalism and other forms of writing. Journalism is not a profession that can be easily compartmentalised. Woodward and Bernstein were deeply influenced by the new journalism which sought to bring an array of fictional and scene-setting devices to the trade. Meanwhile, even the most experienced journalists, such as Nick Davies or Seymour Hersh, succeed because of deeply personal attributes: persistence and intelligence, an ability to win the trust of insiders, experts and witnesses and getting them to talk. It's not rocket science – it's rather more impressive than that. These are deep values of communication hard to formulate or theorise, but they shouldn't need a walled garden of restrictive practices to protect them.

Most revolutions are discontinuous and parallel: newspapers didn't destroy book reading, TV didn't destroy either of them and the internet has not led to the complete disappearance of print any more than the computer led to a completely paperless office. Indeed, if there's any one consistent thread to these three revolutions, it's the triumph of literacy. The 500-year development of print, from Gutenberg to the iPad, has seen writing move from a hieratic handcraft through mechanical mass production back to your own personalised printing press and global delivery system. The electrification of the word has liberated text. Words can be copied and disseminated at virtually no cost, at the click of a mouse. They can be retrieved, searched and analysed just as rapidly. Constructed out of code, the digital domain makes sound, word, image all legible, editable and rewritable. Every day, billions of thoughts and conversations, formerly lost to the ether, are now recorded in text messages, chat boxes, emails, blog comments, tweets and Facebook updates. Now that a quarter of the world's population are online means nearly two billion people are commenting, arguing, laughing, fighting, debating in searchable, retrievable text; never have we been so literary, never have we read so much and written our history so comprehensively.

The incoherence and chaos of this is often hard to accept, especially for anyone who defines literacy as the orthography and normative grammar of an elite. The vastness of these virtual spaces scares us too: people hang around in small clusters, echo chambers filled with like-minded members, pockets of confirmation bias where the 9/11 conspiracy theory or Islamophobia can flourish. Unlike a bookshop or a newspaper, we don't encounter the unknown unknowns so often, stumbling across the great book we've never heard about or the outlandish opinion which actually makes a lot of sense. We often feel adrift, without bearings or validation. We miss the hierarchy, long for the gatekeepers, tycoons, moguls and press barons who can give us the illusion of authority and belonging.

In the last book of *La Divina Comedia*, Dante imagined heaven to be like a vast library in which our souls are pages in God's book collection. The internet takes that vision to a point of genuine realisation: we've all got the potential to be a webpage in the vast cloud of unknowing of the internet; the only thing missing, however, is a single divine omniscient reader.

Or maybe we have one… *Google*!

NET NEUTRALITY

The salient lesson of the Murdoch story and the rise of New Corp is not just about newspapers or satellite TV; it's a broader warning of the dangers of monopoly media power and how, especially in Britain where that power was most acute, this led to both criminality and a suborning of the state's most senior officials. This lesson is even more urgent and relevant as the digital age is creating even bigger media monopolies like blooms of algae in an oxygen starved sea.

During one of his several spats on Twitter in the summer of 2012, Murdoch tried to defend his reputation from the tarnish of the privacy invasion perpetrated by the *News of the World* by citing the case of Google:

> Privacy! Google just hacked millions of home computers in UK, presumably bank accounts, fotos etc while screening streets for Google maps.

Figure 11.4 Tweet from @rupertmurdoch, 3 June 2012

It takes a certain ethical mindset to see the random gathering of encoded electronic data in the same light as listening to the private messages of terrorist victims or war widows and then using that material to write a story without the user's permission. But Murdoch has a point about the volume of data gathering and its potential misuse.

In May 2012 the *New York Times* revealed how a German data protection official, Johannes Caspar, forced Google to release the data it had accumulated through the specially equipped cars that had photographed the world's streets to make the 'Street View' images on Google Maps. It transpired that these vehicles were also equipped with wireless network scanning devices that literally ripped the data out of the air while the cameras snapped a 360-degree view of the street. A whole new sub-genre of street photography has now grown up around the millions of images recorded on 'street view' and there is a great website that records some of the amusing inadvertent snaps in the visual capture (man with no trousers in Estonia, guy peeing behind hedge in France). But it's the data capture that more concerns privacy advocates: 'Snippets of e-mails, photographs, passwords, chat messages, postings on Web sites and social networks — all sorts of private Internet communications — were casually scooped up as the specially equipped cars photographed the world's streets' (Streitfeld and O'Brien, 2012).

Because Google is – at least at the point of service – free, consumers seem to be willing to allow these privacy violations as a cost of service. Facebook, which has built a similar monopoly in social networking, is also free and users seem happy to allow their private data be sold on in return for the functionality of the site. As the *New York Times* concludes: 'The tale of how Google escaped a full accounting for Street View illustrates not only how technology companies have outstripped the regulators, but also their complicated relationship with their adoring customers' (ibid.). But just as Google snatched those wireless communications from the air with no fixed future purpose, we have no idea what can happen to our private data in the hands of a company accountable to no one but the profit motives of its shareholders. Cool people might run Google and Facebook now, but will they always be so relaxed? And who might acquire those companies from them?

The European Competition Commission, which waived through the BSkyB News Corp merger without conditions, is now reported to be looking at the search engine monopoly enjoyed by Google, and that could spell trouble. The last time a major internet service was analysed behind the doors of the Brussels commission, it was Microsoft, which was forced to stop bundling its Internet Explorer with its Windows operating system software and the rest is history: along came Firefox and then Google Chrome, which have now overtaken Internet Explorer, the Microsoft browser.

In publishing and book distribution, another monopoly has managed to escape all regulation. Bezos's Amazon has devastated the large chain bookshops (which had already devastated the independent high street bookshops). Thanks to an almost limitless selection of titles, union-free labour and a phenomenally organised and automated distribution system, the online retailer has closed Borders and weakened Barnes & Noble in the US and Waterstones in the UK. The growth of ebooks seems set to complete the trend. Just three years ago, only 2 per cent of Americans had an e-reader or a tablet such as Kindle, Nook or iPad; by January 2012 the figure was 28 per cent. If this trend follows anything like the trajectory of internet uptake, many traditional bookshops will be out of business within a few years. With Amazon also moving into the publishing business, a raft of publishing houses could follow the fate of the book chains. The whole configuration of content production, distribution and retail is becoming compressed into one moment – that of online choice.

Previously, publishing revolutions took centuries, perhaps decades: Amazon has been selling hardbacks for 15 years at the time of writing, but the ebook has only been on sale on Amazon for 33 months.

These cold winds of structural change, felt by the printers in Wapping a quarter of a century ago, are sweeping through so many sectors of the media and publishing that no one sector is secure. Everyone knows what happened to music publishers and CD sales after the advent of Napster and file sharing. Fewer people perhaps know what's happened to hard-core porn since the rise of amateur porn swaps and the culture of 'free'. As Louis Theroux (2012) wrote in 'How the Internet killed porn': 'In essence, as with every other media evolution of the last 30 years, from VHS to DVDs to the birth of the internet, porn was once again leading the way, only this time into obsolescence.'

In the post-war consumer boom, 'built in obsolescence' applied to white goods, cars, consumer appliances, fridges and TVs. Now that built-in obsolescence applies to immaterial goods and services and the brands that once supported them can rise and fall in years rather than decades.

One of the revolutions yet to roll out, but rumbling in the wings, is the decline of tradition broadcasting TV channels. Just as newspapers have fallen off a cliff, with a drastic decline in their advertising income, traditional cable and terrestrial broadcasts are beginning to show the same steep declines in audiences and revenues. Except for the spectacular world crisis or live spots event, we are consuming more and more news and entertainment content on demand and bypassing the ads. This form of me-TV is becoming the preferred means of viewing, mainly because we can avoid the distractions of advertising sequences and create our own preferred schedules. It's not even narrowcasting – the consumer becomes his or her own TV scheduler and controller. The network brand is becoming increasingly meaningless. Most of the bandwidth of cable companies – the hundreds of channels we don't watch – is wasted, while the broadband internet is used constantly. None of the current pricing reflects this: the broadband is usually an add-on to all the other unused premium channels. Not only are we wasting our money, but the advertisers are too, because we're not watching their ads.

The passive image of mass media – German youth mesmerised by Hitler's broadcasting, British children getting square-eyed in front of American cartoons – was a brief moment of centralised electronic hegemony. It didn't last long. We're going back to becoming avid readers and active writers. We don't need schedulers or listings editors telling us what to watch, when and how. As Henry Blodget (2012) explains in *Business Insider*: 'The traditional "network" model is likely to break down and be replaced with far larger "libraries" of content and far more efficient content production, acquisition, and distribution.' Another little bit of Dante's heaven is offered to us – the electrified library. We still don't know who will be the Amazon of the audio-visual world, but YouTube, Netflix and iTunes are already beginning to fight it out. But it's the triumph of literacy. We want pages on the web. We want vast libraries of content that we can access at will. We want Dante's *Parad-*

iso, but with us as the omniscient all-seeing one.

Against this terrific and terrifying revolution, James Murdoch's tragic over-reach with the Rubicon process makes complete sense. The patent evisceration of the once cash-rich publishing business, like the latent evisceration of the profitable pay-TV market, left him with little choice but try to copy his father's disruptive innovations. As Greg Callus (2011) pointed out: 'Rupert Murdoch's genius — and I mean this with sincerity — has always been in identifying new distribution channels and manipulating them for commercial advantage. He is not, with respect, a great content visionary'. And therein lay the problem with the whole BSkyB deal even before it was launched: in this future of electrified literacy and on-demand libraries in the cloud, content finally is king and the role of distributor — News Corp's key business — is really under attack.

Before the hacking scandal exploded, Callus was one of the few people to understand the Murdochs' ultimate strategy and the Rubicon process intended to make the internet world of free finally pay. Though the bundling of newspapers and pay-TV was important, the real holy grail of the BSkyB takeover was its internet business, the fourth largest in the UK. Complete control would have allowed News Corp to form a digital hub. Sky News could be sold off and ring-fenced to keep to the plurality test and bundling of free newspapers was a side issue. It was the brand identification and content of newspaper titles, the *Sun*, *News of the World*, *The Times* and *The Sunday Times* that were key to the joint web identity. Newspapers provide important portals. As Callus explains:

> …*my employer, the Guardian, sells 220,000 physical newspapers a day, but reaches almost 50 million unique visitors a month online. Which do you think matters more? And remember, the internet is barely 6,000 days old — reliance on the internet as the primary distribution channel for all media outlets is still in its infancy.*

(Ibid.)

With more and more TV stations and newspaper titles converging on the web, News Corp had the unique advantage in the UK of a combined text and multimedia operation.

But how to get people to pay? The history of paywalls and the decline of pay-TV suggest that people are more and more reluctant to pay up front for access. This is where the distribution genius of the Murdoch family comes into play. Just as much of News International has been a form of anti-news, the internet strategy wasn't about service provision, according to Callus, but service denial. In a level and open playing field, the paywalled *Times* and *Sun* stand no chance against the open journalism platforms like the *Guardian* and *Daily Mail* online. The only way to make this work would be to radically tilt the playing field in their direction.

Because it owned an ISP, four newspapers and the monopoly satellite channel, News Corp could carve up three important tranches and then package them together in collateralised digital product which would provide privileged access. By undermining the concept of 'Net Neutrality' whereby every content provider gets equal access to the audience, or vice versa, Murdoch's digital hub could create a fast lane for his own content and a slower access for rivals (unless they paid for it). With nearly four million subscribers, that could put a big dent already in many online UK brands. As we have seen, it is precisely through such distribution deals that Murdoch built up a fifth US TV network. According to Callus, Ed Vaizey, the minister of state at Jeremy Hunt's DCMS department, was already considering dropping the Net Neutrality agreement in 2011. The political leverage around changed legislation would once again be key.

There is a term for what would have resulted – a vertical monopoly. Measured horizontally as a snapshot of similar companies at the same point in the supply chain, the merger of News International with BSkyB might not have caused obvious monopoly problems. But the snapshot is out of date as soon as it is developed and regulation has barely caught up with the changing realities of this sector; under EU competition law a newspaper and a TV station are as different as detergent and dog food. The digital crunch, the centripetal forces which are driving all media into the same event horizon, make this view dangerously redundant.

Perversely, Brussels is reportedly investigating BSkyB's vertical control of Hollywood film rights, because this could breach supply chain competition law. Yet the BSkyB takeover would have made that vertical integration look like peanuts. The best parallel is again with the case of Standard Oil before trust-busting legislation. The oil company's monopoly didn't come about by dominating drilling or refining, but owning the downstream transport and retail. It was a monopoly of distribution and the lack of competition in carriage that mattered. Had the BSkyB deal gone ahead, News Corp would have had a powerful vertical monopoly in the supply chain in Britain, and by expanding Sky in Germany and Italy, a dominant position on the continent.

Most of this book has been devoted the abuses that have arisen from News International's newspaper market dominance in the UK; one can only imagine what would have happened if those monopolistic and uncompetitive practices had encompassed the country's digital domain. Forget Dante's *Paradiso* or the family copy of Orwell's *Nineteen Eight-Four*. James Murdoch's full-size Darth Vader on the executive floor of Wapping would no longer be a joke. For British media, the new satellite publishing operation would have been a Death Star.

19 July 2011

Rupert, J'accuse…!

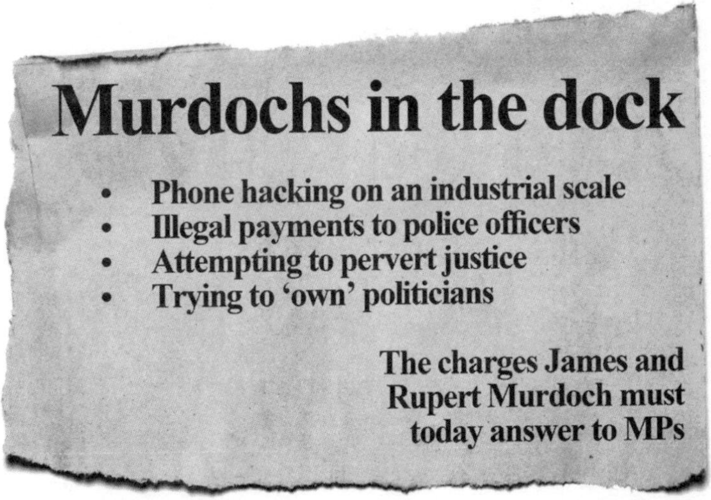

Murdochs in the dock

- **Phone hacking on an industrial scale**
- **Illegal payments to police officers**
- **Attempting to pervert justice**
- **Trying to 'own' politicians**

The charges James and Rupert Murdoch must today answer to MPs

Figure 12.1 Independent, *19 July 2011*

My Daily Kos diary from Tuesday 19 July 2011:

> *FALL OF THE HOUSE OF MURDOCH IX: Showdown in Parliament: the Play and Players: RM No responsibility*
>
> DRAMA IN THE HOUSE?
>
> *So it's finally here: the day I never thought I would see. Around 2.30 BST*

Rupert and James Murdoch will appear before the Culture Select Committee to answer questions on the hacking and corruption charges now facing Newscorp, followed by Rebekah Brooks an hour later. Live House of Commons Coverage here and apparently this will also be covered by C-Span.

HOC CULTURE, MEDIA AND SPORT COMMITTEE
Tuesday 19 July
Wilson Room
Meeting starts at 2.30pm

As everyone is warning, it might be disappointing theatrically: Brooks and the Murdoch's will both be heavily lawyered up and PR air brushed; expect no killer blows or sudden confessions; MPs are not trained examiners either. As Tom Watson, the courageous MP who along with Chris Bryant doggedly pursued the hacking allegations despite being ignored, ridiculed and then threatened has said:

'There is not going to be a killer blow on Tuesday. Expectations are way too high,' [Watson] told the Guardian. 'We will get the symbolism of parliament holding these people to account for the first time. We will look for facts, and not just offer rhetoric. This story has been like slicing a cucumber, you just get a little bit closer to the truth each time.'

Chris Bryant himself has just reiterated on the BBC:

'The theatre of [today's appearance] is irrelevant. In the end we've got to get to the bottom of what is a very murky pool. And I tell you Rebekah Brooks was right. We're only half way into that pool at the moment.'

[...]

I actually find this quite moving, and a Panorama documentary about Murdoch actually bought me to tears last night. This will always be a significant day, because after 42 years, the man who was rumoured to be, and now revealed to be, the most powerful man in Britain finally having to face its elected representatives.

[...]

For my generation (born in the 60s) not only has Murdoch dominated our entire adult lives in terms of news, but his model of the media has disfigured politics. Of my college friends in the 80s, many got siphoned off into the financial services to earn lots of money in entirely unproductive asset bubbles. But a large number also got sucked into journalism, PR, media. I know my journalists — the mother of my children was a very senior BBC News executive — and while all of them were excellent, clever, committed people: I knew something was wrong.

I'd often ask TV presenters or news investigators why, given their passions and interest in politics, they didn't go into politics themselves, and become and [sic] MP. Generally, the answers were awkward. They couldn't say it, but they knew they would earn less money, and the route — being selected and then elected by the people — would be long, arduous and unpredictable. But one senior figure was bluntly honest with me:

'Why would I become an MP, Peter? They have no power.'

So that's part of the problem here, a system dysfunction that goes beyond the Newscorp empire to the wider world of the blogosphere. Pundits and opinion writers make much more noise, more money, and an easier route to political influence than the normal political careers. I have no problem with it as such — except this one anomaly. Politicians are ultimately accountable for their power — at the ballot box. As former Home Secretary Jack Straw has just said

'Parliament should be the cockpit of the nation and not the newspapers'

Today it looks like it will be.

So let's celebrate today whatever happens. The people's representatives are finally confronting the unaccountable 'state within a state' which Newscorp is. Whatever the outcome, I can't help think of It's A Wonderful Life *and the way George Bailey stands up to Henry F Potter. The confrontation isn't direct. Indeed, at the end of the movie, the grasping monopolist — who would have turned Baileys [sic] hometown into a sleazy tabloid Potterville — basically just disappears. The collective goodness of the community, which saves Bailey, makes Potter irrelevant. He keeps his riches. There is no denouement. Potter just fades away into moral oblivion and narrative insignificance.*

This is how I guess the Murdochs will eventually depart, not with a bang but a whimper.

ETHICAL VOID

Though that diary was written in haste on the day, months before I embarked on this book, I still stand by the sentiments expressed then, especially my concern that the political process should have primacy over the media world. Too many of my friends and colleagues have devoted their professional lives to becoming member of the commentariat, when they would have had brilliant careers in politics. But public service – with its lower salaries and high expectations of accountability – is much less attractive than punditry or media production, which doesn't have to submit itself to the vicissitudes of the electorate and – as my friend once said – has considerably more power.

So in another way we are complicit. For my cohort, coming of age in the eighties, I see precious few involving themselves in politics. For the highly numerate, potential engineers, mathematicians, chemists and physicists, financial services provided the lure and they were sucked up into quantitative analysis and the immensely lucrative debt and derivative trading of the City of London. Meanwhile, the highly literate, those who could have been expected to inspire by their oratory or passionate cultural engagement, the pay cheques and kudos of media production were just too great.

The one thing about that diary that reads as naïve and excessively partisan to me now is the analogy of News Corp with Potterville: Murdoch is bigger than that. If one was to judge Murdoch's legacy solely by the *News of the World* or the *New York Post*, then the comparison might have merit. But there is much more, for a good and ill, to Murdoch's media empire than just tabloid sleaze. He has created some extraordinary delivery systems across the world and has even delivered through them some excellent content, examples that he himself has cited, such as *The Times* or *The Simpsons*. Any judgement on his political influence can't absent the politicians themselves who deferred to him. Any criticism of his papers and news channels can't excuse the audiences who read and watch them. Any post-mortems on the social effect of his ideas and ideology can't avoid the fact that we didn't have effective arguments to counter them; the numerate should have explained to us the economic realities of monopoly power; the literate the captious rhetorical devices of *Sun*speak.

Looking back on that day, the warnings of Chris Bryant and Tom Watson also seem quite prescient. There was no smoking gun, no gotchas, no 'The truth, you can't handle the truth!' courtroom drama. Instead there was an old man, his corporate executive son and a near miss with a foam pie. In the end it was a bit of let-down, but that's how it was supposed to be. The mystique of power is often in the eye of the beholder, who projects meaning in the absences, significance in the unseen intent. As Murdoch's tabloids have recognised so profitably, we elevate public figures and celebrities into icons and supercharge them with our own obsessions. Murdoch's appearance before the DCMS select committee – as I was not alone in noticing – was more like the end of *The Wizard of Oz*. After flashes of fire, claps of thunder, a booming voice and a huge ferocious face projected on the wall, the dog pulls away the curtain and sees a little old man manipulating it all. Dorothy accuses the unmasked 'Great Oz' of being 'a very bad man'. But he replies: 'Oh, no, my dear. I – I'm a very good man. I'm just a very bad Wizard.'

The Wizened of Oz

Figure 12.2 Metro, *20 July 2011*

As I said in my foreword, I have no personal animosity towards Rupert Murdoch or any of his family. His appearance at the DCMS select committee in July 2011 and his subsequent day-long grilling by Robert Jay QC at the Leveson Inquiry in April 2012, revealed a man uncomfortable in the limelight, hard of hearing, torn between anger and shame. Though it was clearly a rehearsed line, I suspect that the appearance in Parliament did feel to him like 'the most humble day' of his life – though the grammar is revealing.

THE MOST HUMBLE DAY OF MY LIFE

Figure 12.3 Sun, *19 July 2011*

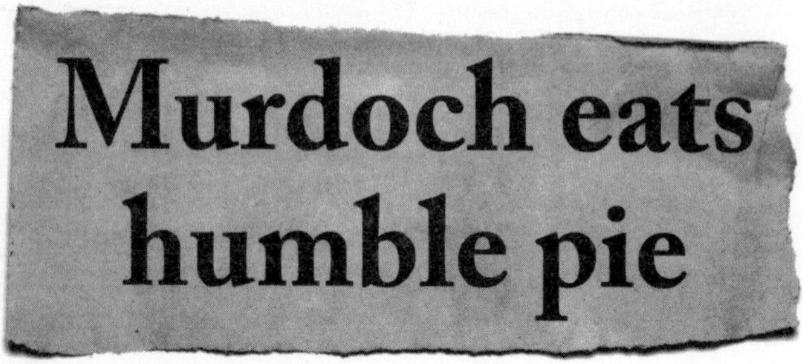

Murdoch eats humble pie

Figure 12.4 Daily Telegraph, *20 July 2011*

Did he mean it was the humblest day of *his* life? Or perhaps the day was humble and he wasn't? Hidden in the solecism was a more personal statement struggling to get out 'this is the most *humiliating* day of my life'. Though it is psychological speculation and risks falling foul of the biographical fallacy again, I can't help detecting – just as in the 'this is the worst day of my life' outburst to the Dowler family – a reversion to some deep childhood shame. After all, no matter how rich and powerful now, Murdoch was once a child, small and helpless and without a voice in a world of giants.

I hold no malice toward the Rupert Murdoch for who he is, but I do have a strong objection to many things he has done. Of course, this could have nothing to do with him being a very bad man, just a very bad wizard. I hope that the eye-catching opening gambit – Rupert Murdoch ruined my life – is more justified and resonant now. From the lost vigour and insight of *The Sunday Times*, the sexism of Page Three, the social polarisation of the Thatcher years, the media obsession of New Labour, the fawning semi-celebrity circus of politics in the last decade or so, the culture he initiated, albeit exceeded by others, has done explicit and undeniable damage to our political process, our police and of course to the media itself. As someone who has made a living in that world of the media and whose entire creative life has been overshadowed by the mores and values of News International, I have principled objections to the overall trajectory of the media, much of it driven by Murdoch. Ultimately, it has changed my life, a lot of it for the worse. But I am not a direct victim of hacking, personal intrusion or public monstering (though as I was writing this book I learned that a close relative had been contacted by Operation Weeting because personal data had been found in Mulcaire's notebooks): it's still for the victims to speak of the pain of that.

The imperial world that Murdoch was born into and the post-colonial world he came of age in, had very different values from the one we live in now. The calls of duty and cliquish gentlemen's codes were accompanied with widespread matey misogyny, outright racism, not to mention – barely hidden behind the polite surfaces – the brutalising effect of two world wars. On several of those fronts, Murdoch has moved with the times quite impressively, so it's not so much the content of his beliefs I'd criticise, but the form he has used to wield them to the expense of others. These are evident in his business practices, the manipulation of lawmakers, the anticompetitive urge to trounce rivals through predatory price wars and backdoor access to legislators. Murdoch shows no signs of liking a free market nor indeed of the principle of shareholder value. He may not treat News Corp, as some of his shareholders have accused him, as a family 'candy store', but he certainly has run it like a family business, eschewing many of the rules of corporate governance vital to a modern organisation and setting such a competitive bar for his employees to jump over that they were almost bound to break the law.

That unreformed will to power, the implicit desire to dominate and brook no dissent, has been one of the most recurrent traits in Murdoch's business practices for over half a century now. It led one Australian prosecutor to describe the behaviour of his company (during an attempted surreptitious takeover of the Australian Football League) as demonstrating an 'ethical void' (Chenoweth, 2001). Harry Evans, who I know from personal experience to be a generous and un-judgemental spirit, called his influence 'malign'. When Murdoch developed prostate cancer, *Private Eye* ran the front page headline 'Cancer has Murdoch' – a cruel headline but no worse than many that have appeared in Murdoch's press. Anthony Barnett, the campaigning writer who founded Charter 88 and Democracy Now, depicts any connection with the Murdochs as potentially contaminating and concludes that the current coalition government is tainted beyond hope: 'They know no moral limits and we had let them into Downing Street, this has to stop.'

Judging Murdoch by other people's standards is deeply political and objectivity impossible, but there is one tighter less ideological test: did he live up to his own standards?

The hard question, the one that will exercise historians in the future just as it currently taxes lawyers, investigators and commenters today is to what extent Murdoch was aware of the well-documented practices of his employees. It's the same question (writ much smaller of course) that haunted Gitta Sereny when she interviewed Albert Speer after he had spent two decades in Spandau prison for war crimes and crimes against humanity committed carrying out his role in Adolf Hitler's Third Reich. Though Speer confessed to many crimes he continually maintained he had no knowledge of the genocidal aims of the Holocaust. As Sereny put it in a *Times* interview in 1981:

> *Even now, after long talks about his guilt, which he felt to such an over-whelming degree, I am still not certain how much he knew and how much he deliberately hid from himself or how much his psyche simply rejected as unacceptable.*

Looking back at the accounts of the Milly Dowler story in the *News of the World* in April 2002 (see Chapter 1) the sourcing of the story from intercepted phone messages is obvious. There are dozens of such stories in his Sunday tabloid. No matter how remote Murdoch then was from his best-selling paper, is it really credible he never saw one of those stories and never asked the editor what the source was? Given the tight rein on budgets, the hundreds of thousands allegedly paid to public officials must have also, at some time, attracted some notice. Maybe Murdoch was lied to by his lieutenants or was just too remote to see the detail. But the lieutenant who had been with him for fifty years, Les Hinton, was much closer to the source of these activities and in charge during the crucial years 1995–2005. All these questions had been put to Hilton, along with Coulson and Brooks, by parliamentary hearings (as well as a court case). It defies common sense that Murdoch didn't ever pursue these topics with his longest serving employee. If we believe his obscure line 'people we trusted let us down' then the next question arises: why did he trust these people in the first place?

This is the best-case scenario, in moral terms. Whatever Murdoch did or didn't know, he should have found out. And if he wasn't aware of the consequences of the culture he created, he should have imagined. And this is where the ethical void really begins – in a failure of imagination, an absence of insight into the foibles of others and lack of perspective and distance to see his own. Had he remedied some of these deficiencies, he might have set up structures within his own company – a charter for whistle-blowers, some kind of proper union representation, real shareholder accountability and transparency. But no. He tried to keep a global corporation a family company and lost both control and perspective.

If he'd gone through a phase of real intellectual inquiry instead of faux Leninist idolatry, Murdoch might have seen that a corporation isn't a person but an institution, which needs to be governed by comprehensible principles and mechanisms of accountability, rather than the whims of its CEO and the cabals around its chairman.

OUR DREYFUS

What makes the hacking scandal and all that follows different from the Watergate case is not the scope of corruption. Like the bungled Watergate burglary in Washington in 1972, a specific localised crime – in this case phone hacking – became the point of examination that uncovered other crimes, which in turn provoked a backlash of public denials and private cover-up, until the escalating dialectic revealed the entire culture, ethics and practice of an organisation. In the case of Richard Nixon, his closest advisors and parts of his presidential administration and the Republican party were eventually held to account by the FBI, which investigated the localised crime from the start: the Senate, which voted unanimously to hold what became known as the Watergate Hearings; the Supreme Court, who obliged the President to release the secret tapes of his conversations with his aides to the hearings; and, eventually, by the TV networks which unprecedentedly took turns foregoing regular broadcasts and commercials to provide uninterrupted coverage. In Britain by contrast the press, the police, and Parliament all failed, with only the High Court eventually forcing a trickle of disclosure. As Harry Evans said in a statement to the Leveson Inquiry: 'When Parliament and press fail in their responsibilities, we can but look to the judiciary to restore integrity in public life and defend the rule of law.'

During Watergate, too, the fall from grace was relatively precipitous and complete: only two years and two months after the break-in Nixon had resigned and two aides already had prison sentences. This is not true of the broader scandal still raging around News International and the role of Murdoch. He remains Chair and CEO of News Corp; though the company is to be split up between news and entertainment, Murdoch still plans a controlling interest. Though over fifty people have been arrested in direct connection with phone hacking and corruption, only a handful have been charged and none of the cases tried. Criminal trials stretch out for years ahead. On the ethical issue there isn't even a basic consensus among journalists or politicians about anything beyond privacy intrusion. Because of the longevity and contentiousness of the scandal, the closest historical analogy I can find is not Watergate, but the Dreyfus Affair.

In 1894, the French Cavalry officer Captain Alfred Dreyfus was framed by his superior officers when they discovered that one of their number was passing on military secrets to the Germans. Dreyfus was charged with espionage, tried for treason and after being found guilty and stripped of his rank, imprisoned on the desolate French Penal colony of Devil's Island – described as the 'dry guillotine' – spending five years in solitary confinement. Dreyfus's

Jewish family origins and the widespread anti-Semitism of France at the beginning of the last century heavily influenced the miscarriage of justice, but these prejudices were a contributory factor and a proximate cause. *L'Affaire Dreyfus* evolved into a much wider set of arguments than the innocence or guilt of a cavalry officer. Over the decade or so the campaign for Dreyfus's exoneration, the conflict between Dreyfusard and anti-Dreyfusard became a fault line for the most significant conflicts in French society.

To be anti-Dreyfusard meant to defend the values of loyalty to the country and, above all, to the military who would be the ultimate protector from all enemies. To be an anti-Dreyfusard meant standing up for the values of *La Patrie*, of blood, Catholicism, kinship and homeland. Meanwhile the Dreyfusards saw things differently. They contended that the true virtues of citizenship were being tossed away in defence of the corrupt bureaucracies of the Army and of an essentially backward form of nationalism which was always seeing enemies in those who didn't conform. To be a Dreyfusard meant to support the civil liberties of the individual against the wider demands of the collective or the state. Marcel Proust characterised it as a confrontation between two camps: on the one hand Authority, the law and highest institutions of the state; on the other, Morality, Justice and the role of intellectuals. This *cause célèbre* became a flashpoint in French society, igniting a combustible mix of social, political and cultural factors into one large explosive narrative often described as a quasi-civil-war.

When David Cameron set up the Leveson Inquiry during the 'firestorm' of the hacking scandal in the summer of 2011 he probably had little idea that it would end up as an investigation into his own background, his friendships, text messages and equestrian hobbies, let alone threaten the stability of his whole coalition government. The scandal surrounding the hacking of the phone of the murdered teenager Milly Dowler and the closure of Britain's oldest and best-selling tabloid, *News of the World*, developed into a wider scandal, concerning the governance of Britain, the oversight of the police and the social function of the press, and the sense that a small cosy circle of wealthy people controlled both the media and Westminster over recent decades.

Act One of the Leveson Inquiry was dominated by the testimony of the victims of privacy intrusion, not only the parents of Milly Dowler, but also the parents of the missing child Madeleine McCann, accused by the papers of being murderers; or of actress Sienna Miller who described how she was hounded almost every night by a crowd of young men (who would have surely been arrested for stalking and harassment – except that they happened to be paparazzi photographers); or the singer Charlotte Church, whose mother's attempted suicide, provoked by a tabloid exposure of her husband's infidelity, was also parlayed into a front page exclusive by Fleet Street. But this turned out to be only a scene setter.

Act Two concentrated on the cosy relationship between the press and the British police, particularly Murdoch's News International, whose senior executives were shown to be wining and dining senior Metropolitan police officers at expensive restaurants and clubs, even as the news organisation was supposed to be under investigation for phone hacking. In February 2012 DAC Sue Akers suddenly changed the dynamic when she testified there was a 'pattern of corrupt payments' from the *News of the World*'s sister paper, the *Sun*, to a 'network of public officials'. Suddenly, the allegations went from phone hacking to corruption. Even that was only a prelude to what was to come.

The third act of the Leveson Inquiry, dedicated to the relationship between the press and politicians, was even more dramatic, uncovering the bigger issue beyond phone hacking or police corruption. As put by Lord Justice Leveson himself:

> *To be more specific, the purpose of this Inquiry is … to look at the much wider sweep of history across party political boundaries in order to discern any patterns of behaviour that could not be recognised as fitting with the open, fair and transparent decision-making that our democracy requires.*
>
> (Brown, 2012)

Before long, the historical record brought up the case of the Times Newspaper Group takeover in 1981 which Harry Evans directly counterposed as being 'closed, unfair, and secret decision-making inimical to a democracy'. Then all eyes turned to News Corp's proposed $16 billion takeover of the major pay-TV channel BSkyB, long planned by James Murdoch as a bid for dynastic succession and pursued relentlessly immediately after Cameron entered Downing Street.

All the dramatic strands soon converged on the prime minister, David Cameron. He had employed the former *News of the World* editor Andy Coulson, after he had resigned in the wake of the first phone-hacking trial, as head of communications for the Conservative Party in 2007 and then, in May 2010, brought him in to Number 10 as chief spokesman for the whole coalition government, where he remained until early 2011. Cameron was also close friends for years with former News International CEO Rebekah Brooks. Both Brooks and Coulson were arrested within a week of the revelation of the hacking of Milly Dowler's phone in connection with allegations of corruption and phone hacking. Cameron also appointed Jeremy Hunt – a known 'cheerleader' for Rupert Murdoch – to oversee the bid in a 'quasi-judicial' capacity, after having just sacked business minister Vince Cable for being too 'partial' against it.

As the hundreds of emails, texts and entries into government logs recording previously undeclared meetings have made clear, senior Conservative politicians and advisors were in frequent, almost daily, contact with senior News Corp executives during the adjudication of Britain's biggest media merger. The inquiry which was designed to explore the culture of the press had shone a light into the otherwise secret back-door channels of a powerful media corporation and three generations of politicians willing to do deals in return for favourable coverage.

But it isn't over. As I write, after six months of intense revelations by the Leveson Inquiry – a backlash has begun. As Professor Brian Cathcart one of the founding members of the Hacked Off campaign has explained 'Operation Megaphone' is already underway, with Fleet Street's major columnists and newspapers trying to counter any changes after the hacking revelations and the investigations of the Leveson Inquiry. Steven Glover, a founder of the *Independent*, expressed it succinctly in the title of his excoriating book review of Watson and Hickman's *Dial M for Murdoch*: 'Lynching the Last Great Newspaperman'. The title alone actually pays tribute to the Stockholm Syndrome of many senior journalists and Glover goes on to argue that Tom Watson's opposition to Murdoch is the product of resentment because of Murdoch's refusal to help Gordon Brown win the previous election (an argument that actually supports the political monopoly they describe). Glover also fails to mention that Watson and Hickman cite him in their book dismissing the phone-hacking scandal as 'hysteria' in 2009 and calling Nick Davies a 'misanthropic, apocalyptic … the sort of journalist who could find a conspiracy in a jar of tadpoles' (Watson and Hickman, 2012). This is the mixture of guilt and abreaction still dominating the debate. Moving on from 'witch-hunts' and lynching, the former *Times* editor and *Guardian* columnist, Simon Jenkins, went for the full Stalinist hyperbole, decrying the Leveson Inquiry on BBC *Newsnight*, describing it as a 'show trial for the Murdochs'. The fight back campaign was summarised by the pleading title of a piece by Peter Preston, the former *Guardian* editor: 'We moan about Rupert Murdoch – but we may well miss him if he goes'.

All these recurrent plaints evoke the same nightmare scenario for the newspaper industry: Murdoch subsidised so many loss-making broadsheet papers, who will subsidise them now? As has been pointed out before, when these same commentators also laud Murdoch's ruthless culling of inefficient print unions in the past while denouncing the unprofitability of the public sector, they show cognitive dissonance of a self-serving kind. The other frequently deployed defence 'would you prefer a Russian oligarch owning *The Times*?' is just as flawed. If nationality was a bar to ownership, then the last century of the British press would have very different as a large number of proprietors have been 'outsiders' in this respect: several expatriate Canadians, an Australian, even a Czech. It's not the nationality of the owner that matters, but the number of them relative to the number of their readers. I wouldn't want to see the *Guardian* controlling over 40 per cent of the newspaper readership: I'd be just as concerned if the *Daily Mail* attempted to takeover BSkyB. As these pages have sought to prove, it's the concentration of ownership and with it unaccountable political influence, that has led to catastrophic abuse of power.

That dominance is provably dysfunctional. After Milly Dowler's phone was hacked in 2002, the British media failed to report on the phone-hacking scandal for nearly a decade; it was only the legal process of other phone-hacking victims' civil suits which eventually exposed the scandal. For three decades the political class had been cowed and awed by the media in general and by its most powerful player in particular and once again it is only the legal process of the Leveson Inquiry that has exposed the subservience of the British political class to one large media company. As the *New Statesman* legal blogger David Allen Green tweeted: 'The Leveson Inquiry has done more to expose wrongdoing by genuinely powerful people than any newspaper title.'

There will be no easy resolution to this debate within British society – nor should there be. The wounds are deep. The issues are profound and connect with the way we've conducted our political social, economic and personal affairs for thirty years. The Murdoch scandal could develop into a long-running focal point for rancour and contempt, of a society divided against itself, yet with no reconciliation or common acceptance. In a provocative article titled, 'The Murdoch and News Corporation scandal wasn't about Conservative Party sleaze – but it is now', the Conservative commentator Peter Oborne (2012) suggested: 'Politicians can now be divided into two categories: those who bought into the News International culture and methodology, and those who did not.'

But it doesn't have to be this way. There is nothing about the Murdoch scandal which should automatically polarise anyone to the left or right. The wider premises of pluralism in the media and the right to a government that doesn't change its policies or legislation to favour one powerful commercial interest, should form a common ground for all the major political parties. This is not just a Labour Party issue nor a Conservative Party issue nor for just the Liberal Democrats. In the eighteenth century, when Britain became one of the world's first market-based economies, British economists formed a broad and long-running consensus about the market failures of monopoly capitalism. A 'free' market in these classical liberal economic terms did not mean a 'free for all' but an open, accessible economy which could not be dominated by cartels or monopolies, but ensured fair competition on commonly held (and legally enforced) rules.

When it came to anti-competition and ownership laws, Murdoch has consistently pushed the boundaries and circumvented them; so it's probably no surprise that his employees should follow this example and break other laws too.

Ultimately, it is hard to resist the conclusion that the failure of many British institutions to cope with phone hacking derived from the far reaching power News Corp has accumulated in this country, especially in publishing and television. In the wake of the Parliamentary Media Committee's 'not fit' report the Tory Foreign Secretary William Hague went on a BBC Radio report to praise Rupert and James Murdoch as 'great business people'. When in opposition, Hague had been commissioned to write a column for the now shuttered *News of the World* and received two substantial book commissions from the News Corp publishing subsidiary Harper-Collins. Similarly, the current education minister, Michael Gove, who was praised for his intelligence by Murdoch both on Twitter and during the Leveson Inquiry, receives an annual salary of over £60,000 from News International for infrequent newspaper columns in *The Times*, where his wife is a fashion editor. HarperCollins also paid him an undisclosed sum for a political biography in 2004, which was never delivered. The same publisher also publishes the romantic comedies of Tilly Bagshawe, the sister of the Conservative MP Louise Mensch, who denounced her colleagues on the media committee for the 'not fit' conclusion of their report. Even British cultural guru Melvyn Bragg, who interviewed Dennis Potter in his dying day when the TV dramatist said he had named his pancreatic cancer after Rupert Murdoch, recently defended the media mogul in an interview on ABC Television, saying Murdoch had 'redeemed and restored' the British press. Bragg's long-running arts documentary series, *The South Bank Show*, was bought up by Sky Arts in 2011 after it was axed by ITV.

These conundrums are the inevitable social symptoms of a particular form of monopoly power News Corp exercises in Britain. For writers, producers, journalists, directors the company has become a monopsony in terms of hiring people and paying their fees as salaries. As Claire Enders told me in an interview for the Daily Beast:

> *I don't think Murdoch owns more than 10 per cent of any U.S. market, where there are stable oligopolies in most media markets. But in the U.K. it is very different. The BBC is very big. BSkyB is dominant in sports and movies. … Any creator of a work has a limited choice of outlets which talented people obviously gravitate towards.*

(JUKES, 2012B)

Many talented people have gravitated towards the country's biggest newspaper group, largest publisher and wealthiest broadcaster. How could they not?

Given the reality of this monopoly power, rather than revert to some kind of McCarthy-esque 'Are you, or have you ever been, a Murdoch employee?' we ought to place the blame on badly-written, or poorly enacted, competition legislation which, in the hands of easily bidden ministers, failed to protect us from monopoly power in the media and all the chilling social and political consequence that flow from it. Media plurality should be a principle both right and left can accept. Ed Miliband has suggested reverting to the old media and cross-ownership rules which prevent – as in America – any proprietor controlling more than a quarter of any given market.

This principle of diversified media ownership has nothing to do with regulating the press, nor with increasing or getting rid of the licence fee, nor with nationality of the owner or their political persuasion. The special problem of monopoly was most notably highlighted by that socialist called Adam Smith and anti-monopoly law is nowhere more strongly propounded than in that great bastion of state control called the United States. Liberals, libertarians, conservatives, democrats and socialists should be able to rally around this principle of basic equality before the law. Pluralism isn't just about a news channel or a political candidate; it is about maintaining a level playing field, politically, culturally and economically. It was the law in British newspapers, until it was broken in 1981. A modernised competition law should cover the new emerging and converging markets in digital media, before it's too late. The abuse of power so apparent over the last decade stems from the original moment of capturing that power.

By the same token, no one should be denigrated or categorised because they were subject to monopsony and worked for some company that was held by the same parent company as News International. There should be no guilt by association. When monopolies of power occur, they have a self-reinforcing nature of an either/or and accepting that binary premise is a form of acquiescence. It is entirely possible to accept that Murdoch has done many good things, without ignoring the bad – or vice versa. But the fact that, as many defenders (including Stephen Glover) point out, Murdoch losing £100 million supporting *The Times* since 1981 is not a justification either way. News International's control of Fleet Street earned it many more millions over many years. And £3 million a year for the captive gratitude of Britain's journalists and leader writers is a pretty good bargain.

To assume that anyone who has worked for Murdoch is somehow compromised in their judgement would fly in the face of the facts. Over the years, many of Murdoch's sternest critics have been former employees such as

Harold Evans (former *Times* editor), Andrew Neil (former *Sunday Times* editor) and David Yelland (former *Sun* editor) – all three of whom took a tongue lashing from the 81-year-old media mogul in front of Lord Justice Leveson when he appeared in April 2012, and later provided a battery on informed counter statements.

Instead of that simplistic Manichean form of thinking, we should regain the lost independence of mind where being pro- or anti-Murdoch does not determine the career chances of journalists, broadcasters or writers. We need a form of truth and reconciliation whereby the conflicts of the past are acknowledged and then forgiven and overcome. But to get to that point we need to understand the roots of the conflict.

FREE SPEECH AND DIALOGUE

As I write, the fourth act of the Leveson Inquiry has begun and in a few weeks Lord Justice Leveson will retire for the summer to prepare his final report on a future regulatory press regime that can prevent some of the abuses revealed over the last year. Senior members of the Hacked Off campaign predict that when the report arrives in the autumn, to be passed on to Parliament to be debated, enacted, amended or rejected, there will be mounting opposition to his proposals for reforms. Various parts of the press will unite to try to sway the legislators. This has happened three or four times in the last forty years and invariably the rights of 'free speech' are loudly appealed to (see Chapter 10). The sad truth is that though free speech is part of British law through Article 10 of the European Convention on Human Rights, it doesn't have the same degree of protection afforded by the First Amendment of the US Constitution.

Many will argue that the statutes in place on 4 July 2011 cover most of the offences alleged so far – phone and computer hacking and corruption of public officials. But the fact that until the Milly Dowler revelations these offences went undetected for so long and that just a handful of instances had been brought to light by costly private litigation pursued by either prominent or wealthy individuals, should give us pause. Some of this can be put down to the failure of competition law, but if that law failed it was vulnerable anyway.

The status quo ante was clearly corruptible and the prerogative of the press – power without responsibility – has re-emerged to a point of crisis once again in British history. This is not solely the fault of News International or Rupert Murdoch – far from it – but as the dominant force in the market they bear much of the blame for failures of leadership. Accustomed to untrammelled power, media organisations will not give it up lightly. An almighty battle is set for months, maybe years, ahead: it's unclear which side will win or how.

One of the biggest problems with this whole conversation as it was conducted over the first year of the hacking scandal was that – as I said in Chapter 1 'Captive Minds' – our concepts of free speech have been hardly updated since the eighteenth century. The first pamphleteers feared the censorship of the Church and the Crown and the dichotomies of Enlightenment thinking and nineteenth-century liberalism were framed around the individual's freedom from central authority. In the twentieth century, facing the twin totalitarianisms of Marxist–Leninism and Fascism, the champions of the free speech argument have fixated on the power of the State even more. Orwell's seminal writings, though grounded in an even-handed critique of both the stifling bureaucracy of liberalism and the power of press barons and movie tycoons, fit in this simple framework of state versus individual. As a result they have been consistently conscripted by modern libertarianism which still exercises a powerful sway on the discourse about media in the US and UK. Fairness rules, public subsidy, even basic competition law is viewed from this vantage as a form of socialism. (Mind you, according to most libertarians, everything bad is socialism – Hitler and Mussolini were really communists and liberal fascism is everywhere.) Though useful in some contexts, the binary opposition between 'liberty' and 'authority' easily falls into an arbitrary axis, forgetting the clear limits on the freedom of one person or institution when it infringes on the freedom of another.

To be clear, free speech is everywhere constrained by such limits. You can't defame someone without risking a claim for damages. You can't conspire to commit murder, fraud or incite violence without facing the sanction of the law. You can't shout 'fire' in a crowded theatre, divulge private medical records or legal confidences, falsely advertise goods or services with impunity. Speech is no more free in this regard than any other of our actions. What we mean by free speech is the right to print and be damned: to offend, dissent, deviate, accuse and decry without having to submit to majority opinion. Free speech, no matter how anti-social, preserves a social good by guaranteeing the rights of the individual and the diversity of public discourse. But implicit in this idea of free speech is the right to disagree. My right of free speech exercised in writing this sentence is predicated on your right to completely disagree, hate my style and berate my fatuous thinking. In short, free speech is wrongly named and framed. It should be called free dialogue.

That dialogic imagination is what has underpinned most of Western civilisation since Plato wrote his Socratic dialogues. Socrates didn't lecture – he debated and conversed, joked and occasionally disparaged, sometimes with sex and alcohol to lubricate the discussions, as in *The Symposium*. This ability to argue, persuade or ridicule was what brought him into conflict with the authorities for mocking their gods and he was charged with corrupting the youth of Athens and sentenced to death. It's hard to imagine a modern equivalent – someone losing their life merely by exercising their right to converse – until one thinks of the dozens of journalists killed every year for covering corruption in Russia, the drug cartels in Mexico or the rebellions of the Mashriq and Maghreb. Though these journalists might seem to be exercising free speech, they are actually exercising the rights to dialogue. When *Sunday Times* journalist Marie Colvin was killed in Homs, she was talking to residents who were being targeted by the shells and sniper fire of the Syrian army and its militias. Her reports were printed in *The Sunday Times* to stir up a debate in the UK and abroad. As a result of her work, ambassadors were called, campaigns were established, Arab league observers were sent and there were discussion of sanctions and other interventions in the Security Council. Speech is an intra-personal act, not an isolated outpouring of monad in prison cell – or if it is – that in itself is a political statement, a dialogue with the authorities.

Freedom of speech, as enshrined in Article 10 of the European Convention on Human Rights, is an individual right: it is therefore not identical to the freedom of the press, which is a collection of corporations and companies and other impersonal interests. In the early days of the printing press, freedom of the press could be equated with freedom of speech, since the unfettered right to publication was first exercised as an individual right against the state, Crown or Church. But as publication has gone from being a means of self-expression to a key part of the information economy, that space has been occupied by large corporate interests, with the press being a prime example of that. As the media converges and companies merge and consolidate, the idea that only the state or the Church censors freedom of speech becomes increasingly anachronistic. There are forms of power apart from the state and international corporations which can threaten national governments by moving the headquarters overseas, avoid taxes, arbitrage varying national laws and thereby escape any kind of democratic accountability. Economically, many of them are already bigger than a lot of nation states. Or as Nick Davies wrote:

> In a totalitarian state, media lies stand up proud and insult their readers
> direct to their faces. In the free society, the lies rest quietly and in comfort
> inside clichés – clichés of language and of fact and of value – and slip gently
> past their readers' defences with the ease of a familiar friend on the door-
> step. … In a democracy, the ideology is still there in every sentence, but it
> lies down and hides beneath the surface. There is no need for a totalitarian
> regime when the censorship of commerce runs its blue pencil through every
> story. … This isn't a conspiracy. It's just a mess.

(DAVIES, 2008)

According to *Business Insider* in 2011 the value of the top 25 companies in the US alone exceed the GDP of many countries: Yahoo is bigger than Mongolia, Visa is bigger than Zimbabwe, eBay is bigger than Madagascar, Nike is bigger than Paraguay, Consolidated Edison is bigger than the Democratic Republic of Congo, McDonald's is bigger than Latvia, Amazon is bigger than Kenya, Morgan Stanley is bigger than Uzbekistan, Cisco is bigger than Lebanon, Pepsi is bigger than Oman, Apple is bigger than Ecuador, Microsoft is bigger than Croatia, Costco is bigger than Sudan, Proctor and Gamble is bigger than Libya, Wells Fargo is bigger than Angola, Ford is bigger than Morocco, Bank of America is bigger than Vietnam, General Motors is bigger than Bangladesh, Berkshire Hathaway is bigger than Hungary, General Electric is bigger than New Zealand, Fannie Mae is bigger than Peru, Conoco Phillips is bigger than Pakistan, Chevron is bigger than the Czech Republic, Exxon Mobil is bigger than Thailand and Walmart is bigger than Norway. If Walmart were a country it would be 25th in terms of GDP, surpassing 157 smaller countries.

Despite the recent US Supreme Court 'Citizens United' ruling, there is no 'personhood' in a corporation: if we accede a company the same rights as the individual then we are tacitly undermining 200 years of civil liberties and by the back door conceding the Church rights to silence us or landowners the right to turn us into serfs.

Whatever the conclusion about press regulation made by Lord Justice Leveson, the fact that free speech is a dialogue should not be overlooked. One of the egregious abuses of power by newspapers is their failure to accept that free speech also presupposes a right to reply. Newspapers are still immensely powerful megaphones and though the online world is providing some kind of right of redress and correction, the apology system currently in place in Britain, which after a lie is published on the front page and the apology hidden away somewhere in a one-inch column, is breaking the reciprocity of free speech – i.e. the right to put an opposing point of view. If the newspapers really want to preserve individual freedom of speech, rather than their corporate freedom of the press, they should recognise the rights of the individual in their principles.

TAKING THE NEWS OUT OF NEWS CORP

This book is called *The Fall of the House of Murdoch* for good reason. The contradiction inherent in Murdoch's project, that he could somehow pass on intact the publicly traded corporate empire he had built up to his heirs, was destined to be an unresolvable dilemma and, as it turned out, an impossible dream. News Corp will survive. So will the Murdoch family. But by the summer of 2013 they will become separate for the first time in nearly half a century.

In what was to be the biggest upheaval in its history, News Corp confirmed in late June 2012 that it was planning to hive off its publishing interests from its lucrative pay-TV and entertainment business. Such a split had been rumoured for years, even before the phone-hacking scandal erupted, but on the day top News Corp executives met to discuss the planned breakup the NWSA shares leapt nearly over 8 per cent. The publishing division had long been regarded by investors as a drain on the company – something known as the 'Murdoch discount' – and the potential shedding of his beloved newspapers added billions to the value of News Corp.

A separately listed news and publishing company would include the book publisher HarperCollins, and 175 newspapers including the *New York Post*, the *Wall Street Journal*, the *Australian* and *The Times*, all four of which make annual losses. Spinning off the publishing interests would not, however, divest the parent company of its potential legal liabilities either in the UK for civil suits for privacy intrusion, nor possible fines in the US for violating the Foreign Corrupt Practices Act. In the last eight months of the fiscal year beginning 2011, only 10 per cent of the company's profits came from publishing. The smaller news company was estimated to be worth somewhere between $2 billion and $5 billion, while the giant pay-TV, cable and broadcasting arm was valued around $50 billion.

Though Murdoch said he planned to remain chairman of both companies, he revealed that he would not be CEO of the smaller newspaper company, thus bringing to an end the saga that began sixty years ago when he inherited the downmarket Adelaide *News* from his father. He then created News Ltd in Australia during the fifties, News International in Britain in the seventies and then the vast News Corp in the US in the nineties. The one consistent theme to Murdoch's extensive global media holdings has been the concept of 'news'.

At the same time as he convinced many that he is the last great newspaperman, Murdoch has managed to reinvent and pioneer the concept of 'infotainment'. Back in 1983, after the exposure of the *Sunday Times*'s Hitler diaries as fakes, he famously responded, 'After all, we are in the entertainment business.' That statement has become truer over time. Just as the old style commercial newspaper had 'bundled' advertising, comment and news, News Corp itself had bundled profitable activities with loss leaders and vanity projects. Quite apart from the hacking scandal, the information revolution would have caused Murdoch's empire to fray anyway.

But now the 'news' is leaving News Corp – what is left?

'After all, we are in the entertainment business': the use of the first person plural has always been awkward here: is it a royal 'we' or a corporate 'we' or a family 'we'? If the latter, those days are surely over as Murdoch confirmed that his oldest son Lachlan was unlikely to take over the hived-off publishing venture. Even as he conceded 'news' would no longer be at the heart of News Corp, simultaneously Murdoch made his first big public admission that a family member would no longer be at the helm of the publishing arm. As for the remaining entertainment giant – dubbed by commentators as 'Fox Corps' – there is little chance that either of his sons will manage it to anything like their father's degree of power, having each made an abortive bid for the top table. The fall of the House of Murdoch started as a fall from grace and now looks almost certain to become a fall from power.

On the day of the announcement of the corporate split, Murdoch also effectively announced his retirement from British public life. Ruling out any further BSkyB bid, Murdoch told an interviewer on his own Fox News Channel he'd prefer to invest his money in the US:

> *There are billions and billions of dollars. If Britain didn't want them, we've got good places to put them here. I am a lot more bullish on the US than on the UK. I would be a lot more reluctant to invest in new things in Britain today than I would be here.*
>
> (HICKMAN, 2012)

The interviewer asked if his reluctance to return to reinvesting in the UK was down to the phone-hacking scandal, to which Rupert replied: 'No, just the English.'

'*Just the English*'!

So this explains this establishment enmity. With much of his adult life devoted to influencing British politics and dominating its political discourse, Murdoch has been running an anti-colonial campaign all along. Other brief outbursts – about how 'they' never forgave his father for Gallipoli, how the English like a good kicking – now make even more sense and reveal a hidden hinterland of resentment. Murdoch still sees himself as the scion of Scottish Presbyterianism, a poor colonial boy, fighting against elites and the snobbish establishment.

Old men are often obsessed by their lineages and attuned to ancestral voices and Murdoch's emergent Scottishness provides some fascinating connections to the anti-establishment theme. Many of the avatars of the rhetoric of the American New Right have Scots–Irish roots: Newt Gingrich, Glenn Beck,

Ann Coulter, even Richard Nixon himself. They trace their heritages back to a wave of immigration from mountainous periphery of the British Isles, who migrated along the marginal lands of the Appalachians to the mountainous back country of the South, through Tennessee and the Ozarks to Oklahoma and then followed through to Southern California in the Depression. There they formed what the writer Wade Graham calls 'California's neo-Scottish new conservatives' who became dominant under Ronald Reagan (Murdoch's favourite politician). The Southern Strategy then became not only Obama's 'Appalachian problem' but metamorphosed into the Tea Party, a fierce insurrectionary movement within the Republican Party that shows no signs of abating.

According to Steven Pinker, those who still live in the mountainous back country of the South still demonstrate the 'culture of honour' found in cultures based on sheep or cattle herding:

> Not only does a herder's wealth lie in stealable physical assets, but those assets have feet and can be led away in an eyeblink, far more easily than land can be stolen out from under a farmer. Herders all over the world cultivate a hair trigger for violent retaliation. … Though contemporary southerners are no longer shepherds, cultural mores can persist long after the ecological circumstances that gave rise to them are gone, and to this day southerners behave as if they have to be tough enough to deter livestock rustlers.

(PINKER, 2011, P. 234)

The historical migration now makes some sense. Murdoch's anti-establishment Australian roots are therefore deeply entangled with his American co-descendants; but still, it's a perverse historical atavism for someone who now lives in a remote corporate world, who slips across the Mediterranean in private yachts and glides through the stratosphere in private jets.

So much for News Corp nation and the high finance globalism Murdoch has practiced and preached. Untethered, unrooted in any national loyalty (or indeed tax regime), the need for belonging returns as even narrower ethnic nostalgia. Despite all the jingoism of 'Gotcha' in the *Sun*, the anti-European rhetoric of his other papers in the UK, notwithstanding the endless meetings with British ministers and prime ministers, Murdoch hated 'the English' all along and is now abandoning them.

As the news leaves News Corp and the dream of a guaranteed dynastic succession dims, the long lost roots of Murdoch's phenomenal anti-establishment energy are revealed. He may have some justification for this feeling. In the post-

Leveson world those left behind to guard his legacy in Britain can see that the rewards of their loyalty might be short-lived. As Murdoch has shown by his abandonment of the country where he made his fortune, his deracinated life-style leaves him with no loyalty to any country or tradition other than his own mythic roots.

A DIALOGUE WITH RUPERT

In accordance with my earlier proposition that free speech is really a form of dialogue, it's only right since his career has been the main subject of this book that I afford Mr Rupert Murdoch a right to reply.

Of course, he'd have to read this book in the first place – which is un-likely. Then he'd have to bother to articulate his objections – which is im-probable. The idea that Murdoch, one of the most powerful and wealthy men on the planet, protected by bodyguards, ushered around in special SUVs and executive jets, could talk to me is impossible… Hold on… wait. Rupert's back again on Twitter.

The paradox of one of the world's most powerful media moguls needing to take to social media to be heard has already been noted. While Murdoch's enthusiasms, odd observations, consistent outbursts, threats, iPad illiteracy and misunderstanding of the role of the internet has not necessarily endeared him to me, it has made me realise: Murdoch too is trapped in a velvet prison, a captive mind suffering from Stockholm Syndrome, even if it's of his mak-ing. He too feels traduced, hounded and misrepresented.

Welcome to the club, Rupert. Now we can talk.

For all these anti-competitive tendencies so amply demonstrated in Mur-doch's fifty-year ride through the media of the English-speaking world, there has clearly been a desire to be challenged, to find a border he can't break, a person to argue with and debate who won't be charmed or intimidated. Only the urge to escape the stifling effects of eminence, the flunkies, yes-men and hangers-on, can explain some of his friendships, many of his tabloid decisions and that meritocratic desire to get down and dirty with the rest of us.

The famed Shakespearean note returned in late March 2012 after the broadcast of the *Panorama* allegations about TV piracy and Neil Chenoweth's follow-up piece in the *Australian Financial Review*. Murdoch's tweet tirades, railing at other news outlets and threatening dire incoherent payback, recall King Lear raging on the heath ('I shall do such things, I know not yet what they are, but they shall be the terror of the earth!').

Enemies many different agendas, but worst old toffs and right wingers who still want last century's status quo with their monoplies.

Figure 12.5 Tweet from @rupertmurdoch, 29 March 2012

Seems every competitor and enemy piling on with lies and libels. So bad, easy to hit back hard, which preparing.

Figure 12.6 Tweet from @rupertmurdoch, 29 March 2012

The mention of 'right wingers' is completely baffling given Murdoch's avowed Conservative beliefs – though his libertarian streak might somehow explain it. The mention of 'monopolies' is even more perplexing. Then the 'toffs' line reveals his real anger. It goes back to his personal mythology of his father being hated by the British for telling the truth about Gallipoli – when he was in fact immediately rewarded by being welcomed into the inner circles of political elite. It triggers the emotion of the poor little rich boy, with his fast car and easy money, arriving from Geelong Grammar school to be taunted by the public school crowd at Oxford. A week later we learned who the 'toffs' were and what the 'hitting back hard' would be when his *Sunday Times* ran an exclusive bit of undercover reportage showing a deputy Conservative Party chairman providing access to the prime minister and chancellor in return for piles of cash for party donations. Murdoch twisted the knife into the Tory leader on 26 March 2012 on Twitter: 'Great Sunday Times scoop. What was Cameron thinking? No-one, rightly or wrongly, will believe his story.'

Anyone who doubts the blackmail effect of Murdoch's newspaper coverage on politicians, the way he uses it chastise, punish and correct those who cross him, should read his tweets. He told Lord Justice Leveson not to 'take them too seriously', but then proceeded to demonstrate how revealing off-the-cuff communication can be by placing 163 pages into the evidence of the Inquiry that put culture secretary Jeremy Hunt right into the frame over his handling of the BSkyB bid. That email dump almost cost Hunt his job and provoked intense and withering scrutiny of Cameron and Osborne for the rest of the year.

Apparently Steve Jobs was to blame. According to Walter Isaacson's biography, Murdoch met Jobs a couple of times around the launch of the iPad (Isaacson, 2011). He thought it was a 'game changer' for publishing and newspapers – obviously someone gave him an iPad for Christmas 2011 and Murdoch fired up his tweet app. The rest was a gift for historians and comedians.

When Murdoch started tweeting in the first few days of 2012 there was much incredulity in the Twittersphere. Though the account was verified, so was another account from Wendi Deng (which turned out to be fake) and Murdoch's initial forays into social media were full of so many unintentional moments it verged on parody. But whatever the incoherence of many of the tweets, there was no doubt they showed that Murdoch still had relish for the fight. Though he rarely responded to replies, it was clear he was reading them ('Re complaints about my spelling! Problem is my pathetic typing. Sorry, if anyone really cares,' 9 January 2012).

Murdoch's desire to make himself heard through Twitter was either the disinhibition that comes with age, a second wind of combative polemic or just a chance to do what he'd always wanted to do: to communicate his ideas, without the encumbrances of editors or producers, PR managers and spin. At first, you wanted to laugh. You wanted to shake your head. You wanted to lead this man carefully away from his iPad and put him on a deckchair somewhere in the sun. It seemed as if Twitter might well destroy Murdoch's reputation and mystique, not because it made him disreputable, bad or mad, but because we ceased to fear him.

Michael Wolff, Murdoch's semi-official biographer who, five years ago, noted how Murdoch was irritable, slightly deaf and liable to go off the reservation without a cohort of media handlers, initially thought the tweets were a PR disaster. But over the months, the media mogul seemed to get the hang of it and soon carved out a distinct and influential persona for himself: cranky, opinionated, given to bursts of generosity, often amazingly lacking in self-knowledge or current political awareness. Sometimes, this very reck-lessness was a breath of fresh air, as when – after the announcement of the split between Katie Holmes and Tom Cruise – he took to Twitter to de-nounce Scientology: 'Watch Katie Holmes and Scientology story develop. Something creepy, maybe even evil, about these people.' Within days, several of Murdoch's newspaper titles were following his lead and publishing damn-ing pieces about the movement founded by L. Ron Hubbard.

Twitter had suddenly removed all those layers of management, politeness and corporate censorship to reveal the partisan activist Murdoch of decades ago – the man who got his hands dirty with printers' ink in order to have an impact on the public stage.

On other occasions, Murdoch has shown a slightly thinner skin, as when he complained: 'Seems impossible to have civilised debate on twitter. Ignorant, vicious abuse lowers whole society, maybe shows real social decay.' To which Jon Snow, the presenter of Channel 4 news, brilliantly replied: '@rupertmurdoch I find that in life one reaps what one sows...'

That the promulgator of *Sun*speak, the man who made the shock-jock doctrine dominant in British newspapers and US cable news, should complain about verbal abuse online is like Brooks complaining about 'personal and gossipy' questions in the Royal Courts of Justice. But there are worse faults in the moral calculus than hypocrisy. It's perfectly conceivable that just as Brooks is not used to having her privacy intruded upon, Murdoch is not used to being monstered by people online. If the tactics are wrong, then turning them on their perpetrators just compounds the error. However, there might be some salutary advantage to this turning of the tables: now they know what it feels like, they might think again.

As Eric Boehlert has noted in the article 'The Self-Destruction of Limbaugh, Murdoch and Beck' Murdoch's online flameouts roughly coincide with the explosion of two of the biggest American practitioners of the right-wing school of on-air trollery. Rush Limbaugh, a cigar chomping, former prescription drug addict, has spent a career in reactive Southern strategy, oddly elevating liberal opinion by constantly insulting it, until he went too far and called a law student, Sandra Fluke, a 'prostitute' and a 'slut' on a.m. radio merely for speaking at a private meeting of Democratic members of congress in favour of a private mandate for contraception coverage for female students. He suffered a massive advertising boycott and lost listeners. Meanwhile, Glenn Beck, who veered to the crazy conspiracy preacher end of right-wing troll was quietly dropped by Murdoch from Fox after he found himself obliged to defend the 'Obama is anti-White racist' line of his talk-show host.

Of course Twitter does not spell the end of *Sun*speak or shock-jock idiocy, but the interactive nature of new media means that we can respond to these assertions, counter the arguments or the lies. We don't need someone to channel our outrage: we can do it for ourselves. This could have never happened in the analogue age of mass media – or at least not in public. Twitter is – for all its limitations in character length – a perfect example of peer-to-peer communication. Like mass media it is broadcast, live, throughout the world to millions. Unlike the one-way transmissions of the past, people can answer back. Twentieth-century communications were mainly one-way channels. Twitter, like so many of the best new media innovations, has created a two-way channel. It doesn't make us better people in terms of content – in fact we can be offensive and nasty as ever. But in terms of form, it adds a communication protocol deeper into our psyches – a two-way protocol. It has helped to remind us of an old truth we almost forgot in the broadcast age: that free speech is not the monologue of the megaphone, but a dialogue.

Just one example of this occurred between Murdoch and Martin Hickman, the co-author of *Dial M for Murdoch*, in July 2012. Soon after the former editor of *The Sunday Times* submitted his evidence to the Leveson Inquiry, Hickman tweeted: 'Heartily recommend Andrew Neil's evidence to #Leveson for a pithy summary of Rupert Murdoch's influence on UK politics.' Within minutes, Murdoch replied: '@martin_hickman anyone taking any notice of Andrew Neil on me is an idiot. Neil treated bestof all ex-employes now shows true colors.'

It's a marvel of the online world that the public can watch a debate – even in 140 characters – between the CEO of News Corp and one of his most trenchant critics. It is also a credit to Murdoch that he should drop the one-way megaphone for the to and fro of Twitter. He clearly prefers it.

Of course, tweeting and blogging can promote the worst of human speech acts – the prevalence of trolling, either on a personal or a racist or sexist basis makes many online forums virtually unusable at times. This is what John Gabriel has dubbed the Greater Internet Dickwad Theory and can be expressed in a very simple equation:

$$\text{Internet} + \text{Audience} + \text{Anonymity} = \text{Dickwad}$$

Even the pioneers of online political blogging can find the dialogic equality of new media difficult. During education secretary Michael Gove's appearance at the Leveson Inquiry, Paul Staines (aka Guido Fawkes) tweeted that Gove was the only person standing up for a free press. I tweeted back a counter argument and Staines's comeback was deeply edifying: '@peterjukes You are too stupid to be allowed internet access.' He subsequently deleted the tweet, but blocked me from any further interactions with him.

Free speech can be hard to master, even by those who vaunt it the loudest.

Compared with the genteel manicured pages of the *Financial Times*, comment sections and Twitter feeds are like an unruly urban wasteland, with general vandalism and graffiti and racist or misogynist trolls popping out from under railway bridges.

This unruliness itself is a source of creativity, like the unlicensed London Southwark in the late sixteenth century, where Shakespearean tragedy was born amid the brothels and bear-baiting pits; or the film business which began in porno peep shows and penny arcades; or indeed the modern press and the modern novel, which were created from the riot of absurd, scurrilous pamphleteering which occurred with the advent of the printing press. Out of marginalised forms of entertainment and gossip, new means of communication, even art, arise. Social media open up a direct channel between individuals in a way impossible only a few years ago: that communication will always result in conflict, but it also offers the resolution to it too. The fact that someone as powerful as Rupert Murdoch goes online and engages in argument is one of the most positive developments of the whole hacking scandal and the rise of new media. It holds out the hope in the power of dialogue: the human capacity to listen and perhaps to be persuaded and change one's mind.

After all, Rupert, your whole empire has been built on that promise.

FACTS ARE SACRED

The Russians got it wrong: it turns out there is truth in news and news in truth.

For all the fun of debate, the play of rhetoric and the art of controversy there is something beyond the mere exchange of subjective views in the media. Though more honoured in the breach rather than the observance, that fundamental separation of fact from comment underpins modern democracy. Though we might never reach any absolute truth, it absolutely matters whether this mushroom is poisonous or not, if the evidence of weapons of mass destruction is hard or soft or that the Holocaust was Adolf Hitler's planned policy. Our whole historical, legal and scientific system is based on that idea of truthfulness (and our journalism used to be too). A secular information-based economy is founded on the availability of accurate evidence and verifiable statements that subject themselves to proof. Comment is free but facts are sacred.

This book has been a sample of the history of Rupert Murdoch's career in the media and – without conducting an exhaustive cost–benefit analysis – it has tried to audit some of the promises and premises of his extraordinary career. By his own standards, News Corp and News International have often failed their stated core purpose – i.e. delivering the news – and there are many examples of them proving to be 'not fit' in this regard. For nearly a decade after Milly Dowler's phone was hacked, News International became an anti-news organisation: in Northcliffe's terms suppressing something it didn't want others to know. The parent company, News Corp, charged with governance and oversight, failed in their remit. As for the company's Chair and CEO of the holding company, Murdoch set his own test to be measured by:

> We have more responsibility than power I think. The newspaper can cre-
> ate great controversies, stir up a (unintelligible) in the community, discus-
> sion, throw light on injustices—just as it can do the opposite. It can hide
> things, and be a great power for evil.

('WHO'S AFRAID OF RUPERT MURDOCH?', 1981)

Thanks to Murdoch's appearance before Parliament on 19 July 2011 and the subsequent disclosures of the Leveson Inquiry, this record has been subject to intense cross questioning and interrogation in a court of law. Sworn affidavits have now taken the place of newspaper columns, internet blogs and volumes of biography. We now have competing testimonies to judge Murdoch's claims at face value.

Of the many forceful remarks Murdoch has made during his half century career there are two declarations, made under oath at the Royal Courts of Justice, that ring out as emphatic and important to him. When he appeared before Lord Justice Brian Leveson in April 2012, Murdoch was unequivocal about how he separated politics and business: he was shocked that other papers used their editorial positions to advance their commercial interests ('We have never pushed our commercial interests in our newspapers') and that he had never intervened in the British political process: 'I've never asked a prime minister for anything!'

In the calm atmosphere of Court 73, outside the partisan thunderdome of the press, these assertions were then subject to some quite intensive scrutiny.

Of the five prime ministers who have governed Great Britain since Murdoch achieved dominance in Fleet Street in 1981, only four could attend the hearings (the fifth, Margaret Thatcher, was too ill). Their evidence, supported by statements from other senior figures, has cast doubt on these two closely-related assertions.

Andrew Neil, who was one of Murdoch's key lieutenants throughout most of Thatcher's rule, sets the scene in his written submission, where he wonders if Murdoch 'had forgotten he was testifying under oath' when he claimed he had never asked politicians for anything:

> In the run up to the Wapping dispute he made it clear to me one night in late 1985 in my office that he had gone to Mrs Thatcher to get her assurance – to 'square Thatcher' in his words – that enough police would be made available to allow him to get his papers out past the massed pickets at Wapping once the dispute got underway. She was fully 'squared', he reported: she had given him assurances on the grounds that she was doing no more than upholding the right of his company to go about its lawful business. I remember this because he added that he could never have got the same assurances from the Mayor of New York or the NYPD, which was why, he told me, he could not 'do a Wapping' on his US newspapers, despite the grip of the print unions there too.

(NEIL, 2012)

Sir John Major, who succeeded Thatcher as prime minister in 1990, claimed Murdoch had told him that News International would only support the Conservative leader if he took a tougher line on the European Union. '[I]t became apparent in discussion that Mr Murdoch said that he really didn't like our European policies … and he wished me to change our European policies,' Major told the Inquiry. 'If we couldn't … his paper could not and would not support the Conservative government' (Major, 2012). True to his alleged word – Murdoch's papers turned viciously on Major and supported New Labour at the next election.

Major's successor, Tony Blair, denied any explicit or implicit deal with the media mogul had ever been made. Just a few weeks later, however, Blair's close adviser and chief press spokesman, Alastair Campbell, published another volume of his diaries and described one of Murdoch's several phone calls to the prime minister on the eve of the Iraq invasion in 2003. 'Both TB [Tony Blair] and I felt it was prompted by Washington,' Campbell wrote in *The Burden of Power*, 'and another example of their over-crude diplomacy.' Murdoch was urging Blair to make a swifter commitment to an Iraq invasion, while the prime minister was still waiting for a UN resolution and a potentially fateful vote in the House of Commons which could have toppled the Labour government. The next day Campbell added, 'TB felt the Murdoch call was odd, not very clever.' If asking a prime minster to speed up an invasion of a foreign country isn't 'asking for something', it's hard to imagine what is.

Gordon Brown's testimony was an even more incriminating as he alleged that News International's support for his premiership in the run-up to the 2010 election was conditional on acquiescing to News Corp's commercial interests. Brown produced a Labour Research document that correlated James Murdoch's demands for the abolition of the broadcast regulator Ofcom and a reduction in subsidy towards the BBC and the media policies adopted by the opposition Conservative party, led by Cameron. However, with no direct evidence that the Conservatives knew about James Murdoch's plan to takeover BSkyB, since the bid was only launched in June 2010 after the coalition government was in place, the suggestion of political support in return for commercial collusion was circumstantial. It left Prime Minister David Cameron and his chancellor George Osborne the space – despite the astonishing volume of contact between them and senior News Corp figures over the previous five years – to dismiss the allegations as 'utter nonsense' and 'pure fantasy'.

However, the deputy prime minister in the coalition government, Nick Clegg, finally swung the balance against Murdoch and indissolubly connected the quid pro quo of favourable editorials with the BSkyB bid. Another senior Liberal democrat minister, Vince Cable, had previously told the Inquiry that News International had threatened to 'do over' the Lib Dems if they didn't accede to the Rubicon plan, though he wouldn't name names. When quizzed on this, Clegg supported Cable and named names: 'Norman Lamb, a friend and a colleague of mine, a Liberal Democrat MP had been told … it would be good for the Liberal Democrats to be open to the bid, otherwise we would expect no favourable treatment from the Murdoch press and Norman was quite agitated about that,' Clegg told Lord Justice Leveson.

Two weeks later Lamb, a political adviser to the deputy prime minister, took the stand and produced contemporaneous notes of a meeting with the chief European lobbyist for News Corp, Frédéric Michel. During that meeting, Lamb alleges that Michel told him that the Lib Dems could expect to receive far less favourable coverage, especially in the *Sun*, if they failed to support the BSkyB bid. 'It was brazen,' Lamb noted at the time. 'VC (Vince Cable) refers case to Ofcom—they turn nasty.'

The evidence is overwhelming: one proprietor, five prime ministers, five refutations – *Rupert, J'accuse…!*

It could not be more clear-cut: you made a declaration of non-intervention, only to be countered by testimonies of three living prime ministers. You made a protestation that your commercial interests never affected your newspaper coverage and that is completely contradicted by one of your most senior former editors and a senior News Corp lobbyist, a man who you have not yet fired for representing you.

If these – some of your most vociferous statements on oath – can be contradicted by so many others as misleading and incorrect, how many more of your more qualified statements are credible? Are there many more lies that have still to be exposed?

Yet there is another explanation beyond conscious mendacity: a scarier but equally plausible argument that you're not deceiving us, but deceiving yourself.

'Wilful blindness', the term carefully inserted into the DCMS report on phone hacking in early 2012, is an important indicator of moral and legal responsibility. We may never demonstrate beyond a reasonable doubt that Murdoch or his son knew about their employees' phone or computer hacking and condoned other forms of bribery and corruption by way of a nod and a wink, but neither intention, nor provable knowledge is the ultimate standard here. In terms of corporate governance, of the responsibilities attributed to those who have great corporate power and wealth (often with other people's money) there is another standard, spelt out by Judge Simeon Lake in the Enron Judgement:

> You may find that a defendant had knowledge of a fact if you find that the defendant deliberately closed his eyes to what would otherwise have been obvious to him. Knowledge can be inferred if the defendant deliberately blinded himself to the existence of a fact.

(HEFFERNAN, 2011)

Wisdom has been defined as knowing that you don't know something and inquiry begins when you seek to fill that void with more information. That is the essence of all good journalism and our exaltation of the free press as the oxygen of democracy. This is the standard Murdoch himself has set his outlets many times over his fifty-year ascension: to probe, investigate and disclosure, despite social discomfiture and invasiveness. In the end, he failed to investigate himself.

However, through those decades, he was enabled by us. Murdoch's power has only accrued by our sitting back and doing nothing. To accuse him of wilful blindness makes no sense without our own complicity and myopia. Our elected representatives and public officials, focused on our democratic tastes, were convinced that we were captivated by his logic and became too scared to take him on. We, the people, misled by those who were supposed to inform us; unprotected by those we entrust to look after our national interest; beguiled by the cruel humour of his headlines and diverted by the daily spectacle of scandals, allowed ourselves to be blind. When we fought back, it was with the same weapons of personal attack and partisan spin, so that the net effect of the defence was more cynicism, a game which his newspapers could always beat us at. So we walked away, indifferent, only to find the power and influence spread further behind the scenes than we could have imagined. We gave up our brains, our heart and courage and only came to our senses just in time when the curtain was pulled away and we saw through the noise and smoke to the wizard pulling the levers.

Had Murdoch's dynastic monopoly power been bequeathed to his children and extended from print to broadcast to the digital domain, the hacking scandal and corruption of public officials would not only have been suppressed, there's every indication these kinds of practices would have proliferated in the competitive frenzy of new media and convergence. That is nothing to do with the character of James Murdoch and his generation, but the hard realities of unchecked power which inevitably lead to abuse.

If News Corp's Rubicon process had succeeded, the Murdoch family would be much more powerful in Britain than Berlusconi in Italy and with the added protection of not even being citizens of the country they dominated. Britain would have just been one of the many provinces of these absentee landlords and their corporate power – both actively and by default – might have jeopardised free speech. To have access to the airwaves, to get your voice heard, to become a successful politician or have your policy passed, would require the permission of this dynasty in some way or another. Maybe you'd get to meet a courtier or maybe just a consul or commissioner to approve. But the real decisions would be made somewhere in the air, in that far flung imperium which is News Corp nation, hovering between Hong Kong, Los Angeles, Sydney or New York.

Members of the family would visit us occasionally, maybe to advise or congratulate our legislators or tax officials. Maybe they would open a school or a new newspaper or give a speech in Edinburgh. Their progress around the country would be accompanied by choruses of paid retainers singing paeans to freedom of speech and global liberty. And we would bring gifts to lay at their feet, tributes for infotainment, first view films, rising share prices and the latest gossip. And we would pave the road of our own serfdom through monthly subscriptions. And we would have no one to blame but ourselves.

Leveson Amnesia

My colleague Chris Brace has compiled a graph of what Harold Evans has called 'festival of forgetfulness' of many of the key respondents of the first three modules of the Leveson Inquiry. The winners are: in first place Adam Smith; in second Andy Coulson; James Murdoch and David Cameron basically tied for third place.

% of Not Remembered

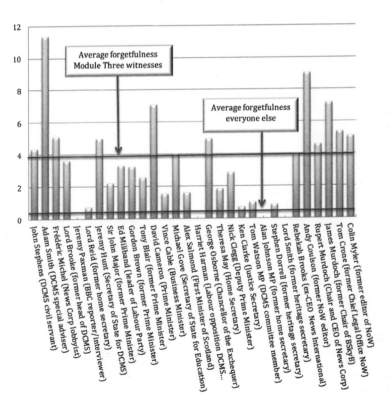

As Brace explains, his preliminary analysis of the evidence by speakers at the Leveson Inquiry shows some interesting deviations from the standard.

1. In the whole of module one, there were around 17,000 questions asked by the various lawyers and Lord Leveson. In reply witnesses failed to remember only on 54 occasions, less than the total number of times Adam Smith managed to fail to remember in his sessions. In percentage terms module one witnesses had memory problems with 0.3 per cent of questions 1/10 of the rate of module three witnesses, 1/19 of employees of News International and 1/22 of those people involved in the Jeremy Hunt decision.

2. The memory of the average witness failed in roughly half of 1 per cent of their replies. However, with politicians and senior employees of News International, the amnesia increases drastically.

3. Politicians in general average just over 3 per cent memory loss: perhaps they should eat more carrots.

4. The average percentage of forgetfulness for senior News Corp executives was even worse at 5.8 per cent.

5. Further dividing this down, there seems to be a critical line at 4 per cent. Anyone involved in Jeremy Hunt's oversight of the BSkyB bid on the government side (post Vince Cable) or employed as a senior News Corp executive scores displayed an amnesia factor around 5.9 per cent, nearly four times greater than those not involved.

6. Moreover government ministers and staff who gave evidence on Jeremy Hunt's dealings with the BskyB deal averaged a massive 6.6 per cent memory loss – the highest of all.

7. It may be argued that government ministers had harder questions than other witnesses, but it should also be taken into account that the events they were questioned over were some of the most recent of those under investigation by the Inquiry – i.e. no more than a year. The events discussed should have been very fresh in witnesses' minds.

Conclusion: being a politician is bad for your memory. Working for News International or dealing with them as a politician is particularly prone to induce forgetfulness. Involvement in the BSkyB bid induces dangerous memory loss.

Arrests

An updated version of the comprehensive list of arrests related to phone hacking and corruption can be found on Wikipedia as of June 2012:

> *This is a chronological listing of individuals charged or arrested in conjunction with the illegal acquisition of confidential information by employees and other agents of news media companies referred to as the 'phone hacking scandal'. Dates indicate approximately when arrests were made. The Met investigation ('Operation') under which arrests were made are shown in parentheses.*
>
> (ARRESTS, 2012)

1. Thurlbeck, Neville (1999) arrested for allegedly bribing a police officer and for conspiracy. Prosecution alleged Thurlbeck paid Detective Con Farmer to supply information on people whose details were kept on a confidential police computer. Both were tried in 2000 and acquitted when the judge directed the verdict due to lack of evidence. Arrested again (5 April 2011); chief reporter at *News of the World*; suspicion of unlawfully intercepting mobile phone voicemail messages (Weeting).
2. Boyall, John (2004) private investigator.
3. Whittamore, Steve (2004) private investigator.
4. King, Alan (2004) retired police officer.
5. Marshall, Paul (2004) former civilian communications officer.
6. Gunning, John (2005) private investigator.
7. Dewse, Christopher (2005) private investigator.
8. Maskell, Mark (2005) private investigator.
9. Lyle, Andrew (2005) private investigator.
10. Jones, Paul (2005) private investigator.
11. Jones, Taff (2005) private investigator.
12. Goodman, Clive (8 August 2006 and 8 July 2011) former royal corr
13. spondent for *News of the World*; suspicion of corruption (Elveden).
14. Mulcaire, Glenn (8 August 2006) private investigator; arrested again (7 December 2011) on suspicion of attempting to pervert the course of justice (Weeting).

15.   Craig, David (August 2006) editor of the Weekly News.

16.   Edmondson, Ian (5 April 2011) former news editor at *News of the World*; suspicion of conspiring to intercept communications and unlawful interception of voicemail messages (Weeting).

17.   Weatherup, James (14 April 2011) assistant news editor at *News of the World* arrested on suspicion of unlawfully intercepting communications (Weeting).

18.   Taras, Terenia (23 June 2011) freelance journalist who contributed stories to *News of the World*; suspicion of conspiring to intercept communications (Weeting).

19.   Elston, Laura (27 June 2011) worked for the Press Association as royal correspondent; arrested on suspicion of phone hacking (Weeting).

20.   Coulson, Andy (8 July 2011) former Chief Press Secretary to David Cameron and former *News of the World* editor; suspicion of conspiring to intercept communications (Weeting and Elveden).

21.   63-year-old man (8 July 2011) arrested and bailed. Arrested 'on suspicion of corruption allegations contrary to Section 1 of the Prevention of Corruption Act 1906' (Weeting and Elveden).

22.   Wallis, Neil (14 July 2011) former *News of the World* executive editor; taken for questioning on suspicion of conspiring to intercept communications (Weeting).

23.   Brooks, Rebekah (17 July 2011) former CEO of News International, former editor of the *Sun* and former editor for *News of the World*; suspicion of conspiring to intercept communications and on suspicion of corruption, i.e., illegal payments to police; arrested again (13 March 2012), this time on suspicion of perverting the course of justice (Weeting and Elveden).

24.   Kuttner, Stuart (2 August 2011) former managing editor of *News of the World*; suspicion of conspiring to intercept communications and on suspicion of corruption (Weeting and Elveden).

25.   Miskiw, Greg (10 August 2011) former *News of the World* news editor; suspicion of unlawful interception of communications and conspiring to intercept communications (Weeting).

26.   Desborough, James (18 August 2011) former *News of the World* Los Angeles-based, Hollywood US editor; suspicion of conspiring to intercept communications, contrary to section 1 (1) of the Criminal Law Act 1977 (Weeting).

27.   Evans, Dan (19 August 2011) former reporter for *News of the World* arrested on suspicion of phone hacking (Weeting).

28. 51-year-old man (19 August 2011) police detective at Metropolitan Police Service; 'on suspicion of misconduct in public office over alleged unauthorised leaks from the Operation Weeting phone-hacking inquiry.' Has not been charged but has been suspended.

29. Hall, Ross (2 September 2011) aka Ross Hindley, former reporter for *News of the World* who reportedly transcribed hacked voicemails included in the 'For Neville' email. Arrested 'on suspicion of conspiracy to intercept voicemail messages and perverting the course of justice' (Weeting).

30. Simons, Raoul (7 September 2011) deputy football editor of *The Times*, 'on suspicion of conspiracy to intercept voicemail messages, contrary to Section 1 (1) Criminal Law Act 1977' (Weeting).

31. Pyatt, Jamie (4 November 2011) district editor of the *Sun*; arrested in conjunction with Operation Elveden 'on suspicion of corruption allegations in contravention of section 1 of the Prevention of Corruption Act 1906' (Elveden).

32. 52-year-old man (24 November 2011) arrested regarding alleged computer hacking by the press (Tuleta).

33. Usher, Bethany (30 November 2011) Former journalist with *News of the World* on suspicion of intercepting voicemail messages. Cleared and released with Scotland Yard saying no further action would be taken (Weeting).

34. Panton, Lucy (15 December 2011) former crime editor of *News of the World* believed to have been arrested in relation to alleged payments to police officers (Elveden).

35. 52-year-old woman (21 December 2011) serving police officer, believed to be a royal protection officer arrested regarding possibly receiving payments from journalists (Elveden).

36. Carter, Cheryl (6 January 2012) personal assistant to former News International chief executive Rebekah Brooks; arrested in relation to phone hacking on suspicion of attempting to pervert the course of justice (Weeting).

37. 29-year-old man (28 January 2012) a police officer arrested on suspicion of corruption, aiding and abetting misconduct in a public office and conspiracy (Elveden).

38. Sullivan, Mike (28 January 2012) crime editor of the *Sun*; arrested on suspicion of corruption, aiding and abetting misconduct in a public office and conspiracy (Elveden).

39. Dudman, Graham former managing editor of the *Sun* arrested on suspicion of corruption, aiding and abetting misconduct in public office and conspiracy (Elveden).

40. Shanahan, Fergus (28 January 2012) executive editor of the *Sun* arrested on suspicion of corruption, aiding and abetting misconduct in a public office and conspiracy (Elveden).

41. Pharo, Chris (28 January 2012) news desk executive of the *Sun* arrested on suspicion of corruption, aiding and abetting misconduct in a public office and conspiracy (Elveden).

42. Webster, Geoff (11 February 2012) deputy editor of the *Sun* arrested on suspicion of corruption, aiding and abetting misconduct in a public office and conspiracy (Elveden).

43. Kay, John (11 February 2012) chief reporter of the *Sun* arrested on suspicion of corruption, aiding and abetting misconduct in a public office and conspiracy (Elveden).

44. Edwards, John (11 February 2012) picture editor of the *Sun* arrested on suspicion of corruption, aiding and abetting misconduct in a public office and conspiracy (Elveden).

45. Parker, Nick (11 February 2012) chief foreign correspondent for the *Sun* arrested on suspicion of corruption, aiding and abetting misconduct in a public office and conspiracy (Elveden).

46. Sturgis, John (11 February 2012) deputy news editor of the *Sun* arrested on suspicion of corruption, aiding and abetting misconduct in a public office and conspiracy (Elveden).

47. 39-year-old man (11 February 2012) police officer from the Surrey police force arrested on suspicion of corruption, aiding and abetting misconduct in a public office and conspiracy (Elveden).

48. 39-year-old man (11 February 2012) employee at the Ministry of Defence arrested on suspicion of corruption, misconduct in a public office and conspiracy (Elveden).

49. 36-year-old man (11 February 2012) member of the armed forces arrested on suspicion of corruption, misconduct in a public office and conspiracy (Elveden).

50. Brooks, Charlie (13 March 2012) husband of Rebekah Brooks believed to have been arrested on suspicion of perverting the course of justice (Weeting).

51. 39-year-old man (13 March 2012) Hampshire man arrested on suspicion of perverting the course of justice (Weeting).

52. 46-year-old man (13 March 2012) West London man arrested on suspicion of perverting the course of justice (Weeting).

53. 38-year-old man (13 March 2012) Hertfordshire man arrested on suspicion of perverting the course of justice (Weeting).

54. 48-year-old man (13 March 2012) East London man arrested on suspicion of perverting the course of justice (Weeting).

55. Larcombe, Duncan (19 April 2012) royal editor of the *Sun* arrested on suspicion of conspiracy to corrupt and to cause misconduct in public office (Elveden).

56. 42-year-old man (19 April 2012) former member of the Armed Forces arrested on suspicion of misconduct in public office (Elveden).

57. 38-year-old woman (19 April 2012) arrested on suspicion of aiding and abetting misconduct in public office (Elveden).

58. 57-year-old (3 May 2012) retired officer from Scotland Yard's Specialist Operations command, with responsibilities including protecting members of the royal family and countering terror operations, arrested on suspicion of misconduct in public office (Elveden).

59. 50-year-old man (15 May 2012) employee of HM Revenue and Customs (Elveden).

60. 43-year-old woman (15 May 2012) from same address as 50-year-old man arrested on same day (Elveden).

61. 37-year-old woman (25 May 2012) News International journalist by appointment at Bromley police station (Elveden).

62. 40-year-old man (14 June 2012) former employee of the prison service arrested in Corby on suspicion of corruption, misconduct in a public office and money laundering (Elveden).

63. 37-year-old woman (14 June 2012) also arrested at home in Corby, on suspicion of aiding and abetting misconduct in a public office and money laundering (Elveden).

64. 31-year-old man (14 June 2012) arrested in Croydon on suspicion of conspiracy to corrupt and conspiracy to cause misconduct in a public office (Elveden)

65. 31-year-old man (28 June 2012) former nurse at Broadmoor secure psychiatric hospital, arrested in Uxbridge on suspicion of conspiracy to corrupt and conspiracy to cause misconduct in a public office (Elveden).

66. 46-year-old man (4 July 2012) a prison officer arrested in south-east London on suspicion of conspiracy to commit bribery and conspiracy to cause misconduct in a public office (Elveden).

67. 37-year-old man (4 July 2012) a former *Daily Mirror* reported arrested in Morden, Surrey, south-east London on suspicion of corruption, on conspiracy to corrupt and conspiracy to cause misconduct in a public office (Elveden).

68. 50-year-old woman (4 July 2012) arrested in Kent on suspicion of corruption, on conspiracy to corrupt and conspiracy to cause misconduct in a public office (Elveden).

69. Penrose, Justin (11 July 2012) crime correspondent for the *Sunday Mirror* arrested in Kent on suspicion of corruption and conspiracy to cause misconduct in a public office (Elveden).

70. Savage, Tom (11 July 2012) deputy news editor of the *Daily Star Sunday* arrested in south-east London on suspicion of corruption and conspiracy to cause misconduct in a public office (Elveden).

71. 55-year-old man (13 July 2012) arrested in Cardiff on suspicion of committing offences under the Computer Misuse Act 1990 and Regulation of Investigatory Powers Act (Tuleta).

72. Phillips, Rhodri (19 July 2012) reporter at the *Sun* arrested in north London on suspicion of handling stolen goods (Tuleta).

Acknowledgements

First off, I'd like to thank the internet. Without its depth, range and immediacy, I would never have been able to drill down into all those news sources and quotations in the six months it took to write this book: to trawl through newspaper cuttings libraries and archives would have taken an eternity. So though I raise concerns about the power of Google, I still couldn't have written this book without you. Cheers.

Many other virtual personas lay behind the creation of this book. I would have never have got back into the groove of non-fiction, or the politicised world of online debate and fact checking, without having found a lively bunch of kindred in the US, mainly on MYDD during the 2008 Primary Wars of the Obama Campaign. Kudos and love particularly to my fellow founders and writers on the *Motley Moose*: Blasky, Gandalf, Kysen, Sricki, Fogiv, Spacemanspiff, Strummerson, Appleby, Virginislandguy, HappyinVT et al: you know who you really are.

With the support of my fellow Mooq, I felt more emboldened to enter the roaring forum of 'the Great Orange Satan', also known as Daily Kos. Markos Moulitsas's phenomenally successful community blog not only gave me the chance to speak to a wider audience, but it also supplied a noble band of 'Murdochgate' investigators under the FOTHOM tag. Forgive me if I miss anyone out but I'm indebted to: ericlewis0, Ceebs, BlueStateRedhead, AnnetteK, Mnemosyne, glitterscale, KenBee, Lib Dem FoP greenbird, Unenergy, blue aardvark, grapeshot, Creosote, Vinnie Vegas, Larsstephens, translatorpro, Word Alchemy, Vatexia, cotterperson, beancounter, dances with beagles, jimstaro, dweb8231 and many others too numerous to mention.

Two of my fellow Kossacks have since become completely indispensable to this book. Hélène Lipstadt's keen eye, historical knowledge and constant interrogation of the more questionable parts of my text, kept me honest and my prose less rambling. Chris Brace has been like a one-man reconnaissance unit, providing advance warning of breaking news as well of analysis of contradictory statements and factual details others completely missed. His brilliant database on the Leveson Inquiry will be invaluable for years to come.

I've been hard on the worst of journalism in this book, but perversely I've met many of the best in the process of writing it, all of whom make me doubly regret I didn't join their ranks many years ago. I'd like to thank James Hanning,

Martin Hickman, Peter Kellner, Heather Brooke, Siân Kevill, Brian Cathcart, Deborah Orr, Michael Wolff, Neil Chenoweth, Richard Peppiatt and David Aaronovitch for all their kindness and tolerance. Jonathan Heawood, Claire Enders, Edyta Zalewska and Lara Carmona also added insight and expertise. Many contributed comments and corrections often under great time pressure, though it should be said they did not always endorse my opinions and any remaining factual errors are entirely my own. There are also several unnamed sources who I can only thank privately. A special word of thanks to Newsweek's London correspondent, Mike Giglio, and Foreign Editor, Louise Roug, for trying to teach me what real journalism is about. The fact I got to correspond with and eventually meet Sir Harry Evans, who unwittingly had such an influence on my formative years, made the writing of this book worthwhile before I'd even finished. Hats off to you, Sir.

Two special thanks go to two direct victims of this story: Alastair Morgan and Richard Horton.

Though it's bad form to thank your publishers or editors in acknowledgements, Unbound is such a unique and unconventional form of publication I feel honour-bound to break that rule and thank the 'Mayor of Little Italy' John Mitchinson for having faith in me in the first place and Dan Kieran and Justin Pollard for being so easily fooled.

If Tony Judt was still around, I would thank him for encouraging me to return to non-fiction and to always try for the most difficult and complex topics. It was at a memorial at King's College Cambridge attended by Tony's father, his former collaborator Jair Kessler, his wife Jennifer Homans and his sons Daniel and Nicholas, gave me heart and inspiration to carry on with this endeavour.

When it comes to family matters my children Alexander and Katherine have not only tolerated their father's obsessions and mental absences, but also reminded him that we have a wise, witty and kind generation to come, who are unlikely to repeat our mistakes – especially if they find out about them.

Where we fell, may they fly.

BIBLIOGRAPHY

A Point of View: Power of the Press (2012) BBC Radio 4, presented by David Cannadine, 16 March. Available at: http://www.bbc.co.uk/programmes/b01d5r25#programme-broadcasts.

Alterman, E. (2011) 'How Rupert Murdoch buys friends and influences people', *The Nation*, 10 August [Online]. Available at: http://www.thenation.com/article/162670/how-rupert-murdoch-buys-friends-and-influences-people.

Alterman, E. (2012) 'Think again: Murdoch "unfit?" ya think?', *Center for American Progress*, 3 May. Available at: http://www.americanprogress.org/issues/2012/05/ta050312.html.

Andrews, A. (2009) 'James Murdoch targets BBC "land-grabbing"', *Telegraph*, 28 August [Online]. Available at http://www.telegraph.co.uk/finance/6107233/James-Murdoch-targets-BBC-land-grabbing.html.

'Arrests' (2012) *Wikipedia*. Available at: http://en.wikipedia.org/wiki/Phone_hacking_scandal_reference_lists#Arrests.

Bakunin, M. (1971) *Bakunin on Anarchy*, translated and edited by Sam Dolgoff, Vintage Books.

Barrett, W. (2011) 'Rudy's cozy Murdoch ties', *Daily Beast*, 21 July. Available at: http://www.thedailybeast.com/articles/2011/07/21/rupert-murdoch-scandal-rudy-giuliani-s-ties-to-news-corp.html.

BBC News (2011) *Transcript of Nick Clegg interview*. Available at: http://news.bbc.co.uk/1/hi/programmes/andrew_marr_show/9540688.stm.

Bennett, D. and Townend, J. (2012) 'Press "omerta": how newspapers' failure to report the phone hacking scandal exposed the limitations of media accountability', in Keeble, R. L. and Mair, J. (eds) *The Phone Hacking Scandal: Journalism on Trial*, Suffolk: Abramis Academic Publishing.

Bernstein, C. (2011) 'Murdoch's Watergate?', *Daily Beast*, 9 July. Available at: http://www.thedailybeast.com/newsweek/2011/07/10/murdoch-s-watergate.html.

The Big Questions (2012) BBC One Television, 27 February.

Blodget, H. (2012) 'Don't mean to be alarmist, but the TV business may be starting to collapse', *Business Insider*, 3 June [Online]. Available at: http://www.businessinsider.com/tv-business-collapse-2012-6.

Boehlert, E. (2012) 'The self-destruction of Limbaugh, Murdoch and Beck',

Media Matters, 9 March. Available at: http://mediamatters.org/blog/2012/03/09/the-self-destruction-of-limbaugh-murdoch-and-be/185562.

British–American Project (2010) *News in a Digital Age*, 17–18 June. London: Chatham House Rule.

Brown, G. (2012) Oral evidence to the Leveson Inquiry. Available at: http://www.levesoninquiry.org.uk/wp-content/uploads/2012/06/Transcript-of-Morning-Hearing-11-June-2012.txt.

Burden, P. (2008) *News of the World?: Fake Sheikhs and Royal Trappings*, London: Eye Books.

Callus, G. (2011) 'Murdoch's critics are their own worst enemy', *Dale & Co.*, 28 June. Available at: http://www.iaindale.com/posts/murdochs-critics-are-their-own-worst-enemy.

Carr, D. and Arango, T. (2010) 'A Fox chief at the pinnacle of media and politics', *New York Times*, 9 January [Online]. Available at: http://www.nytimes.com/2010/01/10/business/media/10ailes.html?_r=3.

Carter, G. (ed) (2011) *Rupert Murdoch: The Master Mogul of Fleet Street*, Vanity Fair: Conde Nast.

Cathcart, B. (2012) 'Phone hacking victims deserve a monument to their courage', *Guardian*, 19 January [Online]. Available at: http://www.guardian.co.uk/commentisfree/2012/jan/19/phone-hacking-victims-monument-courage.

Chenoweth, N. (2001) *Virtual Murdoch: Reality Wars on the Information Highway*, London: Secker & Warburg.

Chippindale, P. and Horrie, C. (1990) *Stick it Up Your Punter!: The Uncut Story of the Sun Newspaper*, London: Simon & Schuster.

Coleridge, N. (1993) *Paper Tigers: Latest Greatest Newspaper Tycoons and How They Won the World*, London: Heinemann.

Curtis, S. (ed.) (1998–2000) *The Journals of Woodrow Wyatt*, London: Macmillan.

Dale, I. (2010) 'Coulson's accusers can go to hell', *Iain Dale's Diary*, 4 September. Available at: http://iaindale.blogspot.co.uk/2010/09/coulsons-accusers-can-go-to-hell.html?spref=tw.

Dale, I. (2011) 'Could Cameron be next?', *Dale & Co.*, 17 July. Available at: http://www.iaindale.com/posts/could-cameron-be-next.

d'Ancona, M. (2007) 'Tories back to school with clever Mr Coulson', *Telegraph*, 3 June [Online]. Available at: http://www.telegraph.co.uk/comment/3640327/Tories-back-to-school-with-clever-Mr-Coulson.html.

Davies, N. (2008) *Flat Earth News: An Award-winning Reporter Exposes Falsehood, Distortion and Propaganda in the Global Media*, London: Vintage.

Davies, N. (2010) 'Are Scotland Yard scared of Rupert Murdoch?', *Nick Davies: Journalism and Books*, 6 April. Available at: http://www.nickdavies.net/2010/04/06/are-scotland-yard-scared-of-rupert-murdoch/.

Davies, N. and Dodd, V. (2011) 'Murder trial collapse exposes News of the World links to police corruption', *Guardian*, 11 March [Online]. Available at: http://www.guardian.co.uk/media/2011/mar/11/news-of-the-world-police-corruption?intcmp=239.

Debrouwere, S. (2012) 'Fungible', *stdout.be*, 4 May. Available at: http://stdout.be/2012/05/04/fungible/.

Dodd, V. and Davies, N. (2012) 'Man convicted in conspiracy case also accused of hacking computer for NoW', *Guardian*, 20 February, [Online]. Available at: http://www.guardian.co.uk/technology/2012/feb/20/news-world-hacking-suspect-conspiracy?newsfeed=true.

Dover, B. (2008) *Rupert Murdoch's China Adventures: How the World's Most Powerful Media Mogul Lost a Fortune and Found a Wife*, Tuttle Publishing.

Elliott, F. and Hanning, J. (2012) *Cameron: Practically a Conservative, London*: Fourth Estate.

Ellison, S. (2011) 'Murdoch and the vicious circle', *Vanity Fair*, October [Online]. Available at: http://www.vanityfair.com/business/features/2011/10/murdoch-201110.

Evans, H. (2011) *Good Times, Bad Times*, Bedford Square Books.

Fallows, J. (2003) 'The age of Murdoch', *Atlantic Magazine*, September [Online]. Available at: http://www.theatlantic.com/magazine/archive/2003/09/the-age-of-murdoch/2777/?single_page=true.

FCPA Professor (2011) 'News Corp and the FCPA', 18 July. Available at: http://www.fcpaprofessor.com/news-corp-and-the-fcpa.

Financial Times (2011) *News International letter of apology*, 14 July. Available at: http://www.ft.com/cms/86624338-aef1-11e0-9310-00144feabdc0.pdf.

Fitzsimmons, J., Fong, J., Shere, D. and Theel, S. (2012) 'Fox News resumes perennial gas price charade', *Media Matters*, 16 February. Available at: http://mediamatters.org/research/2012/02/16/fox-news-resumes-perennial-gas-price-charade/184524.

Fowler, N. (2012) 'In the post-Murdoch era, we must reform media ownership', *Guardian*, 11 May [Online]. Available at: http://www.guardian.co.uk/commentisfree/2012/may/11/post-murdoch-reform-media-ownership.

Frontline (1995) 'Who's afraid of Rupert Murdoch?'. Available at: http://www.pbs.org/wgbh/pages/frontline/programs/transcripts/1404.html.

Fyfe, N. (1930) *Northcliffe: An Intimate Biography*, New York: Macmillan, p. 83.

Gleick, J. (2011) *The Information*, London: Fourth Estate.

Goldmann Rohm, W. (2002) *The Murdoch Mission: The Digital Transformation of a Media Empire*, New York: John Wiley & Sons.

Great Britain. Parliament. House of Commons (2012a) *Daily Hansard Debate*,

25 April [Online]. Available at: http://www.publications.parliament. uk/pa/cm201212/cmhansrd/cm120425/debtext/120425-0002.htm.

Great Britain. Parliament. House of Commons (2012b) *News International and Phone-hacking from the Culture, Media and Sport Committee*, Eleventh Report of Session 2012–12, vol. 1 [Online]. Available at: http://www.publi cations.parliament.uk/pa/cm201012/cmselect/cmcumeds/903/903i.pdf.

Green, D.A. (2012) 'The Nightjack case'. Interviewed by Peter Jukes, March.

Greenslade, R. (2007) 'Vote, vote, vote for Kelvin MacKenzie', *Guardian*, 28 February [Online]. Available at: http://www.guardian.co.uk/media/ greenslade/2007/feb/28/votevotevoteforkelvinmack.

Greenslade, R. (2009) 'Why all journalists should read Cudlipp's Publish and be Damned!', *Guardian*, 8 December [Online]. Available at: http://www.guardian.co.uk/media/greenslade/2009/dec/08/ daily-mirror-sundaymirror.

Groskop, V. (2010) 'David Yelland: "Rupert Murdoch is a closet liberal"', *LondonEvening Standard*, 29 March [Online]. Available at: http:// www.standard.co.uk/lifestyle/david-yelland-rupert-murdoch-is-a-closet-liberal-6732847.html.

Hames, J. (2012) Witness statement to Leveson Inquiry. Available at: http://www.levesoninquiry.org.uk/wp-content/uploads/2012/02/Witness-Statement-of-Jacqueline-Hames.pdf.

Harding, J. (2011) Witness statement to Leveson Inquiry, 14 October. Available at: http://www.levesoninquiry.org.uk/wp-content/uploads/2012/01/Witness-Statement-of-James-Harding.pdf.

Harris, R. (1983) *Gotcha!: The Media, the Government and the Falklands Crisis*, London: Faber and Faber.

Harris, R. (1986a) *Selling Hitler: The Story of the Hitler Diaries*, London: Faber and Faber.

Harris, R (1986b) 'Wapping Dispute', *Newsnight*, BBC, 1986.

Heffernan, M. (2011) *Wilful Blindness: Why we Ignore the Obvious at our Peril*, London: Simon & Schuster.

Helm, T., Doward, J. and Boffey, D. (2011) 'Rupert Murdoch's empire must be dismantled – Ed Miliband', *Guardian*, 16 July [Online]. Available at: http://www.guardian.co.uk/politics/2011/jul/16/rupert-murdoch-ed-miliband-phone-hacking.

Hencke, D. and Evans, R. (2008) 'Memo shows how Blair aided Murdoch', *Guardian*, 1 November [Online]. Available at: http://www.guardian. co.uk/politics/2008/nov/01/media-rupertmurdoch.

Hickman, M. (2012) 'Rupert Murdoch attacks "the English" as he rules out Sky bid',

Independent, 29 June [Online]. Available at: http://www.independent. co.uk/news/media/press/rupert-murdoch-attacks-the-english-as-he-rules-out-sky-bid-7897225.html.

HM Government (2011) *Prime Minister's press conference*, 8 July. Available at: http://www.number10.gov.uk/news/prime-ministers-press-conference/.

Holland, T. (2003), *Rubicon: The Triumph and Tragedy of the Roman Republic*, London: Abacus.

Horton, R. (2012) 'The Nightjack case'. Interviewed by Peter Jukes, 17 June.

Hurst, I. (2011) Oral evidence to the Leveson Inquiry. Available at: http://www. levesoninquiry.org.uk/wp-content/uploads/2011/11/transcript-of-Morning-Hearing-28-November-20111.txt.

Isaacson, W. (2011) *Steve Jobs: The Exclusive Biography*, London: Little, Brown.

Judt, T. and Snyder, T. (2012) *Thinking the Twentieth Century*, New York: Random House.

Jukes, P. (1991) *A Shout in the Street: An Excursion into the Modern City*, London: Faber and Faber.

Jukes, P. (2012a) 'Murdoch hacking scandal could go global, threaten News Corp.'s core TV business', *Daily Beast,* 28 March. Available at: http://www. thedailybeast.com/articles/2012/03/28/murdoch-hacking-scandal-could-go-global-threaten-news-corp-core-tv-business.html.

Jukes, P. (2012b) 'Rupert Murdoch's political trap', *Daily Beast*, 5 May. Available at: http://www.thedailybeast.com/articles/2012/05/05/rupert-murdoch-s-political-trap.html.

Kiernan, T. (1986) *Citizen Murdoch*, New York: Dodd, Mead & Co.

Kitty, A. (2005) *Outfoxed: Rupert Murdoch's War on Journalism*, New York: The Disinformation Company.

Klein, E. (1993) 'Paper lions', *Vanity Fair*, October, pp. 90–106.

Labour Party (2011) 'Sir Paul has taken a brave and honourable decision', 17 July. Available at: http://www.labour.org.uk/sir-paul-taken-brave-honourable-decision.

Lanchester, J. (2012) 'Marx at 193', *London Review of Books*, 34:7, 5 April. Available at: http://www.lrb.co.uk/v34/n07/john-lanchester/marx-at-193.

Lloyd, J. (2012) 'Murdoch diminished?', *Financial Times*, 5 May [Online]. Available at: http://www.ft.com/cms/s/2/2ab8d1f0-9456-11e1-bb47-00144feab49a. html#axzz1wLXPltcx.

McKnight, D. (2012) *Rupert Murdoch: An Investigation of Political Power*, London: Allen & Unwin.

McMullan, P. (2012) 'Brooks and Cameron out hacking'. Interviewed by Peter Jukes, March.

Major, J. (2012) Oral evidence to the Leveson Inquiry. Available at: http://www.levesoninquiry.org.uk/wp-content/uploads/2012/06/Transcript-of-Morning-Hearing-12-June-2012.txt.

Marr, D. (2012) 'The politics of news: David McKnight's "Rupert Murdoch: an investigation of power"', *The Monthly*, February [Online]. Available at: http://www.themonthly.com.au/david-mcknight-s-rupert-murdoch-investigation-power-politics-news-david-marr-4515.

Mellor, D. (2012) Witness statement to Leveson Inquiry. Available at: http://www.levesoninquiry.org.uk/wp-content/uploads/2012/06/Witness-Statement-David-Mellor.pdf.

Michel, F. and Smith, A. (2011) Emails submitted as witness exhibit to the Leveson Inquiry. Available at: http://www.levesoninquiry.org.uk/wp-content/uploads/2012/05/Exhibit-JH12-MOD300008035-MOD300008088-docs-524-550.pdf.

Morgan, A. (2012) 'Daniel Morgan murder'. Interviewed by Peter Jukes, March.

Morgan, P. (2005) *The Insider: The Private Diaries of a Scandalous Decade*, London: Ebury Press.

Morgan, T. and Marsden, S. (2012) 'Leveson Inquiry: John Yates faces champagne quiz', *Independent*, 1 March [Online]. Available at: http://www.independent.co.uk/news/media/press/leveson-inquiry-john-yates-faces-champagne-quiz-7467906.html.

Mulholland, H. (2012) 'Boris Johnson's former aide takes PR job with News International', *Guardian*, 20 May [Online]. Available at: http://www.guardian.co.uk/media/2012/may/20/boris-johnson-aide-news-international.

Munster, G. (1985) *Rupert Murdoch: A Paper Prince*, Melbourne: Viking.

Murdoch, J. (2009) *The Absence of Trust* [MacTaggart Lecture]. 28 August. Available at: http://image.guardian.co.uk/sys-files/Media/documents/2009/08/28/JamesMurdochMacTaggartLecture.pdf.

Murdoch, R. (2012a) *Twitter*, 4 February. Available at: https://twitter.com/rupertmurdoch/status/165933305810788352.

Murdoch, R. (2012b) *Twitter*, 14 February. Available at: https://twitter.com/rupertmurdoch/status/169598517856321536.

Murdoch, R. (2012c) *Twitter*, 19 February. Available at: https://twitter.com/rupertmurdoch/status/171170893064712192.

Murphy, J. (2011) 'Some MPs suspected a year ago but nobody would've believed it', *Standard*, 7 July [Online]. Available at: http://www.standard.co.uk/news/politics/some-mps-suspected-a-year-ago-but-nobody-wouldve-believed-it-6419561.html.

Myers, S. (2012) 'Monday reality check: journalism is being replaced by lots of non-journalistic things', *Poynter.*, 7 May. Available at: http://www.poynter.org/latest-news/mediawire/172970/monday-reality-check-journalism-is-being-replaced-by-lots-of-non-journalistic-things/.

Neil, A. (1996a) *Full Disclosure*, London: Macmillan.

Neil, A. (1996b) 'Murdoch and me', *Vanity Fair*, December [Online]. Available at: http://www.vanityfair.com/business/features/1996/12/rupert-murdoch-199612.

Neil, A. (2012) Witness statement to Leveson Inquiry. Available at: http://www.levesoninquiry.org.uk/wp-content/uploads/2012/07/Witness-statement-of-Andrew-Neil.pdf.

Oborne, P. (2010) 'Does David Cameron really need this tainted man beside him?', *Guardian*, 4 April [Online]. Available at: http://www.guardian.co.uk/commentisfree/2010/apr/04/david-cameron-andy-coulson-election.

Oborne, P. (2012) 'The Murdoch and News Corporation scandal wasn't about Conservative Party Sleaze – but it is now', *Telegraph*, 2 May [Online]. Available at: http://www.telegraph.co.uk/news/uknews/leveson-inquiry/9241162/The-Murdoch-and-News-Corporation-scandal-wasnt-about-Conservative-Party-sleaze-but-it-is-now.html.

O'Carroll, L. (2012a) 'Charlotte Church on phone hacking: "I don't plan to let this lie"', *Guardian*, 27 February [Online]. Available at: http://www.guardian.co.uk/media/2012/feb/27/charlotte-church-phone-hacking.

O'Carroll, L. (2012b) 'Times editor: statutory press regulation would lead to government controls', *Guardian*, 17 January [Online]. Available at: http://www.guardian.co.uk/media/2012/jan/17/times-editor-statutory-press-regulation.

Page, B. (2011) *The Murdoch Archipelago*, London: Simon & Schuster.

Pinker, S. (2011) *The Better Angels of our Nature: The Decline of Violence in History and its Causes*, London: Allen Lane.

Postman, N. (1985) *Amusing Ourselves to Death: Public Discourse in the Age of Show Business*, London: Penguin.

Press, E. (2012) *Beautiful Souls: Saying No, Breaking Ranks, and Heeding the Voice of Conscience in Dark Times*, New York: Farrar, Straus and Giroux.

Private Eye (2012) Issue 1313, 4 May.

Schell, J. (1976) *The Time of Illusion*, New York: Alfred A Knopf.

Senior BBC Source (2012) 'BBC budget 2010'. Interviewed by Peter Jukes, May.

Senior Labour Party source (2012) 'Background to Hackgate'. Interviewed by Peter Jukes, 10 April.

Senior News International source (2012) 'Rebekah Brooks'. Interviewed by Peter Jukes, March.

Senior *Times* journalist (2012) 'Nightjack outing'. Interviewed by Peter Jukes, March.

Sennett, R. (1986) *The Fall of Public Man*, London: Faber and Faber.

Serle, G. (1986) 'Murdoch, Sir Keith Arthur (1885–1952)', *Australian Dictionary of Biography, National Centre of Biography, Australian National University* [Online]. Available at: http://adb.anu.edu.au/biography/murdoch-sir-keith-arthur-7693.

Shawcross, W. (1992) *Murdoch: The Making of a Media Empire*, London: Simon & Schuster.

Snoddy, R. (1993) *The Good, the Bad and the Unacceptable: Hard News about the British Press*, London: Faber and Faber.

Stott, R. (2003) 'Murdoch's world', *Guardian*, 11 October [Online]. Available at: http://www.guardian.co.uk/books/2003/oct/11/highereducation.news3.

Streitfeld, D. and O'Brien, K. (2012) 'Google privacy inquiries get little cooperation', *New York Times*, 22 May [Online]. Available at: http://www.nytimes.com/2012/05/23/technology/google-privacy-inquiries-get-little-cooperation.html/?pagewanted=all.

Telegraph (2011a) 'Andy Coulson resignation: statement in full', *Telegraph*, 21 January [Online]. Available at: http://www.telegraph.co.uk/news/politics/8273751/Andy-Coulson-resignation-statement-in-full.html.

Telegraph (2011b) 'News of the World to close on Sunday, says James Murdoch', *Telegraph*, 7 July [Online]. Available at: http://www.telegraph.co.uk/news/uknews/phone-hacking/8623589/News-of-the-World-to-close-on-Sunday-says-James-Murdoch.html.

Telegraph (2011c) 'Phone hacking: Sir Paul Stephenson's resignation statement in full', *Telegraph*, 17 July [Online]. Available at: http://www.telegraph.co.uk/news/uknews/phone-hacking/8643975/Phone-hacking-Sir-Paul-Stephensons-resignation-statement-in-full.html.

Theroux, L. (2012) 'How the internet killed porn', *Guardian*, 5 June [Online]. Available at: http://www.guardian.co.uk/culture/2012/jun/05/how-internet-killed-porn.

Tucker, R.C. (ed.) (1978) *The Marx-Engels Reader*. Princeton.

Turner, T. (1996) '"60 Minutes" & commercial ad up to inadvertent laugh', *Daily News*, 27 February [Online]. Available at: http://articles.nydailynews.com/1996-02-27/entertainment/17997526_1_mary-e-schmidt-rupert-murdoch-national-press-club.

Watson, T. and Hickman, M. (2012) *Dial M for Murdoch: News Corporation and the Corruption of Britain*, London: Allen Lane.

'Who's Afraid of Rupert Murdoch?' (1981) *Panorama*, BBC One, 16 February.

Wilson, J.K. (1996) *Newt Gingrich: Capitol Crimes and Misdemeanors*, Maine: Common Courage Press.

Wolff, M. (2008) *The Man Who Owns the News: Inside the Secret World of Rupert Murdoch*, London: Bodley Head.

Wolff, M. (2012) 'Rupert Murdoch's Sun on Sunday sets on his empire', *Guardian*, 24 February [Online]. Available at: http://www.guardian.co.uk/commentisfree/cifamerica/2012/feb/24/rupert-murdoch-sunday-wsun-sets-empire?INTCMP=SRCH.

SUBSCRIBERS

Unbound is a new kind of publishing house. Our books are funded directly by readers. This was a very popular idea during the late eighteenth and early nineteenth century. Now we have revived it for the internet age. It allows authors to write the books they really want to write and readers to support the writing they would most like to see published.

The names listed below are of readers who have pledged their support and made this book happen. If you'd like to join them, visit: www.unbound.co.uk.

David Adler
Bruce Alcorn
John Allen
Robert Andrews
Dan Andrews
Martin Archer
Marc Armsby
Andrew Arnold
Sigrid Asmus
Michael Atkinson
Simon Austin
Paul Baldwin
Emory Baldwin
Katherine Baldwin
John Band
Hani Barghouthi
Arpinder Baryana
Kenny Beer
Joseph Bell
Andy Bentley
Jane Bentley
Dan Benton
Scott Berridge

Les Bessant
James Beston
Chris Bird
Linda Black
Edrie Blackwelder
Phil Blaney
Peter Bogg
Jennifer Bowden
Chris Brace
Phil Brachi
Debra Brackett
Alexandra Brito
Sheena and Paul Brockett
Aleksander Bromek
Joan Brooker
Joel Brown
Ste Brown
Kala Brownlee
Helen Buckingham
Laura Buddine
Katy Buss
Marcus Butcher
Richard Butchins

Ian Buxton
Ed Caesar
David Callier
Greg Callus
Clare Cambridge
Lysa Campbell
Richard Canning
Xander Cansell
Mark Carlisle
Derek Carrillo
Seth Chandler
Aaron Chandra
Peter Chapman
Hannah Charlton
John Clark
Paul Clarke
Robert Clements
Lisa Cohen
Stephen Colegrave
Liz Conlan
Ryan Conway
Lewis Cook
Edward Cook
Anthony Cooke
Jake Cox
Catherine Craddock
Andrew Craig
Ian Creamer
Dave Crennell
James Cridland
Matthew Cro
Saorcha Cuffe
Ruth Curtis
River Curtis-Stanley
J-F Cuvillier
Krzysztof Czyzewski

Geoff Dahl
Peter Dalling
Tash Daly
John Dausilio
Bruce Davidson
Brid Davis
Andrea Davis
Catherder Davis
Jon Davison
Marcos D'Cruze
Ryan Dearlove
Simon Denman
Vici Derrick
John Dexter
Ian Dickson
Alex Ding
Dionne Donnelly
Lawrence Doyle
Vikki Drummond
Christian Drury
Fintan Dudleston
Ian Dunn
Vivienne Dunstan
Juliana Dutra
David Edwards
David Ellis
Robert Ellis
Thor-Dale Elsson
Simon Enright
Christian Eriksen
Allyson Evans
Ginny Felton
Charles Fernyhough
Mau Fildes
William Fisher
Dakers Fleming

John Fogerty
Becky Foreman
Iain Forsyth
Christopher Fowler
Craig Francis
David Francis
Alan Freeman
Art Friendly
Jan Frohman Atallo
Jim Galbraith
Kenneth Gallaher
Ina Gallo
Jorge Garzon
Daniel James Gibbons
Simon Gibson
Cyrus Gilbert-Rolfe
Ian Gilhespy
Daniel Gochnauer
Howard Gooding
Linda Goodspeed
Dave Gorman
Laura Graf
Wade Graham
Carin Green
Kath Green
Rick Greene
Matthew Greybrook
Julie Gribble
Matthew Grice
Cathy Griffiths
John Grindrod
Dan Groenewald
Thorhalla Gudmundsdottir Beck
Katrina Gulliver
Eric Guy
Jelena Hadziosmanovic

Thomas Haenen
Christopher Haine
Nikki Hall
Shelley R Hamilton
Balls Hampton
Simon Hanks
Nick Harbourne
Mike Hardcastle
Ruth Harris
Jacqueline Hartnett
James Haskin
Graham Hassell
Jolyon Hedges
Lisa Henderson
Mark Henderson
Vicky Henly
Richard Hesketh
Diane Hewson
Martin Hickman
Stuart Higgins
E O Higgins
Matthew Hilton
Richard Hoare
Rebecca Holbourn
Iain Holder
Jill Hopkins
Stephen Hoppe
Matt Huggins
Suzanne Immerman
Johari Ismail
Marjorie Johns
Jessica Jones
Helen Jones
Daniel Jones
Russell Jones
Jackie Jukes

John Jukes
Haje Jan Kamps
Katspjamas
William Keane
Neil Kelleher
Roberta Kelm
Annette Kenlay
David Kernohan
Sian Kevill
Jan Kewley
Dan Kieran
Chloe King
Cara Louise King
Russ Kirkpatrick
Steve Kirtley
Matt Knight
Shelley Knight
Joseph Kondrot
Cheryl Krauss
Els Krusel
John Langton
Nic Lavroff
Craig Lawrence
Jimmy Leach
Stevie Lee
Mark Leiren-Young
Jack Lenox
Masha and Klim Levene
Jerrick Lim
Sheila Livingston
Serena Lloyd
James Lloyd
Alys Lougher
Alison Lowe
Magdeline Lum
Edie Lush

Tiger M
Ken MacLauchlan
Michael Maclay
Terri MacMillan
Andy MacRae
Maria Maguire
John Malone
Philippa Manasseh
Jose Luis Martinez
Andrew Matangi
Matthew May
Brendan May
Sophie McAllister
Michaela McCaffrey
Charles McCluer
Dan McCurry
Steven McKay
Malcolm Mckay
Stuart McKears
Gavin McKeown
Donna McLean
Virginia McLeod
Colin McMaster
Kevin McNally
Rob Medford
Malini Mehra
Nalini Meir
Deeivya Meir
Benjamin Melançon
Nick Mellish
Nicole Mezzasalma
Nicole Mickey
David Middleton
Richard Milligan
Margo Milne
Karen Mitchell

Ronald Mitchinson
John Mitchinson
Ken Monaghan
Stephanie Montilla
Lloyd Morgan
Paul Mortimer
Simon Murphy
Al Napp
Robert Naylor
Dagmar Nearpass
Allison Newbould
Rebecca Newman
Alex Newsome
Julie Niven
Lola Non
Sam North
Kathlene O'Brien
James O'Doherty
Maureen O'Doherty
Denny O'Fallon
Kaylene O'Neill
Erwin Oosterhoorn
Dana Oren
Dorothy Otnow Lewis
Stuart Owen
David Owen
Torsten Pagel
Wayne Palmer
Ernest Panychevskyy
Kevin Parker
Kevin Parr
Susan P Parris
Clive Peaple
Joel Pearce
Neil Pearce
Mary Peate

Reuben Philp
Ed Picton
Jonathan Pierpoint
Maxime Pons Webster
Hazel Potter
Stephen Potts
Brad Power
Robert Preece
Helen Purves
Alix Rabin
Paul Raymond
Colette Reap
David Rees
Kathryn Richards
Mark Richards
Chris Richards
Ben Rilot
Dave Rimmer
Laura Roberts
David Rosenthal
Catherine Rowlands
Joseph Ruffles
Cecilia Ryan
Georgina Rycyk
Nina Sabillon
Any Salyer
Sharon Salzberg
Sharon Salzberg
Lisa Sargood
S Sarkar
Gert Schepens
Andrew Scheuber
Andrew Schofield
Eileen Schuyler
Ryan Scott
James Scott

Matthew Searle
Elizabeth Segrave-Daly
Larry Seiler
Raj Seshadri
Jonathan Sharpe
Joe Shaun
Richard Shepherd
Emma Shepherd
Rebecca Sickinger
River Skybetter
Elena Smith
Russell Smith
Eric Smith
Adam Smithson
Maddi Sojourner
Mate Soric
Una Spenser
Jeremy Steel
Spencer Steers
Red Stella
Tracey Stern
Roy Stilling
Max Stirk
Francine Stock
Darrell Storey
Jack Tams
Martha Teitelbaum
Corin Tentchoff
Christine Teo
Iain Thomas
Alexander Thompson
David Thornton
Mike Totham
Ned Trifle
Matthew Trow

David Tubby
Daniel Tumilty
Clark Tyler
George Tzilivakis
John and Lindsay Usher
Christine Valverde
Maddie Voke
Steve Wadsworth
Steven Wagenseil
Colette Waitt
George Walker
Mark Walker
Naomi Ward
Paul Wayper
Peter Wells
Laura Wensley-Greaves
Paul Whelan
Ben Whitehouse
Andrew Wiggins
Andrew Wilcox
Brendon Wilkins
Hélène Wilkinson
Stuart Williams
Iain Wilson
Mark Wilson
Robert Wilton
Tim Winstanley
Simon Withers
Steven Wooding
Steve Woodward
Sharon Wright
Claire Yim
Edyta Zalewska
Amanda Zuydervelt

A NOTE ABOUT THE TYPEFACE

This book is set in Monotype Bembo Book. Originally drawn by Stanley Morison for the Monotype Corporation in 1929, the design of Bembo was inspired by the types cut by Francesco Griffo and used by Aldus Manutius, the great scholar-typographer of Renaissance Italy. In 1495, Aldus used it to print Cardinal Bembo's tract *de Aetna*, an account of a visit to Mount Etna. Not intended to be a facsimile of Manutius' work, Morison's Bembo was drawn to embody the elegance and fine design features of the original but marry them with the consistency of modern production methods so it would work with high speed printing techniques.

The Bembo used here is the new digital version, called Bembo Book, designed by Robin Nicholas and released in 2005. It is slightly narrower and more elegant than other digital versions of the typeface and was drawn to produce a closer match to the results achieved using the hot metal version when letterpress printed.